ITALIAN PAINTINGS

from the Richard L. Feigen Collection

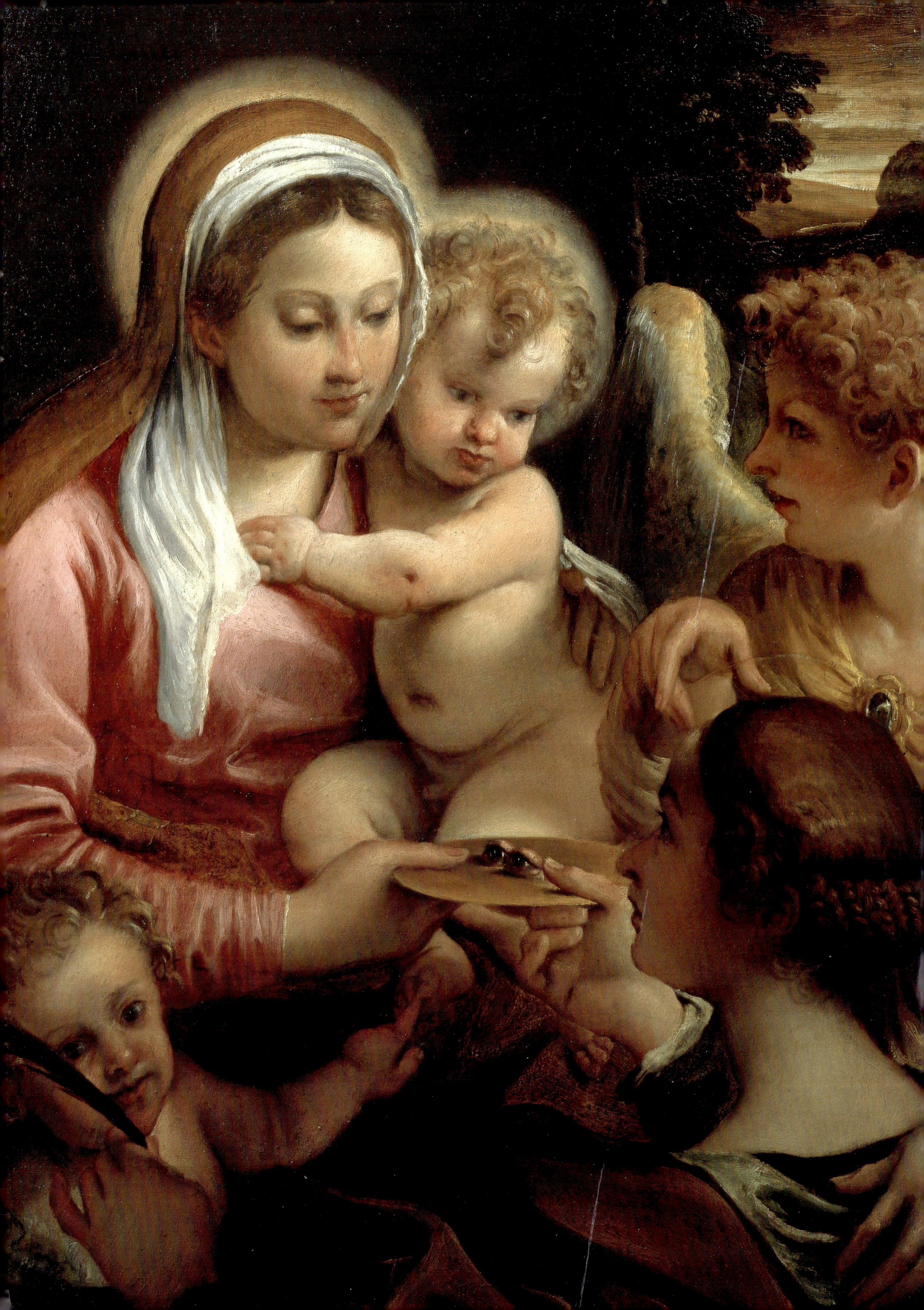

ITALIAN PAINTINGS
from the Richard L. Feigen Collection

LAURENCE KANTER

JOHN MARCIARI

Yale University Art Gallery, New Haven
in association with
Yale University Press, New Haven and London

First published in 2010 by the Yale University Art Gallery
P.O. Box 208271 New Haven, CT 06520-8271
www.artgallery.yale.edu

in association with Yale University Press
P.O. Box 209040 New Haven, CT 06520-9040
www.yalebooks.com

Published in conjunction with the exhibition *Italian Paintings from the Richard L. Feigen Collection*,
organized by the Yale University Art Gallery.

Yale University Art Gallery
May 28–September 12, 2010

Exhibition and publication made possible by the Robert Lehman Exhibition and Publication Fund and
an endowment created with a challenge grant from the National Endowment for the Arts.

Tiffany Sprague, Associate Director of Publications and Editorial Services

Designer: Bruce Campbell
Set in Aldus LT type by Aardvark Type
Printed in Singapore by CS Graphics

Library of Congress Cataloging-in-Publication Data

Kanter, Laurence B.
Italian paintings from the Richard L. Feigen collection / Laurence Kanter, John Marciari.
p. cm.
Published in conjunction with the exhibition held May 28–Sept. 12, 2010, Yale University Art Gallery.
Includes bibliographical references and index.
ISBN 978-0-300-11488-1 (hardcover : alk. paper)—ISBN 978-0-89467-975-9 (pbk. : alk. paper)
1. Painting, Italian—Exhibitions. 2. Feigen, Richard L., 1930– —Art collections—Exhibitions.
3. Painting—Private collections—United States—Exhibitions. I. Marciari, John.
II. Yale University. Art Gallery. III. Title.
ND614.K36 2010
759.5074′7468—dc22
2009033734

10 9 8 7 6 5 4 3 2 1

Jacket illustrations: *(front)* "Barna"/Lippo Memmi, *Virgin and Child Enthroned with Saints Peter and Paul and Ten Angels*,
ca. 1330–35 (detail, no. 13); *(back)* Giovanni di Paolo, *Christ as the Man of Sorrows*, ca. 1460–65 (no. 31)
Frontispiece: Annibale Carracci, *Virgin and Child with Saint Lucy and the Young Saint John the Baptist*, ca. 1587–88 (no. 39)
Page vi: Orazio Gentileschi, *Danaë and the Shower of Gold*, 1621–22 (detail, no. 47)
Page x: Fra Angelico, *Saint Sixtus*, ca. 1453–54 (detail, no. 23)

Contents

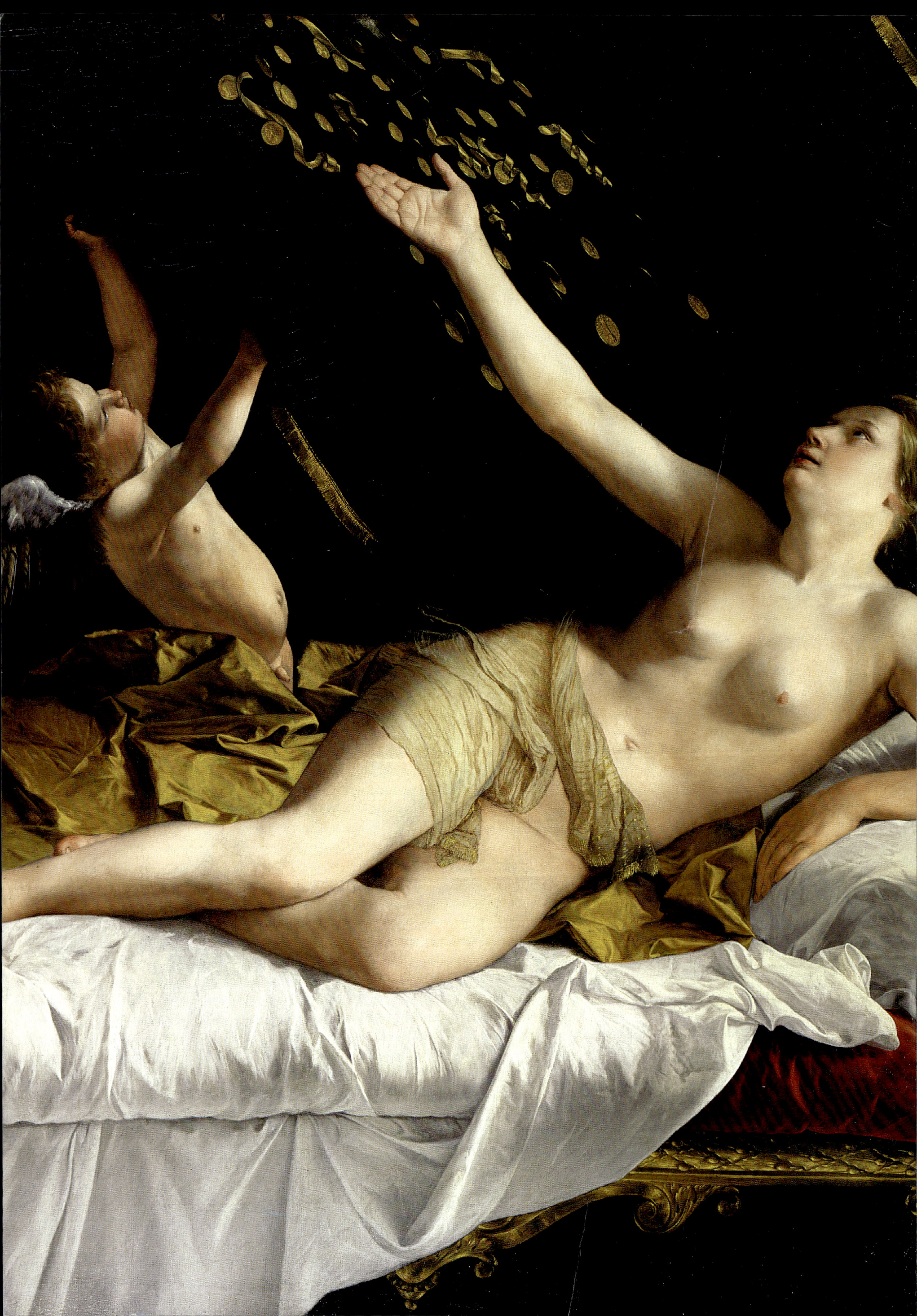

DIRECTOR'S FOREWORD

In 1871, with the acquisition of the collection of paintings formed by James Jackson Jarves, Yale College became only the second public institution in this country (following the New-York Historical Society) to own and display a significant number of works of art from the earlier Italian Renaissance, the then-undervalued and certainly underappreciated periods of the thirteenth, fourteenth, and fifteenth centuries. Since then, these precious objects have come to be esteemed as cultural icons: they are coveted and pursued by museums throughout the country and around the world, yet few museums anywhere have amassed the range and quality of works of art from the early Renaissance represented in Yale's collection. That this is so is a testament to the energies, enthusiasm, and commitment of many generations of Yale alumni—of the likes of Maitland Fuller Griggs, B.A. 1896, and Robert Lehman, B.A. 1913—who recognized the passion that works of art can inspire in undergraduates. It is a unique pleasure now to be able to present this latest chapter in an ongoing legacy, the exhibition and catalogue of Italian masterpieces lent to Yale by another distinguished alumnus collector, Richard L. Feigen, B.A. 1952.

Only Richard could possibly say whether it was studying near the great examples on view here that encouraged him to begin collecting on his own, or whether it was memories of the Jarves, Griggs, and Rabinowitz collections that moved him inexorably toward adding early Italian panels to his world-famous Italian seventeenth-century, British nineteenth-century, and German twentieth-century paintings. Wherever the whisper of inspiration came from, it was pursued with determination and genius, resulting after a remarkably short time in a collection of astonishing breadth and depth that we are very fortunate at Yale to be able to show publicly for the first time ever.

All collectors have their share of misadventures to relate, the tales of prized objects that got away and of opportunities unrealized. Richard no doubt has an ample stock of his own stories, but I am convinced that no matter how many he may tell, they are easily outnumbered by the laments of other collectors and of major museums who will sigh over the treasures they missed once Richard turned his attention in this direction. How many institutions, let alone private collectors, can boast three works by Fra Angelico in their holdings? How many can claim so coherent a display of Florentine fourteenth-century panels, or such rare masterpieces as the examples here by "Barna da Siena" (no. 13) or the Master of the Piani d'Invrea Cross (no. 15)? How many collections are so rich in precious, small-scale coppers by major Mannerist and Baroque masters? Where in the world is to be found a painting as aesthetically compelling, I don't hesitate to say perfect, as Annibale Carracci's *Virgin and Child* (no. 39) or Orazio Gentileschi's *Danaë* (no. 47)? The level of taste and discernment that brought these works and others like them together is impossible to categorize by simple descriptive phrases except to point out the single characteristic that unifies everything presented in this exhibition and catalogue: an unyielding insistence on quality. That is the trademark of Richard's taste, in each of the many fields that have caught his interest over the years: quality, together with the patience and perseverance to seek it out wherever it might be found.

A great collection deserves a great catalogue, and we are proud at Yale to have been able to rely on two of our own to produce this admirable book: Laurence Kanter, the Lionel Goldfrank III Curator of European Art here at the Gallery, and John Marciari, formerly the Nina and Lee Griggs Associate Curator of Early European Art here and now Curator of European Art and Head of Provenance Research at the San Diego Museum of Art. Behind every great book and its distinguished authors lurks an army of supporting actors who rarely appear in the limelight. In this case, special thanks are due to Linsey LaFrenier, Senior Museum Assistant in the Department of European Art at the Gallery, who has orchestrated all the demanding and time-consuming tasks of collecting and collating photographs and comparative material, editing texts, checking and rechecking references, even before the manuscript could be handed to our expert editor, Tiffany Sprague, Associate Director of Publications and Editorial Services, and our always-appreciated, invaluable partners at Yale University Press, including publisher Patricia Fidler; senior production editor Kate Zanzucchi; and production manager Mary Mayer, as well as designer Bruce Campbell, copy editor Linda Truilo, proofreader June Cuffner, and indexer Cathy Dorsey. To all these people, to the many more I have neglected to mention by name, and to the even greater numbers of staff who have contributed to the success of this exhibition, my heartfelt thanks.

A final word of gratitude must be reserved for Richard Feigen. It is no small thing to agree to live without one's personal treasures for even a short space of time, but Richard has never balked at the prospect of sharing his private pleasures with the greater public, and he has from the beginning steadfastly supported the idea of doing so at Yale. Andrew Ritchie, then-director of the Gallery, mounted a memorable series of exhibitions at Yale in the 1950s entirely composed of loans from alumni collections. Sadly, the practice did not become an ongoing tradition, even though Yale alumni could (and still can) boast among their number many of the foremost collectors of art from virtually every period and culture around the globe. Richard's generosity may just be the spur to revitalizing this tradition, a harbinger of many wonderful things to come. Thank you, Richard.

Jock Reynolds
The Henry J. Heinz II Director
Yale University Art Gallery

Preface

The effort and scholarship vested in this catalogue are humbling; I am frankly embarrassed to have been asked to write anything for it at all. The more I reflect on the objects I have managed to accumulate, the more I wince over the ones that got away . . . a Lorenzo Monaco *Lamentation*, a Simone Martini *Madonna*, a putative Duccio . . . and so on. I never believed in money, only in the objects into which it could be converted. Although masterpieces are increasingly unavailable, I never encountered one that was overpriced, only ones I couldn't afford.

There is no program here. My favorite artists and periods reoccur. My focus has shifted in recent years: my passion for fourteenth- and early fifteenth-century Florence and Siena has overwhelmed the *maniera* and Baroque.

As Laurence Kanter knows better than anyone, I remain unrequited, and so the cataloguing chore kept piling on, constantly revised and extended, ultimately terminated not by Larry's unflagging energy and commitment or even by John Marciari's departure for San Diego, only by printer's deadlines.

In the midst of all this, the satisfaction that these paintings give me was enhanced by my marriage to Isabelle Harnoncourt in 2007, giving me someone with whom to share them. However, the fact is that without Larry Kanter's guidance and brilliant scholarship, I would not have ventured into many of these acquisitions. Fortunate I was to have such a mentor.

With some of the early panels studied here, like the Fra Angelico *Saint Joseph* and *Saint Lucy*, the "Barna da Siena," or the Orcagna *Saint Benedict*, I did not know exactly what they were until after I had bought them and Larry Kanter told me. With a few, like the early *Nativity* that some call Ligurian, some Neapolitan, and some Provençal, I still don't know where they were painted.

With academic determination that I sadly lacked as an undergraduate some sixty years ago, I now board the train weekly for Larry's connoisseurship seminars. The more I learn, the more I am appalled at how much I don't know. But with the seeds that Larry is planting at Yale, I have dreams of it becoming the center for connoisseurship and museology that Harvard was in the 1920s. We need such a place.

With an American president now who seems to value culture as a national asset, our country will hopefully stop "dumbing-down"; culture and scholarship will no longer be trashed as "elitist" and "un-American." That is the dream; Yale is the hope.

My gratitude to Larry Kanter, John Marciari, and all those who expended such effort in cataloguing these objects, which mean so very much to me.

Richard L. Feigen
May 2009

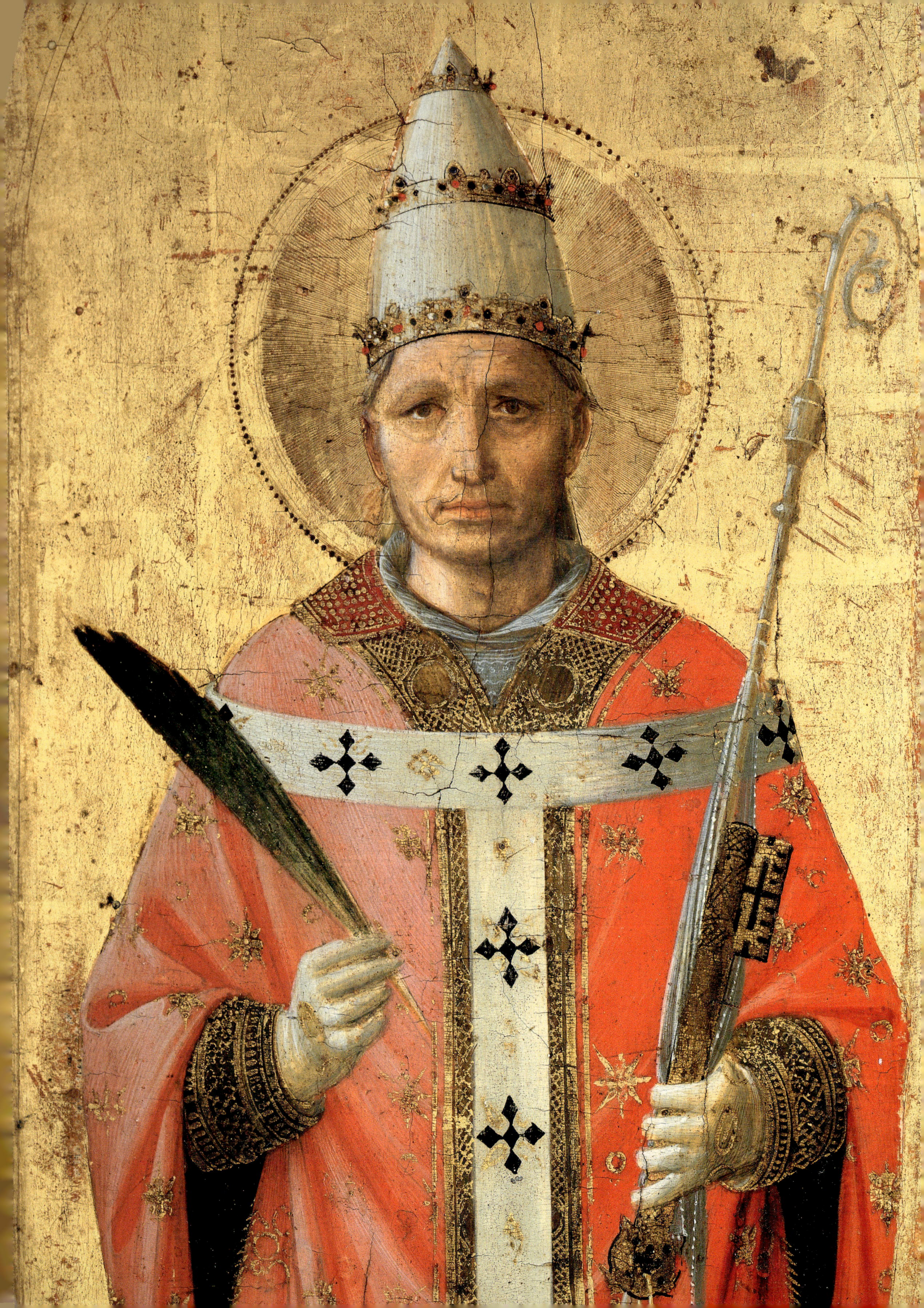

CATALOGUE

For Richard and Isabelle

Taddeo Gaddi

Florence, ca. 1300–1366

1. *Saint John the Evangelist*, ca. 1334–35

Tempera on panel, 53.2 x 31.9 cm (21 x 12½ in.), overall;
53.2 x 29.5 cm (21 x 11⅝ in.), picture surface

PROVENANCE: private collection, England(?) (sale, Sotheby's,
London, December 3, 1978, lot 116, property of a "British
Education Foundation"); Matthiesen Fine Art, Ltd., London;
Piero Corsini, New York (his sale, Christie's, New York,
January 26, 2001, lot 85)

BIBLIOGRAPHY: Andrew Ladis, *Taddeo Gaddi: Critical
Reappraisal and Catalogue Raisonné* (Columbia, Mo., 1982),
p. 202; Matthiesen Fine Art, Ltd., *Early Italian Paintings and
Works of Art, 1300–1480*, exh. cat. (London, 1983), no. 3;
Kristi Wormhoudt, in *Italian Renaissance Art, Selections
from the Piero Corsini Gallery*, ed. Barbara Wollesen-Wisch,
exh. cat. (University Park, Pa., 1987), pp. 18–19; Erling
S. Skaug, *Punch Marks from Giotto to Fra Angelico: Attri-
bution, Chronology, and Workshop Relationships in Tuscan
Panel Painting* (Oslo, 1994), 1: p. 96n.84; Mojmir S. Frinta,
*Punched Decoration on Late Medieval Panel and Miniature
Painting* (Prague, 1998), 1: p. 539

CONDITION: The panel support, of a vertical grain and—
unusually—a soft wood (fir or spruce?), has been thinned
to 16 mm but is not cradled. An export stamp on the reverse
is dated Florence, September 21, 1978. The paint surface has
suffered light overall abrasion and minor scattered flaking
losses but is generally well preserved. The broad craquelure
apparent in the paint film has perhaps been exaggerated by
the greater movement of the soft wood support but has not
resulted in extensive paint loss, and the delicate red and blue
glazed pattern decorating the ends of the pages in Saint John's
book is almost fully intact.

The half-length figure of Saint John the Evangelist was first
recorded at the Sotheby's sale of December 3, 1978, as
"attributed to Pacino di Bonaguida." It was recognized at that
time by Carlo Volpe as a work by Taddeo Gaddi, an attribution
subsequently confirmed by Miklós Boskovits and first published by Andrew Ladis.[1] Ladis proposed a relatively early date
for the panel, ca. 1330–35, by reference to the figure style in
Taddeo Gaddi's frescoes in the Baroncelli chapel in Santa Croce,
Florence, and this appears to be correct. Erling Skaug, who does
not include an examination of this panel in his discussion of
Taddeo Gaddi's punch work, implies by the context of his
observations that it is likely instead to date from the 1340s,
when the rose-and-leaf motif decorating Saint John's halo—a
motif derived from Bernardo Daddi's contemporary practice—
was enhanced by being set off against a granulated ground,

specifically a granulation created with a simple one-point
punch rather than a small ring punch that Gaddi had been
accustomed to using in the previous decade. Skaug's chart of
Gaddi's punch tools, however, records only two paintings that
use the two motif punches occurring in this panel: the Berlin
triptych dated 1334 and a small panel in the Kunstmuseum,
Bern, dated about 1335 by Ladis and Gaudenz Freuler.[2] While
such evidence is more suggestive than conclusive, it is likely
on these grounds and on the grounds of style that the *Saint
John the Evangelist* was painted close to 1334–35.

No other panels that may have formed part of the same
polyptych as the *Saint John the Evangelist* have yet been
found, possibly because the unusual soft-wood support (if it
may be presumed that the entire altarpiece was constructed of
the same material) is more prone to accidental damage from
fluctuations in temperature and humidity and from insect
infestation. An impression of the appearance of the complete
altarpiece may perhaps be gleaned from a fictive altarpiece
painted by Taddeo Gaddi or a member of his studio among
the frescoes decorating the walls of the chapel in the Castello
at Poppi, commonly dated as well to the mid-1330s.[3] There,
five "panels" related in shape and format to Giotto's Badia
polyptych (Galleria degli Uffizi, Florence) portray half-length
figures of the Virgin and Child and Saints Francis, John the
Baptist, John the Evangelist, and Anthony Abbot. The figure
of Saint John the Evangelist, immediately to the right of the
Virgin, is a virtual replica of the Feigen panel, corresponding closely in figure type, pose, and draperies. The present
round-arched shape of the gold ground of the Feigen panel
is likely not to be original but to have been cut to this form
from an ogival or trilobe arch. It is also possible that punched
or engraved decoration once followed the margins of the gold
ground but have since been cut away, cropping the saint's
right elbow at the left edge of the panel.   LK

1. Andrew Ladis, *Taddeo Gaddi: Critical Reappraisal and Catalogue Raisonné*
(Columbia, Mo., 1982), p. 202. Volpe's and Boskovits's verbal opinions were
recorded in the files of the Piero Corsini Gallery; see Kristi Wormhoudt,
in *Italian Renaissance Art, Selections from the Piero Corsini Gallery*,
ed. Barbara Wollesen-Wisch, exh. cat. (University Park, Pa., 1987), p. 19n.3.
2. Marc Fehlmann and Gaudenz Freuler, *Die Sammlung Adolf von Stürler*
(Bern, 2001), pp. 58–61; and Ladis, *Taddeo Gaddi*, p. 130. For the punch
marks, see Erling S. Skaug, *Punch Marks from Giotto to Fra Angelico:
Attribution, Chronology, and Workshop Relationships in Tuscan Panel
Painting* (Oslo, 1994), 1: p. 96; 2: nos. 593, 627.
3. Ladis, *Taddeo Gaddi*, pp. 250–51, fig. 67.

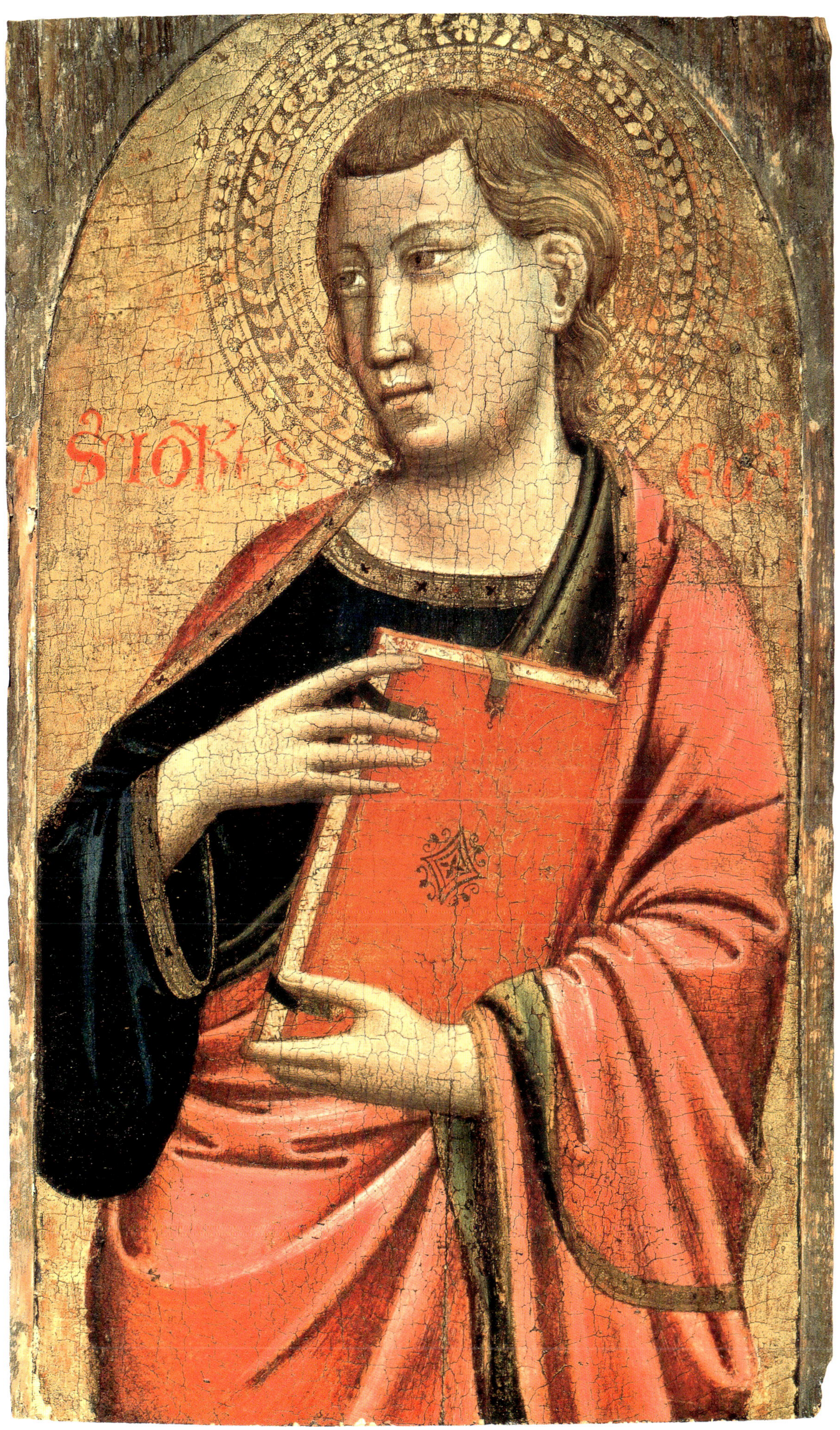
S·IOH·S
EU

Bernardo Daddi

Florence, documented 1312/20–1348

2. *A Prophet*, ca. 1320–30

Tempera on panel, 14.6 x 15.6 cm (5¾ x 6⅛ in.), overall;
14 x 13.8 cm (5½ x 5½ in.), original panel; 8.9 cm (3½ in.),
diameter roundel; 10.2 cm (4 in.), diameter exposed original
surface

PROVENANCE: Marchese Alfonso Tacoli-Canacci, Florence,
ca. 1787(?); Don Ferdinando di Borbone (1751–1802), Duke
of Parma(?); by descent to Princess Caroline of Parma (1770–
1804)(?); by descent(?) to King Johann of Saxony (1801–1873);
by descent to Prince Johann Georg of Saxony (1869–1938);
Professor Robert Oertel

BIBLIOGRAPHY: Staatsgalerie Stuttgart, *Frühe italienische
Tafelmalerei*, exh. cat. (Stuttgart, Germany, 1950), no. 21;
Richard Offner, *A Critical and Historical Corpus of Florentine
Painting: The Fourteenth Century*, sec. 3, vol. 8, *Workshop of
Bernardo Daddi* (New York, 1958), p. 37, pl. 7a

CONDITION: The panel support—poplar of a vertical wood
grain—has been thinned to approximately 1 cm and made
up to a full rectangle by the insertion of two small triangular
wedges in the upper left and right corners. Added strips a
little more than 0.7 cm wide have been affixed to the sides and
top and masked by a coating of gesso painted brown applied
to the panel surface. This coating leaves a 10.2 cm diameter
opening, framed by a pastiglia ribbon-and-stick molding,
through which the original paint surface is exposed. This
comprises a compass-ruled gilt roundel, 8.9 cm in diameter,
in which is painted the half-length figure of a prophet facing
left, holding a white scroll lettered with a pseudoinscription.
The gilding and paint surface are preserved in excellent state,
with minimal abrasion and only microscopic loss from flaking
where the paint overlaps the gold. The roundel is tangent to
the pastiglia frame at the top, and visible below it is the truncated tip of a gilt ogival arch cropped from the top of the panel
this fragment once surmounted. The spandrels outside the
roundel and this arch are silver gilt and very well preserved.

Aside from its notice in the 1950 Stuttgart exhibition,
where it was correctly attributed to Bernardo Daddi,
this exceptionally beautiful and well-preserved roundel is
mentioned only once in the extensive literature on the artist.[1]
It is self-evidently a fragment, cut from the triangular gable
of the right lateral panel of an altarpiece, on the model of
Daddi's 1328 triptych in the Galleria degli Uffizi, Florence,
the polyptych now in San Godenzo in the Mugello, or a dismembered altarpiece now known through surviving fragments in the Nelson-Atkins Gallery in Kansas City, Missouri,
and formerly in the Von Quast collection in Radensleben,
Germany.[2]

In practice, the search for the possible original situation of
this fragment is limited by the small number of such altarpieces
by Bernardo Daddi actually lacking their original framing
gables, and it is further restricted by a consideration of the
engraved decoration of the prophet's halo and the punch decoration of the compass-ruled margin of the roundel. The
punch tool used to create this marginal decoration—number
382 in Erling Skaug's inventory of Florentine punch tools of
the fourteenth and fifteenth centuries—is not recorded in
any work by Bernardo Daddi after 1333, though it recurs
with some regularity in paintings plausibly dated to the
1320s.[3] Among these, the small *Crucifixion* in the Museum of
Fine Arts, Boston, closely approximates the figure style and
emotional tenor of the Feigen *Prophet*, and the two works

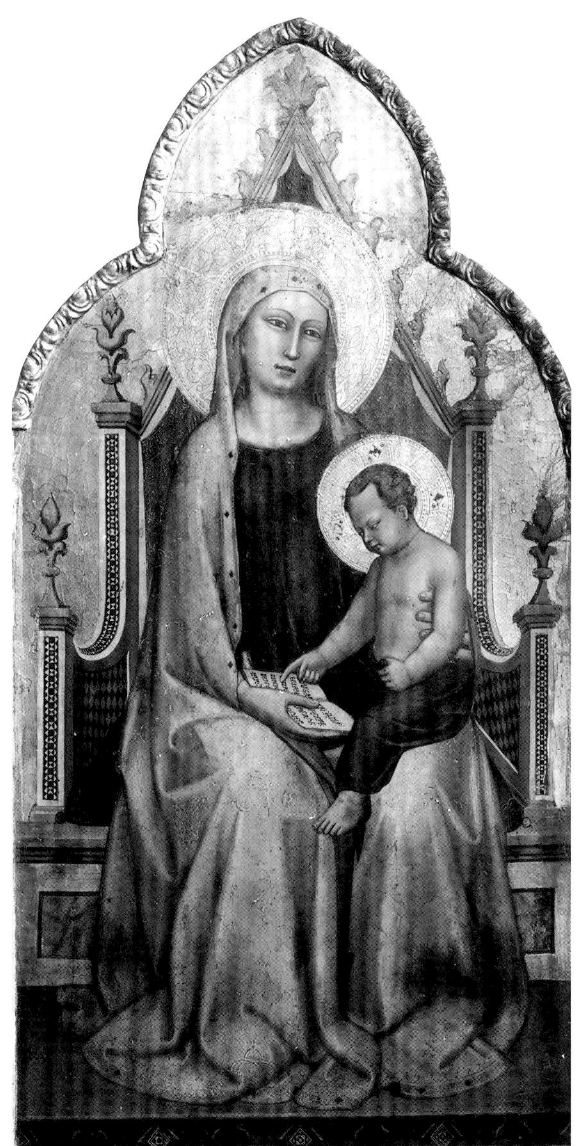

Fig. 1. Bernardo Daddi, *Virgin and Child Enthroned*,
ca. 1320–30. Tempera on panel, 89 x 46 cm (35 x
18⅛ in.). Pinacoteca Nazionale, Parma

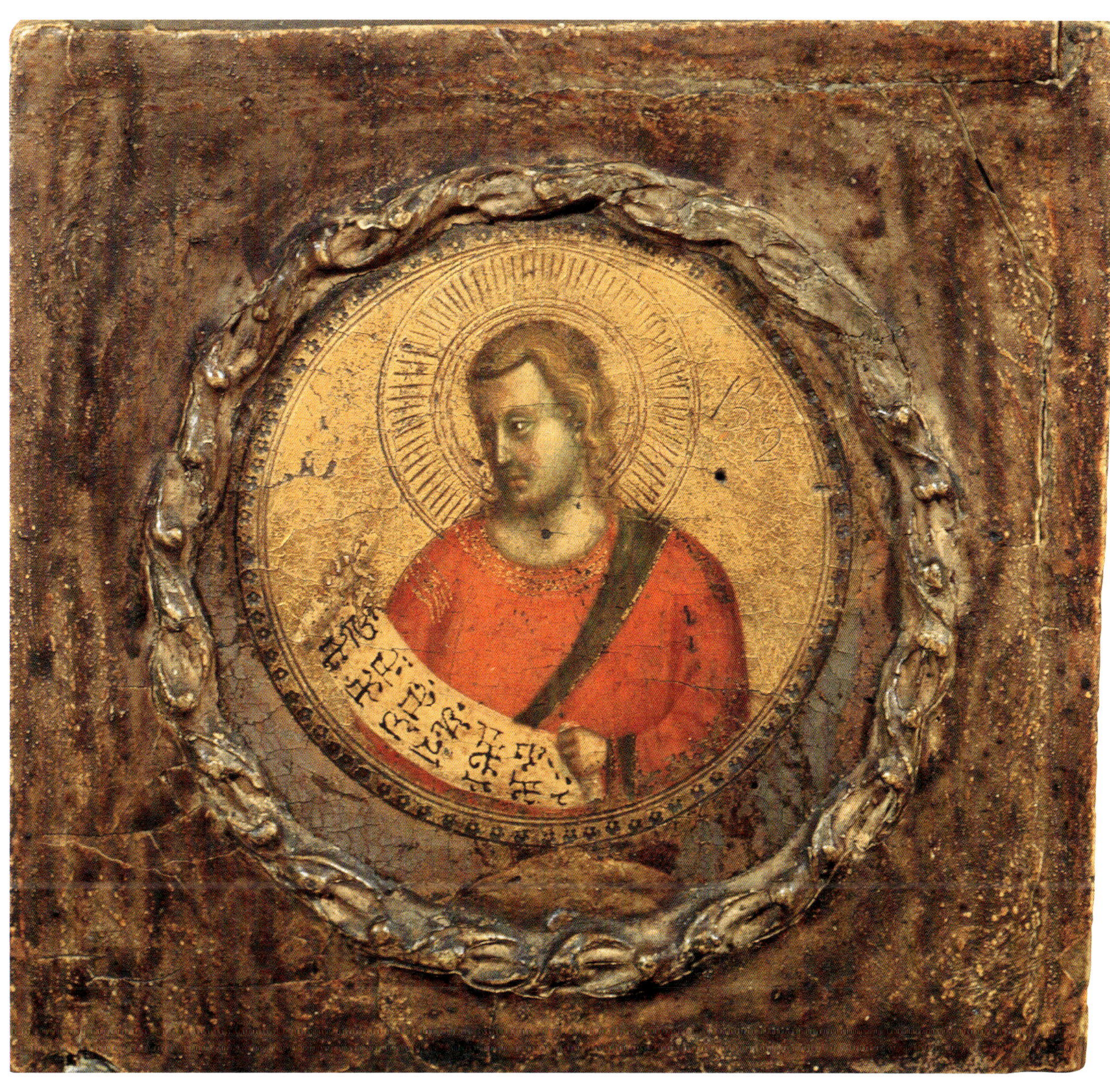

must be considered roughly contemporary.[4] Only a single dated work by Daddi from this decade is known, however—the 1328 triptych in the Uffizi mentioned above—so assigning more than vaguely generic brackets of time to his other early paintings is an intuitive exercise.

One small but important altarpiece from this early period of Daddi's career is lacking its gabled pinnacles, is similar in style to the Feigen *Prophet,* and is decorated similarly to it. It may, furthermore, share an early provenance with the *Prophet,* which could confirm their association as parts of a single complex. The reconstruction of the dispersed altarpiece was initiated by Roberto Longhi, who noticed that a *Virgin and Child Enthroned* in the Pinacoteca Nazionale in Parma (fig. 1) must have been the center panel of a polyptych to which panels representing Saints Peter and Paul in the church of San Vitale in Parma (figs. 2–3) also belonged.[5] Federico Zeri added two more panels to this grouping—a *Saint John the Baptist* formerly in the collection of Amedeo Lia at La Spezia and a *Saint Francis* last recorded in 1917 with the dealer d'Atri in Paris[6]—noting that the provenance of all five panels from the collection formed in Florence around 1787 by the Marchese Alfonso Tacoli-Canacci is confirmed by the gesso spandrels and pastiglia moldings added to their surfaces, typical of the treatment of all the panels in that collection.

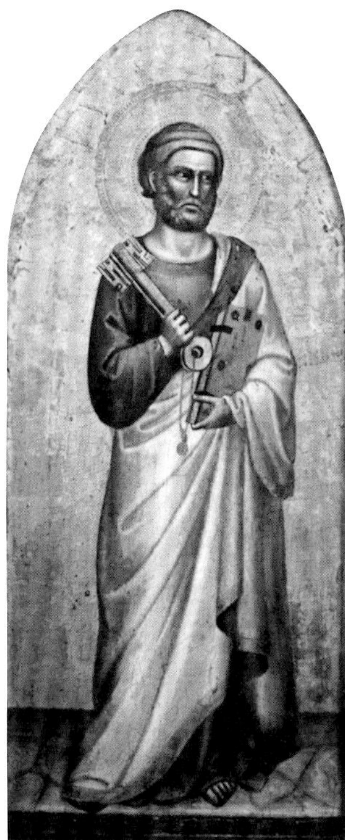 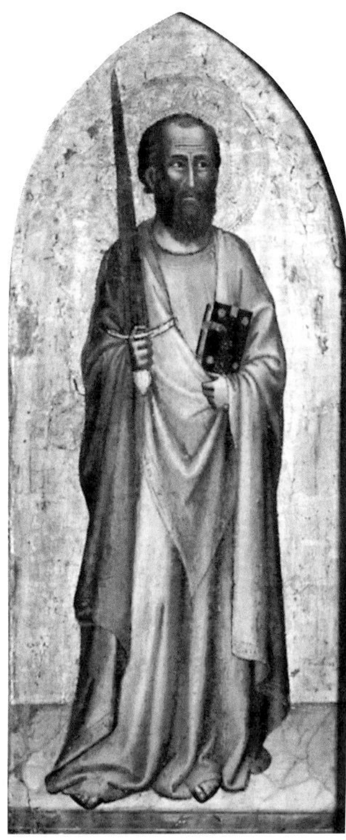

Fig. 2. Bernardo Daddi, *Saint Peter*, ca. 1320–30. Tempera on panel, 77.5 x 33.5 cm (30½ x 13¼ in.). San Vitale, Parma

Fig. 3. Bernardo Daddi, *Saint Paul*, ca. 1320–30. Tempera on panel, 77.5 x 33.5 cm (30½ x 13¼ in.). San Vitale, Parma

The similar treatment of the surround of the Feigen *Prophet* is suggestive evidence of their common origin, as is the fact that King Johann of Saxony, whose collector's mark appears on the back of the Feigen panel,[7] was the grandson of Ferdinando I di Borbone, Duke of Parma, to whom Tacoli-Canacci sold a large portion of his collection of early Tuscan paintings.[8]

All five of the main panels of this altarpiece have been cut across the top within the field of the upper lobe of their ogival framing arches by an amount commensurate with the fragment of such an arch visible at the bottom of the Feigen panel. Extending the diagonal cuts at the top corners of the Feigen panel would produce a triangular fragment approximately 26 cm tall by 25 cm wide at the base (i.e., before trimming to its present nearly rectangular dimensions). The lateral panels to the Tacoli-Canacci altarpiece reportedly measure 77.5 x 33.5 cm (Saints Peter and Paul) and 71 x 34 cm (Saint John the Baptist). Photographs of the lateral panels imply that they too have been made up to full rectangles by the insertion of triangular wedges in their upper corners, then extended by added strips affixed to their side and top edges and incorporated into their painted, gilt, or gesso-covered surfaces. (The photographs do not permit measurement of the original width of the truncated top edges of these panels.)

A putative provenance for the Tacoli-Canacci panels from a Florentine Franciscan church was surmised by Federico Zeri from the presence among them of Saints John the Baptist, patron of Florence, and Francis. Zeri highlighted their strong

Giottesque character, assigning them to Daddi's "preindustrial" phase of production—a nod to Roberto Longhi's contemptuous dismissal of Daddi as a commercially repetitive artist—possibly as early as the beginning of the 1320s and in close proximity to the frescoes in the Pulci Berardi chapel in Santa Croce. Miklós Boskovits refined this suggestion by proposing that the altarpiece may actually have been painted to stand in the Pulci Berardi chapel, though in such a case the absence from the polyptych of Saints Lawrence and Stephen, to whom the chapel was dedicated, would be difficult to explain.[9] A possible alternative might be implied by a faint inscription on the reverse of the Feigen panel: "Fiesole." If not entirely apocryphal,[10] it might indicate a provenance for the complex from the church of San Francesco in Fiesole. This church, however, was ceded to the Franciscans only in 1399, so that if the Tacoli-Canacci altarpiece was indeed removed from there in the late eighteenth century, it must have been transferred there earlier from another Franciscan establishment. Silvia Giorgi interpreted an impresa burned into the back of the panel of the Parma *Virgin and Child Enthroned* as possibly indicating a provenance from the Compagnia di San Pier Maggiore in Florence, the property of which was dispersed in 1784 and 1785.[11] The suggestion is plausible, but perhaps does not account for the presence of Saint Francis in the polyptych: San Pier Maggiore was a convent of Benedictine nuns.

LK

1. Staatsgalerie Stuttgart, *Frühe italienische Tafelmalerei*, exh. cat. (Stuttgart, Germany, 1950), no. 21; and Richard Offner, *A Critical and Historical Corpus of Florentine Painting: The Fourteenth Century*, sec. 3, vol. 8, *Workshop of Bernardo Daddi* (New York, 1958), p. 37.

2. For Daddi's 1328 triptych in the Uffizi, see Richard Offner, *A Critical and Historical Corpus of Florentine Painting: The Fourteenth Century*, sec. 3, vol. 3, *The Works of Bernardo Daddi*, ed. Miklós Boskovits (Florence, 1989), pl. 1; for the polyptych in the Mugello, see Richard Offner, *A Critical and Historical Corpus of Florentine Painting: The Fourteenth Century*, sec. 3, vol. 4, *Bernardo Daddi: His Shop and Following*, ed. Miklós Boskovits (Florence, 1991), pl. 56; for the altarpiece fragment in the Nelson-Atkins Gallery, see Offner III/VIII, pl. 24, and Offner III/IV, add. pl. 9.

3. Erling S. Skaug, *Punch Marks from Giotto to Fra Angelico: Attribution, Chronology, and Workshop Relationships in Tuscan Panel Painting* (Oslo, 1994), 1: pp. 98–117.

4. Laurence Kanter, *Italian Paintings in the Museum of Fine Arts, Boston* (Boston, 1994), pp. 52–54. For the Boston *Crucifixion*, see Offner III/IV, pl. 27.

5. Reported in Giovanni Paccagnini, "Cronaca dei ritrovamenti e dei restauri," *Le arti* 2 (1940): pp. 212–13. The San Vitale panels were subsequently moved into the Pinacoteca and installed as a triptych with the Madonna between them. For the Parma *Virgin and Child*, see Offner III/IV, pl. 57.

6. Federico Zeri, "Qualche appunto sul Daddi—1. Il Polittico Tacoli-Canacci nella sua integrità," in *Quaderni di Emblema—1. Diari di Lavoro* (Bergamo, 1971), pp. 11–14.

7. Frits Lugt, *Les marques de collections de dessins et d'éstampes* (Amsterdam, 1921), no. 1405. Prince Johann Georg's stamp is Lugt no. 1466. An inventory number, "155 M," is also painted on the back of the Feigen panel.

8. See Vincenzo M. Buonocore, *Il marchese Alfonso Tacoli-Canacci: "Onesto gentiluomo smaniante per la pittura"* (Reggio Emilia, Italy, 2005).

9. Offner III/III, pp. 41–43nn.38–40.
10. A sgraffito marking on the front of the Feigen *Prophet*—"13/2"—might
    be interpreted to imply that it was framed as one of a pair after removal
    from the altarpiece. If so, it is possible that "Fiesole" was not an indica-
    tion of provenance but the remaining fragment of an attribution to Fra
    Giovanni da Fiesole that might have begun on the back of the missing
    companion panel.
11. Silvia Giorgi, in *Galleria Nazionale di Parma: Catalogo delle opere
    dall'antico al cinquecento*, ed. Lucia Fornari Schianchi (Parma, 1997),
    pp. 41–42. Giorgi notes that only a single item listed on the inventory
    of August 17, 1784, could be interpreted as relating to the Tacoli-Canacci
    altarpiece, but this is not necessarily an impediment to her proposal. The
    inventory (Z. Covoni, Inventario di tutti i mobile, arredi sacri . . . ritrovati
    nel Monastero di San Pier Maggiore, 17 agosto 1784, MS "San Pier Mag-
    giore 351," Archivio di Stato di Firenze, Florence) lists only those objects
    not otherwise repatriated to the families owning rights to chapels in San
    Pier Maggiore, one of whom could have reclaimed and subsequently sold
    the altarpiece to Tacoli-Canacci. See also Monica Bietti, "Da confraternità
    a Parrocchia di San Piero Nuovo," in *Quaderni dell'ufficio restauri della
    Soprintendenza BAS a Firenze e Pistoia* (Florence, 1989), pp. 59–61.

Bernardo Daddi

Florence, documented 1312/20–died 1348

3a. *Saint John the Evangelist*, ca. 1337

Tempera on panel, 53.7 x 43 cm (21⅛ x 17 in.)

PROVENANCE: see no. 3b

BIBLIOGRAPHY: Miklós Boskovits, *A Critical and Historical
Corpus of Florentine Painting*, sec. 3, vol. 9, *The Painters of
the Miniaturist Tendency* (Florence, 1984), p. 360, pl. 186b;
Richard Offner, *A Critical and Historical Corpus of Floren-
tine Painting*, sec. 3, vol. 3, *The Works of Bernardo Daddi*,
ed. Miklós Boskovits (Florence, 1989), p. 81; Erling S. Skaug,
*Punch Marks from Giotto to Fra Angelico: Attribution,
Chronology, and Workshop Relationships in Tuscan Panel
Painting* (Oslo, 1994), 1: pp. 101n.112, 110

CONDITION: The panel, of a horizontal grain, is 3 cm thick
and exhibits a slight convex warp. Two panel joins, approximately 21.5 cm from the bottom and 15.5 cm from the top,
have opened in the front resulting in modest paint loss along
their length, at the level of the bridge of the saint's nose and
just above the top corner of his book. A 3 cm wide strip of
gesso and repaint covers scattered losses along the right and
top edges, and smaller irregular losses are scattered along
the left edge. The bottom edge is irregularly damaged, and
a large part of the saint's left hand has been repainted. Two
nails driven into the panel approximately on center, originally
attaching a vertical batten on the back, have resulted in paint
losses approximately 16 cm from the bottom of the panel and
12.5 cm from the top, just above the saint's left eye. The gilding and paint surface otherwise are well preserved, with only
minor flaking losses scattered along the raised edges of craquelure and light abrasion in the saint's rose-colored outer robe.

Andrea di Cione, called Orcagna

Florence, active by 1343–died 1368

3b. *Saint Benedict*, ca. 1337

Tempera on panel, 53.4 x 43.1 cm (21⅛ x 17 in.)

PROVENANCE: private collection (sale, Sotheby's, London,
December 8, 1971, lot 57); Mrs. Alice Low Beer, Epsom,
London; by descent to her granddaughters (their sale,
Sotheby's, London, December 7, 2005, lot 33)

BIBLIOGRAPHY: Miklós Boskovits, *A Critical and Historical
Corpus of Florentine Painting*, sec. 3, vol. 9, *The Painters of
the Miniaturist Tendency* (Florence, 1984), p. 360, pl. 186a;
Richard Offner, *A Critical and Historical Corpus of Floren-
tine Painting*, sec. 3, vol. 3, *The Works of Bernardo Daddi*,
ed. Miklós Boskovits (Florence, 1989), p. 81; Erling S. Skaug,
*Punch Marks from Giotto to Fra Angelico: Attribution,
Chronology, and Workshop Relationships in Tuscan Panel
Painting* (Oslo, 1994), 1: pp. 101n.112, 110

CONDITION: The panel, of a horizontal grain, is 3 cm thick
and exhibits a slight convex warp. Two panel joins, approximately 20 cm from the bottom and 16 cm from the top, have
opened in the front, resulting in modest paint loss along their
length, at the level of the saint's upper lip and just above the
top corner of his book. A 2 cm wide strip of gesso and repaint
covers scattered losses along the left and top edges, and smaller
irregular losses are scattered along the right and bottom edges.
The gold background has been overpainted in oils with dark
green foliage, but bolus and remnants of original gilding are
preserved beneath this layer. Punch-tool impressions are still
apparent through the repainted background at the upper left
corner. The gilding of the halo is well preserved, and the paint
surface is exceptionally well preserved aside from abrasions to
the saint's forehead and temple, in the area of his right cheek,
and at the bottom of his beard. Two nails driven into the panel
approximately on center, originally attaching a vertical batten
to the back, have resulted in paint losses 21.5 cm from the bottom edge of the panel and 10.5 cm from the top edge, at the
level of the saint's left eye.

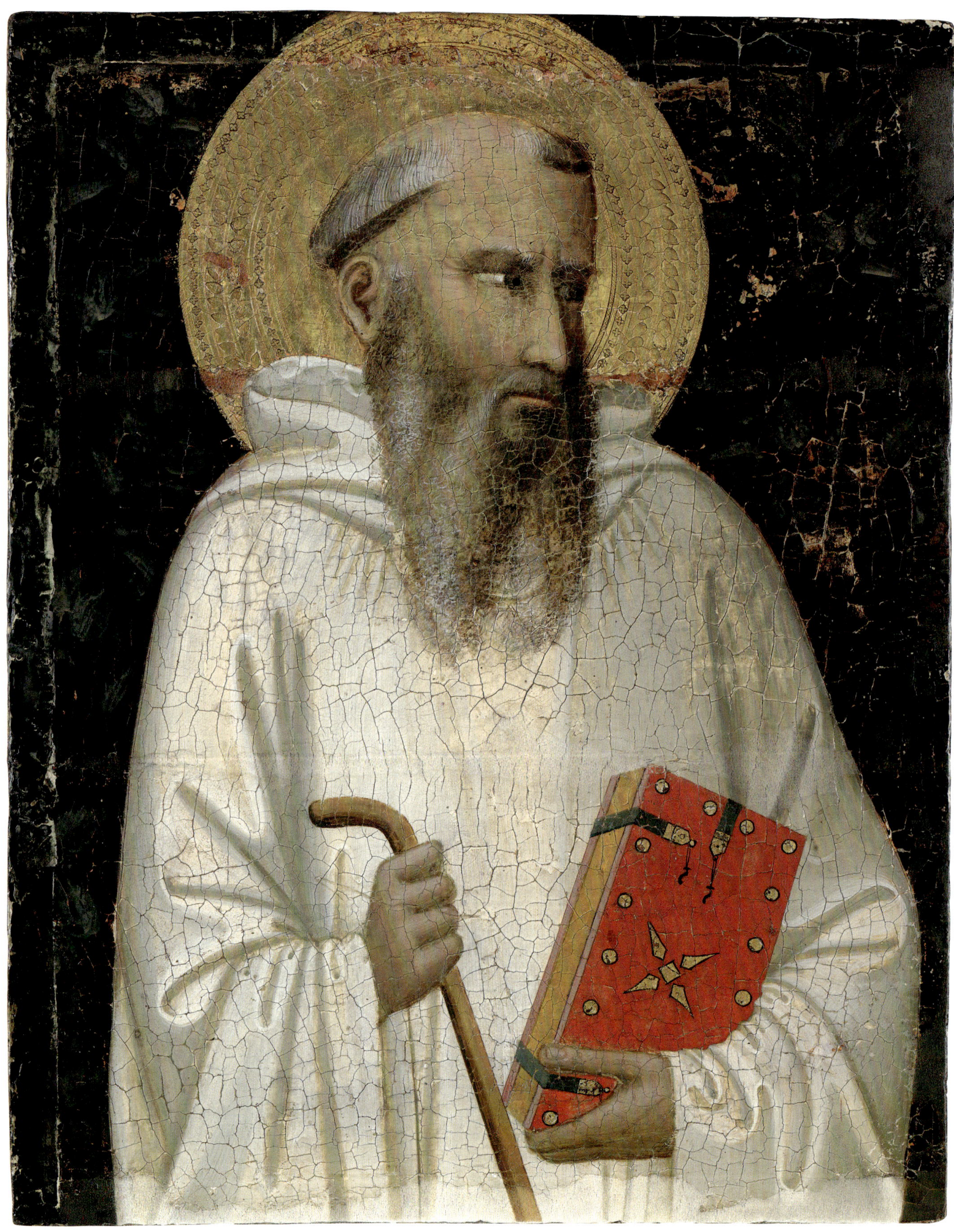

3b During conservation

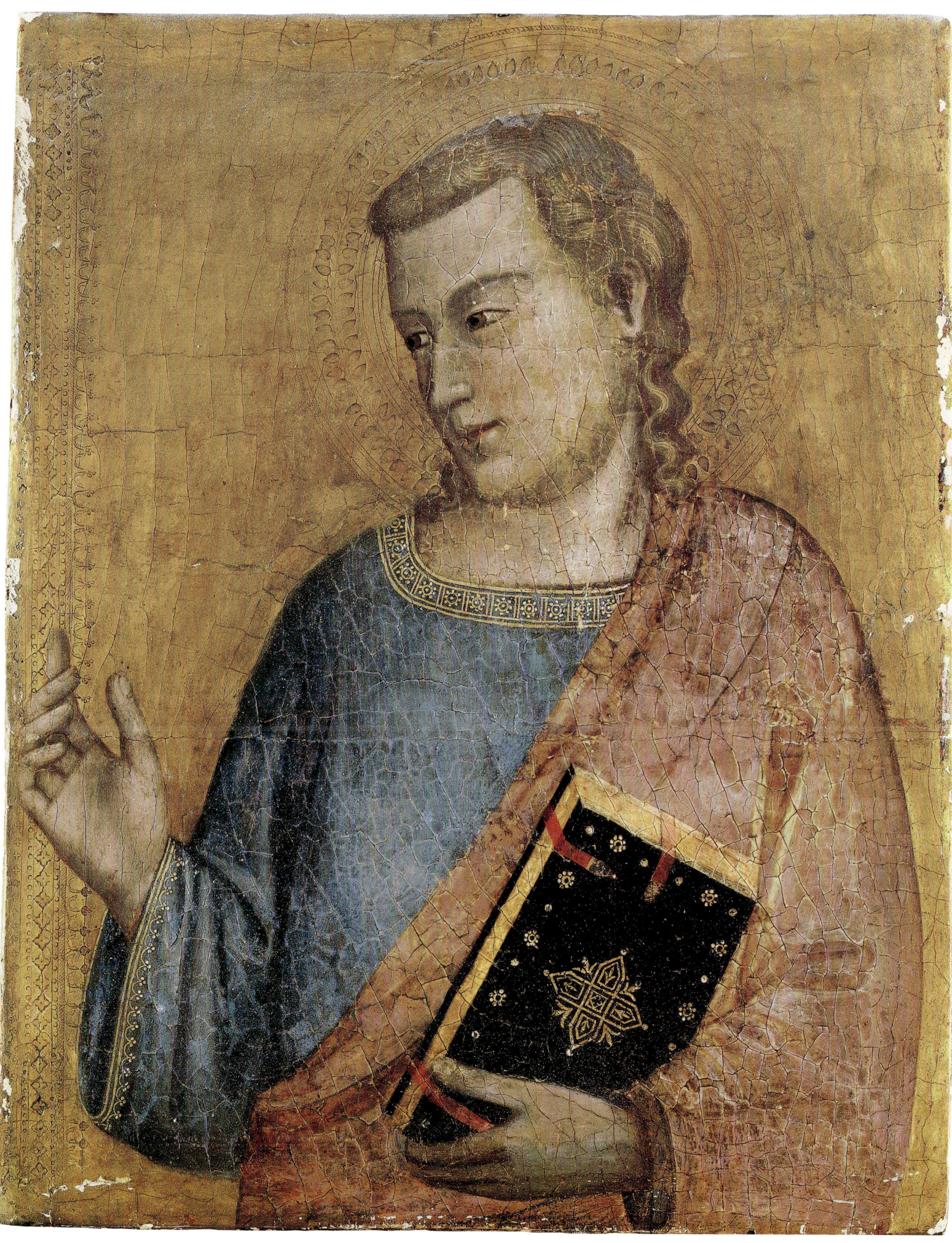

3a Before conservation

These two panels were first published in 1984 by Miklós Boskovits, who attributed them to Bernardo Daddi and recognized them as fragments of an altarpiece that probably also included a much-damaged half-length *Virgin and Child* in the collection of the Yale University Art Gallery (fig. 1), presented there in 1965 as a gift of Hannah Rabinowitz. The association of these three panels was based largely on the correspondence of their punched decoration, confirmed subsequently by Erling Skaug, who adduced as additional evidence the fact that all three paintings had been "semitransferred" from their original supports.[1] This contention is inaccurate. While the linen and paint layers of the Yale *Virgin and Child* have been transferred to a modern support, the Feigen *Saint John the Evangelist* and *Saint Benedict* remain on their original panels. Damages from two panel joins along the horizontal grain of the latter align exactly with major damages to the paint surface of the Yale *Virgin and Child* undoubtedly caused by splits in its original panel support, confirming their reconstruction as parts of a single altarpiece.

While it is certain that these three panels originally stood together, it is less certain that they represent the complete structure of which they formed part. Both Feigen panels have been cropped along their top edges, where not only are the haloes of the saints interrupted at the edge of the panel, but also punch-tool impressions visible beneath repaints (in the *Saint Benedict*) and regilding (in the *Saint John the Evangelist*) of the backgrounds indicate that the panels were originally completed by gabled pinnacles. The Yale *Virgin and Child* has been cropped more aggressively into an arch-shaped picture field, losing both its pinnacle and upper corners, where the figures of two angels placing a crown on the Virgin's head have been obliterated. Additionally, it is possible that two further panels might once have been part of this structure, making it originally a pentaptych rather than a triptych. Both the *Saint John the Evangelist* and the *Saint Benedict* have punched margins along their left edges only, suggesting that each may once have been paired with an additional half-length figure to its right. No such figures have been identified, however, among the surviving paintings attributable to Bernardo Daddi or his followers.

Differences in conception and execution between the figures of Saints John and Benedict, as well as slight differences of scale between them, lead to the suspicion that two different painters must have been involved in their realization. Detail in the *Saint Benedict*, as in the folds of his habit and hairs of his beard, is more finely rendered than in the *Saint John*; the projection of his book in space is more aggressive (lines defining the three visible corners of Benedict's book converge toward a notional vanishing point, whereas those of John's book are roughly parallel to each other); and the bone structure is more angular and the skin tauter in the head and hands of Saint Benedict than in those of Saint John. These differences, which not only distinguish the two panels from each other but also set the *Saint Benedict* apart from the standard production of

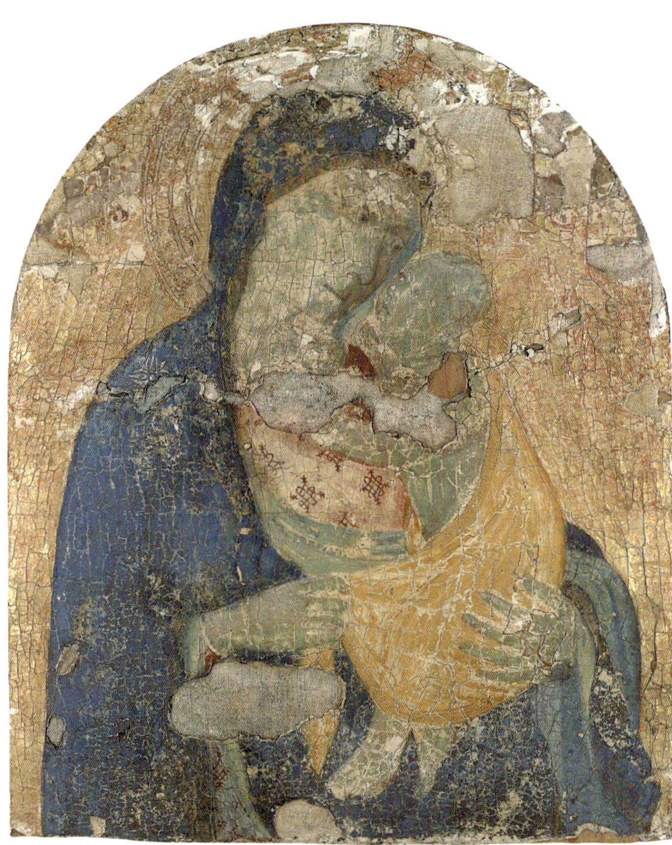

Fig. 1. Bernardo Daddi (or Andrea di Cione?), *Virgin and Child*, ca. 1337. Tempera on panel, 55.7 x 46.2 cm (22 x 18¼ in.). Yale University Art Gallery, New Haven, Conn., Gift of Mrs. Hannah D. Rabinowitz, inv. no. 1965.124

Bernardo Daddi and his shop, are paralleled by very different styles of underdrawing visible on the two panels. The *Saint John* is composed with a thin, delicate, and tentative line drawn probably with a quill pen, while *Saint Benedict* instead uses a broad, sweeping, fluid, and forceful line applied with a brush.

One other important Daddesque work can be identified that shares with the *Saint Benedict* many of its defining characteristics and that diverges in comparable degree from the standard of Bernardo Daddi's acknowledged painting style: the large *Maestà* of 1336 at San Giorgio a Ruballa in Florence, alternately attributed by recent scholarship to Maso di Banco and to Orcagna as a key work in the reconstruction of the earliest career of that Florentine master.[2] The evidence of punch tooling confirms, in a general sense, the association of these panels within a relatively restricted arc of time. The Feigen *Saints* and the San Giorgio a Ruballa *Maestà* share at least two specific motif punches not commonly encountered elsewhere, as well as an overall arrangement of the punch forms and patterns; and on this basis they have been dated in close proximity to each other in Skaug's exhaustive analysis of Bernardo Daddi's use of punch tools. Four of the five motif punches employed in the Feigen panels are inventoried by Skaug among those recurring in paintings from Daddi's shop that were executed between 1335 and 1338: they do not occur in any dated works earlier than this and they disappear from dated works later than this. The fifth punch, Skaug's number 338, was apparently first used by Giotto in his signed polyptych from Santa Maria degli Angeli in Bologna and is found in only one other painting attributed to Bernardo Daddi: a polyptych in the Galleria Communale at Prato.[3] It is suggested by Skaug that this punch was initially borrowed by Daddi from Giotto in 1334, the date usually assigned to the Prato polyptych, and that it may subsequently have been acquired by Daddi after Giotto's death in January 1337, a date he finds appropriate for the Feigen *Saints*.[4]

Discussions of the authorship of the San Giorgio a Ruballa *Maestà* have revolved around its overtly Masesque character, tending to conclude either that Maso was of a generation young enough to have appeared by this date (1336) as an apprentice in Bernardo Daddi's shop or, alternatively, that he was already by this date old enough to have exercised a powerful influence on other artists, specifically on Daddi and on Orcagna. Roberto Bartalini has advanced compelling arguments for considering Maso a member of an older generation than would be compatible with a hypothetical apprenticeship under Bernardo Daddi, and close inspection of the San Giorgio a Ruballa altarpiece reveals a painting technique radically different from that employed by Maso in such works as the Santo Spirito polyptych.[5] Instead, the insistent geometrical abstraction of forms and symmetry of colors in the San Giorgio *Maestà* recall later efforts of the Cione studio more suggestively than they do the work of any other Florentine trecento painters, including Bernardo Daddi, and the proposal to identify this painting (and the Feigen *Saint Benedict* along with it) as the earliest known work by Andrea di Cione seems entirely reasonable.

The problem of identifying the earliest paintings of Orcagna within the workshop of Bernardo Daddi has occupied several generations of scholars with varying, often conflicting results. Prior to the recent association with his name of the San Giorgio a Ruballa *Maestà*, the most persuasive identification was a small *Coronation of the Virgin with Saints* in the Galleria Nazionale di Palazzo Corsini in Rome, but this painting, according to Skaug, would need to be dated on the basis of its punch work to about 1343–44.[6] By this time Orcagna would most likely have been active as a fully independent master, and the Palazzo Corsini *Coronation* therefore, while fully plausible as an attribution to Orcagna, sheds little light on his earliest training as an artist. Closer consideration of the Rabinowitz *Virgin and Child* in the Yale University Art Gallery's collection does not materially aid in this debate. The severely abraded condition of this panel does not permit confident judgments of its style, other than to observe that the emotional interaction between the Virgin and the Christ Child depicted in it is more dramatic than that usually encountered in Bernardo Daddi's many versions of this theme. It would not, therefore, be surprising to learn that the Yale painting had been designed or painted by Orcagna, but it is not possible to aver positively that it was. Traditionally given to Bernardo Daddi, the Yale *Virgin and Child* was reattributed by Offner and Steinweg to Giovanni del Biondo, perhaps an indirect acknowledgment of its Orcagnesque qualities.[7] Charles Seymour, Jr., referred to a later copy of the painting formerly in the Hurd Collection as testimony "to the relative completeness of [Yale's] panel as well as to its importance for its period."[8] The first half of this claim is incorrect, as the remains of two angels and the punched and stippled crown they held above the Virgin's head are still clearly visible cropped at the top edge of the Yale panel. The second contention is undoubtedly true, leading to speculation concerning its possible original provenance in or near Florence, where it is likely to have been publicly, and perhaps prominently, accessible.

The white habit worn by Saint Benedict in the Feigen panel may imply that the altarpiece was a Camaldolese commission. Two chapels in the sacristy of Santa Maria degli Angeli, the principal house of the Camaldolese order in Florence, were endowed by the Spini family in 1336, one with a dedication to Saint Mary Magdalen and one with a dedication to Saint Lawrence. Both of these would have contained altarpieces and either could have included the Feigen *Saints* and Yale *Virgin and Child* if they were originally accompanied by two further panels, one of which would have portrayed either the Magdalen or Saint Lawrence. Another chapel in the sacristy was endowed in 1342 with a bequest of 60 florins by Giovanni di Lottieri Ghitti. The dedication of this chapel to Saint John the Evangelist would be appropriate on iconographic grounds for an association with the Yale/Feigen altarpiece, but the date is too late to advance such a proposal unless, as frequently happened at Santa Maria degli Angeli, the altarpiece was moved there from elsewhere in the monastery and simply "updated" to conform to the circumstances of its new situation. Equally possible but still entirely speculative would be a provenance from the Camaldolese monastery of San Giovanni Evangelista at Pratovecchio, though again no documentation exists for the commissioning of altarpieces there in the fourteenth century. LK

1. Erling S. Skaug, *Punch Marks from Giotto to Fra Angelico: Attribution, Chronology, and Workshop Relationships in Tuscan Panel Painting* (Oslo, 1994), 1: p. 101n.112.
2. For a superficial summary but full bibliography of this important argument, see Ugo Feraci, in *L'eredità di Giotto: Arte a Firenze, 1340–1375*, ed. Angelo Tartuferi, exh. cat. (Florence, 2008), p. 104. For the San Giorgio a Ruballa *Maestà*, see Richard Offner, *A Critical and Historical Corpus of Florentine Painting: The Fourteenth Century*, sec. 3, vol. 4, *Bernardo Daddi: His Shop and Following*, ed. Miklós Boskovitz (Florence, 1991), pl. 20.
3. Offner III/IV, pl. 15.
4. An early dating for the Prato polyptych, which may even be too early for Giotto's ownership of any of the three punches supposedly borrowed from him for use in it, is entirely inferential and is based on the assumption that the polyptych's probable patron, Fra Francesco di Tieri, may have commissioned it to commemorate his appointment in 1334 as rector of the hospital of the Misericordia in Prato. It is worth considering the possibility that the Prato polyptych also dates to 1336 or 1337—especially given the close correspondence in figure type and conception between the

Saints Francis and John the Evangelist depicted in it and the Feigen *Saint Benedict*—and that the punches used in the polyptych were not borrowed from Giotto by Daddi but acquired from him outright. Their disappearance from Daddi's repertoire after 1338 may indicate their transfer to Orcagna's possession, but while plausible, such a contention is neither demonstrable nor in the final analysis necessary to sustain the stylistic arguments raised by the paintings themselves.

5. Roberto Bartalini, "Maso, la cronologia della capella Bardi di Vernio e il giovane Orcagna," *Prospettiva* 77 (1995): pp. 16–35; and Bartalini, "'Et in carne mea videbo Deum meum': Maso di Banco, la cappella dei Confessori e la committenza dei Bardi," *Prospettiva* 98/99 (2000): pp. 58–103.

6. On the Palazzo Corsini *Coronation*, see Miklós Boskovits, "Orcagna in 1357 and Other Times," *Burlington Magazine* 113 (1971): pp. 239–51; and Daniela Parenti, "Studi recenti su Orcagna e sulla pittura dopo la 'peste nera,'" *Arte cristiana* 89, no. 806 (2001): pp. 325–32.

7. Richard Offner and Klara Steinweg, *A Critical and Historical Corpus of Florentine Painting*, sec. 4, vol. 5, *Giovanni del Biondo* (New York, 1969), p. 27.

8. Charles Seymour, Jr., *Early Italian Paintings in the Yale University Art Gallery* (New Haven, Conn., 1970), pp. 28–29. The Hurd *Madonna* is reproduced in Offner IV/V, pl. 4. Miklós Boskovits, in Richard Offner, *A Critical and Historical Corpus of Florentine Painting*, sec. 3, vol. 3, *The Works of Bernardo Daddi*, ed. Boskovits (Florence, 1989), p. 359, claims that after cleaning, the Yale *Virgin and Child* appears to be earlier than the Hurd *Madonna* and was perhaps the prototype on which Giovanni del Biondo based more than one version of the composition; see also Offner IV/V, pl. 9.

Andrea di Cione, called Orcagna
Florence, active by 1343–1368

4a. *The Deposition*, ca. 1360–65

Tempera on panel, 33.6 x 20.3 cm (13¼ x 8 in.), overall; 31.8 x 19.7 cm (12½ x 7¾ in.), picture surface

PROVENANCE: see no. 4b

BIBLIOGRAPHY: see no. 4b

CONDITION: The panel retains its original thickness—13 mm—and has not been cradled, although two walnut(?) battens have been inlaid across its (vertical) grain on the reverse as has a single butterfly join near its lower edge. The back of the panel is painted fictive porphyry, possibly original. Engaged moldings have been removed from all four sides of the panel, and the left edge has been trimmed to the edge of the picture field. Damage from the removal of hinges is apparent at the right edge of the panel approximately 65 mm from the top and from the bottom. The paint surface is well preserved overall, with retouched losses confined to the heads of the Virgin and the female attendant at the left, Joseph of Arimathea's left thigh, and Saint John's right leg. The gold ground inside the punched framing arch has been releafed over the original bolus: the punch tooling along the decorated margins is original but the haloes of the figures have all been reworked.

Andrea di Cione, called Orcagna
Florence, active by 1343–1368

4b. *The Entombment*, ca. 1360–65

Tempera on panel, 33.7 x 21 cm (14½ x 8¼ in.), overall; 31.2 x 19.7 cm (12¼ x 7¾ in.), picture surface

PROVENANCE: Larderel collection, Livorno, until 1945; Silvano Lodi; Barbara Piasecka Johnson, 1989

BIBLIOGRAPHY: Richard Offner and Klara Steinweg, *A Critical and Historical Corpus of Florentine Painting: The Fourteenth Century*, sec. 4, vol. 3, *Jacopo di Cione* (New York, 1965), pp. 99–100, pl. 8; Miklós Boskovits, *Pittura fiorentina alla vigilia del Rinascimento, 1370–1400* (Florence, 1975), p. 326; Thomas Gibson Fine Art, Ltd., *19th and 20th Century Masters and Selected Old Masters*, exh. cat. (London, 1988), p. 8; Ada S. Labriola(?), in *Opus Sacrum: Catalogue of the Exhibition from the Collection of Barbara Piasecka*, ed. Józef Grabski, exh. cat. (Warsaw, 1990), pp. 32–39; Laurence Kanter, "Riconsiderazioni orcagnesche: Due pannelli della Raccolta Crespi attribuiti al Maestro della Predella dell'Ashmolean Museum," in *I fondi oro della collezione Alberto Crespi al Museo Diocesano di Milano: Questioni iconografiche e attributive, atti della giornata di studi, 11 ottobre 2004* (Milan, 2009), p. 53

CONDITION: The panel retains its original thickness—13 mm—and has not been cradled, although two walnut(?) battens have been inlaid across its (vertical) grain on the reverse as have four butterfly joins along an irregular vertical split running the full height of the panel. The back of the panel is painted fictive porphyry, possibly original. Engaged moldings have been removed from all four sides of the panel, and putty repairs of damage from the removal of hinges are apparent at the left edge of the panel. The paint surface is well preserved overall, with retouched flaking losses confined to the draperies of the kneeling women in the foreground, the draperies of the three bottom angels, and the heads of the two top angels. The gold ground inside the punched framing arch has been releafed over the original bolus: the punch tooling along the decorated margins is original, but the haloes of the figures have all been reworked.

The *Deposition* and the *Entombment*—the latter actually a conflation of images of the Lamentation and the Entombment—were first published by Richard Offner and Klara Steinweg among the few paintings that they accepted as autograph works by Jacopo di Cione.[1] The photographs of the panels that they included in the *Corpus* volume dedicated to Jacopo's work showed them in the heavily repainted state typical of works of art from the Larderel collection, and led the authors not unreasonably to propose that they may originally have functioned as pinnacles to an altarpiece, on the analogy to the narrative pinnacles of the San Pier Maggiore high altarpiece by Jacopo now in the National Gallery, London. Miklós Boskovits reiterated an attribution to Jacopo di Cione for the panels but advanced the probable date of their execution from the mid-1370s (following the San Pier Maggiore altarpiece), as proposed by Offner and Steinweg, to 1365–70, that is, possibly before the death in 1368 of Jacopo's older brother Andrea (Orcagna) and Jacopo's emergence as head of the family workshop.[2] He cited similarities of figure style in the panels to that of Jacopo di Cione's small altarpiece of the *Crucifixion* in the National Gallery, London, executed in collaboration with a one-time assistant of Orcagna known

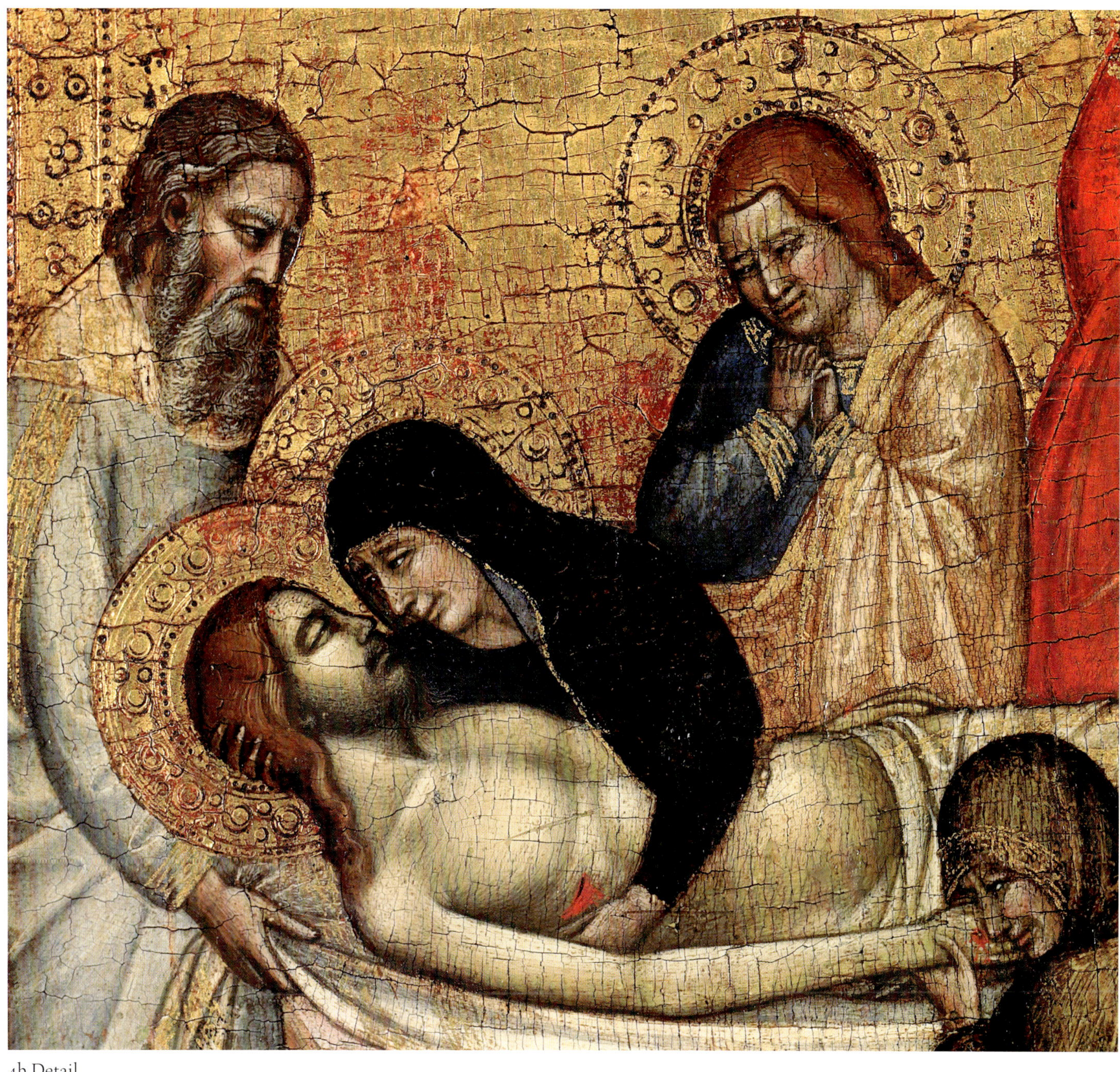

4b Detail

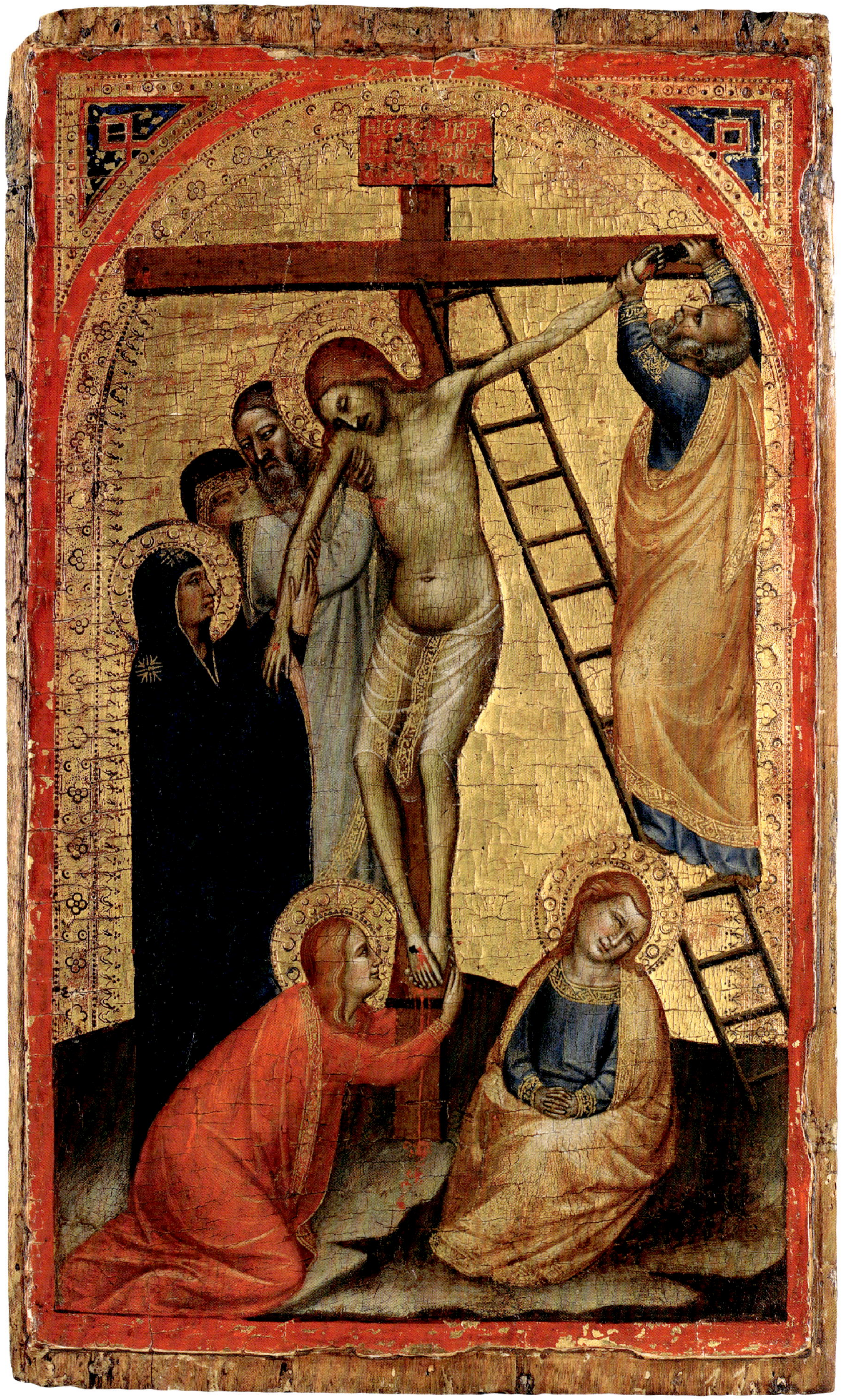

4a

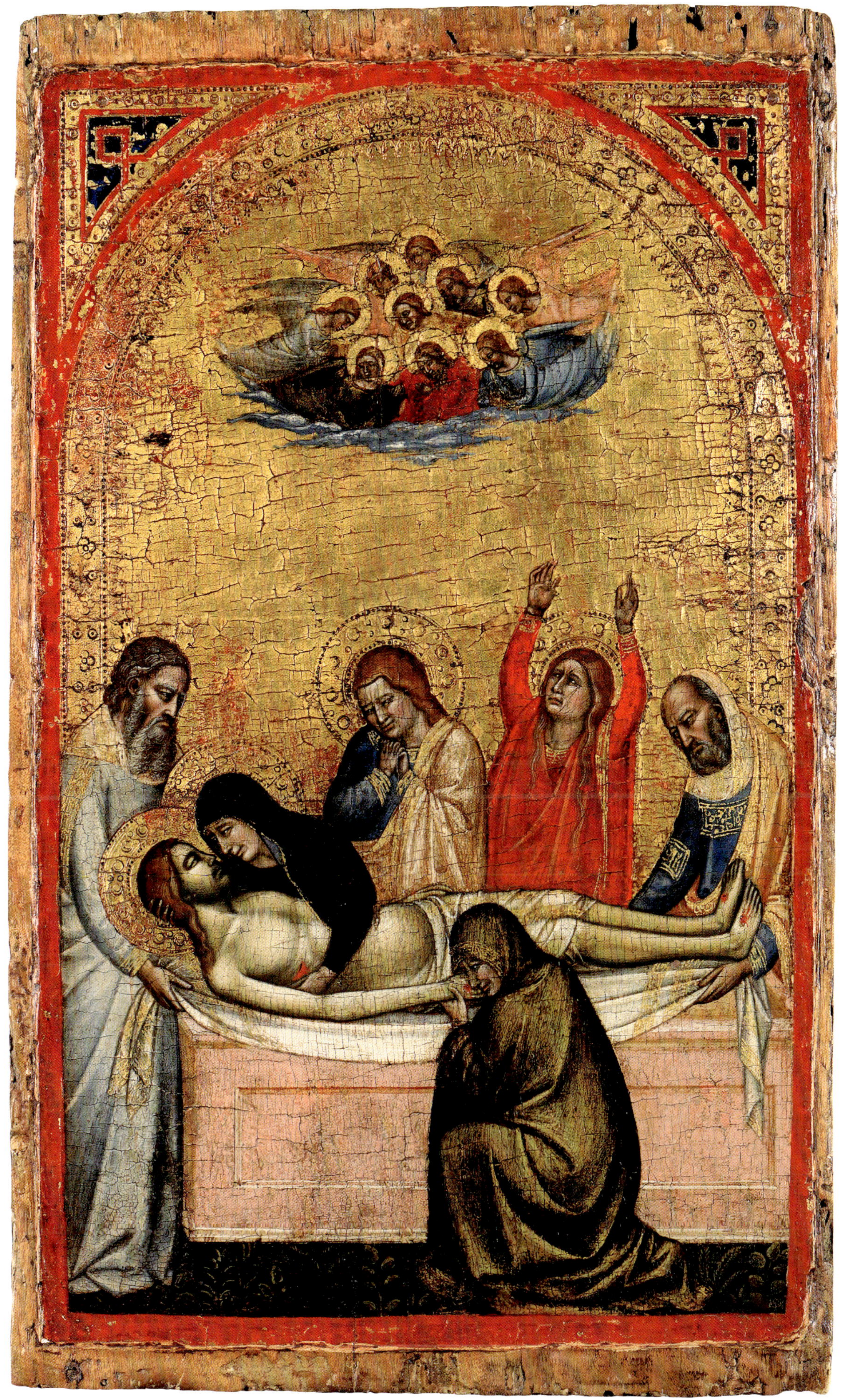

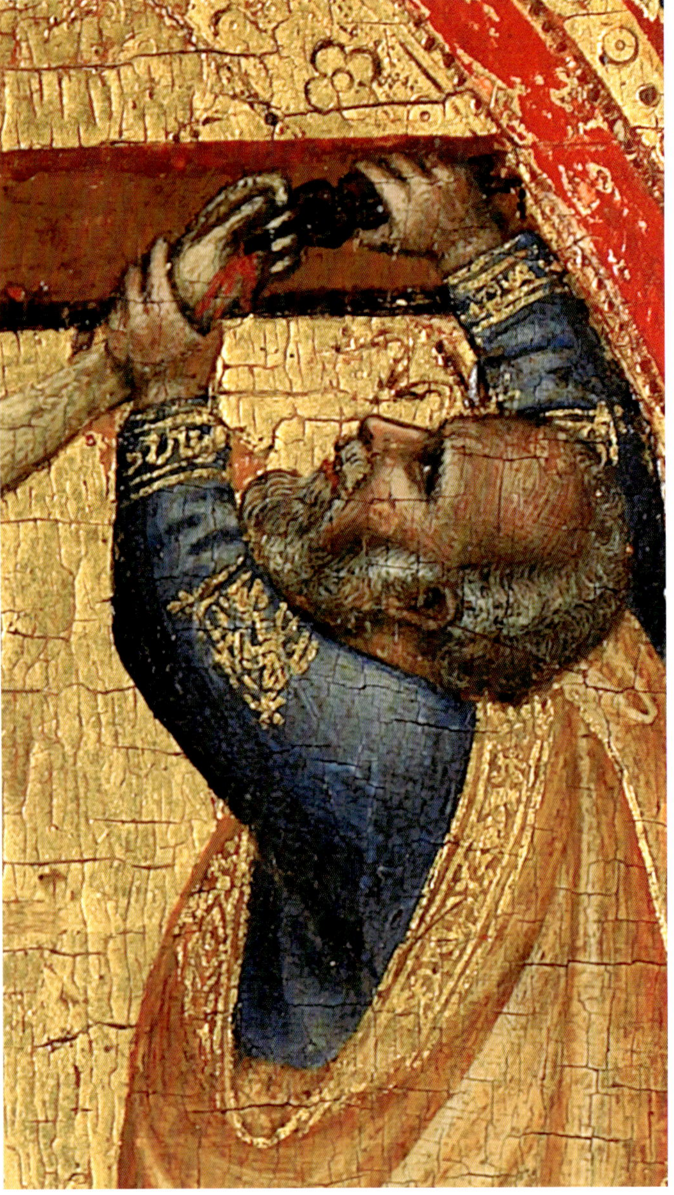

4a Detail

part in any firmly accepted work by Jacopo from the 1370s or later. The sharp, angular, but well-modeled drapery folds, with sophisticated patterns of highlight and shadow; the finely articulated and detailed anatomy; and the highly expressive heads are instead more characteristic of the work of Orcagna himself, while the utterly original iconography of both scenes, combining elements from various earlier narrative prototypes into a novel reformulation not encountered elsewhere in Florentine painting, is difficult to reconcile with Jacopo's usual narrative conservatism. Prior to 1368, however, it is unclear to what extent Jacopo di Cione actually painted independently or whether instead he might have worked all but exclusively as an assistant in his brothers' studios, the operation of which he inherited following their deaths in 1365 (Nardo) and 1368 (Andrea). The execution of the *Saint Matthew* triptych in the Galleria degli Uffizi, Florence—commissioned from Orcagna in 1367 and then transferred to Jacopo di Cione, who received final payment for it in 1369—is a case in point: no consensus has been reached by scholars in defining the role of either painter in its conception or realization. Similarly, a much-restored *Virgin and Child* formerly in the Stoclet collection, sometimes known as the *Parte Guelfa Madonna* and bearing an inscription with the date 1362, has been accepted as a typical early work of Jacopo di Cione, an autograph painting by Orcagna, and an anonymous Daddesque-Orcagnesque effort, none of which are mutually exclusive categories in the present state of our understanding of the confusing nature of collaboration in this highly productive workshop.[4]

Although they show specific points of correspondence to figures in the predella panels from the Strozzi altarpiece in Santa Maria Novella, Florence, of 1357, the *Deposition* and *Entombment* are unlikely to have been designed by Orcagna at that point, or at any earlier point, in his career. No dated works by Orcagna between the Strozzi altarpiece and the *Saint Matthew* triptych are known, and only the 1362 *Parte Guelfa Madonna*—whether it is autograph or not (its condition makes judgments in this respect difficult)—offers a fixed standard for evaluating works within this ten-year period. The perhaps not coincidental resemblance between the figure of Saint John the Evangelist seated on the ground in the *Deposition* and the Virgin in the *Parte Guelfa Madonna* cannot argue for an attribution to Jacopo di Cione for the former but might imply the approximate contemporaneity of the two works. Shortly after 1363, Orcagna, along with his brother Nardo, seems to have adopted the use of a set of punch tools to decorate the gold grounds of his panels that he shared with a number of other Florentine painting studios (significantly, this practice was not continued by Jacopo di Cione when he later assumed control of the studio).[5] These punches appear, for example, in the *Virgin and Child with Six Angels* in the Szépművészeti Múzeum, Budapest, frequently attributed to Jacopo di Cione but clearly executed in Orcagna's studio (possibly, though not certainly, with

as the Master of the Ashmolean Predella. Finally, Ada Labriola, in the exhibition catalogue of religious paintings from the collection of Barbara Piasecka Johnson, elaborated on the comparisons made by Boskovits, though she suggested that the elegant colors, reminiscent of Bernardo Daddi, revealed when the two paintings were cleaned, might imply a date for them even earlier than 1365.[3] Additionally, she noted that the complex psychology and emotive content of the narratives, as well as their delicacy of representational detail, might indicate "that the panels were not intended to function as upper portions of a polyptych."

Labriola's intuition, advancing the date for the two panels earlier than 1365, may be defended on more than the basis of palette alone and raises a complementary issue concerning their attribution. Presumably, their identification as works by Jacopo di Cione is based on a perceived simplification of Orcagna's style, for neither the figure types, drapery forms, nor spatial structure of these panels find a precise counter-

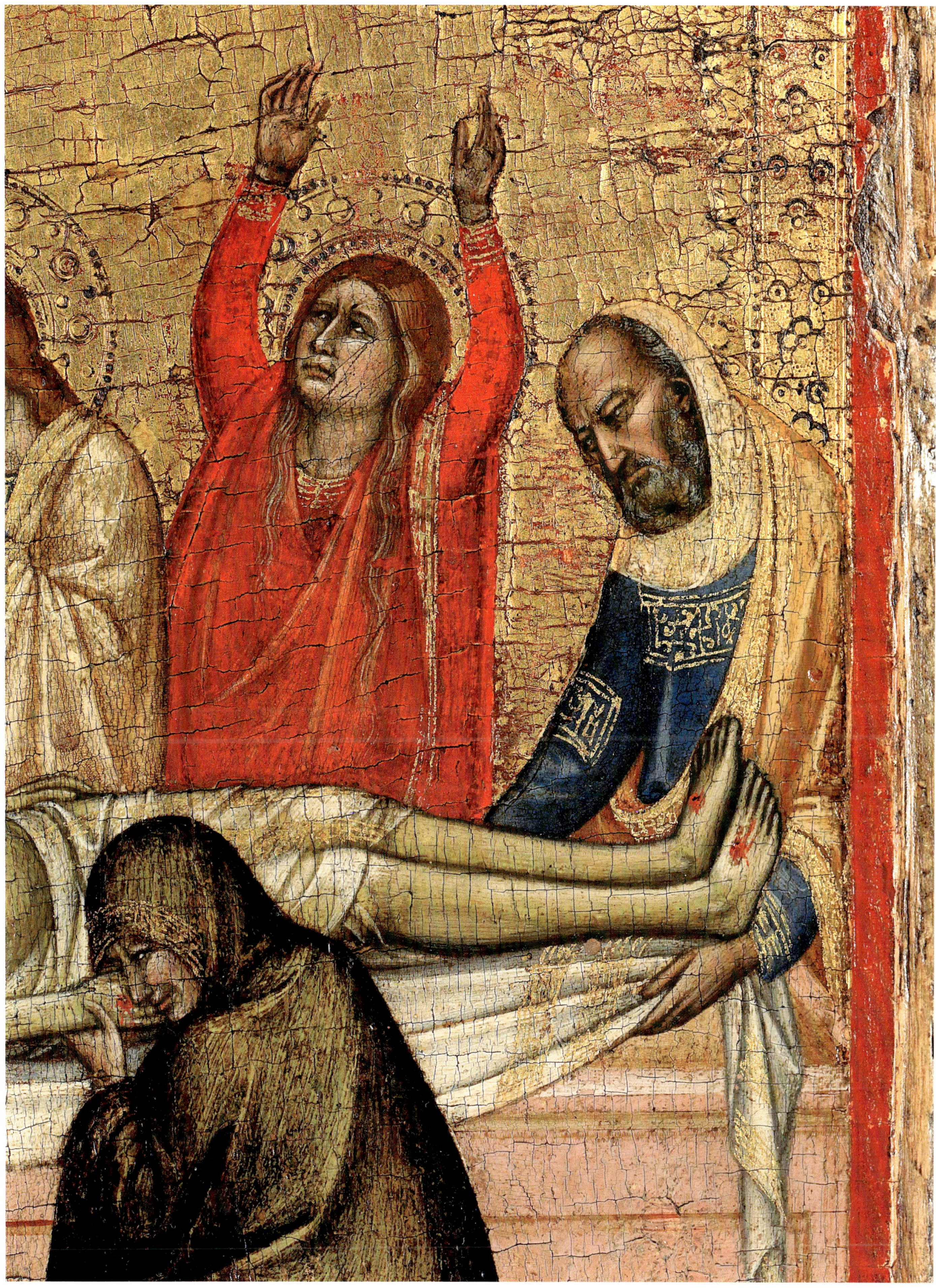

4b Detail

Jacopo's assistance), in the surviving pilasters and pinnacles from an unknown altarpiece painted for Santa Maria degli Angeli,[6] and in the *Saint Matthew* triptych. The punch decoration of the *Deposition* and *Entombment* does not, unfortunately, provide an absolutely certain frame of reference for determining whether they might have been painted before or after 1363, since the gilding of these panels is largely modern. The tooling of the margins that is original includes two punch motifs that may correspond with nos. 94 and 295 in Erling Skaug's lists of Florentine and Sienese punch tools; if the identification of the former is correct, it would imply a date for the panels after 1363.[7]

In the overpainted state in which they were known to Offner and Steinweg, the original function of these two panels would have been difficult or impossible to determine. Too tall and narrow to be predella panels, and seemingly too short and wide to be the wings of a tabernacle triptych, their possible deployment as the pinnacles to an altarpiece was not an unreasonable conjecture. Labriola's objection that their narrative complexity is perhaps inappropriate for such a context is well founded, however. Restoration of their approximately original format, revealed by cleaning, and a consideration of the thickness of each panel, which has not been altered, leads inevitably to the conclusion that they were movable wings of a triptych or some other multipanel structure. Evidence of hinges on the reverse of the panels was largely obliterated by the inset battens applied in an early restoration, but one end of each hinge is still visible on the back of the *Deposition*, and putty repairs at corresponding heights on the *Entombment* must indicate the placement of hinges there as well. Unusually for triptych wings of this period, the panels would, when folded closed, have covered a central panel wider than it is tall. It is possible that they could have functioned as valves of a diptych rather than a triptych—in which case their subjects as well as format are unusual—or they might be presumed to have functioned as the folding doors of a *custodia* or tabernacle cupboard. If that were so, they could originally have been accompanied by further scenes of the Passion, but the number of such scenes and their possible arrangement cannot be ascertained without the fortuitous discovery of further fragments from this hypothetical ensemble.   L K

1. Richard Offner and Klara Steinweg, *A Critical and Historical Corpus of Florentine Painting: The Fourteenth Century*, sec. 4, vol. 3, *Jacopo di Cione* (New York, 1965), pp. 99–100, pl. 8.
2. Miklós Boskovits, *Pittura fiorentina alla vigilia del Rinascimento, 1370–1400* (Florence, 1975), p. 326.
3. Ada S. Labriola(?), in *Opus Sacrum: Catalogue of the Exhibition from the Collection of Barbara Piasecka*, ed. Józef Grabski, exh. cat. (Warsaw, 1990), pp. 32–39.
4. See Boskovits, *Pittura fiorentina*, p. 32; Daniela Parenti, "Studi recenti su Orcagna e sulla pittura dopo la 'peste nera,'" *Arte cristiana* 89, no. 806 (2001): pp. 329–30; Gert Kreytenberg, *Orcagna, Andrea di Cione: Ein universeller Künstler der Gotik* (Mainz, Germany, 2000), pp. 164–66; and Offner IV/III, p. IIIn.2.
5. Erling S. Skaug, *Punch Marks from Giotto to Fra Angelico: Attribution, Chronology, and Workshop Relationships in Tuscan Panel Painting* (Oslo, 1994), 1: pp. 168–80, 193–200.
6. These fragments comprise a pinnacle in the National Gallery, London, representing the *Noli me tangere*, a pinnacle of the *Crucifixion* in the Robert Lehman Collection at the Metropolitan Museum of Art, New York, six half-length *Angels* framed together with the Lehman *Crucifixion*, six pilaster panels of full-length *Saints* published by Offner IV/III, pl. 3, incorrectly as parts of the San Pier Maggiore altarpiece, and six unpublished pilaster figures of *Saints* currently on loan to the National Gallery, London.
7. See Skaug, *Punch Marks*. The trefoil punch possibly identifiable as no. 94 might instead be no. 102, identified by Skaug among the punches used by the Master of San Lucchese in a *Coronation of the Virgin* in the Lindenau Museum, Altenburg, Germany. This painting is more closely related to the early style of Orcagna than is commonly acknowledged, but the precise identification of the trefoil punch used by Orcagna (no. 94, for example, appears in the Lehman *Angels* mentioned in n.6, above) is elusive and its confusion with other punches of similar shape and size renders unreliable conclusions based on its occurrence alone.

Andrea Bonaiuti

Florence, documented 1346–79

5. *Saints John the Baptist and James,*
ca. 1350–55

Tempera on panel, 23.4 x 14.9 cm (9¼ x 5⅞ in.)

PROVENANCE: Adolphe Stoclet, Brussels, by 1927; Mme Feron-Stoclet, by 1956, and by descent until 2001; Brimo de Laroussilhe, Paris

BIBLIOGRAPHY: Pierre Bautier, "I primitivi italiani della collezione Stoclet a Bruxelles," *Cronache d'arte* 4 (1927): p. 314; Raimond van Marle, *Le scuole della pittura italiana* (The Hague, 1934), 2: p. 326; D. Lion-Goldschmidt, *Collection Adolphe Stoclet: Choix d'oeuvres appartenant à madame Feron Stoclet* (Brussels, 1956), p. 98; Miklós Boskovits, *Pittura fiorentina alla vigilia del Rinascimento, 1370–1400* (Florence, 1975), p. 277; Richard Offner, *A Critical and Historical Corpus of Florentine Painting: The Fourteenth Century, Supplement, a Legacy of Attributions*, ed. Hayden B. J. Maginnis (New York, 1981), p. 25; Serena Romano, "Andrea di Bonaiuto," in *Allgemeines Künstlerlexicon*, ed. Thieme-Becker (1986): 2, p. 980; Serena Romano, "Andrea Bonaiuti," in *Enciclopedia*

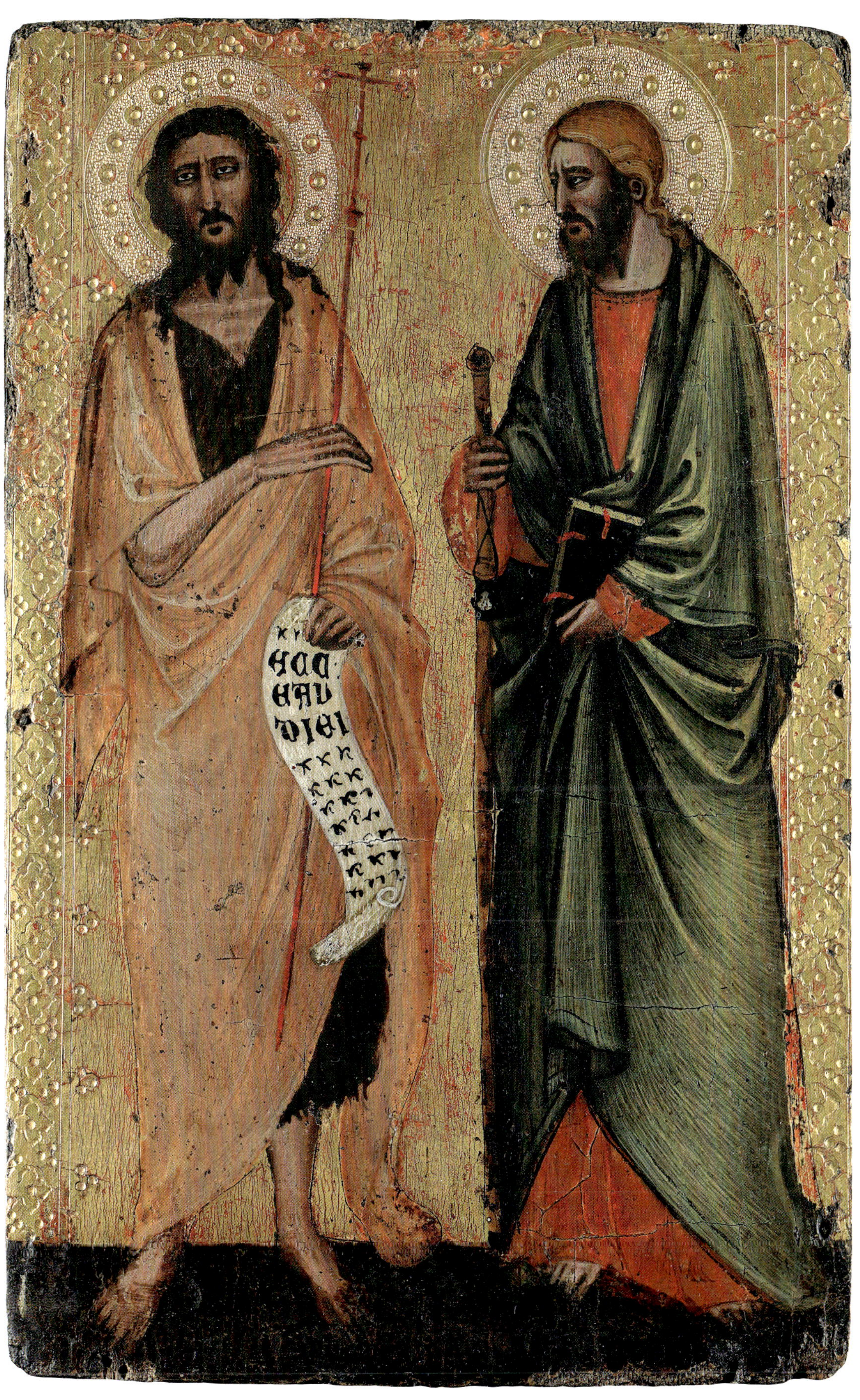

dell'arte medievale (1991), 1: p. 602; Erling S. Skaug, *Punch Marks from Giotto to Fra Angelico: Attribution, Chronology, and Workshop Relationships in Tuscan Panel Painting* (Oslo, 1994), 1: pp. 161–64; Johannes Tripps, *Tendencies of Gothic in Florence: Andrea Bonaiuti*, A Critical and Historical Corpus of Florentine Painting, sec. 4, vol. 7, pt. 1 (Florence, 1996), p. 105; Mojmír S. Frinta, *Punched Decoration on Late Medieval Panel and Miniature Painting* (Prague, 1998), 1: pp. 387, 390

CONDITION: The panel, of a vertical wood grain, has been thinned to 9 mm and cradled. The paint surface is in an excellent state of preservation. Scattered pinpoint flaking losses (retouched) across the "pavement" at the bottom of the panel interrupt the profile of the figures' feet, and two small gilding losses in the Baptist's halo and at the center of the top edge of the panel have been repaired. A narrow strip of gilding at the back of Saint James's robe has flaked away: the exposed bolus in that area now reads confusingly as a stripe of red paint. The panel bears no trace of hinges or of scars from their removal.

This exceptionally refined little panel was long considered to be Sienese and attributed to the artist conventionally known as Barna da Siena (see no. 13), before being recognized by Miklós Boskovits as the work of Andrea Bonaiuti of Florence.[1] Any attribution to Andrea Bonaiuti must in the first instance be based on similarities to the frescoes in the Spanish Chapel at Santa Maria Novella (1365–67), the artist's only fully documented undertaking, and such similarities do exist in this instance, especially to figures such as Job and David at the left of the *Triumph of Saint Thomas Aquinas* on the west wall of the chapel. At the same time it must be acknowledged that the Feigen *Saints John the Baptist and James* is in many respects different from any other panel painting plausibly attributed to Andrea Bonaiuti, principally in its darker emotional range, more attenuated figure types, and finer, more agitated drapery patterns. These aspects of the painting, which account in great measure for its earlier attribution to Barna da Siena, find their closest parallels— although not absolutely compelling analogues—in the fragments of a dispersed triptych by Andrea Bonaiuti now divided between the Statens Museum in Copenhagen and the Museum of Fine Arts in Houston. Those panels were recognized by Richard Offner as works by the same artist as the Feigen (then Stoclet) *Saints John the Baptist and James*, an artist he christened the Statens Nardesque Master.[2] Following Offner, Boskovits contended, probably correctly, that the Statens Nardesque Master is not to be considered an independent painter but a phase of the early career of Andrea Bonaiuti. The strongly Orcagnesque character of the Copenhagen, Houston, and especially Feigen panels argues in support of this contention, and for a dating close to or shortly after 1350 for the group.

In his sphragiological study of the paintings attributed to Andrea Bonaiuti, Erling Skaug grouped the Feigen *Saints John the Baptist and James* together with a panel formerly in the van Gelder collection, now also in the Feigen collection (no. 6), and another in the Boymans van Beuningen Museum, Rotterdam, the Netherlands, as late works by the artist, painted after 1363, based on the occurrence among them of punch marks made by tools thought to have been brought to Florence from Siena in that year.[3] A date of ca. 1365–70 for the ex–Van Gelder panel is entirely convincing on stylistic as well as sphragiological grounds, while the Rotterdam panel forms part of a small, coherent group of paintings isolated by Offner under the name "Master of the Blue Crucifix" that appear all to be late works by Andrea Bonaiuti, possibly executed after 1370, in the final decade of the artist's career. The *Saints John the Baptist and James*, however, has nothing in common with any of these works, and the one motif punch found in its border constitutes, as even Skaug recognized, a special case among those purportedly deriving from Siena in 1363. This punch mark first occurs much earlier in the century on Florentine panels, migrating from the workshop of Giotto himself to that of Bernardo Daddi around 1337 (see no. 3), or possibly as early as 1334, and from there to the workshop of Andrea di Cione or artists closely associated with him (such as the Master of San Lucchese). Its sole occurrence on a Sienese panel is coincident with this last stage of its migratory history: the punch mark was used to decorate the gold ground of an altarpiece by Pietro Lorenzetti now in the National Gallery of Art, Washington, D.C., and it is on this basis that it is presumed to have joined the other punches demonstrably present in Sienese workshops until 1363, and only thereafter in Florence. Five of the six punches used in the Washington painting, however, do not recur in any other painting by Lorenzetti, nor in any other Sienese painting, and the shape of the panels comprising the Washington altarpiece is also more typical of Florentine than of Sienese carpentry work. It might be argued that the Washington altarpiece was perhaps painted in Florence, where Pietro could have made use of the studio property of a local master, rather than that it constitutes evidence of this particular tool having been in circulation in Siena and unavailable to Florentine craftsmen until later in the century.[4]

The size and shape of *Saints John the Baptist and James* argue for its being a fragment of the wing of a devotional triptych—presumably the right wing—where it would have been surmounted by another panel approximately the same size and shape, possibly portraying two more standing saints, and by a triangular or half-arched pinnacle probably portraying the Annunciate Virgin. No such fragments by Andrea Bonaiuti are known, however, nor are any panels that might have stood alongside it in the center or left wing of such a triptych. For the present, *Saints John the Baptist and James* is both physically and stylistically a *unicum* within the accepted oeuvre of the artist.   LK

1. Miklós Boskovits, *Pittura fiorentina alla vigilia del Rinascimento, 1370–1400* (Florence, 1975), p. 277.

2. Richard Offner, *A Critical and Historical Corpus of Florentine Painting: The Fourteenth Century, Supplement, a Legacy of Attributions*, ed. Hayden B. J. Maginnis (New York, 1981), pp. 25–26; see also Carolyn C. Wilson, *Italian Paintings XIV–XVI Centuries in the Museum of Fine Arts, Houston* (Houston, 1996), pp. 79–90, where the Houston and Copenhagen panels are catalogued as "Circle of Andrea Orcagna [*sic*] and Nardo di Cione."

3. Erling S. Skaug, *Punch Marks from Giotto to Fra Angelico: Attribution, Chronology, and Workshop Relationships in Tuscan Panel Painting* (Oslo, 1994), 1: pp. 161–64.

4. There is, furthermore, some confusion over the exact punch used in the Feigen *Saints John the Baptist and James*. The painting is listed by Mojmir Frinta twice, although only a single motif punch occurs in it; and similar punches are documented by Frinta in a variety of Sienese and Florentine panels of approximately overlapping dates. The difficulties of precise measurement of the punch strikes and of slight differences to the center "dot" in this particular motif make all but impossible a determination of the actual number of punch tools involved. See Mojmir S. Frinta, *Punched Decoration on Late Medieval Panel and Miniature Painting* (Prague, 1998), 1: pp. 387, 390.

Andrea Bonaiuti

Florence, documented 1346–79

6. *Eight Saints*, ca. 1365–70

Tempera on panel, 112.1 x 51.7 cm (44⅛ x 20⅜ in.)

PROVENANCE: Captain Annesley Gore, London; Gaston Newmans, Brussels (his sale, Galerie Fievez, Brussels, November 26–27, 1924, lot 8); Mme M. van Gelder, Belgium; Brimo de Laroussilhe, Paris

BIBLIOGRAPHY: Stedelijk Museum, *Italiaansche Kunst in Nederlandsch Bezit*, exh. cat. (Amsterdam, 1934), no. 260; Millard Meiss, *Painting in Florence and Siena after the Black Death* (Princeton, N.J., 1951), p. 47; Miklós Boskovits, *Pittura fiorentina alla vigilia del Rinascimento, 1370–1400* (Florence, 1975), p. 277; Richard Offner, *A Critical and Historical Corpus of Florentine Painting: The Fourteenth Century, Supplement, a Legacy of Attributions*, ed. Hayden B. J. Maginnis (New York, 1981), p. 63; Serena Romano, "Andrea Bonaiuti," in *Allgemeines Künstlerlexicon*, ed. Thieme-Becker (1986): 2, p. 980; Serena Romano, "Andrea Bonaiuti," in *Enciclopedia dell'arte medievale* (1991), 1: p. 602; Erling S. Skaug, *Punch Marks from Giotto to Fra Angelico: Attribution, Chronology, and Workshop Relationships in Tuscan Panel Painting* (Oslo, 1994), 1: pp. 162–64; Johannes Tripps, *Tendencies of Gothic in Florence: Andrea Bonaiuti*, A Critical and Historical Corpus of Florentine Painting, sec. 4, vol. 7, pt. 1 (Florence, 1996), pp. 39, 158; Mojmir S. Frinta, *Punched Decoration on Late Medieval Panel and Miniature Painting* (Prague, 1998), 1: p. 453

CONDITION: The panel retains its original thickness of 3 cm and is only moderately warped. It has been cut along the outer profile of the arch at the top, excising the cusps of its pastiglia framing and leaving two areas of exposed wood from the removal of engaged corbels. Exposed gesso at the left and right vertical edges implies that these are original and were covered by attached colonettes. An 11 cm wide batten is secured across the back of the panel 46 cm from the bottom edge. Two small nails, 99 and 100 cm from the bottom edge, may have secured a second batten at that height. The paint surface is exceptionally well preserved, displaying modest abrasion near the edges of the composition and local retouching in Saint Bartholomew's white draperies, especially in the lower left corner.

The panel, clearly the left lateral of an altarpiece triptych of not inconsiderable size, portrays eight saints—seven male and one female—kneeling in adoration facing to the viewer's right. Saint Bartholomew, furthest forward in the bottom row, holds a knife, symbolic of his attempted martyrdom by flaying, and a book, in reference both to his status as an apostle of Christ and to his mission to evangelize Armenia. Next to him is a saint usually identified as Matthew, though his attributes are not unequivocally clear, and completing the bottom row at the right edge of the panel is Saint Peter, wearing his conventional colors of blue and yellow with a priest's alb over his shoulders, and holding the silver and gold keys in his right hand and a volume of his epistles in his left. Above Saint Peter is Saint John the Baptist, pointing to the scene or figures on the contiguous center panel of the altarpiece and holding in his left hand a scroll lettered EC/CE A/NGN/I[S] [*sic*] DEI/ ECC/E Q/UI T[OLLIT] (Behold the Lamb of God . . .). Alongside the Baptist are Saint James the Lesser(?) and a young apostle usually identified as Saint John the Evangelist. In the top row of the panel are Saint Paul, holding the sword of his martyrdom, and a female saint usually identified as Mary Magdalen, but particularized by no attributes other than her red dress.

This panel first appeared at public sale in 1924 with an attribution to Giovanni del Biondo proposed by Osvald Siren, and it was subsequently exhibited in Amsterdam in 1934 as

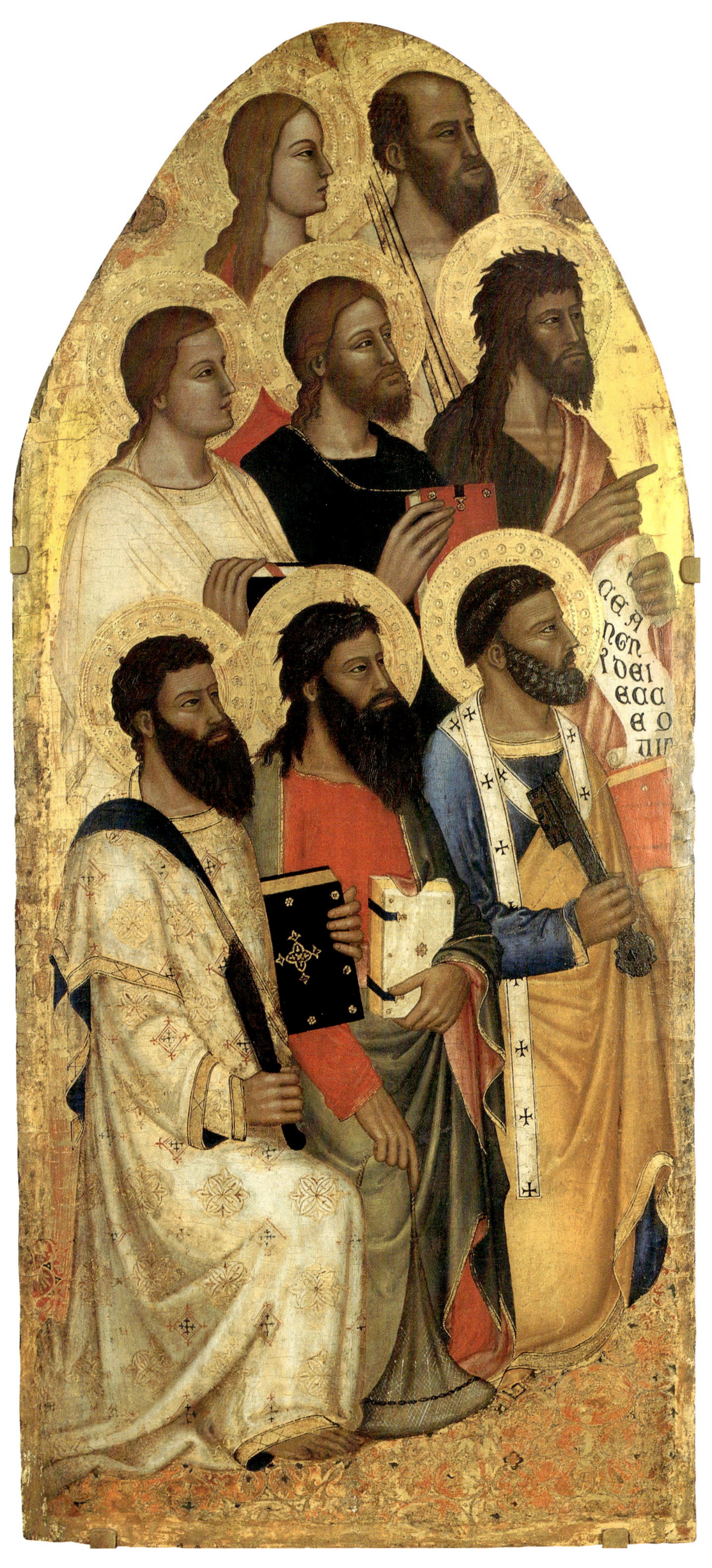

ecca
non
i dei
eaa
e o
uir

by Allegretto Nuzi. The name of Andrea Bonaiuti was tentatively associated with it by Millard Meiss, who described it as a work from the artist's circle possibly on the suggestion of Richard Offner, in whose posthumous lists it appears as "Workshop of Andrea Bonaiuti."[1] Bonaiuti's name and a date around 1365–70 were advanced firmly by Miklós Boskovits and have been largely accepted since.[2] The attribution and dating are based on the identity in style between the figures in this panel and those in the frescoes in the Spanish Chapel at Santa Maria Novella in Florence, the only fully documented work by Andrea Bonaiuti, for which payments are registered from 1365 to 1367 and which are commonly dated 1366–68. Johannes Tripps singled out resemblances to the fresco of the *Resurrection* in the chapel vaults, one of the first works painted there, but even closer parallels are evident to the figures in the upper half of the *Triumph of Saint Thomas Aquinas* on the west wall of the chapel.[3]

Given the size and enormous complexity of the Spanish Chapel frescoes and the limited time allotted to Bonaiuti for their completion, it has been argued that they cannot have been executed without extensive assistance. The overall uniformity of their conception, spatial projection, and figure style, however, does not permit too close a division of hands among the various scenes and consequently does not beg the question of attributing to Bonaiuti panel paintings such as the present altarpiece wing, but it does urge caution in depending exclusively upon comparison to the frescoes to establish dating and chronology. To this end, Erling Skaug's observations are more useful. Skaug catalogued three punch tools used in the decoration of the gold ground on the present panel, all of which he identified among a group of punches brought to Florence from Siena around 1363 and thereafter shared among a group of Florentine painters until the middle of the following decade.[4] It would follow that 1363 may be taken as a *terminus post quem*, and the range 1365–70 seems entirely satisfactory.

Following a formula first popularized by Bernardo Daddi and subsequently by Orcagnesque masters of the following generation, it is likely that the missing center panel of Bonaiuti's altarpiece portrayed the Coronation of the Virgin, while the right lateral panel would have contained eight more saints kneeling in three rows, completing a symmetrical composition with the present panel. No panels or fragments of panels by Bonaiuti that match this description are known. The identities of the saints in the missing right lateral panel might help specify a likely provenance for the altarpiece, but in their absence it is possible only to make a few generic observations that may or may not bear upon the question. The present panel includes no monastic saints or saints representative of liturgical (deacons, bishops, popes) or civil (kings, princes, knights) orders. Saints Peter, John the Baptist, and Paul are aligned vertically and closest to the sacred scene in the center panel, but it might be significant that saints as important as John the Baptist and Paul are relegated to lesser prominence in the back rows, perhaps suggesting that either Saint Peter or, more likely, Saint Bartholomew in the front row may be related to the dedication of the church or chapel for which the altarpiece was painted. One possibility in such a case might be the parish church of San Bartolommeo al Corso degli Adimari in Florence, also known since the thirteenth century as San Bartommeo dei Pittori, which was secularized in 1768.[5] Another possibility could be the hospital of San Bartolo a Mugnone, which was founded in 1310 in the Piazza Vecchia di Santa Maria Novella, Andrea Bonaiuti's parish.[6] A hospital known as San Bartolommeo or San Martino a Mugnone was located outside the Porta al Prato, and if Saint Martin occupied a prominent position in the missing right lateral panel of this altarpiece, a strong case could be made for a provenance from the church of that institution.[7] Equally, it is possible that the five apostles present in this panel were joined by seven others in its missing companion, and a dedication to the Santi Apostoli might be presumed. Barring the recovery of this companion panel, however, or some fortuitous documentary discovery, the original provenance of the altarpiece must remain a matter of conjecture.   LK

1. See Millard Meiss, *Painting in Florence and Siena after the Black Death* (Princeton, N.J., 1951), p. 47; and Richard Offner, *A Critical and Historical Corpus of Florentine Painting: The Fourteenth Century, Supplement, a Legacy of Attributions*, ed. Hayden B. J. Maginnis (New York, 1981), p. 63.
2. Miklós Boskovits, *Pittura fiorentina alla vigilia del Rinascimento, 1370–1400* (Florence, 1975), p. 277.
3. Johannes Tripps, *Tendencies of Gothic in Florence: Andrea Bonaiuti, A Critical and Historical Corpus of Florentine Painting*, sec. 4, vol. 7, pt. 1 (Florence, 1996), pp. 39, 158.
4. Erling S. Skaug, *Punch Marks from Giotto to Fra Angelico: Attribution, Chronology, and Workshop Relationships in Tuscan Panel Painting* (Oslo, 1994), 1: pp. 162–64.
5. Walter and Elisabeth Valentiner Paatz, *Die Kirchen von Florenz* (Frankfurt-am-Main, Germany, 1940–54), 1: pp. 333–36.
6. Vincenzo Fineschi, *Memorie sopra il cimitero antico della chiesa di S. Maria Novella di Firenze* (Florence, 1787), pp. xxix, 116, 276.
7. Paatz and Paatz, *Kirchen von Florenz*, pp. 131–32.

Cenni di Francesco di Ser Cenni

Florence, active by 1369–ca. 1415

7. *Saint Benedict*, ca. 1370–80

Tempera on panel, 23.5 x 22.2 cm (9¼ x 8¾ in.)

PROVENANCE: Leonardo Mondadori, Milan (Semenzato, Florence, May 29, 2002, lot 381)

BIBLIOGRAPHY: unpublished

CONDITION: The panel support, of a horizontal grain, has been neither thinned nor cradled and measures 21 mm in depth. It retains what appears to be its original top and left edges, though it has clearly been trimmed at the bottom and cut at the right. The gold background of the painting is well preserved within the upper half of the punched and engraved arch that surrounds the saint, including the repeated three-dot motif that lines the arch, while the arch itself and the spandrels in the upper corners of the panel are regilt. Similarly, the lower corners of the panel are regessoed and regilt, and new gilding laid over the original gesso extends halfway up the panel along its outer edges. The lower parts of the saint's robes are repainted, and his hands have been restored. The face and beard and most of the upper parts of the draperies are in excellent state, with negligible loss from abrasion and minimal retouching of flaking losses. A large number "99" is painted in black on the reverse.

This unpublished panel was sold at auction in 2002 as representing a Dominican saint and with an attribution to Giovanni del Biondo. Such attributions are, however, often generic, and Giovanni del Biondo's accepted oeuvre has been inflated by the inclusion of a number of paintings only superficially related to his aggressively Orcagnesque style. This panel, for example, is much softer in handling than is usual for the artist, lacking the exaggerated prismatic forms for which he is known; and the modeling of the draperies, especially of the cloak pulled back over the saint's raised left arm, is achieved with a depth of shadow otherwise not encountered in his work. The projection of the saint's left arm forward in space and the turn of his head and glance back across the axis of his body are also atypical of Giovanni del Biondo, though the figure type and proportions are indeed reminiscent of his paintings from the late 1360s and early 1370s.

The particular manner of drawing the saint's left hand, with elongated fingers bent, at right angles, at the second knuckle only, may instead indicate the authorship of Giovanni del Biondo's most gifted pupil and sometime collaborator, Cenni di Francesco, whose intervention here is also implied by the refined execution of the saint's beard and tonsure and

the simple but expressive rendering of his features, with a continuous stroke of highlight defining the bridge of the nose and brow and a single dark line indicating the upper lid of the eye. If this attribution is correct, the painting would be datable to the decade of the 1370s, when Cenni's work was still closely allied to that of Giovanni del Biondo and before he developed the exaggeratedly attenuated figure canon and crisper delineation of forms that characterize his later works. Comparable examples from this early period include the predella panel of the *Assumption of Saint John the Evangelist* in the Accademia, Florence (inv. no. 446) that Cenni di Francesco painted in collaboration with Giovanni del Biondo, and the small group of works assembled by Richard Offner under the rubric "Nantes Master" but recognized by Roberto Longhi and Federico Zeri as by Cenni di Francesco.[1]

The pattern of damages and restoration evident on the surface of this panel implies that originally the saint may have been portrayed within a tondo frame rather than a half-arch, and a suggestion of its former appearance may be derived from a similar, though smaller (16 x 20 cm) panel showing Saint James, sold at Finarte in Milan in 1967 (another tondo, representing Saint Louis of Toulouse, related to this in size and style, though built into a possibly modern raised frame molding, was sold at Sotheby's, New York, in 2006, incorrectly attributed to "Follower of Simone Martini").[2] In such a format, and given the horizontal grain of the support, it is reasonable to assume that the panel is a fragment of a predella, where in all likelihood it occupied the left-most end. No other fragments of the same predella have yet been identified.   LK

1. On Cenni di Francesco and Giovanni del Biondo, see Miklós Boskovits, "Ein Vorläufer der spätgotischen Malerei in Florenz: Cenni di Francesco di Ser Cenni," *Zeitschrift für Kunstgeschichte* 31 (1968): p. 275; and Boskovits, *Pittura fiorentina alla vigilia del Rinascimento, 1370–1400* (Florence, 1975), p. 287, pl. 85. For the group identified by Offner, see Richard Offner, *A Critical and Historical Corpus of Florentine Painting: The Fourteenth Century, Supplement, a Legacy of Attributions*, ed. Hayden B. J. Maginnis (New York, 1981), p. 23. For Longhi and Zeri's attribution of these works to Cenni di Francesco, see Roberto Longi, cited in Michel Laclotte, *De Giotto à Bellini: Les primitifs italiens dans les musées de France*, exh. cat. (Paris, 1956), p. 3; and Federico Zeri, "La mostra 'Arte in Valdelsa' a Certaldo," *Bolletino d'arte* 48 (1963): p. 247.

2. See Finarte, Milan, sale cat. (March 6–9, 1967), lot 242, and Sotheby's, New York, sale cat. (May 18, 2006), lot 71. The *Saint James* was published by Miklós Boskovits, *Pittura fiorentina*, fig. 53, as "Maestro della Cappella Rinuccini," i.e., Matteo di Pacino.

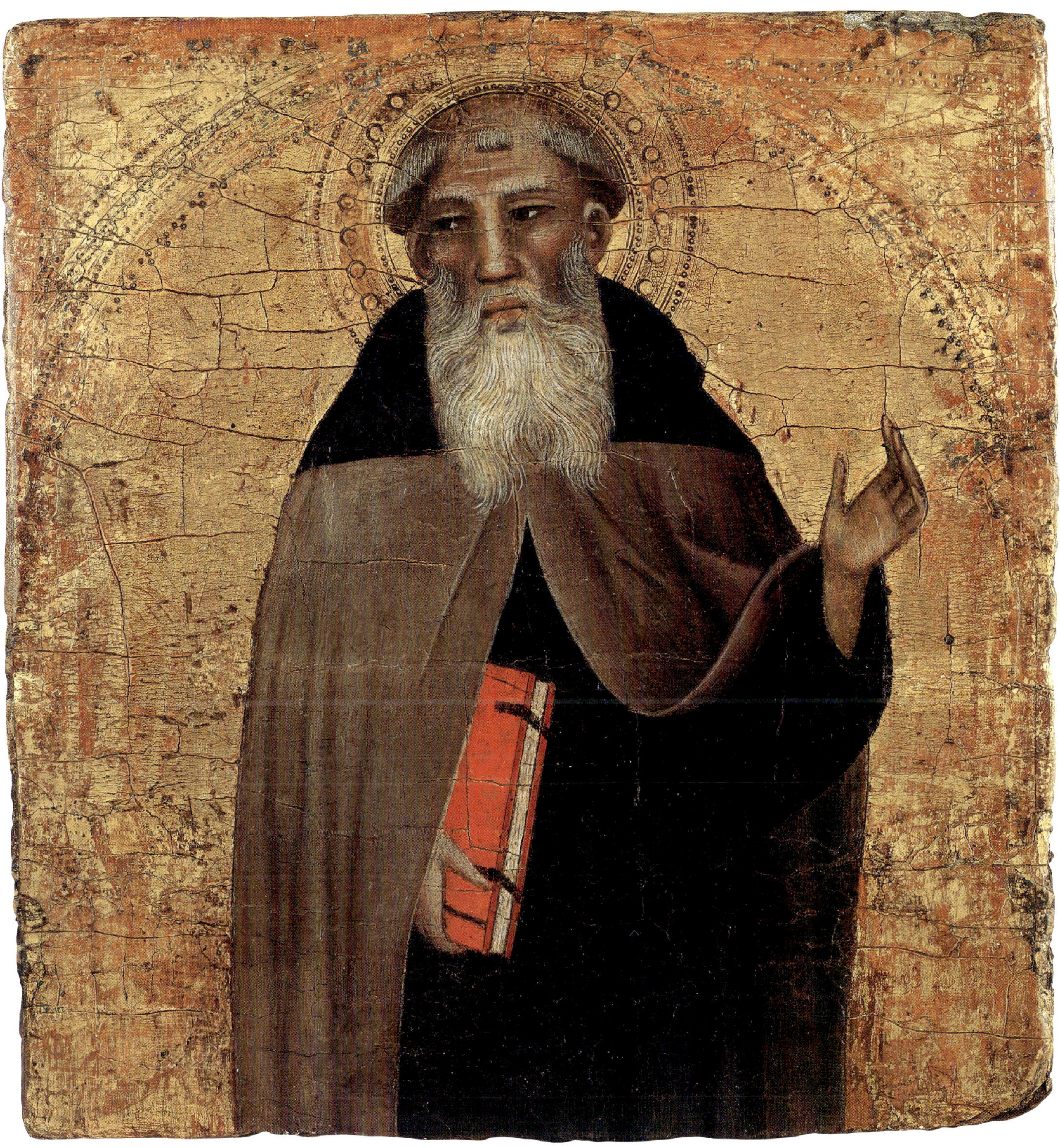

Agnolo Gaddi

Florence, documented 1369–died 1396

8. *The Martyrdom of Saint Andrew,* ca. 1380–85

Tempera on panel, 29 x 38 cm (11⅜ x 15 in.), overall;
26.8 x 36.7 cm (10½ x 14½ in.), picture surface

PROVENANCE: Marchese Alfonso Tacoli-Canacci, Florence,
by 1792; Julius Bohler, Munich, 1929;[1] Marczell von Nêmes,
Munich (his sale, Mensing, Müller, Cassirer, Helbing,
Munich, June 16, 1931, lot 8); private collection (sale, Müller,
Amsterdam, March 18, 1952, lot 781); private collection (sale,
Sotheby's, London, July 8, 1981, lot 87); private collection (sale,
Sotheby's, London, July 8, 1999, lot 62); Rob Smeets, Milan

BIBLIOGRAPHY: Roberto Salvini, "In margine ad Agnolo
Gaddi," *Rivista d'arte* 16 (1934): p. 223; George Kaftal, *The
Iconography of the Saints in Tuscan Painting* (Florence, 1952),
pp. 41–42; Miklós Boskovits, *Pittura fiorentina alla vigilia
del Rinascimento, 1370–1400* (Florence, 1975), pp. 297, 301;
Miklós Boskovits, *Early Italian Painting, 1290–1470: The
Thyssen-Bornemisza Collection* (Milan, 1990), p. 90; Carl
Brandon Strehlke, *Italian Paintings, 1250–1450, in the John
G. Johnson Collection and the Philadelphia Museum of Art*
(Philadelphia, 2004), p. 150

CONDITION: The panel, of a horizontal wood grain, has been
thinned to 6 mm and cradled. Two large areas of damage in
the gold ground to the left of Saint Andrew on the cross have
been repaired, and retouching covers losses in the robe of the
kneeling supplicant at the left. The paint and gilded surfaces
otherwise are extremely well preserved. All painted forms
have been incised freehand along their contours, and underdrawing of the proconsul's hand where it passes behind the
white column is clearly visible.

The story of the martyrdom of Saint Andrew, apostle of
Christ and brother of Saint Peter, is recounted in the
Legenda Aurea of Jacobus da Varagine.[2] Ordered to sacrifice
to idols by Aegeus, proconsul of Achaia, Andrew refused and
was bound to a cross, where he hung for two days. On the
third day, the crowd to whom Andrew was preaching
demanded he be released, but Andrew, preferring to embrace
his martyrdom, forbade Aegeus to free him.

When it appeared at the 1931 sale of the collection of
Marczell von Nêmes in Munich, the *Martyrdom of Saint
Andrew* was catalogued as by a Florentine master ca. 1400.
This was the generic attribution that had been given by
Bernard Berenson to a scene of *Saint Sylvester and the
Dragon* in the John G. Johnson Collection at the Philadelphia
Museum of Art (fig. 1), recognized by Georg Gronau as a pair
to the *Martyrdom of Saint Andrew*.[3] Both paintings were
thought by Lionello Venturi to have been painted by the art-
ist responsible for the frescoes in the Manassei chapel in Prato

Cathedral, and they were grouped by Roberto Salvini under
the name "Vatican Master," referring to a heterogeneous
group of works from the circle of Agnolo Gaddi assembled by
him around a painting of the *Virgin with Seven Virtues* in the
Pinacoteca Vaticana.[4] Miklós Boskovits first recognized the
Philadelphia panel and the *Martyrdom of Saint Andrew* as
autograph works by Agnolo Gaddi of about 1380–85, roughly
contemporary to the frescoes in the Castellani chapel in Santa
Croce in Florence (1383–85).[5] This is unquestionably correct.
It is interesting to note that one of the assistants employed by
Agnolo Gaddi in the Castellani chapel has been identified as the
Master of the Cappella Manassei, to whom Venturi had attrib-
uted the present panel and its companion in Philadelphia.

No further narrative scenes have been identified that
might have belonged to the same predella as the *Martyrdom
of Saint Andrew* and *Saint Sylvester and the Dragon*, nor
have any proposals been advanced to identify surviving fragments of the rest of this altarpiece—other than to specify
that Saints Andrew and Sylvester must have been portrayed
in the lateral panels—or to specify its original provenance. It
had not hitherto been recognized, however, that the *Martyrdom of Saint Andrew* and *Saint Sylvester and the Dragon*
appeared together in the catalogues of the collection formed
in Florence in the last two decades of the eighteenth century
by the Marchese Alfonso Tacoli-Canacci. The *Martyrdom of
Saint Andrew* is listed as no. 26 in the undated manuscript
Catalogo Ragionato dei pittori della scuola toscana: "Tavola. Quadro per traverso con fondo d'oro Rappresentante

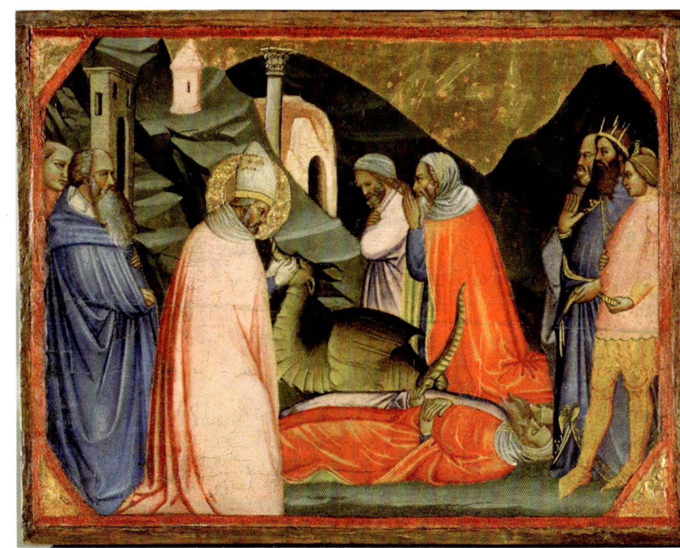

Fig. 1. Agnolo Gaddi, *Saint Sylvester and the Dragon*, ca. 1380–85.
Tempera on panel, 29.2 x 38.4 cm (11½ x 15⅛ in.). Philadelphia
Museum of Art, John G. Johnson Collection, 1917

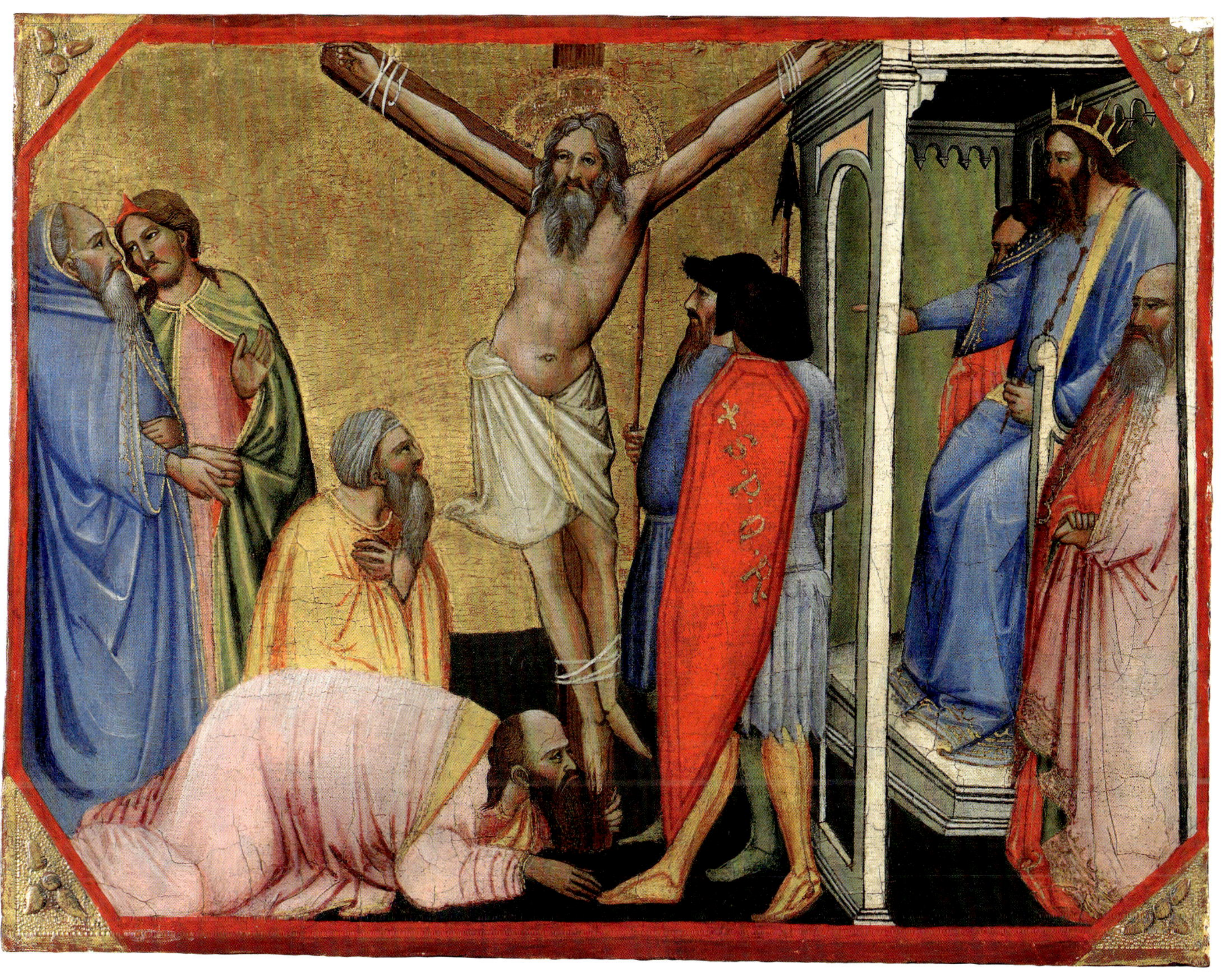

Sant'Andrea Apostolo legato in Croce alla presenza del Tiranno, di Soldati, e di altre figure con veduta di architettura. – B[raccia] ⅔ – B[raccia] ⅔ – Di Giotto di Bondone – Di Cimabue – 1276. 1326 – 2."[6] The following item in the inventory corresponds to the *Saint Sylvester and the Dragon* now in Philadelphia: "Tavola. Quadro Rappresentante San Giustino Vescovo, e due Figure distese per terra, ed'un mostruoso serpente, al quale il detto Santo lega la bocca alla presenza di un Re, e di altri spettatori. – B. ⅔ – B. ⅔ – Di Giotto di Bondone – Di Cimabue – 1276. 1326 – 2." Both listings are repeated in the dated inventories of Tacoli-Canacci's collection of 1792 and 1796, but neither appears in the dated catalogue of 1789, and it might be reasonable to suppose that

they entered his collection after that date.[7] It may also be significant that the painting listed directly after these two in the inventories shares with them Tacoli-Canacci's attribution to "Giotto di Bondone, [scolaro] di Cimabue" and may have been the same height: "Tavola. Quadro per traverso dipinto sopra fondo d'oro rappresentante il Salvatore in Croce nel mezzo ai due Ladroni, con la Madonna svenuta. E sostenuta da Santa Veronica e dalle altre Marie, e San Giovanni Evangelista ed'a piè della Croce quantità di altre Figure, e Soldati. – B. ⅔ – B. 1½."[8] Plausibly the center of the predella from which the present panel comes, no painting of this subject has been identified among the recognized works of Agnolo Gaddi.   LK

1. Notation on the reverse of a photograph of this painting in the Richard Offner photo archive, Institute of Fine Arts, New York University.

2. Jacobus de Voragine, *The Golden Legend: Readings on the Saints*, trans. William Granger Ryan (Princeton, N.J., 1993), 1: pp. 16–18.

3. Bernard Berenson, *Italian Paintings in the John G. Johnson Collection* (Philadelphia, 1913), pp. 7–8, 231. Gronau's observations are cited in Mensing, Müller, Cassirer, Helbing, Munich, *Collections Marczell von Nêmes: Catalogue des tableaux*, sale cat. (June 16, 1931), p. 4.

4. Mensing, Müller, Cassirer, Helbing, *Collections Marczell von Nêmes*, p. 4. For Salvini, see Roberto Salvini, "In margine ad Agnolo Gaddi," *Rivista d'arte* 16 (1934): p. 223.

5. Miklós Boskovits, *Pittura fiorentina alla vigilia del Rinascimento, 1370–1400* (Florence, 1975), pp. 297, 301.

6. Biblioteca della Soprintendenza ai beni Artistici e Storici, Parma, MS 145; transcribed in Vincenzo M. Buonocore, *Il marchese Alfonso*

7. *Tacoli-Canacci: "Onesto gentiluomo smaniante per la pittura"* (Reggio Emilia, Italy, 2005), pp. 210–11.

7. For the 1792 inventory, see Archivio di Stato di Parma, MS 101, nos. 25–26; transcribed in Buonocore, *Il marchese Alfonso Tacoli-Canacci*, p. 211. Tacoli-Canacci's label corresponding to the 1792 inventory, numbered 26, is still attached to the back of the Philadelphia panel. For the 1796 inventory, see J. Bocalosi, *Catalogue raisonné de plusieurs excellens tableaux . . .* (Parma, 1796), nos. 382–83; transcribed in ibid. For the 1789 catalogue, see Real Biblioteca, Madrid, MS II/574; transcribed in *Etruria pittrice* (Florence, 1789).

8. Buonocore, *Il marchese Alfonso Tacoli-Canacci*, p. 211. In the 1796 inventory the measurements are changed to 1¼ braccia by 1½ braccia.

Niccolò di Pietro Gerini(?)

Florence, documented 1368–1414/15

9. *Saint Sigismund*, ca. 1380–90

Tempera on panel, 41 x 26.5 cm (16⅛ x 10½ in.)

PROVENANCE: private collection, France (sale, Palais d'Orsay [Laurin-Guilloux-Buffetaud-Tailleur], Paris, June 15, 1978, h.c.)

BIBLIOGRAPHY: unpublished

CONDITION: The panel, of a vertical wood grain, is approximately 3 cm thick. The back has been coarsely gouged with a broad chisel and is unplaned, though it shows evidence of having once been thicker or attached to a further wooden surface along its right edge (left from the back), where a 6 cm wide strip of exposed worm tunnels runs the full height of the panel. The panel has clearly been reduced by cutting at the bottom and apparently along the sides, but evidence of trimming along the arch at the top is equivocal. The picture surface is in excellent condition, save for scattered damages to the gold ground along the curve of the arch at the top and an 11 x 4 cm area of damage and repaint in the lower right corner of the composition. The saint's face has been vandalized by seven sharp vertical scratches and two blunt horizontal scratches, which have all been inpainted in modern times. Detail in the painting is somewhat obscured by an opaque and discolored varnish.

This unpublished panel was sold in 1978 with a traditional attribution to Niccolò di Pietro Gerini, and its subject was identified as Saint Louis of France. The crown, gilt orb, and ermine cloak clearly identify the figure as a king, but the martyr's palm held in his right hand eliminates the possibility of his being Saint Louis of France. In practice, only one martyred king appears in Tuscan painting from the fourteenth and fifteenth centuries—Saint Sigismund (Sigismondo), and it must be he who is portrayed here.

For most of the medieval period, Sigismund, an obscure sixth-century Burgundian king, was the object of a local cult only, until his relics were presented to Emperor Charles IV (d. 1378) and translated by him to Prague. The emperor acquired the head of the saint during a trip to France in 1354 and had it enshrined in a gilded reliquary in the cathedral in Prague, alongside numerous other relics (including seven complete bodies of saints) that he acquired that year. In 1365, after being crowned king of Burgundy, Charles brought the saint's body back to Prague, proclaiming him patron saint of Bohemia soon after and in 1367 baptizing his son Sigismund. Charles attributed his recovery from serious illness in 1371 to the intervention of Saint Sigismund, and it is only from this moment, and more particularly after 1387, when Charles's son Sigismund was named king of Hungary, that images of Saint Sigismund begin to appear in European

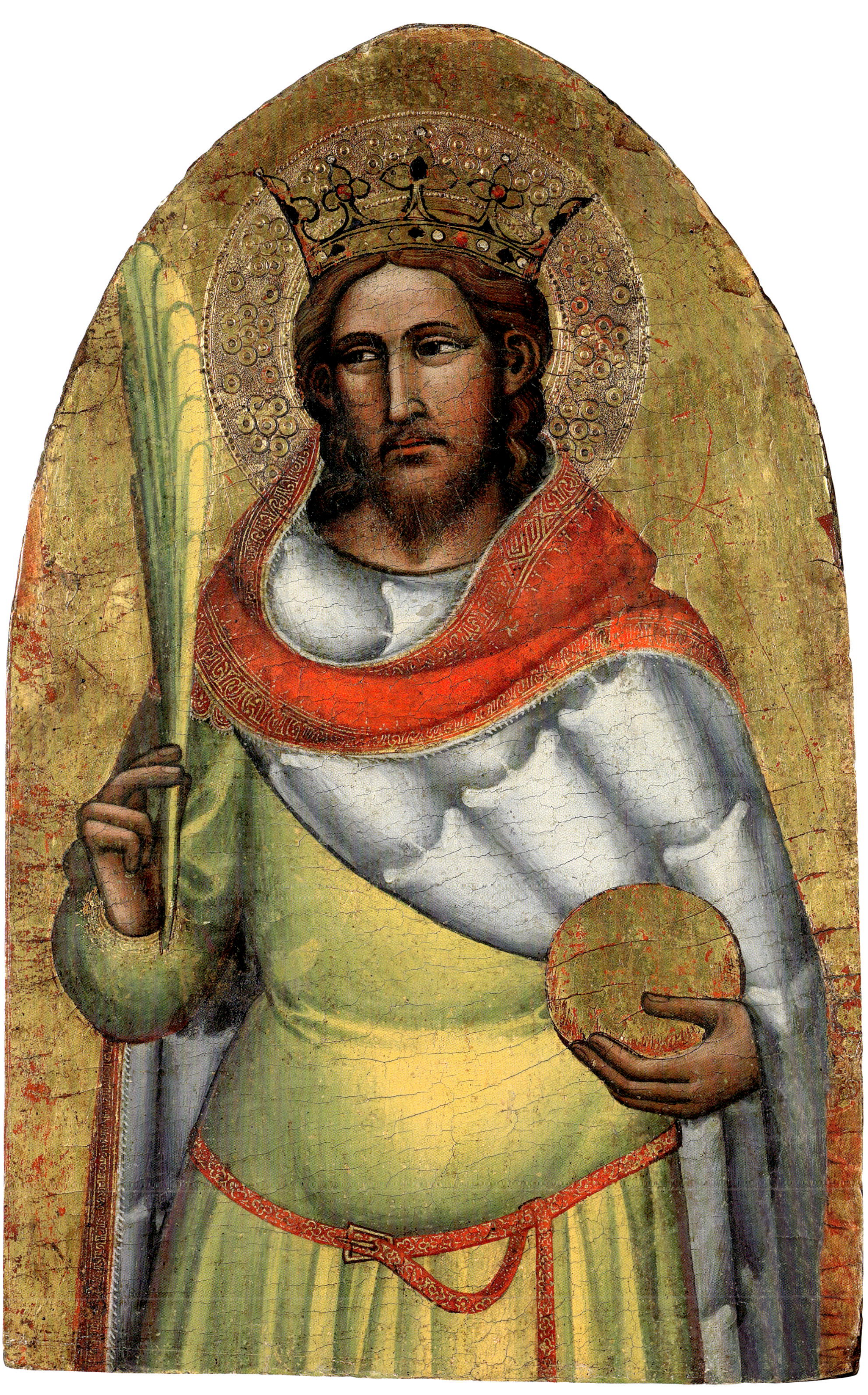

art.[1] Although Sigismund was granted the title King of the Romans in 1410 and elected Holy Roman Emperor in 1433, images of his name-saint commonly occur in Italy only in the last half of the fifteenth century, and then primarily in Ghibelline contexts.[2] The present panel may be the earliest surviving representation of the saint in Tuscan painting, and its attribution and provenance, both unknown, are therefore matters of more than academic interest.

As no general cult of Saint Sigismund is recorded in Italy, it is reasonable to suppose that whatever its original function—the panel appears to have been the lateral of an altarpiece of which no other fragments have yet been identified, although if it were once full length it could also have served as an independent votive image—the subject of this painting must have referred either to the name of its patron or to a Bohemian community or confraternity. It is also possible that it was commissioned in a Ghibelline center: the gouges through the saint's face noted above may possibly be explained by the later subjection of that center to Guelph (presumably Florentine) rule, as such apotropaic vandalism is normally encountered on early panel paintings on the faces of villains—especially executioners—or demons, not saints. If so, this hypothetical change of allegiance is likely to have occurred early enough (that is, before the later fifteenth century) for Sigismund's overtly Ghibelline associations to have been popularly understood. Of the many towns in which the putative author of this painting, Niccolò di Pietro Gerini, was active, Pisa and San Miniato Tedesco best fit this description, though no known record of a commission in either locale can be associated unequivocally with this painting.

The traditional attribution of this panel to Niccolò di Pietro Gerini has been confirmed (verbally) by Miklós Boskovits, who considers it an early work by the artist. The softly rounded contours of the saint do not conform to Gerini's usual sculptural, robust modeling or forceful drawing style, although more than a casual similarity may be remarked to an altarpiece of the *Virgin and Child with Saints John the Baptist, James, John the Evangelist, and Ansanus* at Collegonzi (Vinci), dated 1386. Also attributed by Boskovits to Niccolò di Pietro Gerini, this painting is considered by Sonia Chiodo to be a work by "Gerini and collaborators," though it is possible that it represents instead an as yet imperfectly understood aspect of Gerini's early career.[3]   L K

1. See David Charles Mengel, "Bones, Stones, and Brothels: Religion and Topography in Prague under Emperor Charles IV (1346–1378)" (PH.D. diss., University of Notre Dame, 2003), pp. 325–72; and Barbara Drake Boehm, "Charles IV, the Realm of Faith," in *Prague: The Crown of Bohemia, 1347–1437*, ed. Boehm and Jirí Fajt, exh. cat. (New York, 2005), pp. 30–31.
2. The identification by inscription of one of the royal saints in the Bardi chapel in Santa Croce in Florence as Saint Sigismund is a sixteenth-century repair to the early fourteenth-century figure. It is to be understood as an anachronism irrelevant to the original identity of the figure, who is not portrayed with a martyr's palm; see Nancy Thompson, "Cooperation and Conflict: Stained Glass in the Bardi Chapels of Santa Croce," in *The Art of the Franciscan Order in Italy*, ed. William R. Cook, The Medieval Franciscans 1 (Leiden, the Netherlands, 2005), pp. 257–77. The earliest record of a Saint Sigismund painted in Florence is of 1467, when Neri di Bicci included an image of the saint in an altarpiece he painted for San Felice in Piazza on the commission of Mariotto Lippi; see Bruno Santi, ed., *Neri di Bicci, le ricordanze* (Pisa, 1976), p. 303.
3. Sonia Chiodo, "Il Maestro della Misericordia e Niccolò di Pietro Gerini: Un problema di pittura fiorentina di secondo trecento," *Arte cristiana* 93, no. 826 (2005): p. 56, fig. 19. Another painting published by Chiodo (see "Mariotto di Nardo: Note per un 'egregio pictore,'" in *Arte cristiana* 87, no. 806 [1999]: fig. 1), the small *Virgin and Child with Six Saints and Two Angels* formerly in the collection of R. and J. Jones, London, may relate to this picture as well but is difficult to judge confidently in photograph. It is part of a group of paintings the author wishes to isolate from Gerini as early works by Mariotto di Nardo, though it is clearly by a hand different from all the other panels included by her in this study.

Niccolò di Pietro Gerini

Florence, documented 1368–1414/15

10a. *The Annunciatory Angel*, 1387

Tempera on panel, 61 x 36.8 cm (24 x 14½ in.), overall; 59.8 x 35.8 cm (23½ x 14⅛ in.), picture surface

PROVENANCE: see no. 10b

BIBLIOGRAPHY: see no. 10b

CONDITION: The panel support, of a vertical grain, has been thinned to 12 mm but is not cradled. Its original gabled form was truncated across the top and has been made up to a rectangular format by the insertion of triangular wedges approximately 8 cm tall at the upper left and right corners. Two nails originally securing a horizontal batten are driven through the panel 10 cm from the present top edge. The picture surface is in an excellent state of preservation, apart from minor losses in the gold ground at the right edge of the composition.

Niccolò di Pietro Gerini

Florence, documented 1368–1414/15

10b. *The Virgin Annunciate*, 1387

Tempera on panel, 61.1 x 36.5 cm (24⅛ x 14⅜ in.), overall; 59.8 x 35.8 cm (23½ x 14⅛ in.), picture surface

PROVENANCE: James Fenton (1818–1902), Norton Hall, Chipping Campden, Gloucestershire, England (his sale, Christie's, London, February 26–28, 1880, bought in); Richard Kay Fenton (1853–1915), Dutton Manor, Ribchester, near Preston, Lancashire, England (his sale, Christie's, London, February 16, 1903, purchased by Hartman); private collection, Sweden; Edward Hutton (1875–1969), London; Matthiesen Gallery, London; Wildenstein & Co., New York, before 1975

BIBLIOGRAPHY: Christie's, London, *Catalogue of the Extensive and Valuable Collection of Ancient and Modern Pictures of James Fenton, Esq., Removed from Norton Hall, Gloucestershire,* sale cat. (February 26–28, 1880), lot 137; Christie's, London, *Catalogue of Ancient and Modern Pictures of James Fenton, Esq., Deceased, Late of Dutton Manor, Longridge, Preston,* sale cat. (February 16, 1903), lot 49; Bernard Berenson, *Italian Pictures of the Renaissance: A List of the Principal Artists and Their Works with an Index of Places: Florentine School* (London, 1963), 1: p. 161, pl. 378; Miklós Boskovits, *Pittura fiorentina alla vigilia del rinascimento, 1370–1400* (Florence, 1975), p. 412; Richard Offner, *A Critical and Historical Corpus of Florentine Painting: The Fourteenth Century, Supplement, a Legacy of Attributions,* ed. Hayden B. J. Maginnis (New York, 1981), p. 83, fig. 154; Mojmir S. Frinta, *Punched Decoration on Late Medieval Panel and Miniature Painting* (Prague, 1998), 1: pp. 136, 515

CONDITION: The panel support, of a vertical grain, has been thinned to 12 mm but is not cradled. Its original gabled form was truncated across the top and has been made up to a rectangular format by the insertion of triangular wedges approximately 8 cm tall at the upper left and right corners. Three nails originally securing a horizontal batten are driven through the panel 10.5 cm from the present top edge. The center nail of the three coincides on the picture surface with the area above the Virgin's left eye, where damages have been locally retouched. Minor losses have also been retouched in the Virgin's chin and jaw, right hand, book, and on the back of her bench. The painted and gilded surfaces are otherwise in excellent state.

The *Annunciatory Angel* and the *Virgin Annunciate* were catalogued in the nineteenth century under a generic attribution to Giotto, but they have been correctly known throughout the modern literature as by Niccolò di Pietro Gerini. Their size and format imply that they functioned as lateral pinnacles to a large altarpiece, the central pinnacle of which was first identified independently by both Dillian Gordon and Eliot Rowlands in a panel portraying the *Blessing Redeemer*

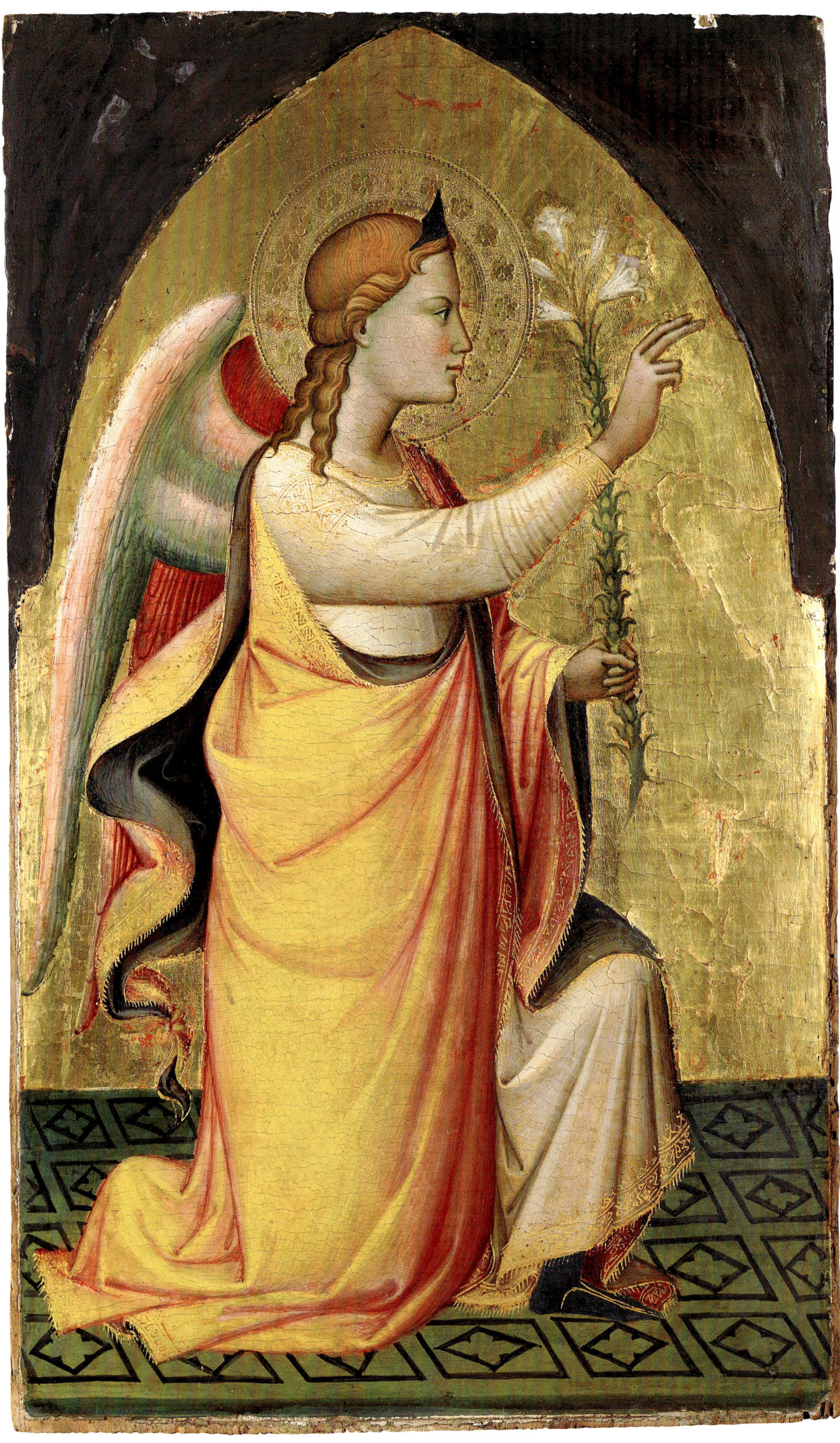

10a

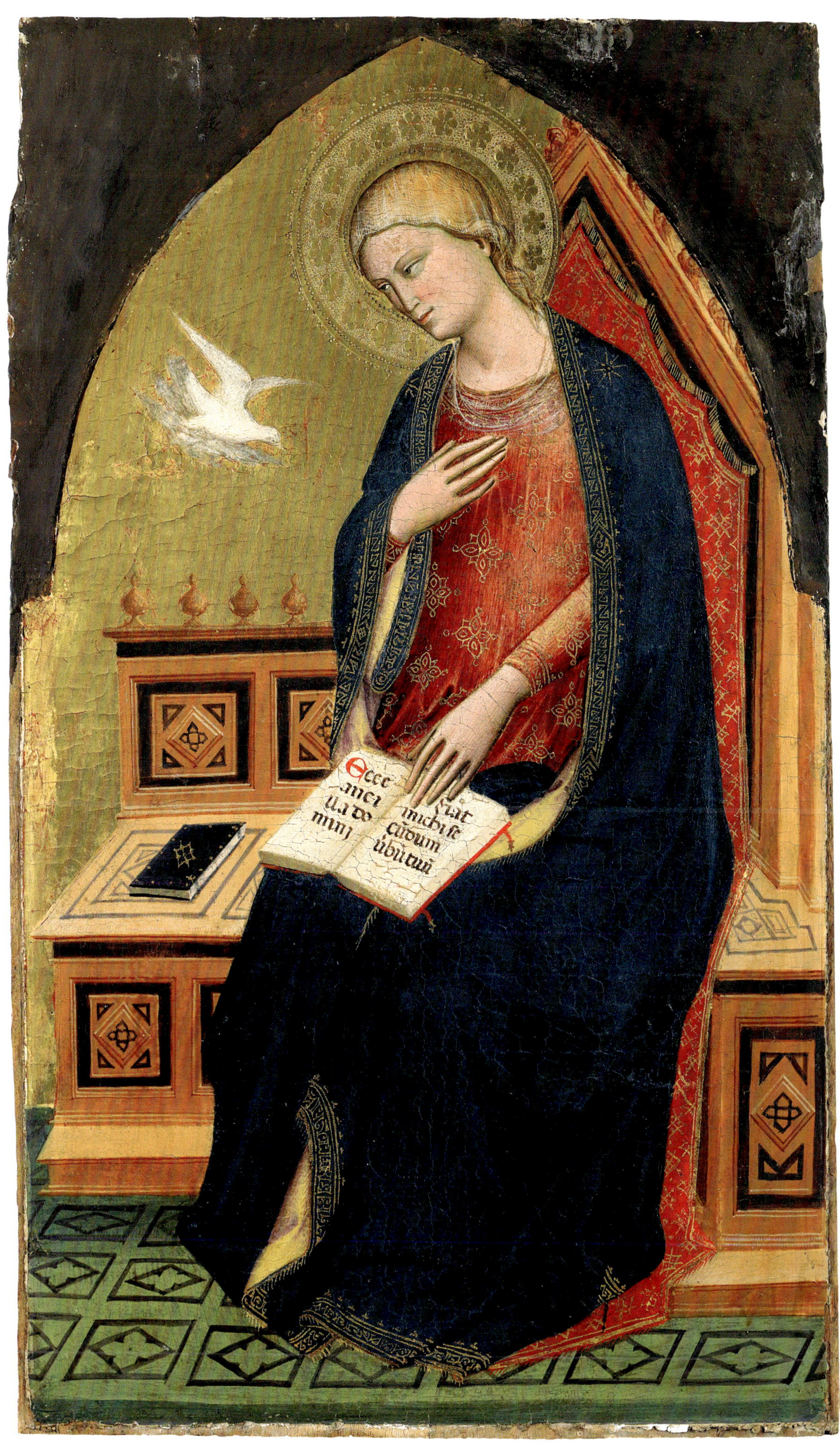

10b

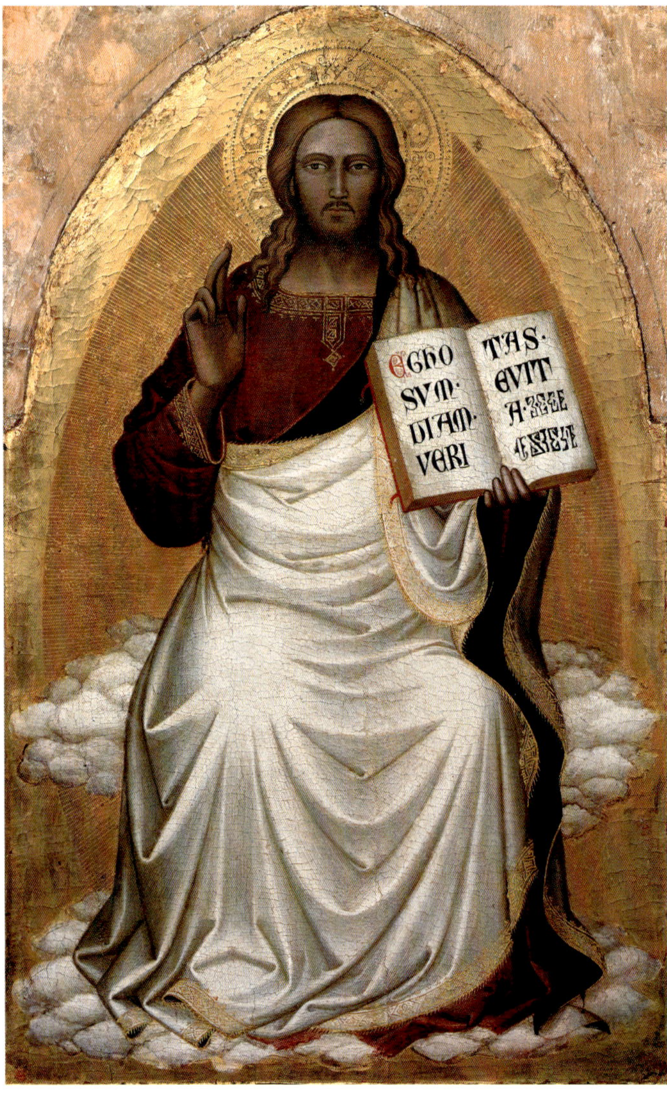

Fig. 1. Niccolò di Pietro Gerini, *Salvator Mundi*, 1387. Tempera on panel, 62.5 x 39.8 cm (24⅝ x 15⅝ in.). Alte Pinakothek, Munich

now in the Alte Pinakothek, Munich (fig. 1).[1] The Munich *Redeemer* is closely related in style to the two *Annunciation* panels; it is nearly the same size (62.5 x 39.8 cm); and it has been truncated across its top in the same fashion, with its upper left and right corners made up to a rectangular format by the insertion of identical triangular wedges. Furthermore, it preserves two nails that once secured a horizontal batten, driven into the panel 9.5 cm from its present top edge.[2] This feature, singularly unusual in altarpiece pinnacles, corresponds exactly to nails present in the *Annunciation* panels and confirms beyond the possibility of doubt that all three originated from a single complex.[3] The original purpose of battens in this position is mysterious, as pinnacle panels in conventional fourteenth-century altarpieces did not directly abut each other. They may have served to secure the panels to an elaborate independent framing structure, but no surviving intact examples are known that could confirm any such hypothesis.

Miklós Boskovits proposed dating both the Feigen *Annunciation* panels and the Munich *Redeemer* between 1385 and 1390, without, however, associating them as fragments of a single complex.[4] He tentatively suggested that the Munich panel might have formed the central pinnacle to the *Baptism of Christ* altarpiece by Niccolò di Pietro Gerini in the National Gallery, London (fig. 2), documented as having been commissioned in 1387 by Filippo di Nerone Stoldi for the chapel of San Giovanni Decollato in Santa Maria degli Angeli in Florence.[5] This suggestion, acknowledged without commitment in catalogues of both museums, is highly plausible, but it has not yet been possible to confirm due to the nineteenth-century rebuilding of the frame of the London altarpiece.[6] The *Baptism of Christ* must once have been a pentaptych, not a triptych as presently constituted. Two additional full-length standing saints must originally have flanked Peter and Paul alongside the central Baptism, possibly Saints Philip and Michael, while a third narrative scene, perhaps an Adoration of the Magi, undoubtedly intervened between the two scenes preserved in the predella today.[7] It is reasonable to suppose that each pair of lateral saints in the main register was framed together beneath a double arcade contained within a single pastiglia-decorated spandrel, leaving adequate space above its entablature to accommodate one of the two *Annunciation* pinnacles.

It should be noted that the punch tools used to decorate the haloes in the Feigen and Munich panels do not recur in the panels of the London altarpiece, but this is not an impediment to their hypothetical reconstruction. The largest punch used in the Feigen and Munich panels, a six-petaled rosette measuring 12 mm in diameter, has not been documented in any other work by Niccolò di Pietro Gerini, but it appears to be identical to a punch used repeatedly by Lorenzo Monaco in paintings from the second and third decades of the fifteenth century.[8] Erling Skaug has observed that for the entirety of his late career, Gerini used only a single punch to decorate his panels, and concluded that at that time presumably "it must mean that Gerini had no other punch at his disposal."[9] This late phase is tentatively said by Skaug to have begun ca. 1392, following the artist's return to Florence from Pisa, though admittedly not on the basis of hard evidence. It could well be that the transition date should be advanced before the Pisan interlude, since the one work documented by Skaug as having been executed in Pisa—the *Annunciation* pinnacles in the Fitzwilliam Museum, Cambridge—was painted there not by Gerini but by Spinello Aretino.[10] That the rosette punch used in the Feigen and Munich panels shortly before this should not recur in later works by Gerini is not, therefore, surprising. The means by which it ultimately came into the possession of Lorenzo Monaco perhaps as much as three decades later are obscure, though it is perhaps not idle to speculate (following Skaug's hypothesis) whether Gerini lost possession of this punch, and Lorenzo Monaco acquired it, in Pisa: all the paintings by Lorenzo Monaco in which it appears postdate his work there in 1415.[11]   LK

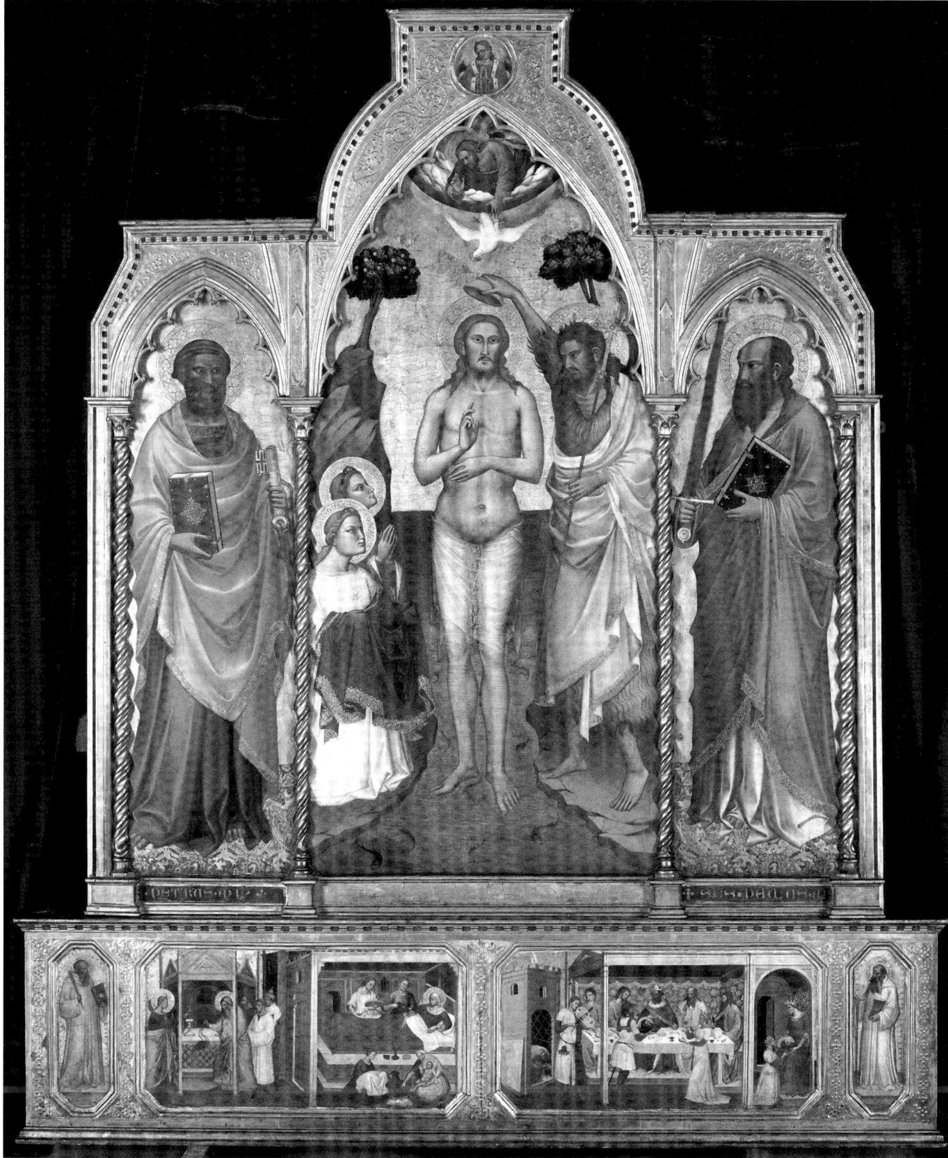

Fig. 2. Niccolò di Pietro Gerini, *The Baptism of Christ with Saints Peter and Paul*, 1387. Tempera on panel, 238 x 200 cm (93¾ x 78¾ in.). National Gallery, London, 1857

1. On the Munich *Redeemer*, see Cornelia Syre, *Frühe italienische Gemälde aus dem Bestand der Alten Pinakothek*, exh. cat. (Munich, 1990), pp. 57–60. Gordon and Rowlands's identifications were made in correspondence with the author.

2. I am grateful to Dr. Cornelia Syre, Curator at the Bayerische Staatsgemäldesammlungen, Munich, for confirming this information.

3. I am informed by Dr. Dillian Gordon, Keeper at the National Gallery, London, that the three altarpiece pinnacles by Giovanni da Milano in that collection (inv. no. 579A) also were originally fitted with horizontal battens, but I am unaware of other examples in which altarpiece pinnacles were treated in this fashion.

4. Miklós Boskovits, *Pittura fiorentina alla vigilia del Rinascimento, 1370–1400* (Florence, 1975), p. 412.

5. Werner Cohn, "Notizie storiche intorno ad alcune tavole fiorentine del '300 e '400," *Rivista d'arte* 31 (1956): pp. 66–67.

6. Syre, *Frühe italienische Gemälde*, pp. 57–58, 60n.6; and Martin Davies and Dillian Gordon, *The Early Italian Schools: Before 1400*, National Gallery Catalogues (London, 1988), pp. 89–90.

7. The suggestion that Saints Philip and Michael might have occupied the two missing lateral panels was advanced by Dillian Gordon, in correspondence with the author, based on the names of the donors of the chapel at Santa Maria degli Angeli in which the *Baptism* stood: Don Filippo di Nerone Stoldi and his mother, Angiola. That the missing central predella scene might portray the Adoration of the Magi is deduced from the fact that the feast of the Epiphany (January 6) commemorates both the Adoration of the Magi and the Baptism of Christ. Commemoration of the Baptism is also observed on the octave of Epiphany (January 13).

8. Mojmir S. Frinta, *Punched Decoration on Late Medieval Panel and Miniature Painting* (Prague, 1998), 1: p. 515. Erling S. Skaug, *Punch Marks from Giotto to Fra Angelico: Attribution, Chronology, and Workshop Relationships in Tuscan Panel Painting* (Oslo, 1994), 1: pp. 284–85, distinguishes two separate punch tools amalgamated by Frinta. This appears to be correct; it is the second, and later, of the two (Skaug no. 503) that seems to correspond to the punch used by Gerini. It should be noted that in a later reconsideration of his research on Lorenzo Monaco, Erling Skaug reaffirmed his belief that "none of Lorenzo Monaco's early punches seems to have been transferred *post mortem* from older artists." Skaug does not discuss Don Lorenzo's later punches in this light. See Skaug, "Notes on the Punched Decoration in Lorenzo Monaco's Panel Paintings," in *Lorenzo Monaco: A Bridge from Giotto's Heritage to the Renaissance*, ed. Angelo Tartuferi and Daniela Parenti, exh. cat. (Florence, 2006), p. 53.

9. Skaug, *Punch Marks*, p. 266.

10. Stefan Weppelmann, *Spinello Aretino und die toskanische Malerei des 14. Jahrhunderts* (Florence, 2003), pp. 232–37.

11. Daniela Parenti, in Tartuferi and Parenti, *Lorenzo Monaco*, p. 202, questions whether Lorenzo Monaco actually worked in Pisa or merely sent paintings there from Florence.

Niccolò di Pietro Gerini

Florence, documented 1368–1414/15

11. *The Martyrdom of Saint Lawrence*, 1404

Tempera on panel, 22.5 x 31.9 cm (8⅞ x 12½ in.)

PROVENANCE: private collection (sale, Sotheby's, New York, January 12, 1995, lot 3); private collection (sale, Sotheby's, New York, January 25, 2001, lot 2); Derek Johns, London

BIBLIOGRAPHY: Reimar F. Lacher, in *Geschichten auf Gold: Bildererzählungen in der frühen italienischen Malerei*, ed. Stefan Weppelmann, exh. cat. (Berlin, 2005), pp. 151–55

CONDITION: The panel has been thinned to 7 mm but is not cradled. It is inscribed on the back: "III s.o a.o." The paint surface is in excellent state except for retouches on the eyes and some of the faces of the executioners that have been scratched through.

Saint Lawrence, archdeacon of Rome under Pope Saint Sixtus II (r. 257–58), was martyred under the emperor Gallienus. For refusing to sacrifice to the Roman Gods and for distributing the wealth of the Church—at Sixtus's command—to the poor rather than surrendering it to the emperor, he was ordered stripped, bound to an iron grill, and tortured over hot coals until he died.

The Feigen *Martyrdom of Saint Lawrence* was unknown to scholars until its appearance at sale in New York in 1995. It was identified as the work of Niccolò di Pietro Gerini by Miklós Boskovits, who suggested that it may have formed part of a predella with an *Adoration of the Magi* by Gerini in the Gemäldegalerie, Berlin (fig. 1).[1] As both panels are the same height and are closely related in style, this proposal is reasonable and was confirmed by their exhibition side by side in Berlin in 2005. The catalogue of this exhibition referred to a *Beheading of the Baptist* by Gerini (fig. 2), noted by Richard

Offner as belonging to a private collection in Florence and by the photographer Girolamo Bombelli as being part of the Saibene collection, Milan, as a possible third panel from the same predella.[2] The size of this panel is unknown, but its figure style, claustrophobic composition, and manner of engraving haloes once again corresponds closely to those in the Feigen *Martyrdom of Saint Lawrence*, and the identification seems likely.

A fourth panel from this predella may now be identified as the *Temptation of Saint Anthony* in the Strossmayer Gallery, Zagreb, Croatia (fig. 3), catalogued there as by Giovanni dal Ponte but correctly attributed to Niccolò di Pietro Gerini by Offner and Boskovits.[3] This panel corresponds closely to the Feigen panel in figure style and in the pattern of its engraved halo, and is nearly identical to it in size (22 x 32 cm). It is possible, though, that all four known panels of this predella have been trimmed slightly in length, as the cropping of figural elements at the lateral borders in all but the Zagreb *Temptation of Saint Anthony* would be somewhat unusual for narrative paintings of this period.

The conjunction within this reconstructed predella of scenes from the lives of Saints Lawrence, John the Baptist, and Anthony Abbot suggests that it is likely to have been painted for the only known altarpiece by Niccolò di Pietro Gerini that includes those three saints among its lateral panels: polyptych no. 8610 at the Galleria dell'Accademia in Florence (fig. 4).[4] This altarpiece measures 178 x 264 cm overall, which is commensurate with the dimensions of the predella panels reunited here. The identity of the remaining figure among the laterals of that altarpiece, Saint Julian, must correspond to the subject of the missing fifth predella panel.

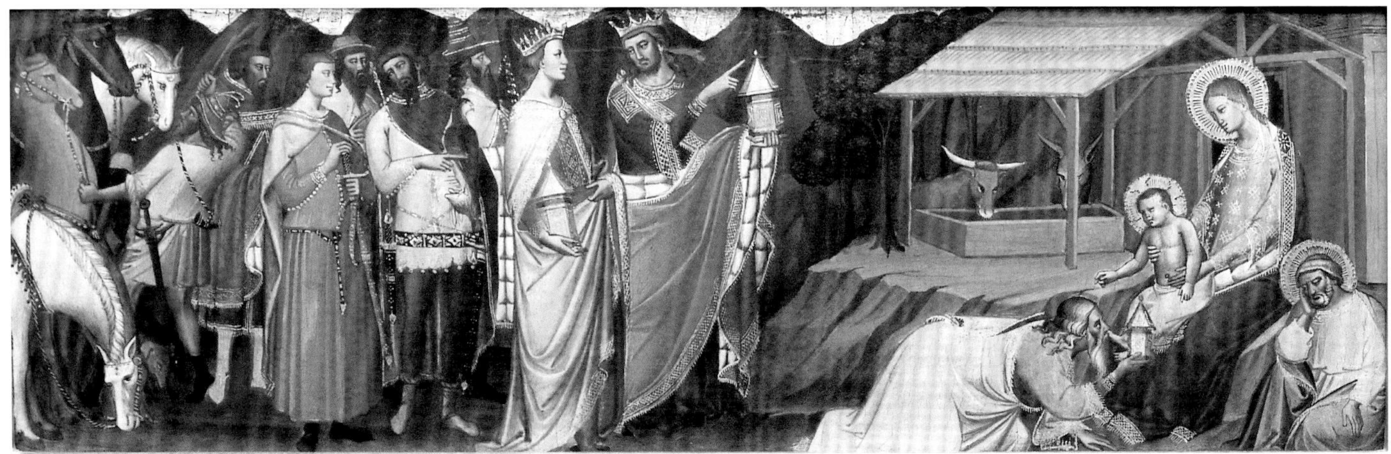

Fig. 1. Niccolò di Pietro Gerini, *The Adoration of the Magi*, 1404. Tempera on panel, 22.5 x 70 cm (8⅞ x 27⅝ in.). Gemäldegalerie, Berlin, inv. no. 1112

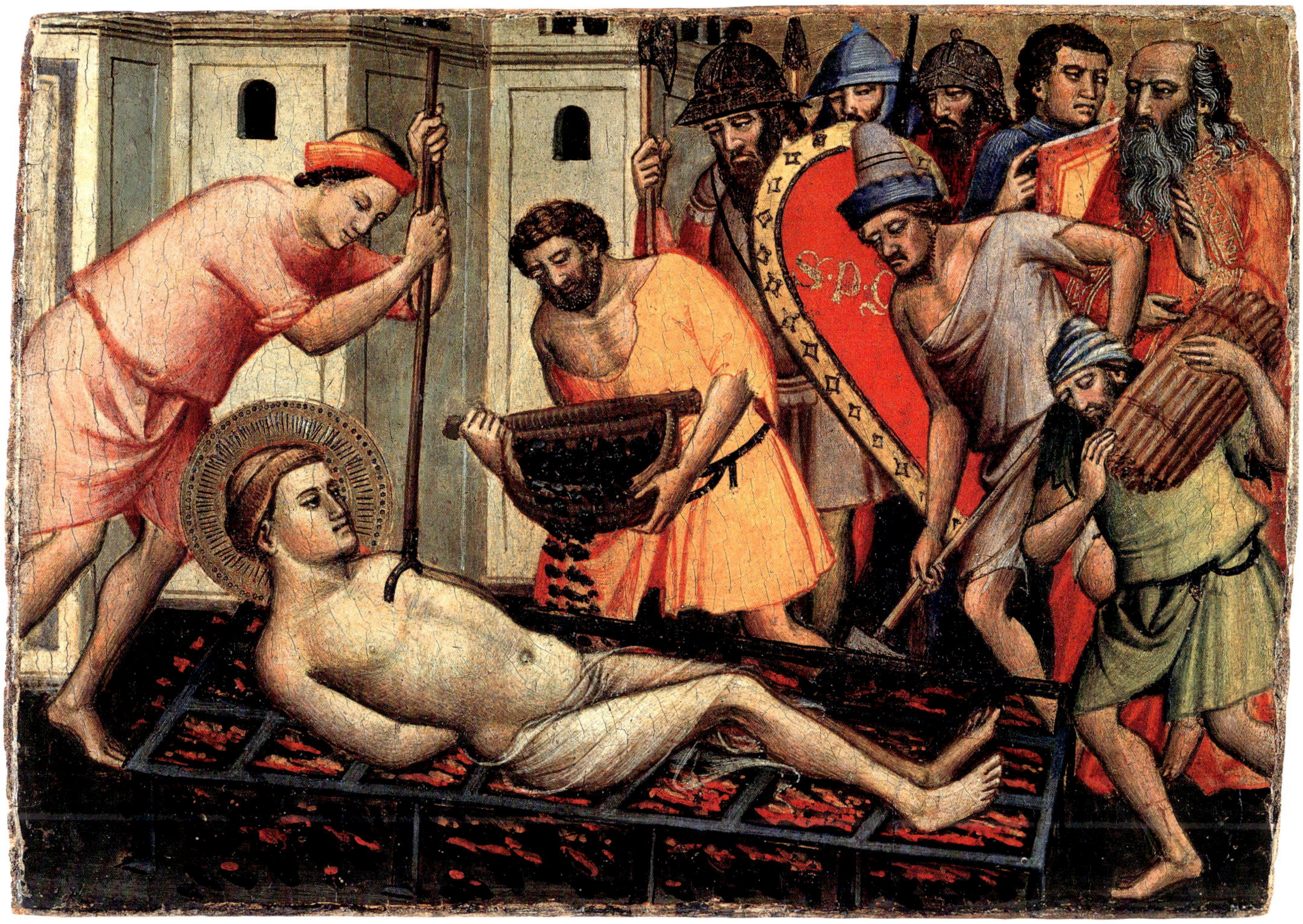

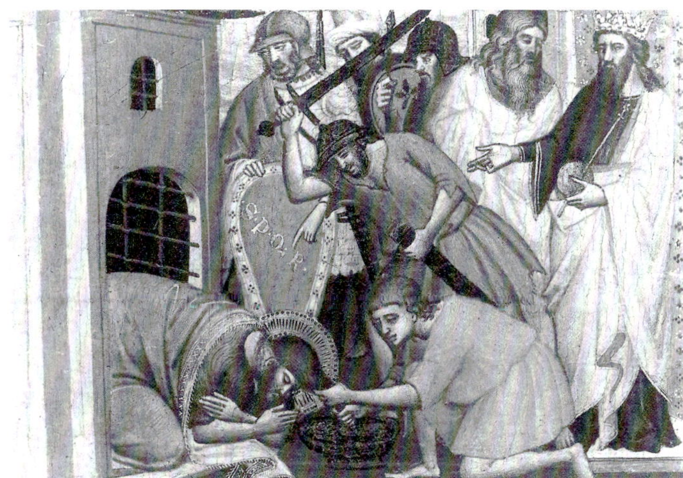

Fig. 2. Niccolò di Pietro Gerini, *The Beheading of the Baptist*, 1404. Tempera on panel, dimensions unknown. Private collection

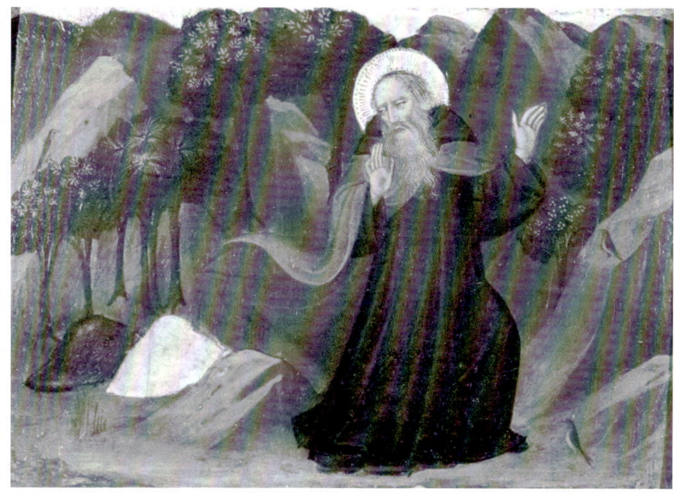

Fig. 3. Niccolò di Pietro Gerini, *The Temptation of Saint Anthony*, 1404. Tempera on panel, 22 x 32 cm (8⅝ x 12⅝ in.). Strossmayer Gallery, Zagreb, Croatia

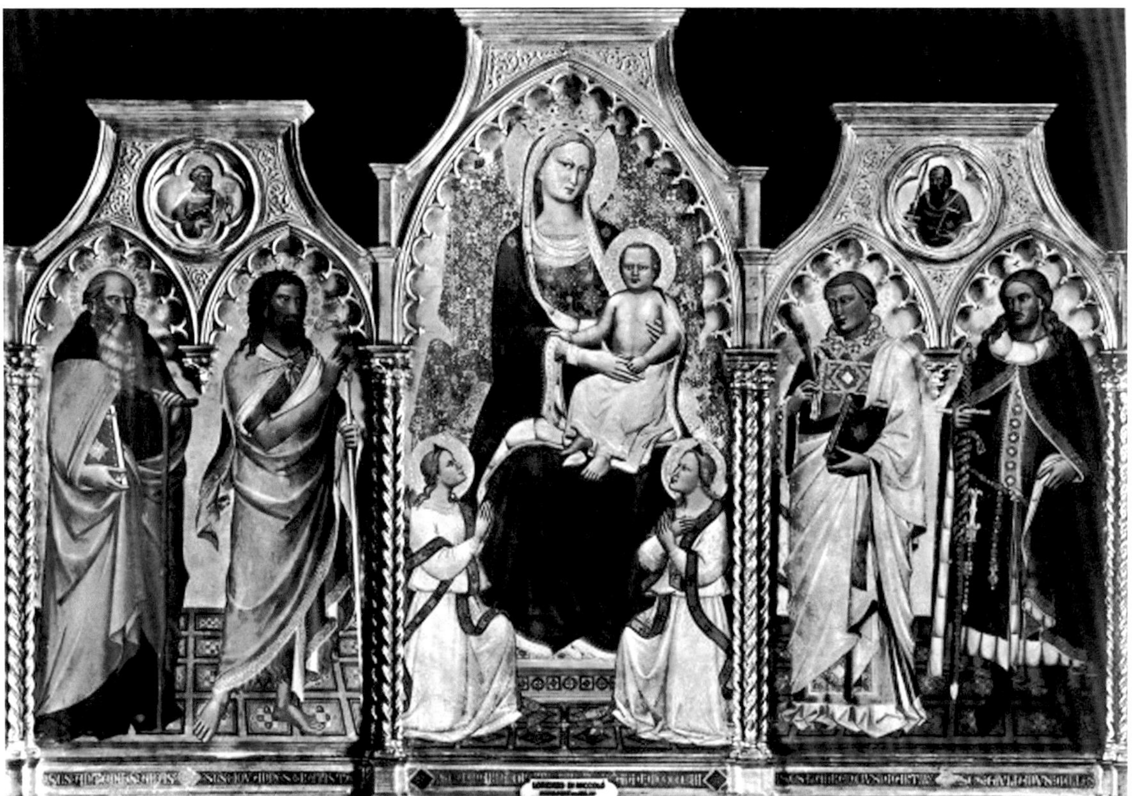

Fig. 4. Niccolò di Pietro Gerini, *The Virgin and Child with Saints*, 1404. Tempera on panel, 178 x 264 cm (70⅛ x 103⅝ in.). Galleria dell'Accademia, Florence, inv. no. 8610

Accademia 8610 is dated by inscription "1404" and was painted originally for the Florentine church of San Benedetto fuori Porta a Pinti. This church was founded in January 1400 as a daughter house of the Camaldolese order. Construction began in 1401 and appears to have been complete by 1407. In 1404 Domenico di Francesco Corsi, a silk merchant, provided an endowment and liturgical furnishings, including Gerini's altarpiece, for the chapel of Saint Anthony Abbot.[5] The church was suppressed in 1529 during the Siege of Florence; all its furnishings were transferred to the Camaldolese church of Santa Maria degli Angeli within the city walls, and it is there that the altarpiece is recorded by all later writers until the nineteenth century. Some confusion persists in modern literature on the altarpiece over its attribution either to Niccolò di Pietro Gerini or his presumed pupil and sometime associate, Lorenzo di Niccolò, but Gerini's authorship has been correctly reaffirmed by Everett Fahy.[6] The identification of the Feigen *Martyrdom of Saint Lawrence* and its companion scenes as fragments of the predella to this altarpiece provides a benchmark for recognizing Gerini's late style in small-scale narrative paintings, nearly all of which had previously been dated to the earlier part of his career.　L K

1. Miklós Boskovits, *Frühe italienische Malerei: Gemäldegalerie Berlin, Katalog der Gemälde* (Berlin, 1988), pp. 142–44, without reference to other panels from the same predella.
2. Reimar F. Lacher, in *Geschichten auf Gold: Bildererzählungen in der frühen italienischen Malerei*, ed. Stefan Weppelmann, exh. cat. (Berlin, 2005), pp. 151–55. Richard Offner, *A Critical and Historical Corpus of Florentine Painting: The Fourteenth Century, Supplement, a Legacy of Attributions*, ed. Hayden B. J. Maginnis (New York, 1981), p. 81, fig. 152, as "Gerinesque–Gerini School." Walter Angelelli and Andrea De Marchi, *Pittura dal duecento al primo cinquecento nelle fotografie di Girolamo Bombelli* (Milan, 1991), p. 155, no. 285 (Bombelli neg. no. E 79051).
3. *Katalog Galerije Slika Jugoslavenske Akademije Znanosti I Umjetnosti* (Zagreb, Croatia, 1947), no. 2, p. 13; Offner, *Supplement*, p. 75; and Miklós Boskovits, *Pittura fiorentina alla vigilia del Rinascimento, 1370–1400* (Florence, 1975), p. 415. The panel is reproduced by Mario Salmi, with a tentative attribution to Lorenzo Ghiberti, in "Lorenzo Ghiberti e la pittura," in *Scritti di storia dell'arte in onore di Lionello Venturi* (Rome, 1956), 1: p. 227, fig. 5.
4. Giorgio Bonsanti, *La Galleria dell'Accademia: Guida e catalogo completo* (Florence, 1987), p. 90.
5. Dillian Gordon, *The Fifteenth Century: Italian Paintings*, National Gallery Catalogues (London, 2003), 1: pp. 186–87n.91.
6. Everett Fahy, "On Lorenzo di Niccolò," *Apollo* 108 (1978): pp. 380–81. Laurence Kanter, *Italian Paintings in the Museum of Fine Arts, Boston* (Boston, 1994), p. 130, incorrectly associated a *Martyrdom of Saint Bartholomew* by Lorenzo di Niccolò with the *Beheading of the Baptist* from the predella reconstructed here, without reference to Accademia 8610.

Master of the Massa Marittima Choirbooks

Siena, active ca. 1290–ca. 1325

12. *The Resurrection in an Initial D*, ca. 1320

Tempera on parchment, 22.1 x 21.2 cm (8¾ x 8⅜ in.)

PROVENANCE: John Pope-Hennessy, by 1977 (his sale, Christie's, New York, January 10, 1996, lot 2); Edwin L. Weisl, Jr., New York (his sale, Christie's, London, June 7, 2006, lot 12)

BIBLIOGRAPHY: Cristina De Benedictis, "Miniature senesi del primo trecento," *Prospettiva* 14 (1978): p. 64; Enzo Carli, "Risurrezioni a Siena," *Antichità viva* 29, no. 5 (1990): pp. 6–7, 9; Carl Brandon Strehlke, in *Leaves of Gold: Manuscript Illumination from Philadelphia Collections*, ed. James R. Tanis and Jennifer A. Thompson, exh. cat. (Philadelphia, 2001), p. 17n.11; Ada Labriola, in *La miniatura senese, 1270–1420*, ed. Cristina De Benedictis (Milan, 2002), pp. 43, 53, 64–65n.113, 66n.148, 291–92; Ada Labriola, in *Dizionario biografico dei miniatori italiani: Secoli IX–XVI*, ed. Milvia Bollati (Milan, 2004), pp. 457, 610–11

CONDITION: The miniature is in excellent condition. There are retouches in the blue background to the left and right of Christ's shoulders, and smaller retouches in the front of the sarcophagus and in the rocks of the landscape. Minor abrasions to the initial letter have not been overpainted.

The initial D probably begins the invitatory for matins on Easter Sunday, which is normally recited "Surrexit Dominus vere" (The Lord has truly risen). It appears that this text may have been rearranged to read "Dominus surrexit vere." On the verso of the cutting are four staves of music and fragmentary lines of text drawn from the first two antiphons of matins on Easter Sunday: [EGO SUM QUI SUM ET CONSILIUM MEUM NON EST CUM] IMPIIS SET IN LEGE DOMINI [VOLUNTAS] MEA EST ALLELUIA. PS. BEATUS VIR. [A. POSTULAV]I PATRI MEO [sic] ALLELUIA. A. [DEDIT MI]HI GENTES ALLELUIA IN HE[REDITATEM ALLELUIA] (I am who I am, and My counsel is not with the wicked, but My delight is in the law of the Lord, alleluia. *Psalm* Happy the man. *Antiphon* I have asked My Father, alleluia; He has given Me the nations, alleluia, for an inheritance, alleluia).

The representation of Christ rising from His tomb is iconographically precocious for Italian manuscript illumination (and panel painting). The hours for Easter Sunday were normally illustrated in the thirteenth and early fourteenth centuries with an image of the three Maries at the tomb of Christ being told of the Resurrection by an angel. This image could appear either in an initial E, accompanying the text of the Benediction antiphon recited during the Mass of the Easter Vigil: "Et valde mane una sabbatorum veniunt ad monumentum orto iam sole" (And very early on the first day of the week they came to the tomb when the sun had just risen); or in an initial A beginning the second responsory at matins, which was recited for those who had not participated in the Mass: "Angelus Domini descendit de caelo et accedens revolvit lapidem et super eum sedit et dixit mulieribus: Nolite timere scio enim quia crucifixum quaeritis iam surrexit" (An Angel of the Lord came down from Heaven and drawing near rolled back the stone and sat upon it and said to the women: Do not be afraid for I know that you seek the Crucified. He has already risen). The risen Christ standing in the empty tomb, normally contained within an initial S ("Surrexit Domini"), begins to appear with some frequency only at the end of the fourteenth century. In the present case it may have been intended as a literal representation of the text of the first versicle at matins: "Surrexit Dominus de sepulcro, alleluia" (The Lord has risen from the grave, alleluia). A related image of Christ walking out of His tomb is sometimes found in graduals, where it fills a letter R ("Resurrexi et ad huc tecum sum"), from the late thirteenth century on, but the frontal image of Christ as it is seen here is not known earlier than this example.[1]

The Feigen *Resurrection in an Initial D* was first attributed by Cristina De Benedictis to a follower of the Sienese artist Memmo di Filippuccio, father of Lippo Memmi and father-in-law of Simone Martini, the author of several frescoes in San Gimignano and, supposedly, an assistant of Giotto working on the frescoes of the upper church in the Basilica di San Francesco at Assisi.[2] A homogeneous body of manuscript illuminations, first isolated by Pietro Toesca, was identified by Giovanni Previtali as the work of Memmo di Filippuccio, an identification that was generally accepted until Miklós Boskovits observed that similarities between the acknowledged works of Memmo di Filippuccio and the miniatures were only superficial and that the latter should instead be recognized as by an anonymous Ducciesque master.[3] This painter was baptized the Master of the Massa Marittima Choirbooks by Ada Labriola, after his most extensive commission: a set of seven antiphonary volumes now divided between the Cathedral and the church of Sant'Agostino in Massa Marittima, as well as numerous cutout fragments removed from these books now in the Vatican Library, the Free Library of Philadelphia, and elsewhere.[4] The artist was characterized by Labriola as among the most sensitive of Duccio's immediate followers, probably active between about 1290 and 1320.

In publishing the *Resurrection in an Initial D* for the first time, De Benedictis intended to situate it close to the group of illuminations then called works by Memmo di Filippuccio but not to extend that attribution to it without qualification. Enzo Carli asserted the high quality of the miniature and the

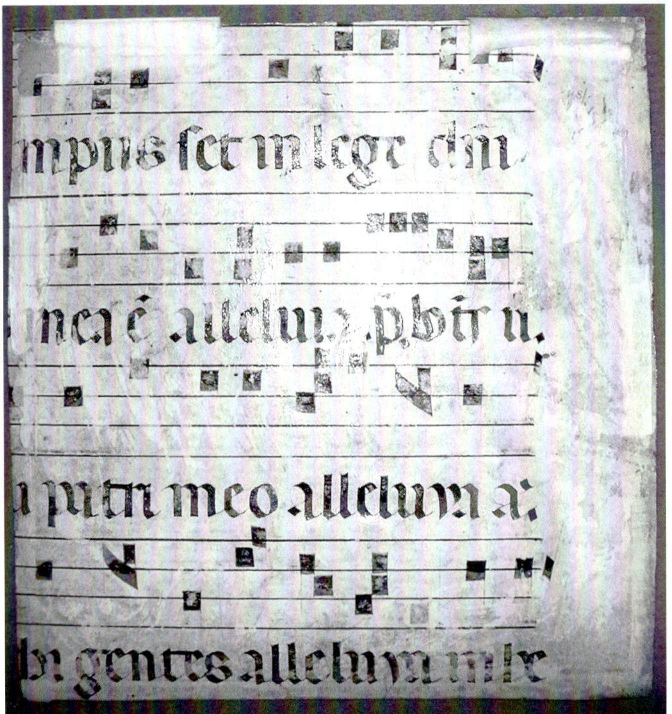

12 Verso

originality of its iconography as probable evidence of its being an autograph creation of Memmo di Filippuccio.[5] Carl Strehlke also accepted the *Resurrection* as an integral member of this group of illuminations while admitting the likelihood that the attribution to Memmo for any of them is tenuous.[6] He furthermore suggested the possibility that the *Resurrection* might have been removed from an antiphonary volume in the church of Santo Stefano in Pane in Florence, along with two cuttings in the Fondazione Giorgio Cini, Venice. Labriola rejected this suggestion on the grounds that the Santo Stefano antiphonary is dated 1302 in an incipit, while supposed borrowings from Duccio's *Maestà*—specifically the motif of Christ's sarcophagus rendered with inset panels on its front face and its opened lid laid askew across its top—imply that the *Resurrection* cannot have been painted before 1311.[7] While the second of these observations may have merit, the first is irrelevant as the date in the incipit refers to the writing of the text of the antiphonary only. The style of its illuminations is instead indistinguishable from that of the Massa Marittima choirbooks, which are dated by common consensus to ca. 1320.[8]

Rejecting its association with the Santo Stefano antiphonary, Labriola also eliminated the *Resurrection* from her list of works by the Master of the Massa Marittima Choirbooks, assigning it instead to an artist of a decidedly younger generation christened by her the Master of the 1337 Statutes. The group of works assembled by her under that name, however, is heterogeneous, as was correctly observed by Giulietta Chelazzi Dini, and there can be no doubt that the *Resurrection* is to be situated within the group of illuminations executed by the Master of the Massa Marittima Choirbooks.[9] Specifically, it may be identified as part of the artist's eponymous works: a missing folio from Corale s.s in Sant'Agostino in Massa Marittima. Another hitherto unidentified page from the same books (Corale 9 at the Cathedral in Massa Marittima) may be recognized in a cutout initial H with Saint Martin dividing his cloak with a beggar in the Museum of Fine Arts, Boston (fig. 1), illustrating the second responsory at matins for the feast of Saint Martin (November 11): "Hic est Martinus, electus Dei Pontifex" (This is Martin, God's chosen priest).[10] Both of these are consonant in figure type and decorative border motifs to all the other works so far identified as by the Master of the Massa Marittima Choirbooks, which at times approach the full Ducciesque style of painters such as the Master of Città di Castello. Most of the works assigned to the so-called Master of the 1337 Statutes instead reveal the tastes of a significantly later generation of artists in their decorative elements, spatial compositions, and figure style and may have been executed closer to the middle than the beginning of the fourteenth century.   L K

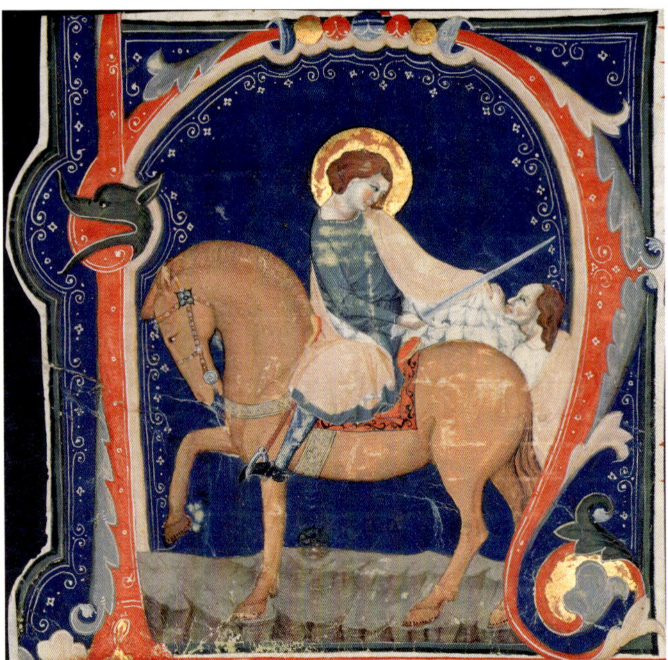

Fig. 1. Master of the Massa Marittima Choirbooks, *Saint Martin Dividing His Cloak with a Beggar*, ca. 1320. Tempera on parchment, 17.6 x 18.2 cm (7 x 7⅛ in.). Museum of Fine Arts, Boston, inv. no. 41.908

1. Enzo Carli, "Risurrezioni a Siena," *Antichità viva* 29, no. 5 (1990): pp. 6–7, 9.
2. Cristina De Benedictis, "Miniature senesi del primo trecento," *Prospettiva* 14 (1978): p. 64. The identification of Memmo di Filippuccio among the assistants of Giotto at Assisi is due to Roberto Longhi, "Giudizio sul duecento," *Proporzioni* 2 (1948): p. 50, and is the basis for most of the subsequent discussion of this artist in later art-historical literature. See also Giovanni Previtali, "Il possibile Memmo di Filippuccio," *Paragone* 155 (1962): pp. 3–11; and Enzo Carli, "Ancora dei Memmi a San Gimignano," *Paragone* 159 (1963): pp. 27–36.

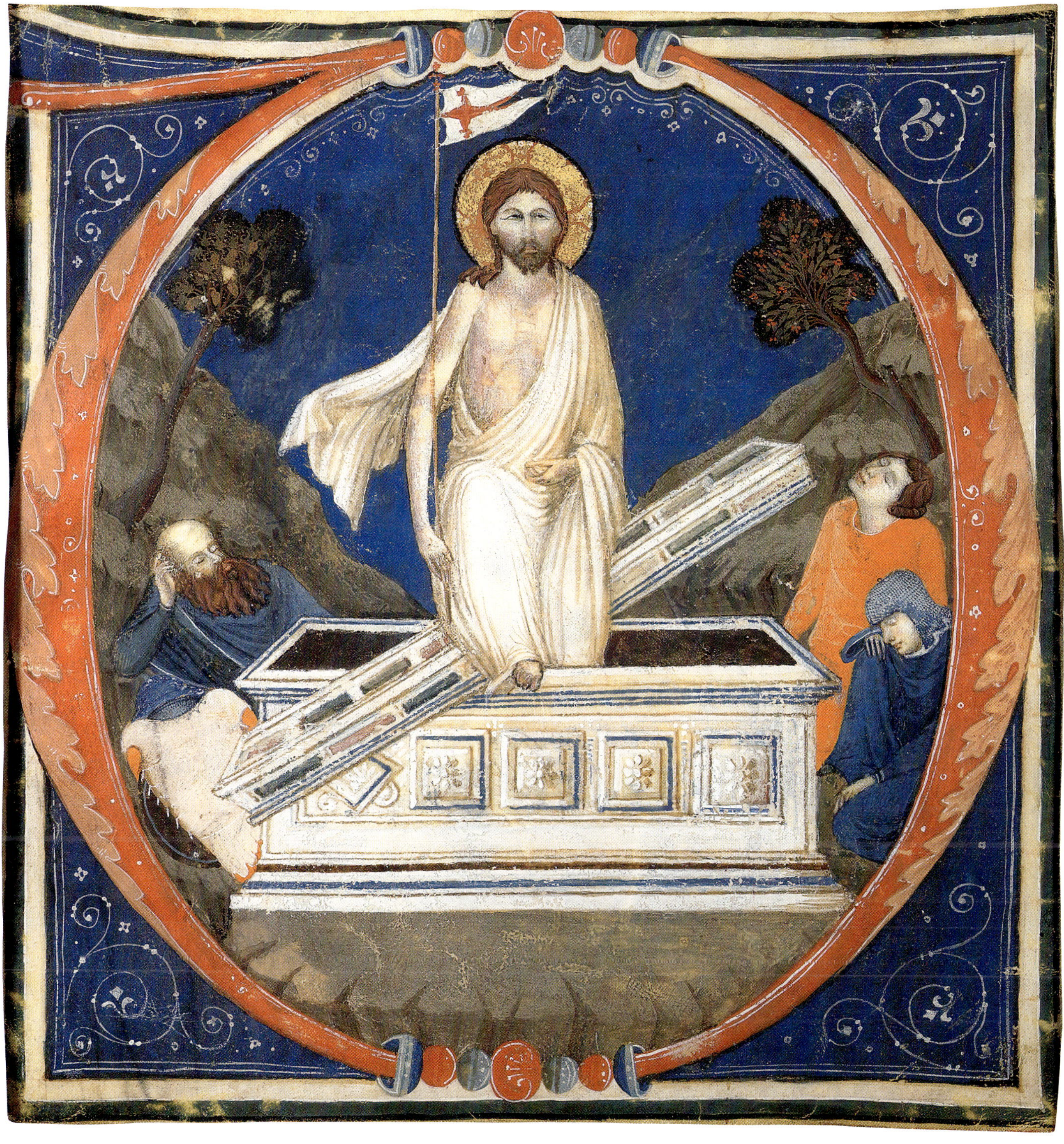

3. For Toesca and Previtali's discussion, see Pietro Toesca, *La collezione di Ulrico Hoepli,* Monumenti e studi per la storia della miniatura italiana (Milan, 1930), pp. 60–62; and Giovanni Previtali, "Miniature di Memmo di Filippuccio," *Paragone* 169 (1964): pp. 3–11. See also Maria Grazia Ciardi Duprè Dal Poggetto, "'L'homo astrologicus' e altre miniature di Memmo Filippuccio," in *Scritti di storia dell'arte in onore di Ugo Procacci* (Milan, 1977), 1: pp. 111–19; Cristina De Benedictis, "Memmo di Filippuccio tra Assisi e Siena," in *Roma anno 1300,* ed. Angiola Maria Romanini (Rome, 1983), pp. 211–16; Anna Maria Giusti, in *Il Gotico a Siena: Miniature, pitture oreficerie, oggetti d'arte,* ed. Giulietta Chelazzi Dini, exh. cat. (Siena, 1982), pp. 66–74; and Anna Rosa Calderoni Masetti, "Sulla datazione dei corali di Memmo di Filippuccio a Pisa," in *Scritti per l'Istituto Germanico di Storia dell'Arte di Firenze,* ed. Cristina Acidini Luchinat (Florence, 1997), pp. 47–50. For Boskovits's

observations, see Miklós Boskovits, "Il Gotico senese rivisitato: Proposte e commenti su una mostra," *Arte cristiana* 71 (1983): pp. 261, 271; and Boskovits, *A Critical and Historical Corpus of Florentine Painting,* sec. 3, vol. 9, *The Painters of the Miniaturist Tendency* (Florence, 1984), p. 37n.121.

4. Ada Labriola, in *La miniatura senese, 1270–1420,* ed. Cristina De Benedictis (Milan, 2002), pp. 43, 53, 64–65n.113, 66n.148, 291–92.

5. Carli, "Risurrezioni a Siena," pp. 6–7, 9.

6. Carl Brandon Strehlke, in *Leaves of Gold: Manuscript Illumination from Philadelphia Collections,* ed. James R. Tanis and Jennifer A. Thompson, exh. cat. (Philadelphia, 2001), p. 17n.11.

7. Labriola, in De Benedictis, *Miniatura senese,* pp. 46, 65n.113.

8. This date is based in the first instance on supposed borrowings from Giotto's Stefaneschi altarpiece for the illumination in the choirbooks

portraying the Decollation of Saint Paul. Although the correspondence between the miniature and the same scene on the altarpiece is not as close as is commonly asserted, an approximate date between the second and third decades of the fourteenth century—after the Pisa choirbooks of 1316–17—is reasonable on stylistic grounds.

9. Giulietta Chelazzi Dini, in *Duccio: Alle origini della pittura senese,* exh. cat. (Siena, 2003), p. 304.

10. Formerly in the collection of Edward Jackson Holmes, Boston. The text on the reverse of the cutting is a fragment from the preceding first and second antiphons at matins: "[MARTINUS, ADHUC CATECHUMENUS, HAC] ME VESTE CONTEXIT. SANCTAE TRINITA[TIS FIDEM MAR]TINUS CONFESSUS [EST, ET BAPTISMI GRATIAM PERCEPIT]" (Martin, still a catechumen, has clothed Me with this mantle. Martin professed his faith in the Holy Trinity and received the grace of baptism).

"Barna"/Lippo Memmi
Siena, active second quarter 14th century

13. *Virgin and Child Enthroned with Saints Peter and Paul and Ten Angels,* ca. 1330–35

Tempera and oil on panel, 32.6 x 29.6 cm (12⅞ x 11⅝ in.), overall; 30.3 x 29.6 cm (11⅞ x 11⅝ in.), picture surface

PROVENANCE: Joseph Lindon Smith, Dublin, N.H., by 1913; Mrs. John Jay Schiefflelin; Sotheby's, New York, January 22, 2004, lot 9

BIBLIOGRAPHY: Bernard Berenson, *Catalogue of a Collection of Paintings and Some Art Objects*, vol. 1, *Italian Paintings* (Philadelphia, 1913), p. 54; Raimond van Marle, *The Development of the Italian Schools of Painting*, vol. 2 (The Hague, 1924), p. 297; Millard Meiss, "Primitifs italiens à l'Orangerie," *Revue des arts* 6 (1956): pp. 141–42; Sam Wagstaff, Jr., in *An Exhibition of Italian Panels and Manuscripts from the Thirteenth and Fourteenth Centuries in Honor of Richard Offner,* exh. cat. (Hartford, Conn., 1965), pp. 22–23; Luciano Bellosi, "Moda e cronologia: B) Per la pittura del primo trecento," *Prospettiva* 11 (1977): pp. 21, 24; Cristina De Benedictis, *La pittura senese, 1330–1370* (Florence, 1979), p. 79; Marianne Lonjon, "Le Maître des Saints du Mans," in *L'art gothique siennois: Enluminure, peinture, orfèvrerie, sculpture,* exh. cat. (Avignon, 1983), pp. 195–97; Alessandro Bagnoli and Luciano Bellosi, eds., *Simone Martini e "chompagni"* (Siena, 1985), p. 100; Pierluigi Leone de Castris, *Simone Martini* (Milan, 2003), pp. 180, 182

CONDITION: The panel, of a vertical wood grain, is 23 mm thick and has not been thinned, except along the vertical edges on the back and across the top and bottom edges on the front. Numerous pinpoint (and some larger) flaking losses interrupt the paint surface, especially in the blues of the Virgin's and Saint Peter's robes, the vaulting on either side of the Virgin's throne, and the hair of some of the angels: the heads of two angels on the right, whose faces are not visible, have been renewed. The paint surface otherwise is in nearly immaculate condition, showing negligible abrasion to pigment layers and completely preserving all mordant gilt decoration and much of its original colored oil glazes. The exceptional oil content of pigment binders has resulted in unusual transparency in some of the color fields, as in the shot greens and reds of Saint Paul's robes, and is perhaps responsible as well for the more aggressive flaking of some darker colors, especially blue. The panel shows no traces of the attachment or removal of hinges or battens on its back or sides.

This remarkable panel was first exhibited publicly in 1926, when it was lent to the Museum of Fine Arts, Boston, by Joseph Lindon Smith of Dublin, New Hampshire. Although it had initially been described by Bernard Berenson as one of the few panel paintings by Barna da Siena, at the time of its exhibition it was reportedly attributed by Richard Offner to the shop of Ambrogio Lorenzetti, possibly with some intervention by the master himself, and this attribution was repeated by Sam Wagstaff in 1965 in the exhibition he mounted at the Wadsworth Atheneum dedicated to Richard Offner.[1] Millard Meiss shifted it closer to the circle of Pietro Lorenzetti when he identified it as the center panel of a small triptych that included as side panels two full-length standing saints in the Musée de Tessé, Le Mans, France (fig. 1).[2] He baptized their author the Master of the Le Mans Saints (Maître des Saints du Mans), to whom he also ascribed a small panel of the *Maestà* loosely related in composition to the present panel that had previously been published by Mina Gregori as a work by Pietro Lorenzetti.[3] Offner, although he never published his opinion regarding the Lindon Smith panel, filed its photograph along with the Le Mans *Saints* under the name "Lindon Smith Barna," a category that included no other paintings. Luciano Bellosi also gave the panel to the artist formerly known as Barna da Siena, but he rejected its association with the Le Mans *Saints*, which he considered earlier, more purely Ducciesque paintings.[4] This distinction has not been accepted by subsequent writers. Cristina De Benedictis and Marianne Lonjon both retained the epithet Master of the Le Mans Saints, suggesting that the painter may have been an Avignonese follower of Simone Martini active in the 1340s.[5]

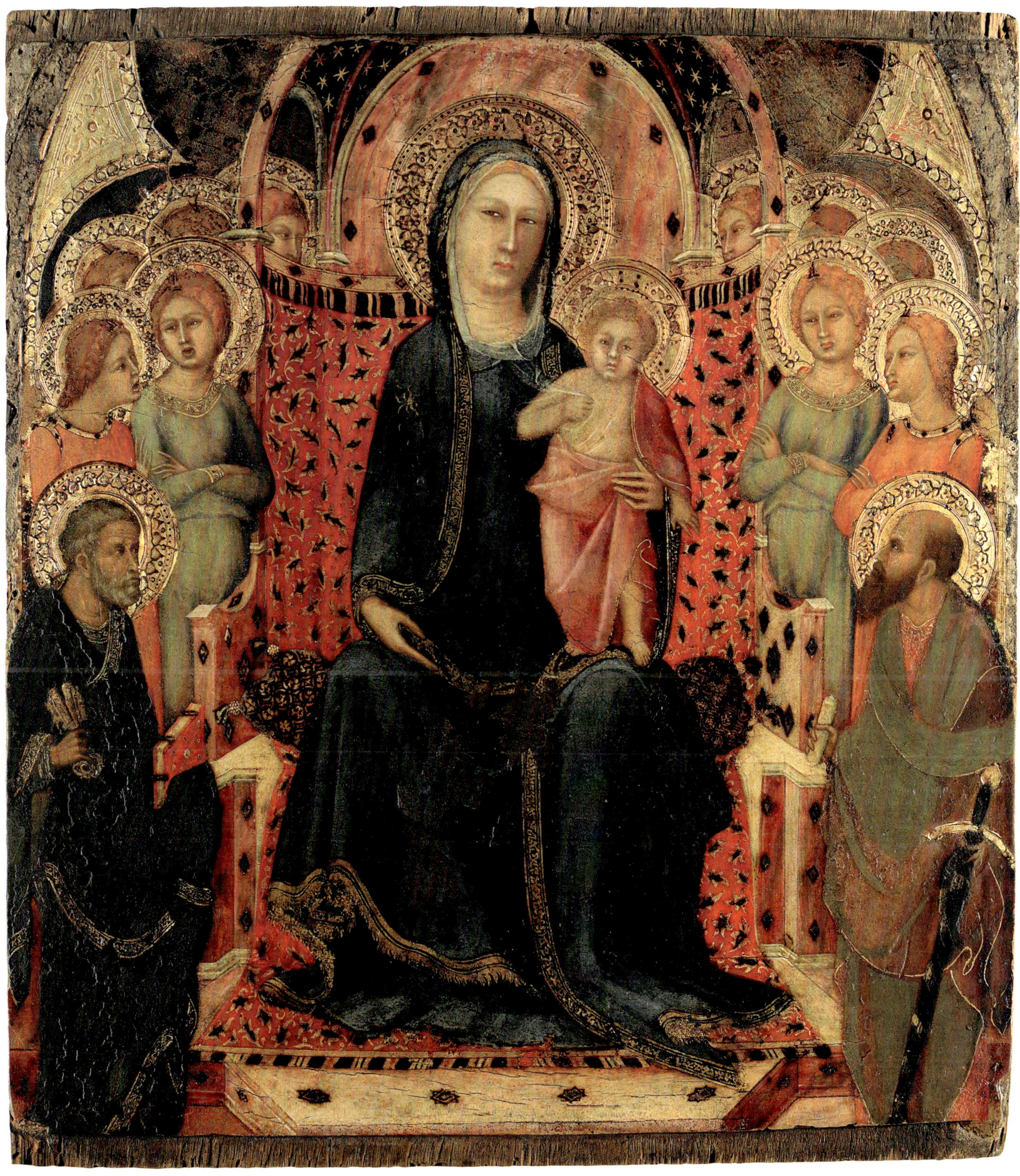

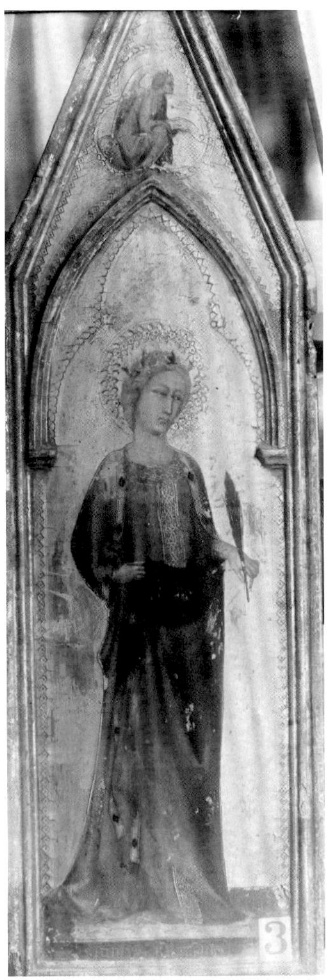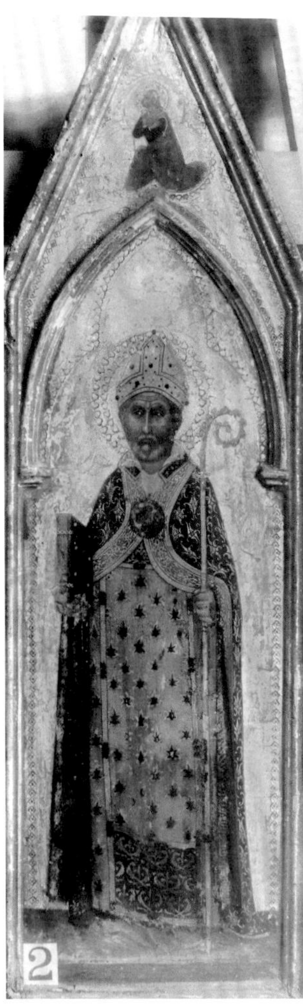

Fig. 1. "Barna"/Lippo Memmi, *Saint Lucy*(?) and *Bishop Saint*, ca. 1330–35. Tempera on panel, 54.7 x 17 cm (21½ x 6¾ in.), each. Musée de Tessé, Le Mans, France

Pierluigi Leone de Castris reaffirmed the association of the three panels with the personality once known as Barna—for him identifiable with Lippo Memmi's brother Tederigo—as early works, still reminiscent of Simone Martini's frescoes in Assisi and probably datable 1320–22.[6]

No topic in the study of early Italian painting has been as contentious nor subject to as wide a variety of opinion as the historical identity of the artist whom Giorgio Vasari called Barna da Siena, supposedly the author of a cycle of New Testament frescoes in the right nave of the Collegiata at San Gimignano and traditionally considered one of the most expressive and most original masters of the Sienese trecento. Alternately expansive and restrictive lists of works were aggregated to his name throughout the first two-thirds of the twentieth century, but no consensus as to the period of his activity—whether in the 1330s and 1340s or the 1360s and 1370s—appeared in scholarly literature. The almost complete absence of documentary references to a painter named Barna, furthermore, coupled with the discovery of late fourteenth- (or early fifteenth-) century sgraffito inscriptions beneath the San Gimignano frescoes claiming them as the work of "Lippo da Siena," led the Sienese archivist Peleo Bacci to conclude

that Vasari's narrative may have been a fiction and that Lippo Memmi should be recognized as the real author of the works otherwise thought to be by Barna da Siena.[7]

Arguments over the past forty years have nearly all supported Bacci's contentions with additional circumstantial evidence tending to conflate the identities of Barna da Siena and Lippo Memmi. This evidence, however, is not unequivocal, and Bacci's original observations need to be considered more carefully in context of the polemical and vituperative nature of his article (with special animus reserved for Emilio Cecchi and Ugo Ojetti), which was meant to discredit judgments of connoisseurship in the face of what he thought to be the completely repainted state of the frescoes. Bacci, furthermore, based much of his speculation on the then-prevalent belief that the San Gimignano frescoes were painted in the second half of the fourteenth century rather than, as is currently believed, before 1340. It would be reasonable to presume that an artist receiving so important a commission at that time ought to have been listed on one of the roles of the Sienese painters' guild, which commence as early as 1363—Barna is not; only a single notice of 1340 referring to a "Barna Bertini dipentore" has ever been associated with his name—while graffiti perhaps dating to the late trecento, possibly not long after completion of the frescoes, might just as reasonably be presumed to carry strong evidential value for determining their authorship (Bacci was an archivist, not an art historian).

The most compelling of recent arguments supporting Bacci's thesis concern an altarpiece always associated with the name of Barna—certainly painted by the author of the San Gimignano frescoes—comprising four panels showing full-length figures of Saints Peter, Paul, John the Baptist, and Andrew seated on faldstools (two in Palermo and one each in Altenburg, Germany, and in Pisa) and four related pinnacle panels (Altenburg, and Avignon and Douai, France) showing half-length figures of the Blessing Redeemer and saints.[8] This is now believed to be identical with a painting described by Vasari in the church of San Paolo a Ripa d'Arno in Pisa and said by him to have borne Lippo Memmi's signature. Yet another group of paintings sometimes associated with the Barna group—though less certainly related in handling to the San Gimignano frescoes—and sometimes labeled as by a Master of the Glorification of Saint Thomas, includes a painting signed by "Lippus de Sena," again supposed to be Lippo Memmi. The tendency of current studies is to accept the aggregate weight of these arguments as "demonstrating" that Barna never existed and that all the works formerly thought to be his are actually by Lippo Memmi. Variations on the theme suggest that the distinctions formerly drawn between Lippo and Barna are valid but that the latter must have been part of the large workshop of the former and therefore that he could have been Lippo's brother Tederigo, known from documents but not from securely identified works of art.

Attributions to Lippo Memmi are all based on the existence of five signed paintings, one of them, the *Annunciation*

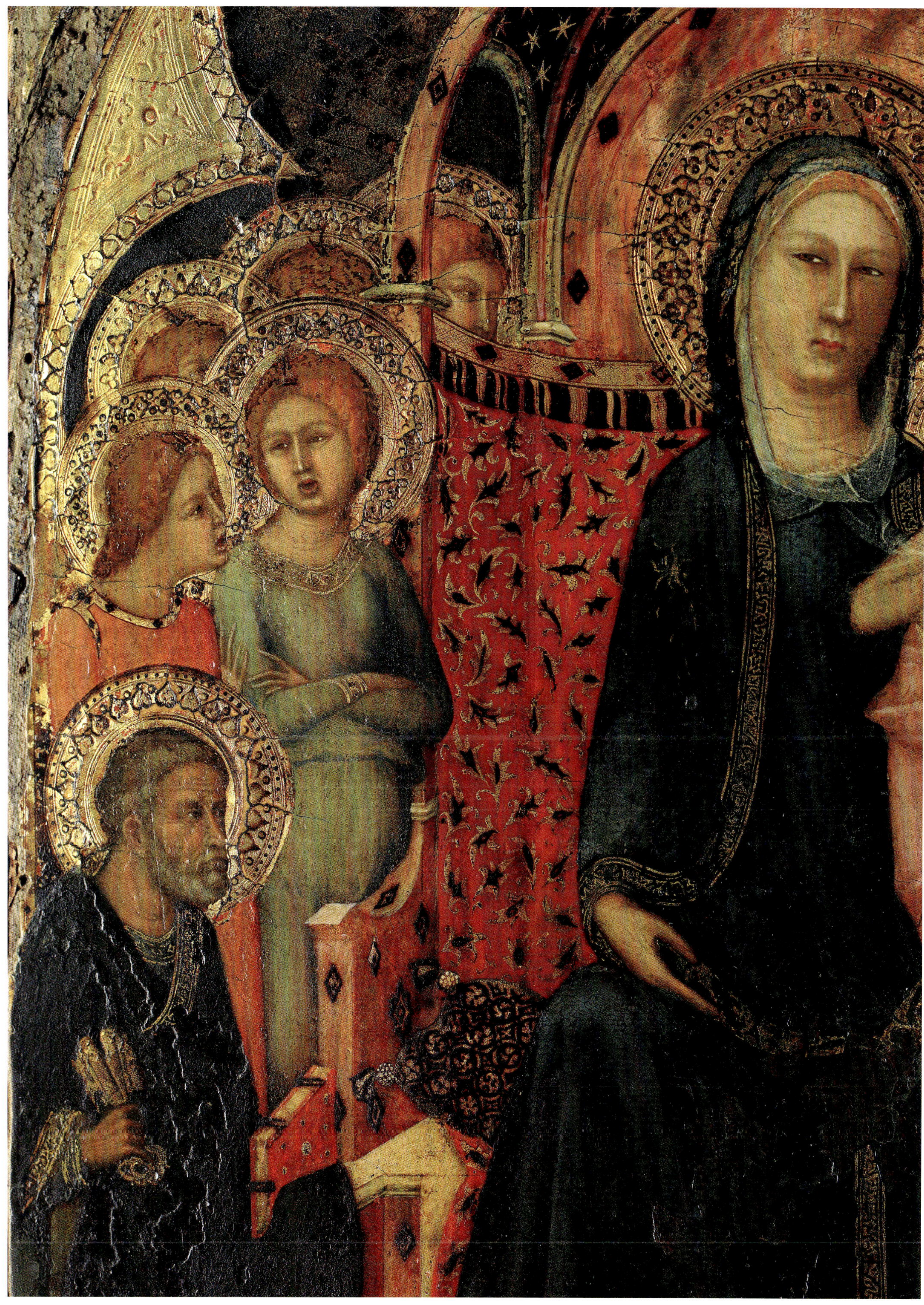

13 Detail

altarpiece of 1333 from Siena Cathedral (now in the Galleria degli Uffizi, Florence) executed in partnership with his brother-in-law, Simone Martini. A second, the so-called *Madonna dei Raccomandati* in Orvieto Cathedral (referred to above), is sufficiently unlike the others to have engendered proposals that another painter named Lippo might have been active in Siena in the first half of the fourteenth century, though a general consensus of recent opinion prefers to accept the painting (along with the other works in the Master of the Glorification of Saint Thomas group) as indicative of Lippo Memmi's early style. The three remaining paintings portray the Virgin and Child: one in Berlin, one in Altenburg, and one formerly in the church of the Servi in Siena, now exhibited in the Pinacoteca Nazionale there. These are again sufficiently unlike each other to permit the assumption either that Lippo was capable of wide variations in quality within his autograph work; that he may have worked with some regularity in collaboration with other artists, specifically Simone Martini, who could have been responsible for designing the Servi *Madonna*; or that he operated a large and productive workshop, which, as seems to have been the case in Florence with the studio of Giotto, used his signature more as a trademark than as an indicator of what today might be considered autograph status.

Although it is of crucial importance, it has not generally been recognized that the signature on the frame of the last of these five paintings, the Servi *Madonna,* is false, having been added to the painting in the fifteenth century.[9] While it is possible that this "signature" reproduces an original inscription and that the painting could indeed have been by Lippo Memmi, it is equally possible—indeed, probable, given the rarity of signatures appended to paintings of this format in the fourteenth century[10]—that it did not. Either way, the attribution of the painting must be demonstrated, not assumed, and the "signature" cannot be used as a basis of comparison for assigning other works to Lippo's name. Furthermore, if it is at least logically possible that Lippo's name could have been added to the painting *ex novo* in the fifteenth century—that his name was, in other words, valuable enough or at least widely enough known at that time to be affixed to a painting that may or may not have been by his hand—it is also logically necessary to disregard or, at the very least, question the evidential value of the graffiti beneath the San Gimignano frescoes.[11] Questions must also be raised about the San Paolo a Ripa d'Arno altarpiece: the identification of that work with the eight panels mentioned above is highly plausible but even so must be understood to be hypothetical, while in the physical absence of the signature reported by Vasari it cannot be determined whether such a signature actually existed, or whether, if it did exist, it was placed there by the artist or added to the work later.[12]

The purpose of this perhaps over-exigent scrutiny of Lippo Memmi's signatures is to underscore their relative rather than absolute value in establishing his artistic identity. It seems to this writer necessary on stylistic grounds to agree with those authors who maintain the integrity of the Barna group as distinct from the larger, more amorphous category of paintings now associated with Lippo's name. The paintings in the Barna group display accomplishments of modeling, composition, and expressive tenor fundamentally at odds with the average production of all the rest of the works of art attributed to Lippo Memmi or to the wider circle of artists close to him, which range from competent to highly refined but not especially innovative diffusions of the general tenets of Simone Martini's style. Aspects of the Feigen *Maestà,* such as the faultless foreshortening of the four inlaid lozenges on the dais of the Virgin's throne; the white dotted highlights at each corner of the cornice moldings on the throne spires; the stenciled glazing on the Virgin's gilt cushion; the view up into the canopy of the throne; or, above all, the transition from a dark blue to a light blue glaze over the gilding on either side of the canopy, as though the pastiglia frame of the painting were casting a shadow within the pictorial space, appear in no works by Lippo Memmi and are, indeed, superior to the accomplishments of almost any other trecento painter both on the level of craftsmanship and intellectual conception. Confusion between "Barna" and Lippo results entirely from their shared repertory of figure types (undoubtedly indicating that they must have worked together for some period of time), but the contrast between the insistently flat drawing of the latter and the spatial sophistication of the former, to mention one point only, is irreconcilable with attributions to a single hand, even presuming these differences to arise from chronological disparities or from the piecemeal intervention within Lippo's production of Simone Martini as a designer. Recognizing, as most scholars do, that the paintings in the Barna group must have been executed over a great part of the range of Lippo Memmi's career makes the gulf between them unbridgeable.

Clearly it is impossible to state categorically that Barna was the historical name of the painter responsible for the group of paintings assigned to him, though with proper qualification "Barna" remains a useful denominator to label it as a distinct set of paintings. That he was heavily dependent on Lippo Memmi's (or at the very least on Simone Martini's) influence is self-evident, but it is possible to suggest that this dependence was not exclusive and that the trajectory of his career was different from Lippo's. It has often been remarked how much his paintings reveal the influence of Pietro and Ambrogio Lorenzetti, which Lippo's conspicuously do not, and now it is possible as well to suggest that he was trained in a different studio than either Lippo's or Simone's. The evidence for this is suggested in the first instance by Luciano Bellosi's astute observation that the Le Mans *Saints* associated with the Feigen *Maestà* are essentially Ducciesque in style, and confirmation is offered by a frequently overlooked panel of the *Virgin and Child Enthroned with Saints Peter, Paul, John the Baptist, and Dominic and a Donor* in the Art

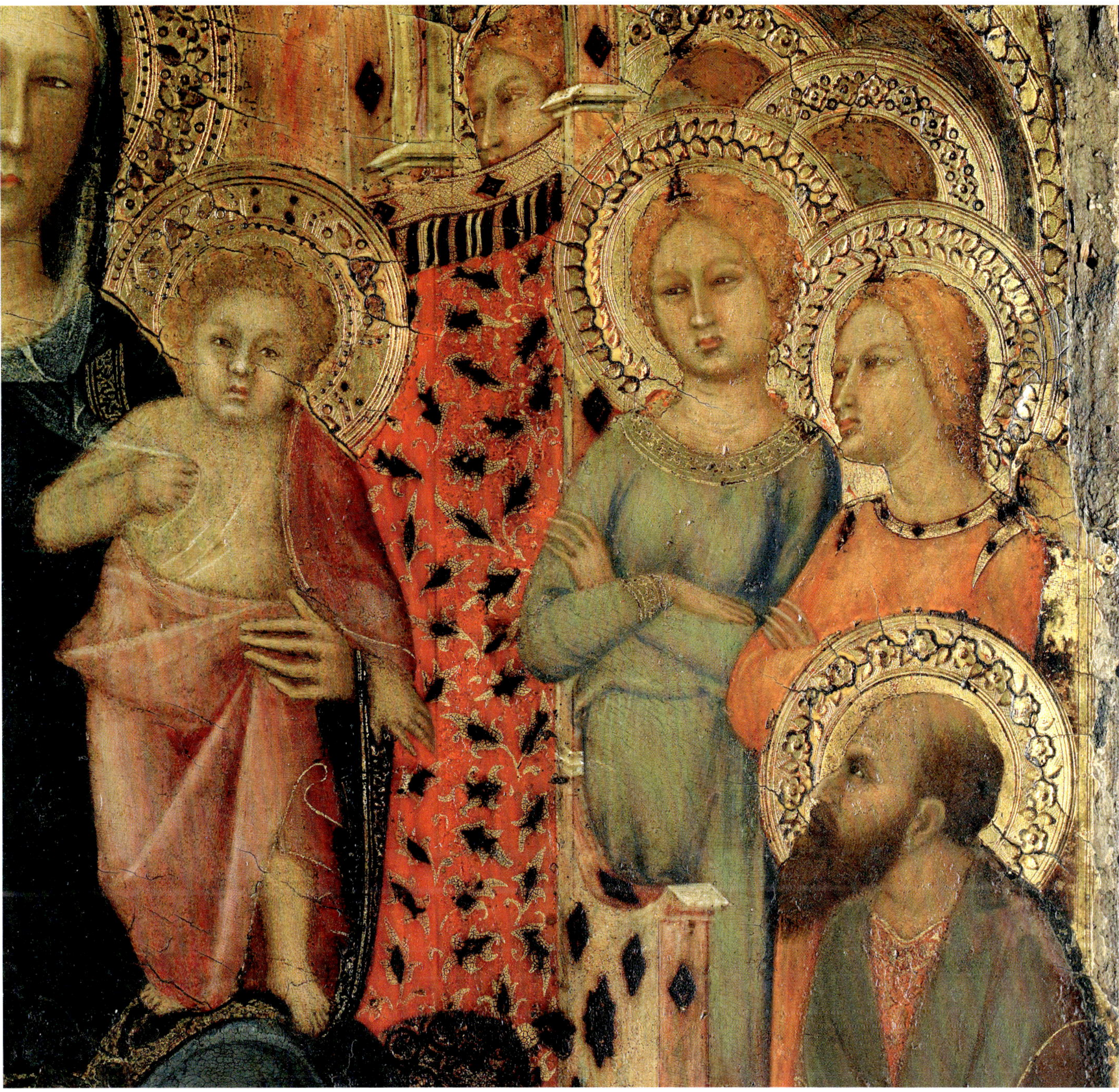

13 Detail

Institute of Chicago (inv. no. 37.1007).[13] Generally attributed to Ugolino di Nerio, the painting displays spatial conceits utterly foreign to Ducciesque painting (especially the extensive and empty foreground) and employs no punch tools found in any other work by Ugolino. These instead all recur in the repertoire of Simone Martini and Lippo Memmi/"Barna,"[14] and closer examination of the well-preserved figures of saints and the donor around the picture's perimeter[15] reveals a correspondence of figure types, detail, and painting technique to works by "Barna." If this panel is to be considered the earliest member of the "Barna" group, or the earliest member so far identified, it may signify an initial training for that artist in the workshop of Ugolino di Nerio, essentially different from and later than the supposed beginnings of Lippo Memmi in the studio of his father, Memmo di Filippuccio.

It is difficult to imagine a date for the Chicago panel earlier than 1320, given the complexity of its punch tooling and its evident debt to the mature style of Ugolino di Nerio. In all likelihood, the further extreme of the career of Barna should be represented by paintings such as the *Mystic Marriage of Saint Catherine* in the Museum of Fine Arts, Boston, or the diptych now divided between the Ashmolean Museum, Oxford, and the Gemäldegalerie, Berlin, both probably executed in the 1340s or close to 1350. Arguments have been advanced, with suitable credibility, for dating the San Gimignano frescoes (whoever their author is thought to be) shortly after 1333, and it is reasonable to suppose that paintings such as the Asciano *Madonna* or the supposed San Paolo a Ripa d'Arno altarpiece were not separated from the frescoes by a wide margin of time. The closest analogies to the Feigen

Maestà and the Le Mans *Saints* among the list of paintings attributable to "Barna" are to be found with the panels that originally comprised the San Paolo a Ripa d'Arno altarpiece. Whether these are to be situated in the later 1320s, as some authors have contended, or after 1333, as others instead prefer, is difficult to judge, although the reminiscences within the Feigen *Maestà* of compositional examples by Pietro Lorenzetti would be easier to explain if the work were given a later date.[16]

There is some discussion regarding the identity of the saints in the two panels at Le Mans. The bishop bears no attributes that would aid in his identification. The female carries a martyr's palm and is inscribed below her feet SANCTA K.TARINA. This inscription was described by Lonjon as probably of a later date, and she proposed instead the possibility that the figure may represent Saint Agatha, though again without her usual attributes.[17] It is possible that the crown of flames worn around her head is not meant to refer to Agatha's martyrdom but rather to indicate her identity as Saint Lucy, who usually carries a flaming oil lamp invoking the Latin root of her name: *lux*, or light.   L K

1. Bernard Berenson, *Catalogue of a Collection of Paintings and Some Art Objects*, vol. 1, *Italian Paintings* (Philadelphia, 1913), p. 54; and Sam Wagstaff, Jr., in *An Exhibition of Italian Panels and Manuscripts from the Thirteenth and Fourteenth Centuries in Honor of Richard Offner*, exh. cat. (Hartford, Conn., 1965), pp. 22–23.

2. Millard Meiss, "Primitifs italiens à l'Orangerie," *Revue des arts* 6 (1956): pp. 141–42.

3. Mina Gregori, "Due opere di Pietro Lorenzetti," *Paragone* 47 (1953): pp. 77–80.

4. Luciano Bellosi, "Moda e cronologia: B) Per la pittura del primo trecento," *Prospettiva* 11 (1977): pp. 21, 24.

5. Cristina De Benedictis, *La pittura senese, 1330–1370* (Florence, 1979), p. 79; and Marianne Lonjon, "Le Maître des Saints du Mans," in *L'art gothique siennois: Enluminure, peinture, orfèvrerie, sculpture*, exh. cat. (Avignon, 1983), pp. 195–97.

6. Pierluigi Leone de Castris, *Simone Martini* (Milan, 2003), pp. 180, 182.

7. Peleo Bacci, "Il Barna o Berna: Pittore della Collegiata di San Gimignano, è mai esistito?" *Balzana* 1 (1927): pp. 249–53.

8. See Daniela Parenti, in *Maestri senesi e toscani nel Lindenau-Museum di Altenburg*, ed. Miklós Boskovits, exh. cat. (Siena, 2008), pp. 27–37, for the most recent and fullest discussion of this complex.

9. The letters of Lippo Memmi's name are each contained within punch decoration on the lower molding of the frame of the painting. It was first noted by Mojmir Frinta ("Unsettling Evidence in Some Panel Paintings of Simone Martini," in *La pittura nel XIV e XV secolo: Il contributo dell'analisi tecnica alla storia dell'arte*, ed. Henk W. van Os and J. R. J. van Asperen de Boer [Bologna, 1983], p. 214) that the tools employed to create this decoration were first used in the mid-fifteenth century in the workshop of Sano di Pietro. Alessandro Bagnoli ("I tempi della Maestà: Il restauro e le nuove evidenze," in *Simone Martini: Atti del convegno*, ed. Luciano Bellosi [Florence, 1988], p. 118n.22) rejected this contention, stating that conservation of the painting demonstrated that the letters of the signature were contemporary with the gilding and punching of the frame, which is integral with the panel. It was not noticed by Bagnoli that the bottom molding of the frame (bearing the signature) is not integral with the panel but is a later replacement. It is curved to follow the warp of the panel and is applied in such a manner as to cover part of the paint surface and interrupt one of the punch strikes at the lower left margin of the gold ground, both impossibilities for originally engaged moldings. The punches used on the bottom molding extend a short distance up the lateral moldings to mask repairs at the corners; they are different from those used on the original engaged moldings at the top and sides of the painting and demonstrably originate from Sano di Pietro's workshop in the fifteenth century.

10. The alterations affected by the frame repairs described in n.9 may imply that the painting was reduced from a full-length to a half-length image in the fifteenth century, or simply that the panel was sufficiently warped to require repairs to the split bottom moldings of its frame. In either event, the intact lateral and top moldings indicate that it was never part of a larger complex, such as an altarpiece, in which a signature or inscription would be less unusual.

11. Although several authors have come to view these graffiti as the equivalent of contemporary signatures, it was not Bacci's intention to portray them as such. They clearly postdate completion of the frescoes, perhaps by as little as a few decades but possibly by as much as a full century, and the fact that the inscription is repeated four times—an unprecedented occurrence in the period—should alone render it highly suspicious as an informed indicator of the authorship of the cycle.

12. Essentially, the identification is based on the recognition of the so-called Hermit Saints in Altenburg as Vallombrosans; on Vasari's description of Saints Peter, Paul, and John the Baptist being included in the altarpiece; and on the absence of surviving candidates with a stronger claim. While all three (especially the first) are permissive conditions, none of them is conclusive: an exceptionally large percentage of Tuscan fourteenth-century altarpieces contain the three saints named by Vasari and an even larger percentage do not survive even in a fragmentary state. The identification of Barna da Siena with Lippo Memmi adds further circumstantial evidence to this argument, but as that identification is largely based on this argument the proposition is circular.

13. Christopher Lloyd, *Italian Paintings before 1600 in the Art Institute of Chicago: A Catalogue of the Collection* (Chicago, 1993), pp. 258–61.

14. It was pointed out by Norman Muller, "Ambrogio Lorenzetti's 'Small' 'Maestà' Reconsidered," in *Conservare Necesse Est: Festschrift til Leif Einar Plahter på hans 70–årsdag*, ed. Erling Skaug (Oslo, 1999), p. 221n.21, that a rarely encountered punch mark found on the Chicago panel, "Frinta Bb8" (see Mojmir S. Frinta, *Punched Decoration on Late Medieval Panel and Miniature Painting* [Prague, 1998], 1: p. 83), is also found on the *Mystic Marriage of Saint Catherine* in the Museum of Fine Arts, Boston, which is nearly always associated with the name of Barna (see Laurence Kanter, *Italian Paintings in the Museum of Fine Arts, Boston* [Boston, 1994], pp. 92–95) and on the reverse of a small *Madonna and Child* in the Ashmolean Museum, Oxford, usually attributed to Naddo Ceccarelli (see Christopher Lloyd, *A Catalogue of the Earlier Italian Paintings in the Ashmolean Museum* [Oxford, 1977], pp. 48–49, where the author professes himself unpersuaded by this attribution). The latter, a painting of exceptional refinement, should be recognized as part of the "Barna" group, as should the unrestored passages in another *Madonna and Child* attributed to Ceccarelli in the Robert Lehman Collection at the Metropolitan Museum of Art, New York; see John Pope-Hennessy and Laurence Kanter, *Italian Paintings*, Robert Lehman Collection 1 (New York, 1987), pp. 24–25.

15. The figure of the Christ Child, the Virgin's hands and draperies, the sgraffito-decorated cloth behind her, and the pillow on which she sits are painted in a coarser technique than the rest of the panel. The style and handling are reminiscent of the work of Sano di Pietro in the mid-fifteenth century. The Virgin's face is original, i.e., conforming to the handling of the four saints and the donor, the marble throne and its dais, and the foreground carpet or pavement.

16. Lonjon, "Maître des Saints du Mans," p. 197, cited Pietro's *Nativity of the Virgin* altarpiece painted for Siena Cathedral in 1342 as a model for the architecture of the Virgin's throne in the Feigen panel.

17. Ibid., p. 195.

Pseudo-Dalmasio

Bologna, active second quarter 14th century

14a. *Four Saints*, ca. 1335–40

Tempera on panel, 14.4 x 56 cm (5⅝ x 22 in.), overall;
10.6 x 10.6 cm (4¼ x 4¼ in.), picture surface, each

PROVENANCE: see no. 14b

BIBLIOGRAPHY: see no. 14b

CONDITION: The two pairs of quatrefoils were probably
painted on a single continuous plank, but it is not possible to
confirm that this was so, as the edges of the reverse have been
taped and large labels from Thos. Agnew and Sons have been
pasted over the seam, obscuring the continuity of the wood
grain. The panel is 2.2 cm thick and has not been thinned.
Like no. 14b, this panel preserves traces of a vertical batten
secured with two nails down the center of each of its sections,
but an additional square-cut nail has been driven into the
panel near the left edge, roughly in the position of the nose
of the Dominican bishop in the left-most quatrefoil. The purpose of this nail is unclear, and its presence has not provoked
any visible damage to the paint surface, the condition of
which is excellent in each of the four quatrefoils. The moldings of the quatrefoils are largely intact and preserve areas of
original gilding, though extensively repaired. The blue background outside the quatrefoils is modern.

Pseudo-Dalmasio

Bologna, active second quarter 14th century

14b. *Four Saints*, ca. 1335–40

Tempera on panel, 14.1 x 56 cm (5½ x 22 in.), overall;
10.6 x 10.6 cm (4¼ x 4¼ in.), picture surface, each

PROVENANCE: Giuseppe Bellesi, London, before 1935;
Thos. Agnew and Sons, London, 1943

BIBLIOGRAPHY: Roberto Longhi, "Prefazione," in *Guida alla
mostra della pittura bolognese del trecento* (Bologna, 1950),
p. 16, reprinted in *Paragone* 5 (1950): p. 11; Roberto Longhi,
Opere complete, vol. 6 (Florence, 1973), p. 160; Daniele
Benati, "Pseudo-Dalmasio," in *Giotto e le arti a Bologna: Al
tempo di Bertrando del Poggetto*, ed. Massimo Medica, exh.
cat. (Milan, 2005), pp. 176–78

CONDITION: The two pairs of quatrefoils were painted on
a single continuous plank, sawn in half in comparatively
modern times. The panel, 2.2 cm thick, has not been thinned
and preserves on its back traces of a vertical batten running
down the center of each of the two halves into which it has
been cut. Each batten was secured with two nails that remain,
cut off, in the panel, driven almost exactly on center between
each pair of quatrefoils. The painted blue background of the
panel is modern, but it is not clear whether it covers original
gilding or a modern repaired surface. The moldings of the
quatrefoils are largely original and preserve areas of original
gilding, though much repaired. The gold ground in each quatrefoil is nicked and scratched and has been locally repaired,
but the paint surfaces are beautifully preserved.

The identities of the eight saints in these panels are not
easily established. The cardinal in the third quatrefoil
of no. 14a is probably Saint Jerome, which could imply a
likely (though not certain) identification of the bishops on
either side of him as Saints Augustine and Ambrose. The
bishop furthest left in that series wears a Dominican habit
and was tentatively identified by Daniele Benati as Saint
Albertus Magnus.[1] The four saints in no. 14b bear no individually distinctive attributes, and they have been presumed
to represent apostles.[2]

These eight figures form part of a series of which twelve
others, identical to these in size and format, are known. One
set of four, not cut into two pairs, is preserved in the collection of the National Gallery of Ireland, Dublin, and represents Saint Ursula, Saint Catherine of Alexandria, a bishop
saint, and Saint Dominic (fig. 1). A second set of four, also
uncut, is now in the Detroit Institute of Arts and is thought
to portray Saints John the Baptist, Thomas Aquinas, Paul,
and Peter (fig. 2). Benati, however, has proposed recognizing
the first of these figures as Saint Andrew rather than John
the Baptist, while the Dominican saint next to him cannot be Thomas Aquinas, since that figure is unequivocally

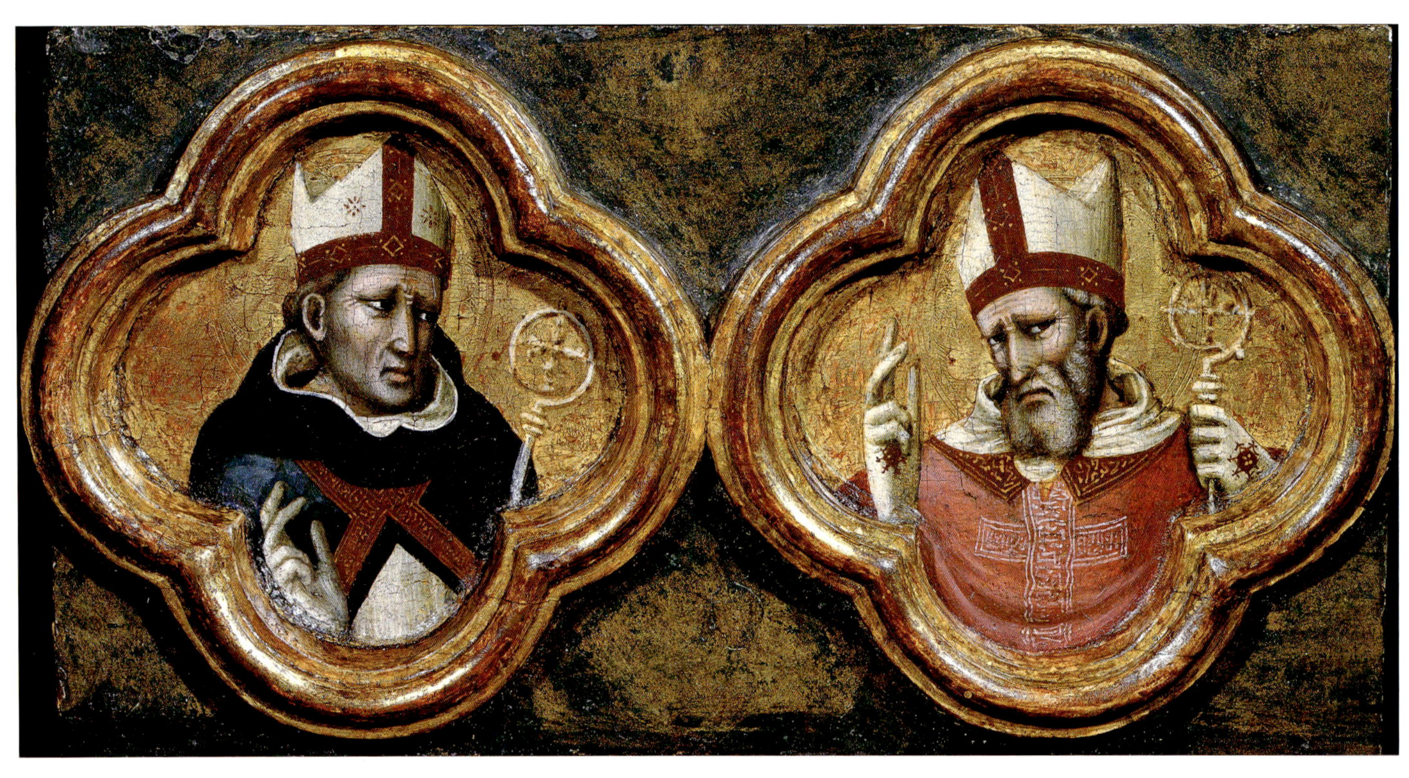

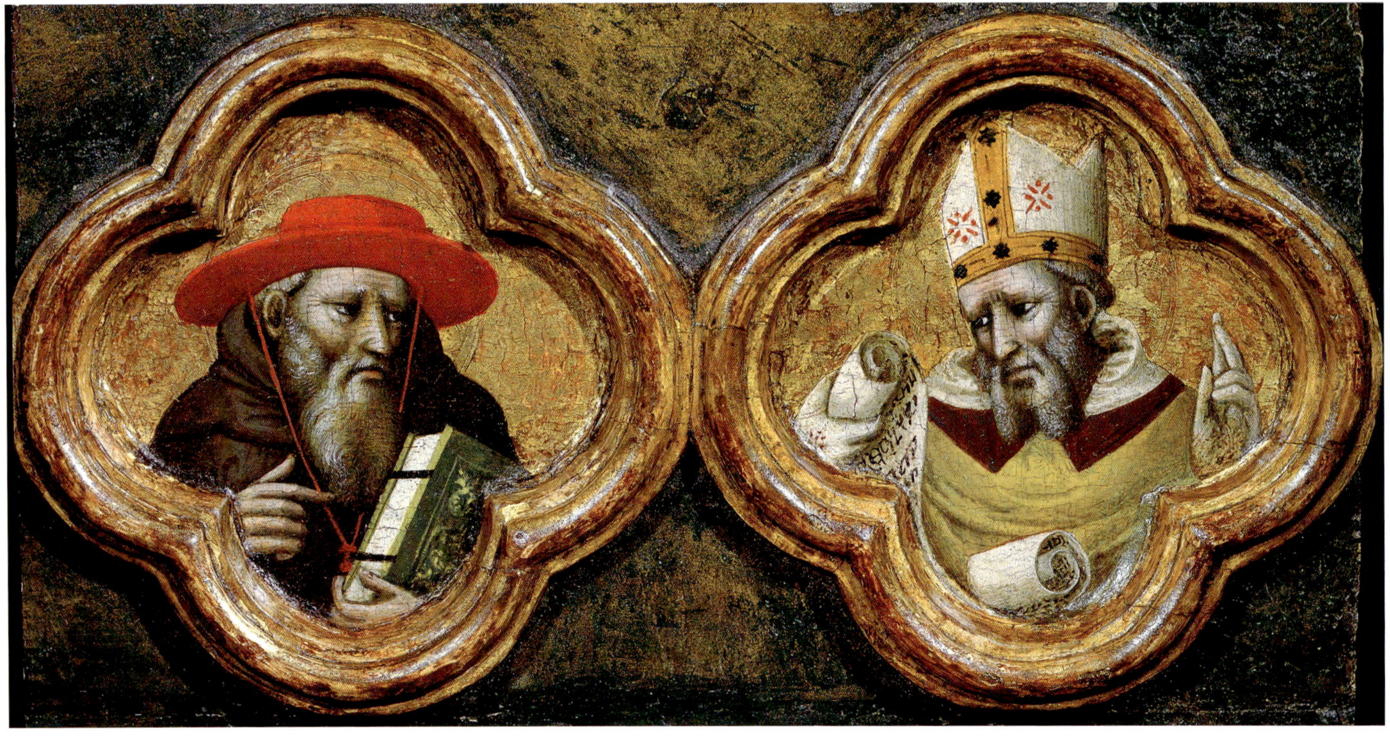

14a

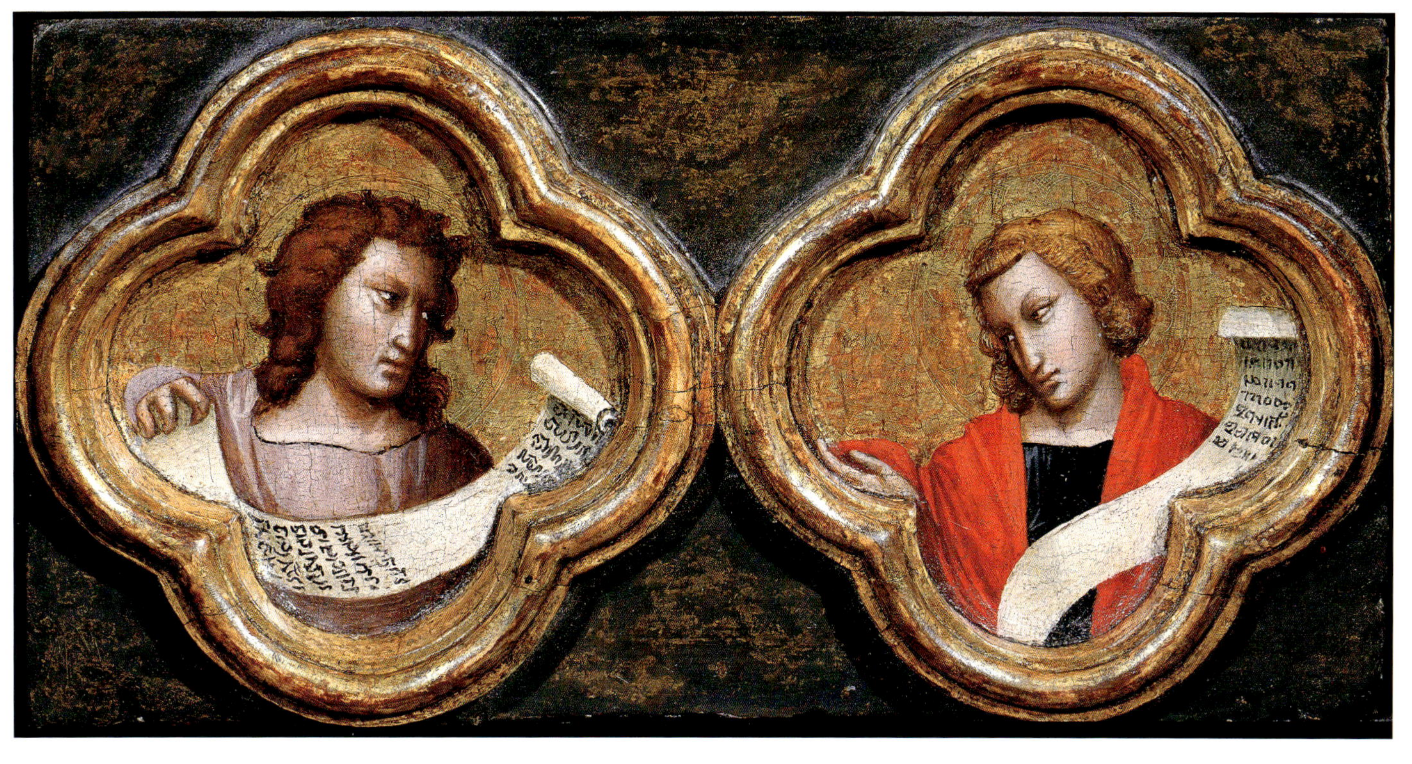

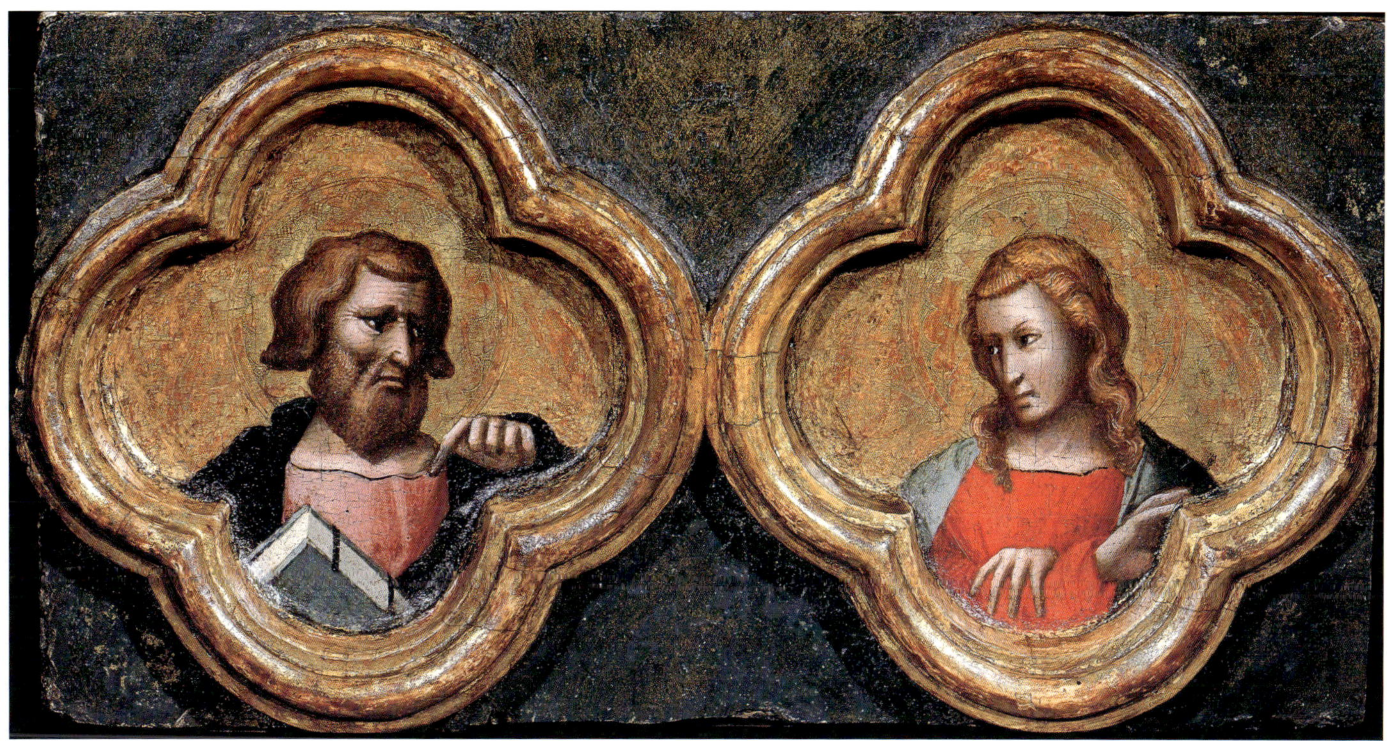

14b

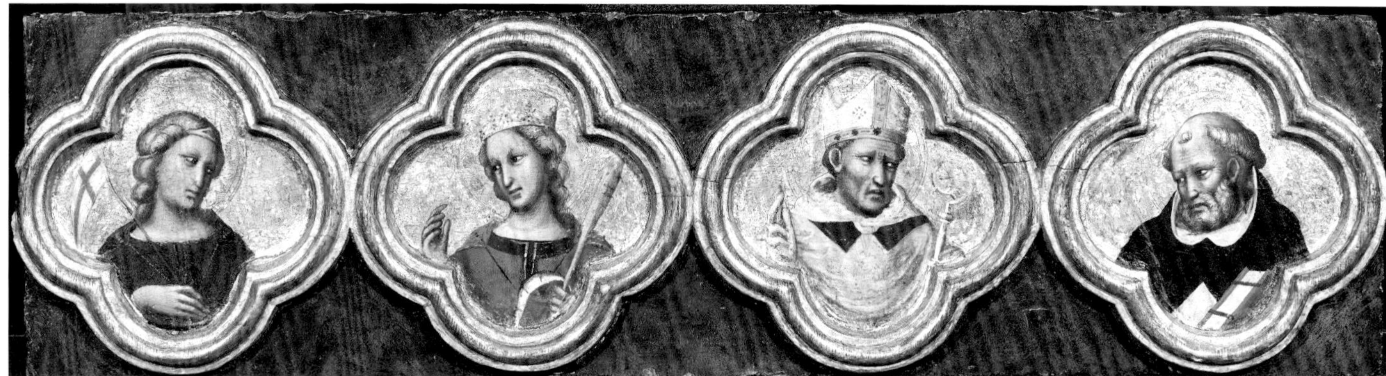

Fig. 1. Pseudo-Dalmasio, *Saint Ursula, Saint Catherine of Alexandria, an Unidentified Bishop Saint, and Saint Dominic*, ca. 1335–40. Tempera on panel, 14.4 x 56 cm (5 ¾ x 22 in.). National Gallery of Ireland, Dublin

included in the fifth set of quatrefoils, formerly together with the others at the dealer Giuseppe Bellesi in London (current location unknown).[3] The panel now in Detroit was acquired in 1937 from Lionello Venturi in Paris, while that in Dublin was purchased in 1943 from the Drey Gallery in London. The other three, including the two catalogued here, were reportedly offered for sale by Agnew's in London in 1944. Agnew's gallery label is pasted to the reverse of each of the Feigen panels, and no. 14a, additionally, has pasted to its back a letter from Colin Agnew, dated April 28, 1943, in which the figures are attributed to Antonio Veneziano.

W. R. Valentiner first recognized the *Four Saints* now in Detroit as Bolognese rather than Tuscan, describing them as "in the style of Vitale or Andrea da Bologna."[4] In 1950 Roberto Longhi arranged to include this panel in the exhibition in Bologna of Bolognese fourteenth-century painting, where he assigned them to the painter identified by him as Dalmasio di Jacopo degli Scanabecchi, a Bolognese artist known from documents to have been active in Pistoia and author, according to Longhi, of the apse frescoes in the church of San Francesco there, of the fresco decoration of the Bardi di Vernio chapel in Santa Maria Novella in Florence, and of a discreet number of highly Giottesque panel paintings. More recent scholarly opinion has recognized that while Dalmasio di Jacopo degli Scanabecchi remains the only Bolognese painter of this period whose activity in Tuscany can be documented, he is unlikely to be the artist responsible for the works reunited by Longhi, since the latter must have been active, indeed well known, by the mid-1330s, whereas Dalmasio appears to have attained his majority only in the early 1340s.[5] Rebaptized the Pseudo-Dalmasio, this painter is now accepted as the author of a singularly important body of work, including the predella to Giotto's signed altarpiece in Bologna, but no further direct or tangential documentary evidence has emerged to clarify any details of his historical biography.[6]

The nature of the object of which these twenty figures contained in quatrefoil medallions may have formed part is mysterious. It is unlikely that they were included in a reliquary or sacristy cupboard: neither of these contexts would account for the rough planing of the backs of the panels,

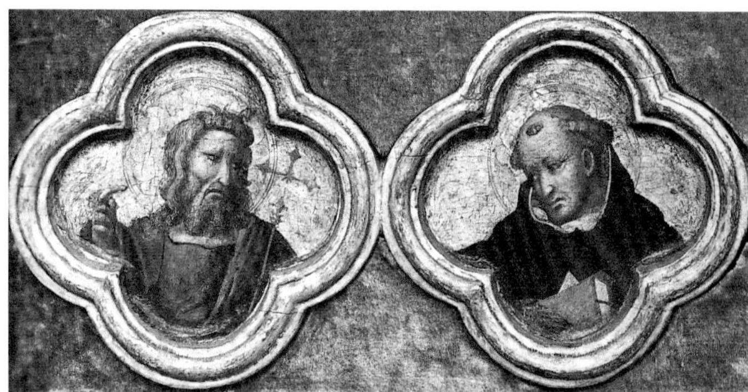

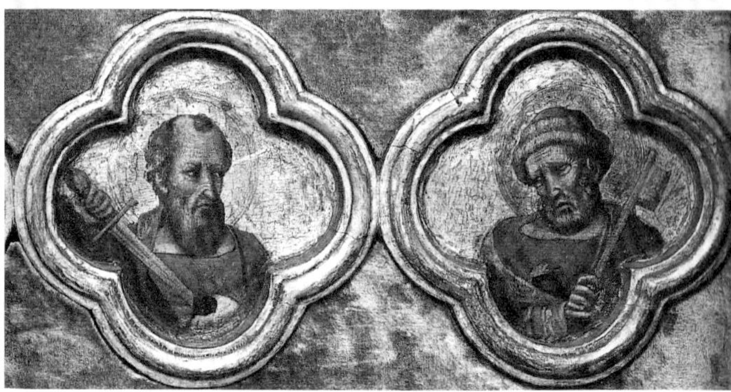

Fig. 2. Pseudo-Dalmasio, *Saint Andrew, a Dominican Saint, Saint Paul, and Saint Peter*, ca. 1335–40. Tempera on panel, 14.4 x 56 cm (5 ¾ x 22 in.). Detroit Institute of Arts

which is original, or for the presence of vertical battens along the center of each of them. Benati suggested they could have combined to form the predella to an altarpiece. Vertical battens are frequently encountered in such a context, but rarely set as close together as is the case here, while the slight variance in height among the panels is difficult to explain in the case of a long, continuous predella. Given the uniform downward direction of the glances of the saints, the panels could have been intended as part of the structure of an altarpiece frame intermediary between the main tier panels and a superimposed set of painted pinnacles. Again, this possibility would seem to preclude the need for battens on the reverse. For the present, this question must be left unresolved other than to stipulate that whatever their original function, the twenty quatrefoils were clearly created as part of a Dominican commission.　　　　　　　　　　　　　　L K

1. Daniele Benati, "Pseudo-Dalmasio," in *Giotto e le arti a Bologna: Al tempo di Bertrando del Poggetto*, ed. Massimo Medica, exh. cat. (Milan, 2005), p. 176.

2. Ibid.

3. For Benati's identification of Saint Andrew, see ibid. The existence of the final set of quatrefoils was attested by W. R. Valentiner, who in a communication in the files at the Detroit Institute of Arts, claimed to have seen all twenty figures together at Bellesi. A photograph of the fifth set, the existence of which was unknown to Benati and other modern scholars, is preserved in the Photographic Archives of Federico Zeri, University of Bologna. Presumably, Roberto Longhi was aware of the complete set of figures, but his reference to "una serie assai più ricca, oggi dispersa in più luoghi," in Roberto Longhi, "Prefazione," in *Guida alla mostra della pittura bolognese del trecento* (Bologna, 1950), p. 16, is unspecific.

4. W. R. Valentiner, *Italian Gothic Painting* (Detroit, 1944), pp. 48–49. See also E. P. Richardson, ed., *Detroit Institute of Arts, Catalogue of Paintings* (Detroit, 1944), p. 67; and W. E. Suida, "Some Bolognese Trecento Paintings in America," *Critica d'arte* 33 (1950): pp. 53–57.

5. Luciano Bellosi, *Buffalmacco e il Trionfo della morte* (Turin, 1974), pp. 84, 104n.62.

6. The most comprehensive discussion of the critical history of studies of the Pseudo-Dalmasio is to be found in Benati, "Pseudo-Dalmasio," pp. 64–70. See also Gian Lorenzo Mellini, "Commento a 'Dalmasio,'" *Arte illustrata* 3, nos. 27–29 (1970): p. 49; Alessandro Volpe, "Frammenti di un'allegoria agostiniana: Quattro 'Filosofi' di Dalmasio," *Paragone* 647 (2004): pp. 3–19; and Carl Brandon Strehlke, *Italian Paintings, 1250–1450, in the John G. Johnson Collection and the Philadelphia Museum of Art* (Philadelphia, 2004), pp. 106–11.

Master of the Piani d'Invrea Cross

Liguria, active ca. 1320–50

15. *The Nativity*, ca. 1340–45

Tempera on panel, 31.4 x 23.2 cm (12⅜ x 9⅛ in.), overall; 28.3 x 20.4 cm (11⅛ x 8 in.), picture surface

PROVENANCE: private collection, France (sale, Robert Hours & L. R. Hugues de Valaurie, Aix-en-Provence, France, December 9, 2006)

BIBLIOGRAPHY: Chantal Humbert, "Une nativité napolitaine," *Gazette de l'Hôtel Drouot* 41 (2006): p. 205; Anna de Floriani, "Pittura del trecento fra Genova e Avignone: Osservazioni in merito ad alcuni studi recenti e un'ipotesi ligure per il trittico di Angers," *Studi di storia dell'arte* 18 (2007): pp. 23–27

CONDITION: The panel support and its engaged frame are carved from a single piece of wood and are extremely well preserved: a shallow wedge 4.5 x 2 cm has detached from the lower left corner and been reaffixed and the raised lower molding is chipped and broken. An original hinge is preserved at the top left while the location of the bottom hinge on that side is indicated by a hole through the outer molding. The outer edges of the panel are painted red and the back fictive porphyry. The paint surface is in an excellent state, with minimal abrasion and virtually no significant areas of loss. A scratch through the head of the ass and minor flaking losses in the Christ Child's halo and outside the perimeter of the Virgin's halo have been retouched.

This previously unknown panel was offered for sale in 2006 with an attribution to a Neapolitan painter, the Master of the Franciscan Temperas, based on its very evident resemblance to a diptych associated with that master now in the J. Paul Getty Museum, Los Angeles (fig. 1).[1] A relationship to the two Getty panels, which are usually known as the Ansouis Diptych after their historical provenance, may be established on the basis of figure style, landscape motifs, spatial structure, punch tooling, and even carpentry. The works are so closely related in this last respect as to suggest the likelihood of having been executed in the same place—the panel supports probably having been supplied by the same carpenter's workshop—and at nearly the same date. Both works, furthermore, were produced for patrons (or possibly the same patron) with Franciscan connections: the Ansouis Diptych includes on one valve a representation of the Stigmatization of Saint Francis while the Virgin in the Feigen *Nativity* conspicuously wears a Franciscan rope belt with three knots (symbolizing the vows of poverty, chastity, and obedience).

In an extended study of the Ansouis Diptych, Carl Strehlke demonstrated its affiliation with the Angevin dynasty as a probable commission of Delphine de Signe ca. 1343, and he underscored both Neapolitan and Provençal aspects to its visual language.[2] Chantal Humbert affirmed the link between the Feigen *Nativity* and the Ansouis Diptych, and extended to the former the attribution to the Master of the Franciscan Temperas that had sometimes been posited for the latter, noting also that in one of that painter's eponymous works in Naples the Virgin is likewise portrayed wearing a Franciscan

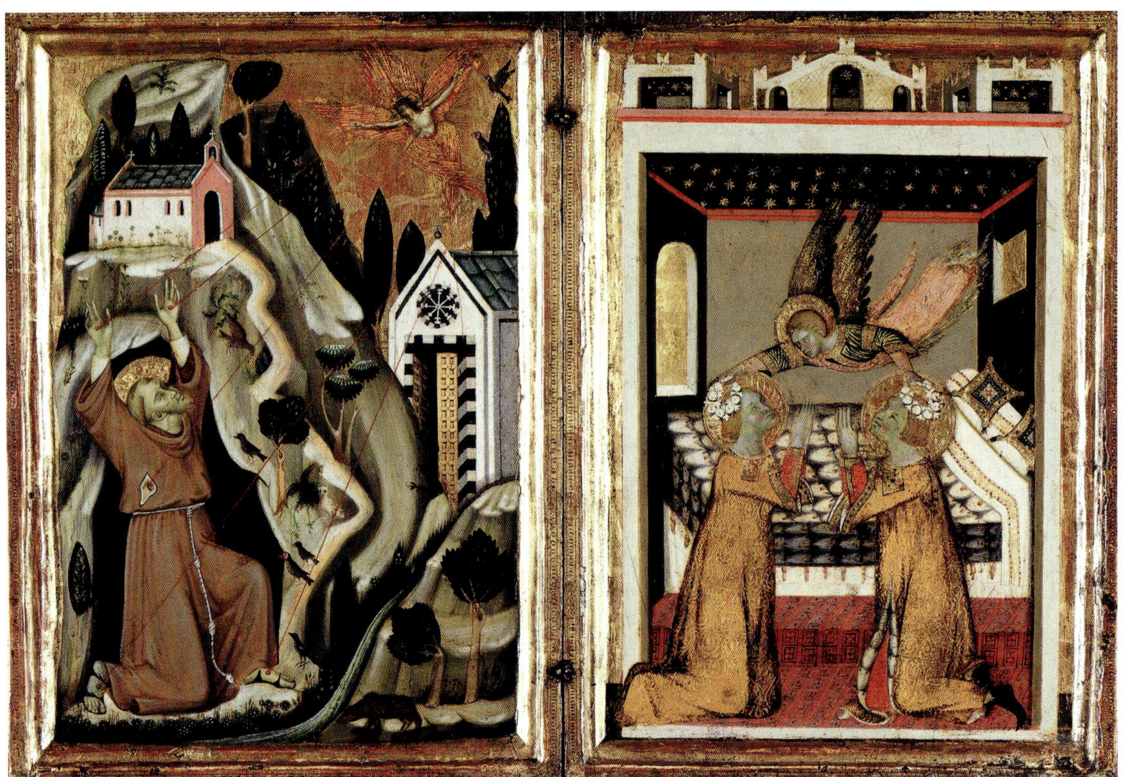

rope belt with three knots.[3] Beyond this shared iconographic motif and their evident connection to the Angevin court, however, it is difficult to see more than a casual stylistic relationship between the Feigen *Nativity* and the Ansouis Diptych on the one hand and the four Franciscan temperas commissioned for the convent church of Santa Chiara in Naples on the other; and it is not possible to insist that the diptychs (the *Nativity* was clearly once the right valve of a diptych) were made for the Angevin court in Naples rather than in Provence. Reflections of both Neapolitan and Provençal style in the panels were acknowledged by Andrea de Marchi, who, however, identified the artist responsible for the Ansouis Diptych as Ligurian (though very likely active in the south of France as well), the author of a small *Crucifixion* now in the Musée des Beaux-Arts, Tours, and of a large painted cross in the oratory church at Piani d'Invrea, near Varazze.[4] It is difficult to judge the Piani d'Invrea Cross on the basis of available photographs, but the Tours *Crucifixion* does bear a striking stylistic similarity to the Ansouis Diptych and the Feigen *Nativity*, and it seems at present justifiable to accept their identification as works by the same artist. Although "Master of the Ansouis Diptych" might be a more felicitous appellation for the group, by reference to its most distinguished member and in acknowledgment that four works by the artist were discovered in France, it would beg the question of the painter's putative Ligurian origins, and there is no reason therefore not to accept the Piani d'Invrea Cross as the master's eponymous work.

A recent discussion of these panels by Anna de Floriani had the virtue of advancing further evidence of a Ligurian origin for the Master of the Piani d'Invrea Cross by adducing echoes of his compositions in an altarpiece dated 1345 now in the Cathedral of Saint-Cécile in Albi, France, transferred there in the nineteenth century from the oratory of San Bernardo at Lavagnola, near Savona.[5] De Floriani's contention that iconographic correspondences between the Ansouis Diptych and the Albi altarpiece argue for an attribution to the Master of the Albi Polyptych for both works—and by extension for the Feigen *Nativity* as well—is mistaken however. The Master of the Albi Polyptych is a derivative painter, elements of whose style were drawn from a number of sources, among them the Master of the Piani d'Invrea Cross. The Albi polyptych does establish a *terminus ante quem* for the Ansouis Diptych and the Feigen *Nativity*, both of which are likely to have been painted in the first half of the 1340s, or possibly at the end of the preceding decade.   LK

1. Pierluigi Leone de Castris, *Arte di corte nella Napoli angioina* (Florence, 1986), p. 459n.5.

2. Carl Brandon Strehlke, "A Celibate Marriage and Franciscan Poverty Reflected in a Neapolitan Trecento Diptych," *J. Paul Getty Museum Journal* 15 (1987): pp. 79–86. See also Adrian Hoch, "A Medieval Franciscan Image of a 'White Marriage' Reconsidered," *Arte cristiana* 88 (2000): pp. 429–38.

3. Chantal Humbert, "Une nativité napolitaine," *Gazette de l'Hôtel Drouot* 41 (2006): p. 205.

4. Andrea de Marchi, "Maître de la Croix des Piani d'Invrea," in *Italies: Peintures des musées de la région Centre*, exh. cat. (Tours, France, 1996), pp. 45–51.

5. Anna de Floriani, "Pittura del trecento fra Genova e Avignone: Osservazioni in merito ad alcuni studi recenti e un'ipotesi ligure per il trittico di Angers," *Studi di storia dell'arte* 18 (2007): pp. 23–27.

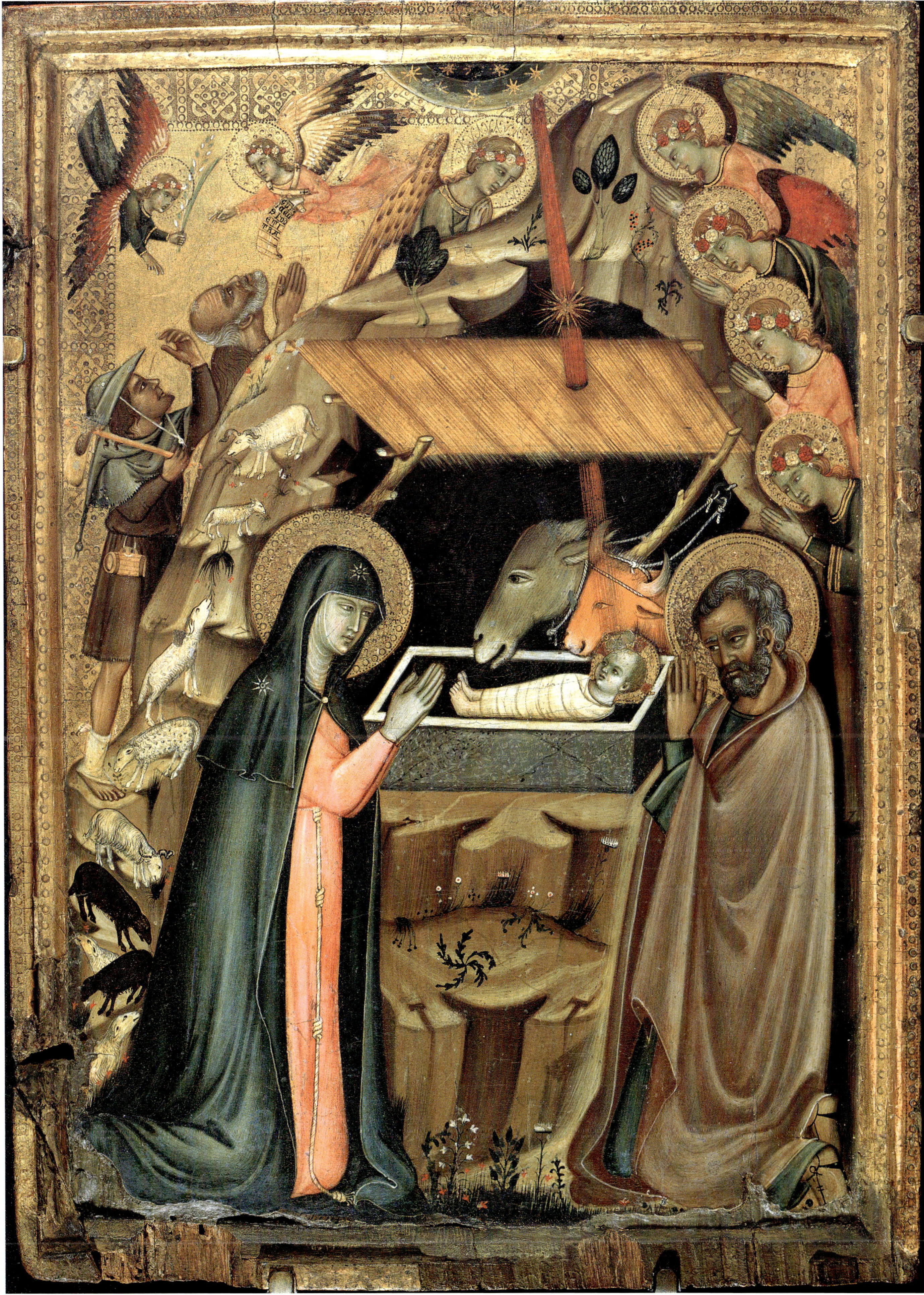

Allegretto Nuzi

Fabriano, ca. 1315/20–1373/74

16. *The Martyrdom of Saint Blaise,* ca. 1350–55

Tempera on panel, 23.2 x 40.3 cm (9⅛ x 15⅞ in.), overall

PROVENANCE: Dr. Fritz Bamberger, Berlin;[1] private collection, New York (sale, Philip Weiss Auctions, Oceanside, N.Y., February 25, 2008, lot 4101)

BIBLIOGRAPHY: Bernard Berenson, *Italian Pictures of the Renaissance: A List of the Principal Artists and Their Works with an Index of Places: Central and North Italian Schools* (London, 1968), 1: p. 305; 2: fig. 211; Everett Fahy, in Christie's, London, *Old Master Pictures,* sale cat. (July 9, 2003), lot 80; Ada Labriola, in *The Alana Collection, Newark, Delaware, USA: Italian Paintings from the 13th to 15th Century,* ed. Miklós Boskovits (Florence, 2009), p. 14

CONDITION: The panel has been thinned to 15 mm but is not cradled. It has been cut irregularly along all four edges such that only the present top right corner is square. The paint surface is in excellent state, exhibiting only mild abrasion and negligible minor flaking losses. Inscribed in ink across the back of the panel is: "Nach Sg. Waagen auf di Florentinische schule."

The story of the martyrdom of Saint Blaise, as it is portrayed in this panel, is recounted by Jacobus da Varagine in the *Legenda Aurea.*[2] After his arrest at the order of the Roman prefect Agricola, Blaise, Bishop of Sebaste in Cappadocia, was tortured and, following his final refusal to recant his belief in Christ, beheaded. Executed with him were two small children—visible to the right of center in the foreground of the scene, one of them cropped at the lower edge of the panel—who had pleaded with their mother not to abandon them in martyrdom but to take them along with her in death. Their mother was one of seven women—visible at the lower left corner of the scene, again cropped at the edge of the panel—who had defied the prefect by collecting the blood shed by Blaise when he was tortured and who were then themselves tortured and beheaded.

This panel was first published by Bernard Berenson as a work by Allegretto Nuzi, though he had not correctly identified its subject.[3] That was subsequently clarified by Everett Fahy, who associated it with two other predella panels by Nuzi showing miracles of Saint Blaise that had been offered for sale by the Galleria Lorenzelli, Bergamo, in 1950.[4] These two panels, attributed to Nuzi by Roberto Longhi, are now in the Alana collection, Delaware, one of them surviving in ruinous state.[5] The first of them, measuring 25.2 x 33.8 cm, represents the arrest of Saint Blaise at the command of the prefect Agricola and two miracles enacted by the saint on his way to prison: his cure of a child who was choking on a

fishbone and his command to a wolf to restore to a poor woman a pig he had stolen from her. The second panel showed the same poor woman bringing to Blaise in prison the head of her pig, her only possession, which she slaughtered to feed him, and the flagellation of Saint Blaise.[6] Completing the narrative cycle would have been at least one more scene from the legend of Saint Blaise, either the saint accepting food from the birds and blessing wild animals at the beginning of the sequence or, more likely, the saint being tormented with iron combs prior to his beheading—the most commonly encountered scene from his legend.

Accepting the relationship of these three episodes from the legend of Saint Blaise as fragments of a single predella and as the work of Allegretto Nuzi, Ada Labriola was unable to suggest the identity of any other fragments from the same complex, either as parts of the predella or of the main register of the altarpiece, nor was she able to propose a likely provenance for the ensemble.[7] Her dating of the panels to the period between 1350 and 1355, on the other hand, is highly persuasive and is based on the reminiscences within them of Florentine influences that Nuzi would have absorbed in the preceding decade in the studios of Bernardo Daddi and of Puccio di Simone. Nuzi is documented in Florence in 1346, although the exact nature of the work he produced there is unclear. In 1354 he collaborated with Puccio di Simone on the execution of an altarpiece for the church of Sant'Antonio Abate fuori Porta Pisana in Fabriano. While no small-scale narrative scenes by Nuzi certainly datable to this period survive, comparisons between the present panels and predella scenes by Puccio di Simone are highly suggestive. By 1360 Allegretto Nuzi evinces the geometrical stylization and obsessive interest in decorative surface patterning that characterize his mature and late styles, and it is reasonable to suppose that the Saint Blaise scenes predate this shift in his aesthetic principles.   LK

1. Notation on the reverse of a photograph of this painting in the Richard Offner photo archive, Institute of Fine Arts, New York University.
2. Jacobus de Voragine, *The Golden Legend: Readings on the Saints,* trans. William Granger Ryan (Princeton, N.J., 1993), 1: pp. 151–53.
3. Bernard Berenson, *Italian Pictures of the Renaissance: A List of the Principal Artists and Their Works with an Index of Places: Central and North Italian Schools* (London, 1968), 1: p. 305; 2: fig. 211.
4. Everett Fahy, in Christie's, London, *Old Master Pictures,* sale cat. (July 9, 2003), lot 80.
5. Cited in George Kaftal, *The Iconography of the Saints in Tuscan Painting* (Florence, 1952), col. 204.
6. This panel reportedly survives in all but illegible state. It was not reproduced in *Old Master Pictures,* in which the two scenes from the legend of Saint Blaise last appeared, and was represented there by the photograph from Kaftal, *Iconography of the Saints.*
7. Ada Labriola, in *The Alana Collection, Newark, Delaware, USA: Italian Paintings from the 13th to 15th Century,* ed. Miklós Boskovits (Florence, 2009), pp. 14–15.

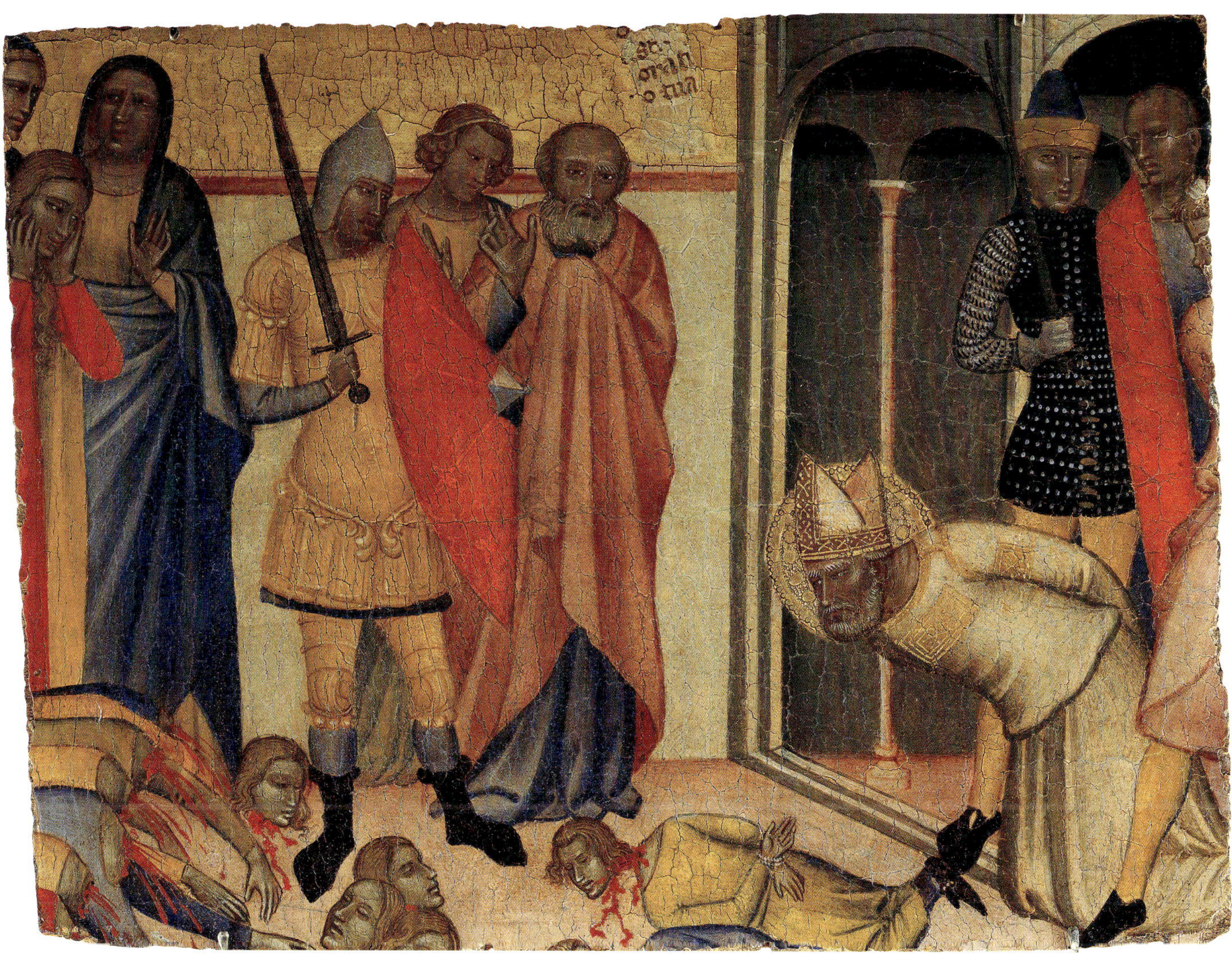
s̄c̄o
oran
o tua

Niccolò di Buonaccorso

Siena, documented 1372–died 1388

17. *Saint John the Evangelist*, ca. 1370–75

Tempera on panel, 35.3 x 25 cm (13¾ x 9⅞ in.)

PROVENANCE: Sir Arthur Henry Hardinge (1859–1933), London; Dr. Brian Lawn, London, before 1950; private collection (sale, Christie's, London, July 4, 1997, lot 71)

BIBLIOGRAPHY: Gaudenz Freuler, *Bartolo di Fredi Cini: Ein Beitrag zur sienesischen Malerei des 14. Jahrhunderts* (Disentis, Switzerland, 1994), pp. 390, 401, 498–99

CONDITION: The panel, of a vertical wood grain, has been thinned to 18 mm and exhibits a very slight warp. The paint surface is extremely well preserved aside from scattered minor flaking losses in the saint's beard, although it is obscured by a thick, uneven, and partially opaque old varnish. Damages around the cropped edges of the panel have been locally over-painted and the background has been regilt, seemingly over an isolating layer of varnish, leaving the original halo intact and fully exposed. Two square-cut nail holes approximately 8 to 9 cm from the top edge of the panel, tapering as they enter the wood from the back, have provoked no visible damage in the paint surface. These indicate the original location of a horizontal batten crossing the panel at this level (nailed back to front) and confirm its identification as the lateral panel of an altarpiece.

This fragmentary bust of a saint was first identified as John the Evangelist and attributed to Bartolo di Fredi by Gaudenz Freuler on the basis of a photograph preserved at Villa I Tatti, sent by its then owner, Brian Lawn, to Bernard Berenson in 1950.[1] The attribution was endorsed by Everett Fahy at the sale of the panel in 1997, but has more recently been doubted by Miklós Boskovits.[2] Freuler, who believed the panel to have been entirely regilt and to have originally por-trayed the saint full length, proposed associating it with an altarpiece of the *Adoration of the Magi* by Bartolo di Fredi now in the Robert Lehman Collection at the Metropolitan Museum of Art, New York, thought by him to be a late work, painted after 1390, probably intended for the Cinughi chapel in San Domenico, Siena.[3] Freuler later emended this proposal to include a head of an archangel by Bartolo di Fredi, formerly in the Erich Lederer collection, Vienna, that had appeared at sale in London on the day preceding the Feigen *Saint John the Evangelist* as a possible fragment from the other lateral panel of the same altarpiece.[4] The ex-Lederer *Archangel* sub-sequently reappeared at sale in New York, where it was cata-logued as portraying the Archangel Gabriel and as possibly part of a larger representation of the Annunciation.[5]

The identification of the figure represented in the Feigen panel as Saint John the Evangelist can be confirmed by com-parison to a full-length panel of that subject by Bartolo di Fredi in the Campana Collection at the Musée du Petit Palais, Avignon.[6] The same comparison, however, reveals the essen-tial dissimilarity of the two figures beyond a superficial rela-tionship of iconographic details, specifically physiognomic type and color of draperies. The hair and beard of the Avignon saint are conceived as ropelike bundles, typical of the pattern used by Bartolo di Fredi for all his elderly male figures, while in the Feigen saint the hairs of the beard, curling around the ear, and at the side of the head are all individually rendered as fine strokes of white paint. The features of the face of Bartolo di Fredi's Saint John the Evangelist are pinched and are drawn with hard, sharp outlines, the wrinkles of the forehead are very differently organized than they are in the Feigen saint, and no veins appear at the temples. Earlier works by Bartolo di Fredi, such as the fragments of his 1382 *Deposition* altarpiece in Montalcino, do incorporate some of these peculiarities, but no painting by him is as reminiscent of the style of his con-temporary Bartolomeo Bulgarini as is the Feigen *Saint John the Evangelist*, and it is necessary to conclude that the attri-bution of the latter to Bartolo di Fredi is mistaken.

No exact parallel for the figure of Saint John the Evangelist in the Feigen panel is known among surviving Sienese paint-ings of the last third of the fourteenth century, but many aspects of its technique—including the exceptionally fine tempera modeling of the flesh tones and hair, the rounded features, the presence of delicately drawn lashes above the eyes, and the exclusive use of a large circular punch in the deco-ration of the halo—recur in works by Niccolò di Buonaccorso, a younger contemporary of Bartolo di Fredi known primarily for precious, small-scale narrative and devotional images. Only four paintings by Niccolò di Buonaccorso painted on the scale of the Feigen *Saint John the Evangelist* are known to survive, and these all portray either the Virgin, the Christ Child, or young male saints, therefore offering no point of compari-son for such distinctive features of the Feigen *Saint John the Evangelist* as the manner of rendering the beard or eyebrows.[7] Of these four, the closest in handling to the Feigen panel is a half-length *Saint Lawrence* in the Glasgow Art Gallery and Museum, which has been convincingly dated by Pia Palladino to the first half of Niccolò di Buonaccorso's career, probably in the early to mid-1370s, when the artist was still strongly influenced by his teacher Jacopo di Mino del Pelicciaio and by Bartolomeo Bulgarini and before he evinced the interest in Bartolo di Fredi's example that would come to characterize his work after 1380.[8] It is possible that the Glasgow *Saint Lawrence* and the Feigen *Saint John the Evangelist* are sur-viving fragments of a single altarpiece, but physical evidence in support of such a possibility is lacking.   LK

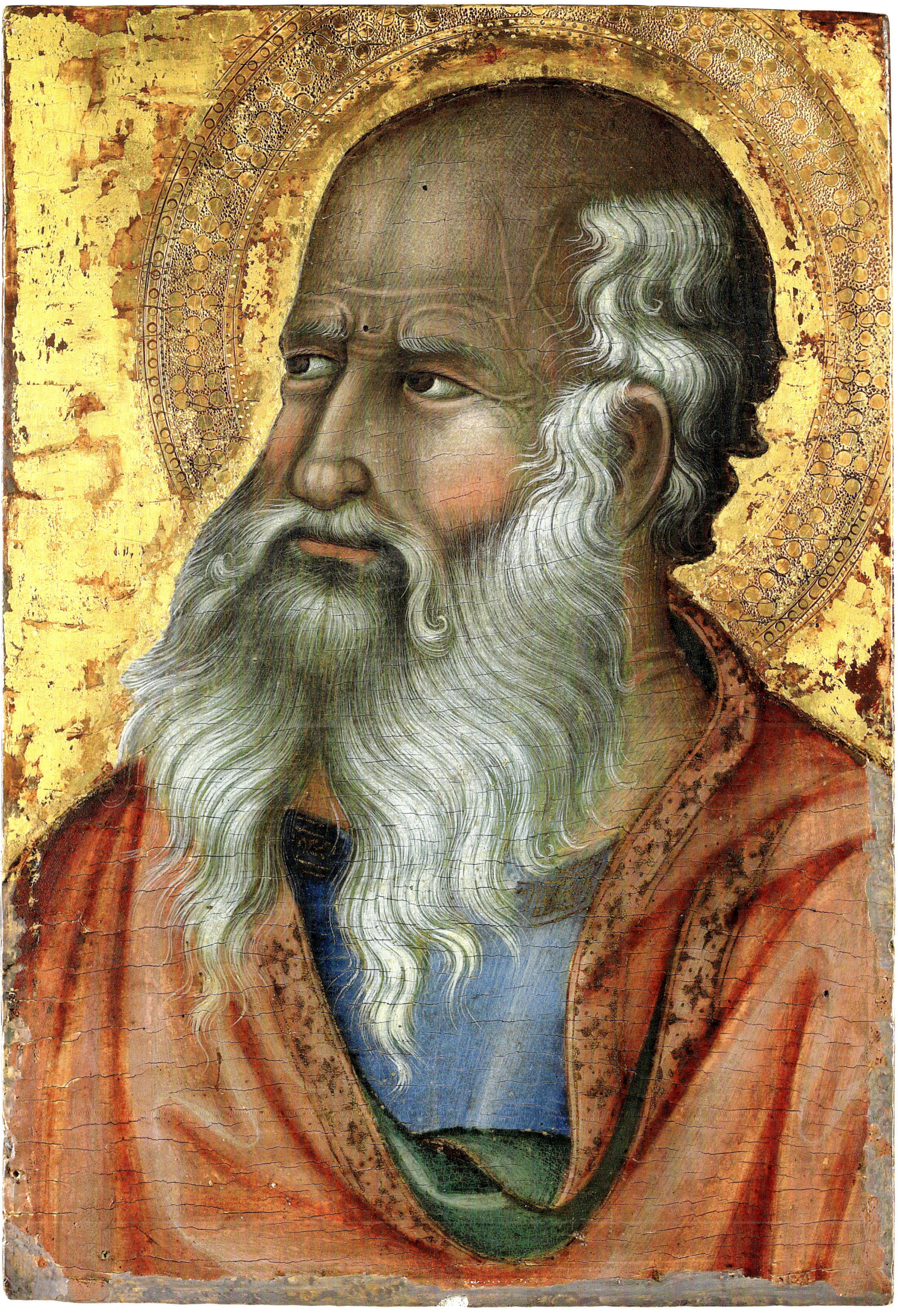

1. Gaudenz Freuler, *Bartolo di Fredi Cini: Ein Beitrag zur sienesischen Malerei des 14. Jahrhunderts* (Disentis, Switzerland, 1994), pp. 390, 401, 498–99.

2. Miklós Boskovits, conversation with the author, 2008.

3. John Pope-Hennessy and Laurence Kanter, *Italian Paintings*, Robert Lehman Collection 1 (New York, 1987), pp. 30–32.

4. Gaudenz Freuler, letter to Richard L. Feigen, August 28, 1997; see Sotheby's, London, sale cat. (July 3, 1997), lot 58.

5. Sotheby's, New York, sale cat. (January 25, 2007), lot 32. It is suggested in the catalogue that this may have been a diptych, in which case the companion panel could have resembled the bust-length *Annunciate Virgin* in Avignon (see Michel Laclotte and Esther Moench, *Peinture italienne: Musée du Petit Palais, Avignon* [Paris, 2005], pp. 65–66), which was recently discovered to be by Bartolo di Fredi, regilt (and formerly repainted) by Giovanni di Paolo. The ex-Lederer *Archangel* is the same width as the Avignon panel; it is 10 cm less tall but could easily have been cropped along its bottom edge.

6. Laclotte and Moench, *Peinture italienne*, pp. 17, 64–65.

7. The other works are: *Virgin and Child Enthroned*, formerly signed and dated 1387, Timken Museum of Art, San Diego; *Saint Lawrence*, companion to the Timken panel, Museo Diocesano, Siena; *Virgin* (fragment), Städelsches Kunstinstitut, Frankfurt; and *Saint Lawrence*, Art Gallery and Museum, Glasgow. The best discussion of these paintings, and of Niccolò di Buonaccorso's work in general, is to be found in Pia Palladino, *Art and Devotion in Siena after 1350: Luca di Tommè and Niccolò di Buonaccorso*, exh. cat. (San Diego, 1997), where a fifth large-scale panel, a full-length figure of Saint Paul in the Metropolitan Museum of Art, New York, is accepted as a work by Niccolò, following its attribution to him by Boskovits ("Il Gotico senese rivisitato: Proposte e commenti su una mostra," *Arte cristiana* 71 [1983]: p. 274n.36). Pursuant to conservation of this painting at the Metropolitan Museum, it was recognized by Palladino as a work by Bartolo di Fredi; see Rudolf Hiller von Gaertringen, *Italienische Gemälde im Städel, 1300–1550: Toskana und Umbrien* (Mainz, Germany, 2004), p. 123n.24.

8. Palladino, *Art and Devotion in Siena*, p. 54; and Hiller von Gaertringen, *Italienische Gemälde im Städel*, pp. 125–28.

Gherardo di Jacopo Starnina

Florence, documented 1387–1409/13

18. *The Presentation of the Christ Child in the Temple*, ca. 1404–5

Tempera on panel, 33 x 51.3 cm (12¾ x 20¼ in.), overall; 31.7 x 49.7 cm (12½ x 19⅝ in.), picture surface

PROVENANCE: Rudolph Schmidt & Co., Berlin; Mr. Gore, London; Sotheby's, London, July 8, 1999, lot 59; Rob Smeets, Milan

BIBLIOGRAPHY: Eliot W. Rowlands, *The Collections of the Nelson-Atkins Museum of Art: Italian Paintings, 1300–1800* (Kansas City, Mo., 1996), pp. 78, 80–82; Gabriele Fattorini, in *Galleria Nazionale di Parma*, vol. 1, *Catalogo delle opere dall'antico al cinquecento*, ed. Lucia Fornari Schianchi (Milan, 1997), p. 62; Andrea de Marchi, "Gherardo Starnina," in *Sumptuosa tabula picta: Pittori a Lucca tra Gotico e Rinascimento*, ed. Maria Teresa Filieri, exh. cat. (Lucca, 1998), pp. 268, 271; Milvia Bollati, in *El Renacimiento mediterráneo: Viajes de artistas e itinerarios de obras entre Italia, Francia, y España en el siglo XV*, ed. Mauro Natale, exh. cat. (Madrid, 2001), pp. 173–78; Carl Brandon Strehlke, *Italian Paintings, 1250–1450, in the John G. Johnson Collection and the Philadelphia Museum of Art* (Philadelphia, 2004), pp. 395–96n.5, 398; Stefan Weppelmann, *Geschichten auf Gold: Bildererzählungen in der frühen italienischen Malerei*, exh. cat. (Berlin, 2005), pp. 143–47; Anneke de Vries, "Opere e giorni: Alcune considerazioni sulla produzione e sul funzionamento della bottega di Gherardo Starnina," in *Nuovi studi sulla pittura tardogotica: Intorno a Lorenzo Monaco* (Florence, 2007), pp. 61–62

CONDITION: The panel, of a horizontal wood grain, has been thinned to 11 mm, and three vertical channels for restraining battens (now missing) have been cut into its back. A split running the length of the panel following the slightly irregular pattern of its grain has been repaired and is visible on the paint surface sloping gradually downward from the prophetess Anna's waist at the right to the knees of the male figure at the left: the second P in the inscription on Anna's scroll is a reconstruction through this split. The paint surface otherwise is extremely well preserved though slightly dulled by a reticulated modern spray varnish.

The *Presentation of the Christ Child in the Temple* portrays an event from the childhood of Christ following the Old Testament ritual of ransoming back from God the first-born male child of Hebrew families. The event, which is celebrated liturgically on the feast of the Purification of the Virgin (February 2), is recounted in full in the gospel of Luke (2:22–38):

> And when the time came for their purification according to the law of Moses, they brought him up to Jerusalem to present him to the Lord (as it is written in the law of the Lord, "Every male that opens the womb shall be called holy to the Lord") and to offer

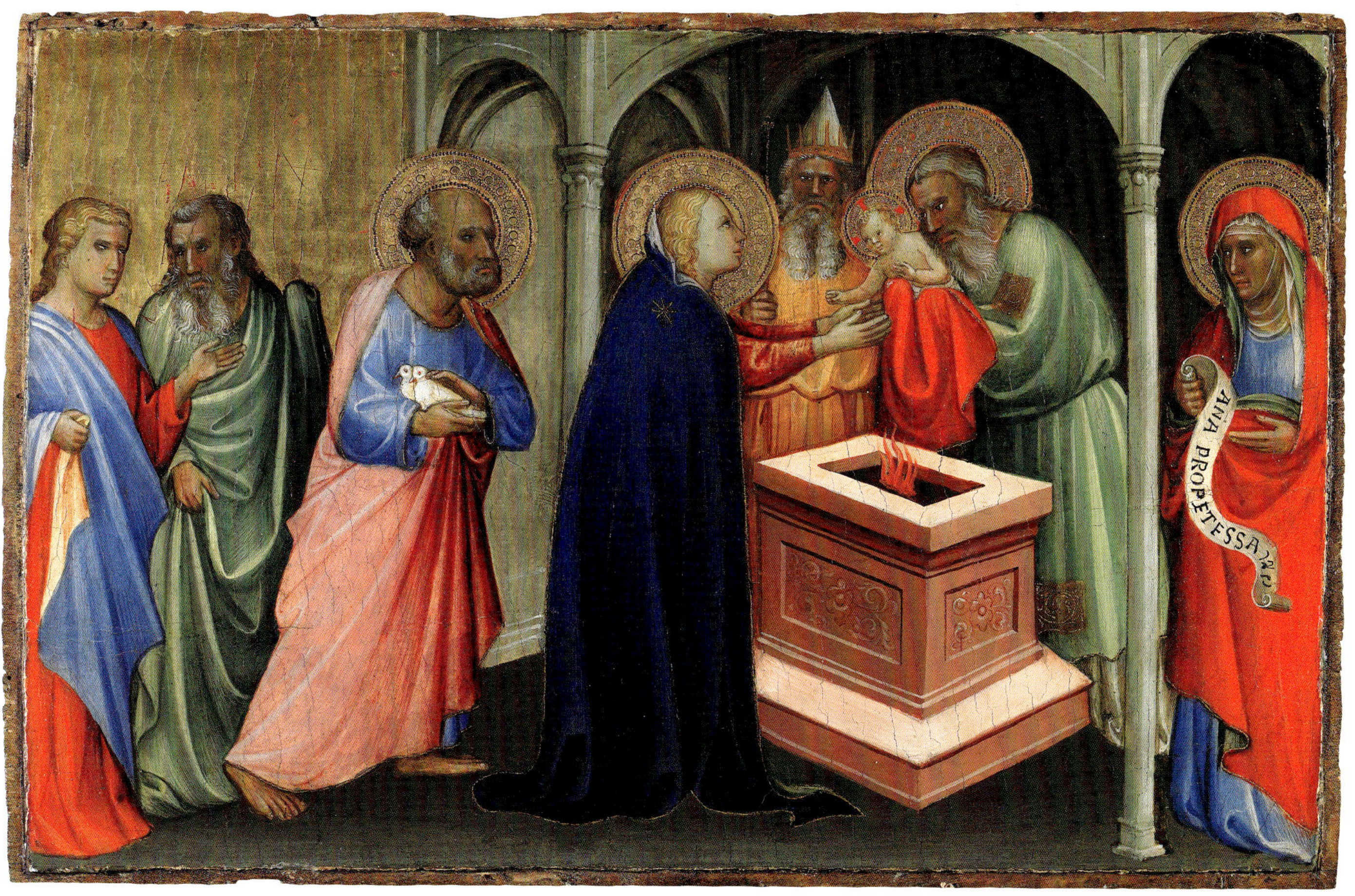

a sacrifice according to what is said in the law of the Lord, "a pair of turtledoves, or two young pigeons." Now there was a man in Jerusalem, whose name was Simeon, and this man was righteous and devout, looking for the consolation of Israel, and the Holy Spirit was upon him. And it had been revealed to him by the Holy Spirit that he should not see death before he had seen the Lord's Christ. And inspired by the Spirit he came into the temple; and when the parents brought in the child Jesus, to do for him according to the custom of the law, he took him up in his arms and blessed God and said, "Lord, now lettest thou thy servant depart in peace, according to thy word; for mine eyes have seen thy salvation which thou hast prepared in the presence of all peoples. . . . And there was a prophetess, Anna, the daughter of Phanuel of the tribe of Asher; she was of a great age, having lived with her husband seven years from her virginity, and as a widow till she was eighty-four. She did not depart from the temple, worshiping with fasting and prayer night and day. And coming up at that very hour she gave thanks to God, and spoke of him to all who were looking for the redemption of Jerusalem.

Along with the revelations to the Shepherds (December 25) and to the Magi (January 6), the testimony of Simeon upon beholding the Christ Child—"Nunc Dimittis servum tuum in pace"—and of the prophetess Anna were the initial affirmations of the divinity of Jesus. In the present panel, Anna, wearing a blue dress and red cloak and identified by her halo and by a scroll lettered ANA PROPETESSA [*sic*], stands at the far right within a portico of the temple. Before her, within the wide central arch of the temple, is the Virgin, dressed in blue, receiving the infant Christ back from the arms of Simeon, who reaches across an altar table with a flame (to receive the sacrifice of redemption) rising from its center. A priest of the temple, dressed in yellow and holding a long staff, stands behind them. Saint Joseph enters the temple at the left bearing the two pigeons prescribed by Mosaic law as the price of ransom for the first-born child. Behind him at the far left are two onlookers bearing witness to the testimonies of Simeon and Anna. In its essential features the scene follows the example of Giovanni del Biondo's 1364 altarpiece of the same subject, painted for Santa Maria degli Angeli and now exhibited in the Galleria dell'Accademia in Florence, although the composition has been rearranged for greater narrative clarity within the horizontal format of a predella panel.

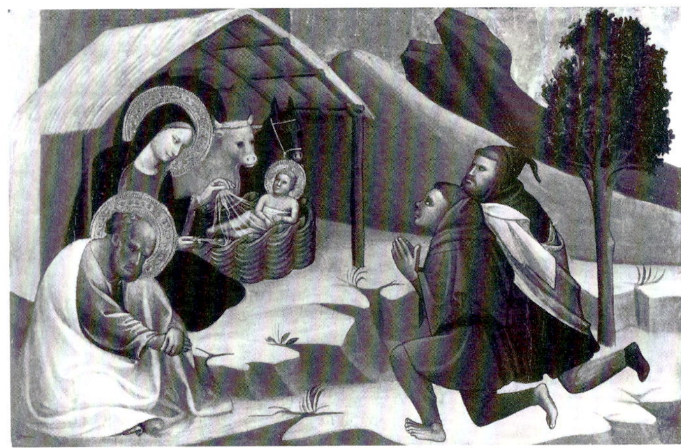

Fig. 1. Gherardo di Jacopo Starnina, *The Nativity*, ca. 1404–5.
Tempera on panel, 31.5 x 49.5 cm (12⅜ x 19½ in.). Private collection

The *Presentation of the Christ Child in the Temple* was recognized by Federico Zeri as a work by Gherardo Starnina and was first published by Eliot Rowlands as completing an altarpiece predella with a *Nativity* formerly in the Viezzoli collection in Genoa (fig. 1) and an *Adoration of the Magi* in the Nelson-Atkins Museum of Art, Kansas City, Missouri (fig. 2).[1] This reconstruction has been accepted by all subsequent scholars and is confirmed by the identical heights of the three panels and the identical widths of the *Presentation* and the *Nativity* (which would have stood at the right and left, respectively, of the *Adoration*), by the correspondence of the setting in the *Nativity* and the *Adoration*, by the similar punch decoration of the haloes in all three panels, and by the conformity of all three panels in style. Rowlands associated this predella with an altarpiece by Starnina comprising the *Dormition and Assumption of the Virgin*, now divided between the Philadelphia Museum of Art (fig. 4) and the Fogg Art Museum, Cambridge, Massachusetts (fig. 3), as its center panel, and lateral panels showing full-length standing figures of Saints Michael, James, and John the Baptist (left) and Saints John the Evangelist, Peter, and Paul (right), now in the Museo Nazionale di Villa Guinigi, Lucca (fig. 5). The Kansas City *Adoration* and Viezzoli *Nativity* had earlier been associated

with this altarpiece, tentatively, by Andrea de Marchi, who however withdrew the suggestion because of the iconographic difficulty of reconciling a Marian altarpiece with a predella portraying scenes from the infancy of Christ.[2] Rowlands argued that such a discrepancy is not unusual, and following his identification of the *Presentation in the Temple* as the third element of the predella, his reconstruction of the complete altarpiece was accepted by de Marchi and all later scholars.[3]

A Lucchese provenance for the *Dormition and Assumption* altarpiece has been presumed since its initial reconstruction—without predella panels—by Alvar Gonzalez-Palacios.[4] The lateral panels now in the Villa Guinigi were found, in the nineteenth century, in the parish church at Tramonte, near Brancoli, outside Lucca, and are said to have been previously in the monastery of San Michele Arcangelo e San Pietro in Brancoli. As both Saints Michael and Peter figure prominently in the Villa Guinigi panels, and as at least one other painting formerly in that monastery was transferred to Tramonte in the early nineteenth century, such an original provenance for the *Dormition and Assumption* altarpiece seems likely and has been accepted, provisionally, by Carl Strehlke.[5] Three other suggestions have also been advanced, however, which all merit consideration pending further archival discoveries. Rowlands observed that the subject of the central panel of the altarpiece would have been appropriate to the high altarpiece from the church of Santa Maria Assunta at Piazza, near Brancoli.[6] Maria Teresa Filieri recorded the commissioning of an altarpiece in 1407 for the parish church of Lammari near Lucca, which in 1647 was described as representing the Burial and Assumption of the Virgin with Apostles and Saints.[7] Finally, Andrea de Marchi suggested that Brancoli and Lammari are both too remote and isolated to have been the original location of an altarpiece as important and influential as Starnina's, and he suggested instead the church of San Michele in Foro in Lucca, for which an altarpiece (no subject specified) is documented as being painted in 1404.[8]

An argument that might incline in favor of one or another of these hypotheses could be the issue of the altarpiece's

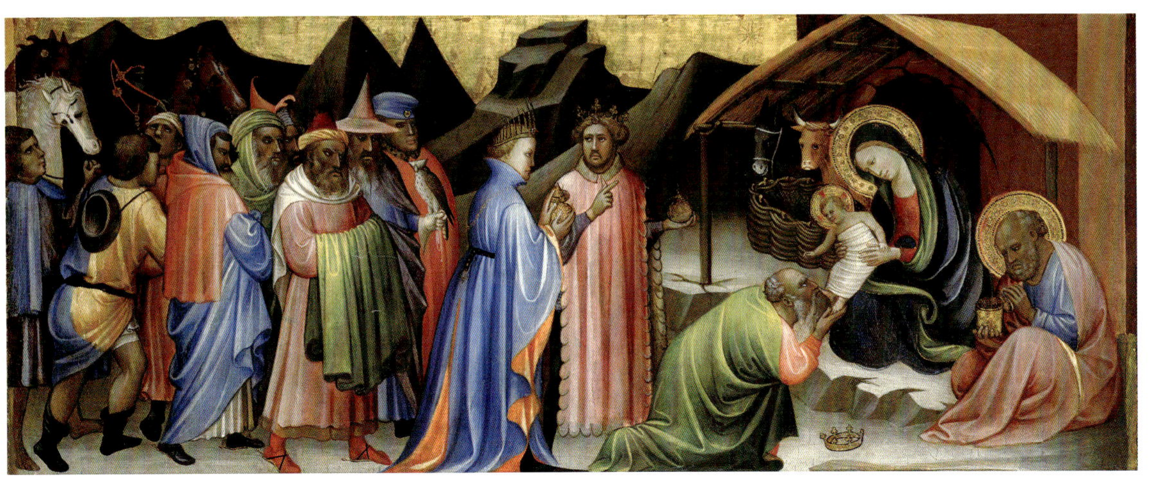

Fig. 2. Gherardo di Jacopo Starnina, *The Adoration of the Magi*, ca. 1404–5. Tempera on panel, 33 x 79.7 cm (13 x 31⅜ in.). Nelson-Atkins Museum of Art, Kansas City, Mo., Gift of the Samuel H. Kress Foundation

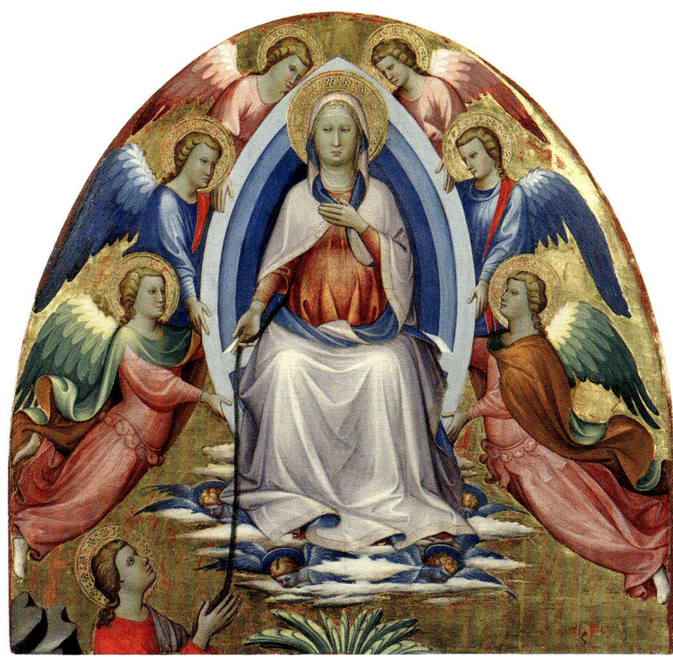

Fig. 3. Gherardo di Jacopo Starnina, *The Assumption of the Virgin*, ca. 1404–5. Tempera on panel, 81 x 83.8 cm (31⅞ x 33 in.). Harvard University Art Museums, Fogg Art Museum, Cambridge, Mass., Gift of Friends of the Fogg Art Museum Fund, inv. no. 1920.1

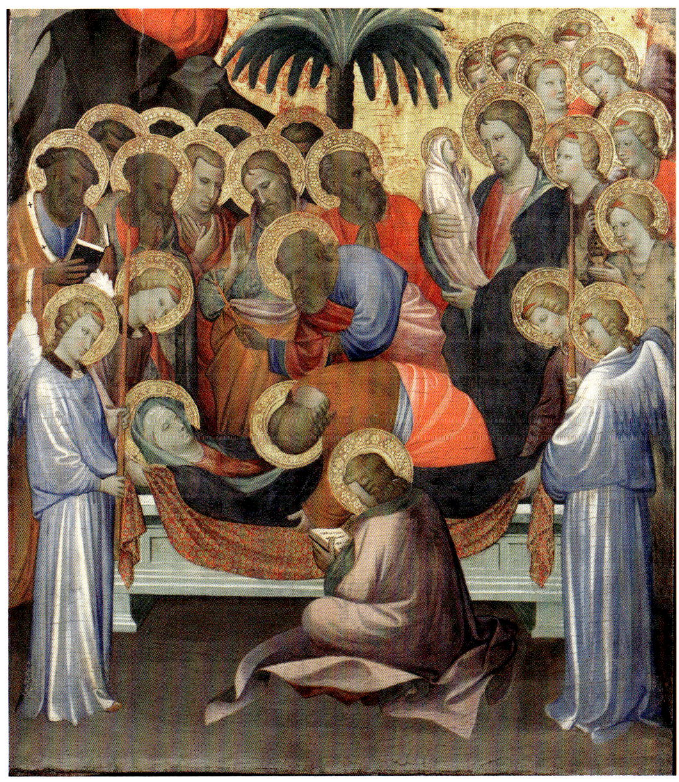

Fig. 4. Gherardo di Jacopo Starnina, *The Dormition of the Virgin*, ca. 1404–5. Tempera on panel, 102.5 x 91 cm (40⅜ x 35⅞ in.). Philadelphia Museum of Art, John G. Johnson Collection, 1917

date, though this would be a circumstantial and certainly not conclusive argument. Strehlke advanced evidence to suggest that if the painting were intended for the monastery of San Michele Arcangelo e San Pietro, it might have been commissioned around or shortly after 1408. In October 1406, the Benedictine nuns resident at this monastery were dispossessed by the local bishop in favor of a group of reformed Augustinian canons, and in 1408 the church of Santa Maria Forisportam in Lucca became part of the same reform movement. It has long been recognized that the overall composition of Starnina's altarpiece is based on one of the same subject painted in 1386 by Angelo Puccinelli for Santa Maria Forisportam, and it is reasonable to suppose that the impetus for this repetition was specifically the unification of the two churches within the same order.[9]

Every writer concerned with Gherardo Starnina has emphasized the difficulty of specifying dates for works produced within the last decade of the artist's career, following his return to Florence from Spain sometime between 1401 and 1403 and preceding his death sometime between 1409 and 1413. The nearly obliterated frescoes in the Carmine in Florence, documented as having been finished by 1404, and the equally fragmentary remains of frescoes in Santo Stefano in Empoli, commissioned in 1409, provide the only firm points in Starnina's chronology but have engendered widely varying proposals for tracing his artistic development. For

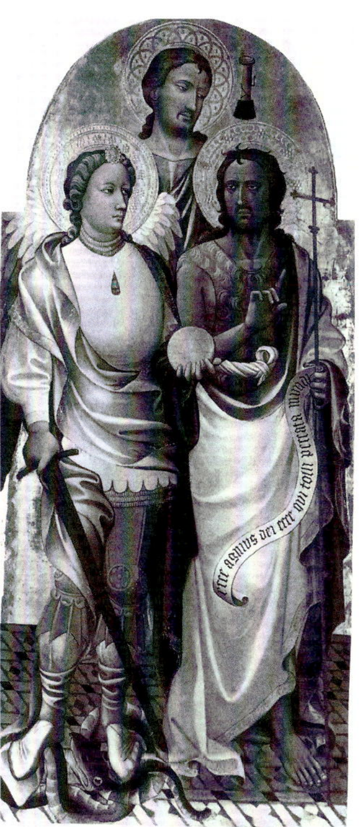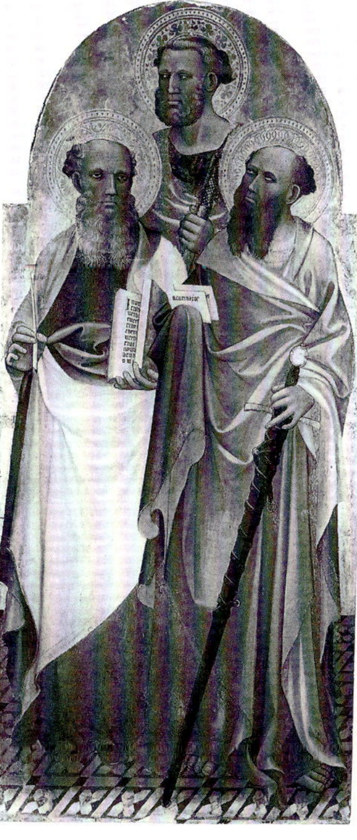

Fig. 5. Gherardo di Jacopo Starnina, *Saints Michael Archangel, James Major, and John the Baptist* and *Saints John the Evangelist, Peter, and Paul*, ca. 1404–5. Tempera on panel, 131 x 60 cm (51⅝ x 23⅝ in.), each. Museo Nazionale di Villa Guinigi, Lucca

some (for example, Strehlke), the stately classicism of a painting such as the Acciaiuolj altarpiece (now divided among collections in Berlin; Stockholm; Dresden; Rotterdam, the Netherlands; Douai, France; and elsewhere) represents the earlier end of this spectrum, while the more agitated and expressive gothicism of the Wurzburg altarpiece indicates Starnina's final and most mature amalgamation of his Iberian experiences with the influences of Lorenzo Ghiberti and Lorenzo Monaco. For others, the pronounced Iberian traits visible in the Wurzburg altarpiece—and the possible identification among its panels of the hand of an Iberian assistant working alongside Starnina—can best be explained by presuming its proximity in date to the artist's return from Spain, making attractive the possibility that it might be an altarpiece commissioned shortly after 1403 by Filippo di Piero Rinieri for Santa Maria in Campo in Florence.[10] The issue, though not at present resolvable, is of some importance in that the *Dormition and Assumption* altarpiece, of all Starnina's major works on panel, is most closely related stylistically to the Wurzburg altarpiece. If the latter were indeed datable ca. 1403/4, it would not be unreasonable to accept de Marchi's hypothesis of a provenance from San Michele in Foro and a date of 1404/5.

One lingering point of contention in the reconstruction of the *Dormition and Assumption* altarpiece concerns the possibility of pinnacle panels that might once have stood above it. Gabriele Fattorini suggested that a *Coronation of the Virgin* in the Pinacoteca Nazionale in Parma might have been a central pinnacle from this complex, since it agrees with the main panels in size and style, is of an appropriate subject to have stood above a scene of the Dormition and Assumption of the Virgin, and has, like the altarpiece, a probable Lucchese provenance.[11] This proposal was not discussed by Strehlke in his catalogue entry for the Philadelphia *Dormition*, and it was rejected by de Marchi who argued that the shape of the Parma *Coronation* is more appropriate to a processional standard than to an altarpiece pinnacle. While it is true that several standards of this format are known from the area of Pisa and Lucca, the similarities adduced by Fattorini, and especially the matter of a Lucchese provenance (which was subsequently demonstrated incontrovertibly by Filieri), are too numerous and too compelling to be dismissed as purely coincidental.[12] It is, however, worth reconsidering in light of Fattorini's and Filieri's discoveries an earlier suggestion by the present author, identifying the Parma *Coronation* as the center panel

of an altarpiece that included full-length figures of Saints Vincent and Stephen (Museum of Fine Arts, Boston), Lawrence (Perkins Collection, Museo-Tesoro della Basilica di San Francesco, Assisi), and Anthony Abbot (whereabouts unknown), that has been rejected by all subsequent writers.[13] The reconstruction is physically plausible: three-cusped center panels of polyptychs are not rare—an example by Taddeo di Bartolo from nearby San Miniato al Tedesco should suffice by way of illustration—and the Boston and Assisi laterals presuppose a central panel exactly the size of the Parma *Coronation*. Furthermore, if this reconstruction is correct, it would suggest a relatively protracted period of activity for Gherardo Starnina in the environs of Lucca and provide additional explanation for the overwhelming impact of his art on later generations of Lucchese painters.   L K

1. Eliot W. Rowlands, *The Collections of the Nelson-Atkins Museum of Art: Italian Paintings, 1300–1800* (Kansas City, Mo., 1996), pp. 78, 80–82.
2. Andrea de Marchi, in *Da Baduino ad Algardi: Pittura e scultura a confronto*, exh. cat. (Turin, 1990), pp. 19, 23.
3. Andrea de Marchi, "Gherardo Starnina," in *Sumptuosa tabula picta: Pittori a Lucca tra Gotico e Rinascimento*, ed. Maria Teresa Filieri, exh. cat. (Lucca, 1998), pp. 268, 271.
4. Alvar Gonzalez-Palacios, "Posizione di Angelo Puccinelli," *Antichità viva* 10, no. 3 (1971): pp. 3–9.
5. Carl Brandon Strehlke, *Italian Paintings, 1250–1450, in the John G. Johnson Collection and the Philadelphia Museum of Art* (Philadelphia, 2004), pp. 395–96n.5, 398. On the additional painting transferred to Tramonte, an altarpiece by Priamo della Quercia, see Linda Pisani, in Filieri, *Sumptuosa tabula picta*, pp. 342–46.
6. Rowlands, *Collections of the Nelson-Atkins Museum of Art*, p. 82.
7. Filieri, *Sumptuosa tabula picta*, pp. 36–37.
8. De Marchi, "Gherardo Starnina," in Filieri, *Sumptuosa tabula picta*, p. 270.
9. See Gonzalez-Palacios, "Posizione di Angelo Puccinelli," pp. 3–9.
10. Dillian Gordon, *The Fifteenth Century: Italian Paintings*, National Gallery Catalogues (London, 2003), 1: pp. 364–75; and Laurence Kanter, "The National Gallery's New Catalogue of Fifteenth-Century Italian Paintings," *Burlington Magazine* 146 (2004): pp. 105–8.
11. Gabriele Fattorini, in *Galleria Nazionale di Parma*, vol. 1, *Catalogo delle opere dall'antico al cinquecento*, ed. Lucia Fornari Schianchi (Milan, 1997), p. 62.
12. Filieri, *Sumptuosa tabula picta*, p. 272.
13. Laurence Kanter, *Italian Paintings in the Museum of Fine Arts, Boston* (Boston, 1994), pp. 130–36; reiterated in Laurence Kanter, "Gherardo Starnina," in *The Treasury of Saint Francis of Assisi*, ed. Giovanni Morello and Kanter (Milan, 1999), pp. 102–3, excluding a spandrel panel of the prophet Hosea in the Museo di Palazzo Venezia, Rome, and definitively excluding lateral figures of Saints John the Baptist and Nicholas, which were mistakenly added to the complex by de Marchi and others.

Lorenzo Monaco

Florence, ca. 1370–1422/23

19. *The Prophet Jeremiah*, ca. 1407

Tempera on panel, 20.8 x 10.4 cm (8¼ x 4⅛ in.), exclusive of
later engaged framing elements

PROVENANCE: Marchese Alfonso Tacoli-Canacci, Florence, by
1792;[1] private collection, Germany (sale, Neumeister, Munich,
March 16, 1994, lot 325)

BIBLIOGRAPHY: Miklós Boskovits, "Su Don Lorenzo, pittore
camaldolese," *Arte cristiana* 82 (1994): p. 353; Laurence Kanter,
*Painting and Illumination in Early Renaissance Florence,
1300–1450*, exh. cat. (New York, 1994), pp. 261–62; Dillian
Gordon, "The Altarpiece by Lorenzo Monaco in the National
Gallery, London," *Burlington Magazine* 137 (1995): p. 724;
Dillian Gordon, "Renaissance Painting and Illumination at the
Metropolitan," *Apollo* 140 (February 1995): p. 51; Dillian
Gordon, *The Fifteenth Century: Italian Paintings*, National
Gallery Catalogues (London, 2003), 1: pp. 177–79; Angelo
Tartuferi, in *Lorenzo Monaco: A Bridge from Giotto's Heritage
to the Renaissance*, ed. Tartuferi and Daniela Parenti, exh. cat.
(Florence, 2006), pp. 167–71; Angelo Tartuferi, "Ancora su
Lorenzo Monaco, dopo la mostra e il convegno," in *Intorno
a Lorenzo Monaco: Nuovi studi sulla pittura tardogotica*,
ed. Daniela Parenti and Tartuferi (Florence, 2007), p. 16

CONDITION: The panel support has been thinned to 8 mm
and displays a pronounced convex warp. It retains a gilded
barb at the left and right edges, and possibly at the bottom,
where the gilding, however, has been repaired. The paint
surface is exceptionally well preserved and is unimpaired
by modern restorations, except over an irregular area across
the top of the panel extending down as far as the peak of the
prophet's cowl. The gilding in the upper half of the panel is
abraded, but three scratches across the prophet's face and
one along his left arm are the only other blemishes in the
picture surface.

Four slotted moldings, rectangular in profile, were engaged
to the panel along its outer edges, presumably at the time
it was cut out of its original context; the top and bottom
moldings have disengaged with the warping of the panel. On
the reverse of the panel are the number "202" painted in black
and two eighteenth-century(?) pieces of paper coeval with the
added moldings. The upper sheet is printed with "ETRURIA
PITTRICE no.," with the number "166" added in red ink,
scored through and replaced with the number "144." On the
bottom sheet is written in ink: "N.o 166 [scored through and
replaced with 144] / Graffione Fiorent. / discepolo di Alessio /
Baldovinetti / + 1448."

The prophet Jeremiah—identifiable by the inscription
on a scroll held in his right hand: [HAEC DICIT DOMI-
NUS] IUX[TA] VIAS GE[N]TIU[M] N[ON] [*sic*] NOL[ITE DISCERE
ET A SIGNIS CAELI NOLITE METUERE QUAE TIMENT GENTES]
("Thus saith the Lord: Learn not according to the ways of
the Gentiles: and be not afraid of the signs of heaven, which
the heathens fear" [Jer. 10:2])—is portrayed half-length and
turned three-quarters to the viewer's left. His beard is short
and curling, his robe is green highlighted in white and yellow,
and his head and shoulders are wrapped in a white cloth. The
gold ground of the panel is closed off by symmetrical trilobe
arches at top and bottom, the spandrels of which are decorated with a black (or dark blue) sgraffito design of a flower
and leaves on a vine tendril.

As one of the four major prophets (along with Isaiah,
Ezekiel, and Daniel) of the Old Testament, Jeremiah is often
included among the ancillary—usually pilaster—figures in
early Renaissance altarpieces, sometimes in the company
of the patriarchs Noah, Abraham, Moses, and David, as wit-
nesses to the divinity of Christ or the purity of the Virgin.
The shape, size, and composition of the present panel argue
that it originally appeared in the right framing pilaster of a
large altarpiece, where its half-length format suggests that
it may have occupied the uppermost position. This was recognized independently, when the panel first appeared at auction, by Miklós Boskovits, who suggested that it may have
been damaged along its upper edges when it was prized from
its original frame moldings; by the present author; and by
Marvin Eisenberg, who thought the damages to the top of the
panel might have been caused by a fire.[2]

When it appeared at auction in 1994, the *Prophet Jeremiah*
was catalogued as from the workshop of Lorenzo Monaco,
possibly attributable to Bartolomeo di Fruosino; it was recognized by Boskovits, the present author, and Eisenberg as an
autograph work by Lorenzo Monaco. Boskovits remarked on
its stylistic similarity to the panels of the *Coronation of the
Virgin* altarpiece by Lorenzo Monaco in the National Gallery,
London (fig. 1), reputedly from the church of San Benedetto
fuori della Porta Pinti, in Florence, all of which he dated
around 1405 but in any event earlier than 1407. The present
author dated the *Jeremiah* ca. 1406–7 in relation to the illuminations in one of the Santa Maria degli Angeli antiphonaries,
now Corale 7 at the Biblioteca Laurenziana, Florence.[3] Noting
the coincidence of this date with a "documentary" reference
to the San Benedetto *Coronation* altarpiece in 1407 (see below),
the present author also suggested that the *Jeremiah* might
have been a fragment of that large complex but observed that
the sgraffito decoration of its spandrels is more commonly
encountered in Lorenzo Monaco's late works. Eisenberg

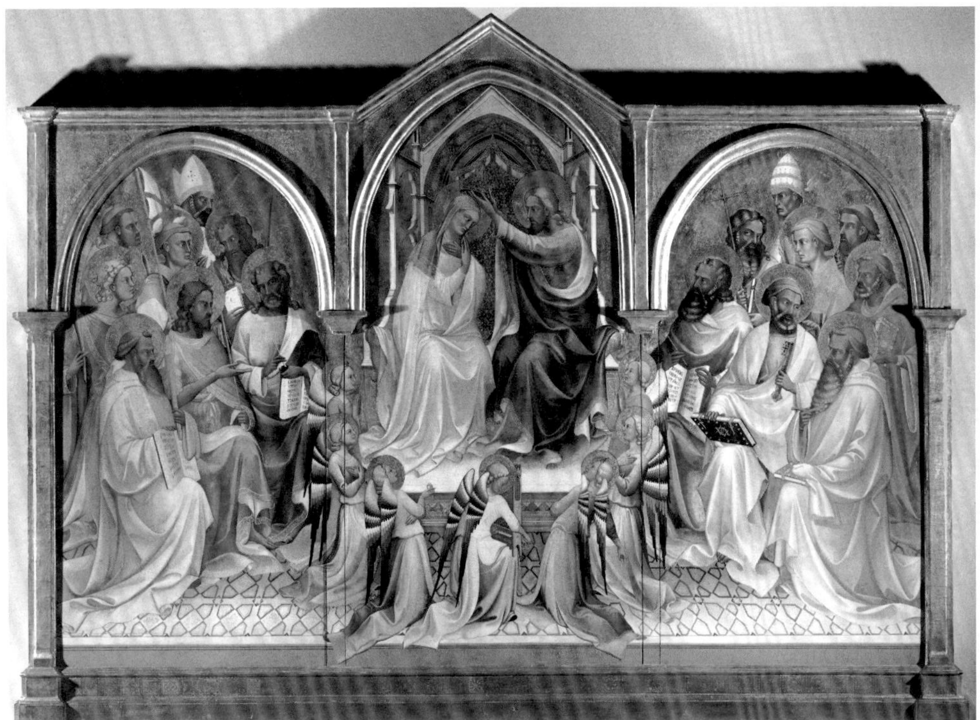

Fig. 1. Lorenzo Monaco, *The Coronation of the Virgin with Saints*, ca. 1407. Tempera on panel, 264.9 x 365.8 cm (104⅛ x 132 in.). National Gallery, London, wings presented by William Coningham, 1848; center panel bought, 1902

rejected the possibility of any connection between the *Jeremiah* and the San Benedetto *Coronation* altarpiece, for which he preferred a date after 1414, whereas for the *Jeremiah* he advanced a date of ca. 1398–1400.

The association of the *Jeremiah* with the *Coronation of the Virgin* altarpiece from San Benedetto fuori della Porta Pinti, specifically as the uppermost panel of the missing right framing pilaster, has been accepted by both Dillian Gordon and Angelo Tartuferi, largely without comment.[4] Other aspects of the reconstruction of that altarpiece and of its dating have instead been subjects of debate. Georg Pudelko and Martin Davies first established a link between the main panels of the structure now in London, all three of which entered the collections of the National Gallery at different times and from different sources, with the reference by Giorgio Vasari to an altarpiece formerly in the Camaldolese church of San Benedetto that had been transferred to the cloister of Santa Maria degli Angeli during the Siege of Florence in 1529.[5] Five predella panels showing the Adoration of the Magi and various episodes from the legend of Saint Benedict—now divided among the National Gallery in London, the Pinacoteca Vaticana, and the National Museum in Poznań, Poland—and a pinnacle panel showing the Virgin Annunciate now in the Norton Simon Museum of Art, in Pasadena, California (fig. 2), have also been accepted by all critics as parts of the same structure. To these panels, Kanter and Boskovits added, in addition to the *Jeremiah*, a central pinnacle of the *Blessing Redeemer* formerly in the Loeser collection and recently purchased by the Italian state on behalf of the Galleria dell'Accademia, Florence (fig. 3).[6] More controversial has been a suggestion that four panels in the Metropolitan Museum of Art, New York, representing the patriarchs Noah, Abraham, Moses, and David, all portrayed full length and seated on stone benches,

might have been included in this altarpiece as an intermediate layer between the main-tier panels and the pinnacles.[7] Initially rejected by Gordon but later tacitly admitted by her and by Tartuferi as a possibility, it was ultimately argued that they are coincident in date to the altarpiece but originate from a different complex as they once included among their number a figure of Saint Peter, who is also portrayed on one of the lateral panels from San Benedetto now in London.[8] Pudelko's suggestion that one of the spandrels at either side of the central *Coronation of the Virgin* in this altarpiece might have been filled by a tondo identified by him as representing Saint Cyprianus is to be rejected: the tondo in question actually represents the prophet Isaiah and may now be shown to have been part of a different altarpiece (see no. 20). Also to be rejected is the suggestion by Mirella Levi d'Ancona that a further part of the predella to this altarpiece might be a fragmentary panel in the National Gallery, London, showing Saint Benedict in the Sacro Speco at Subiaco.[9] This panel has been cropped significantly on the right but has a vertical grain and was probably once part of a large Thebaid showing scenes from the legends of the desert fathers.

Traditionally, with the exception of Osvald Sirén, all writers who discussed the *Coronation of the Virgin* in London considered it a relatively uninspired workshop repetition of Lorenzo Monaco's Uffizi altarpiece of the same subject and therefore placed its execution after 1414, the date inscribed across the base of the Uffizi painting.[10] Boskovits and Kanter, however, both insisted that the style of the London altarpiece could be meaningfully compared only to Lorenzo Monaco's paintings of the first decade of the fifteenth century, and that it should more properly be considered a first experiment with the compositional structure that would ultimately be resolved in the Uffizi altarpiece, which is by general consensus the

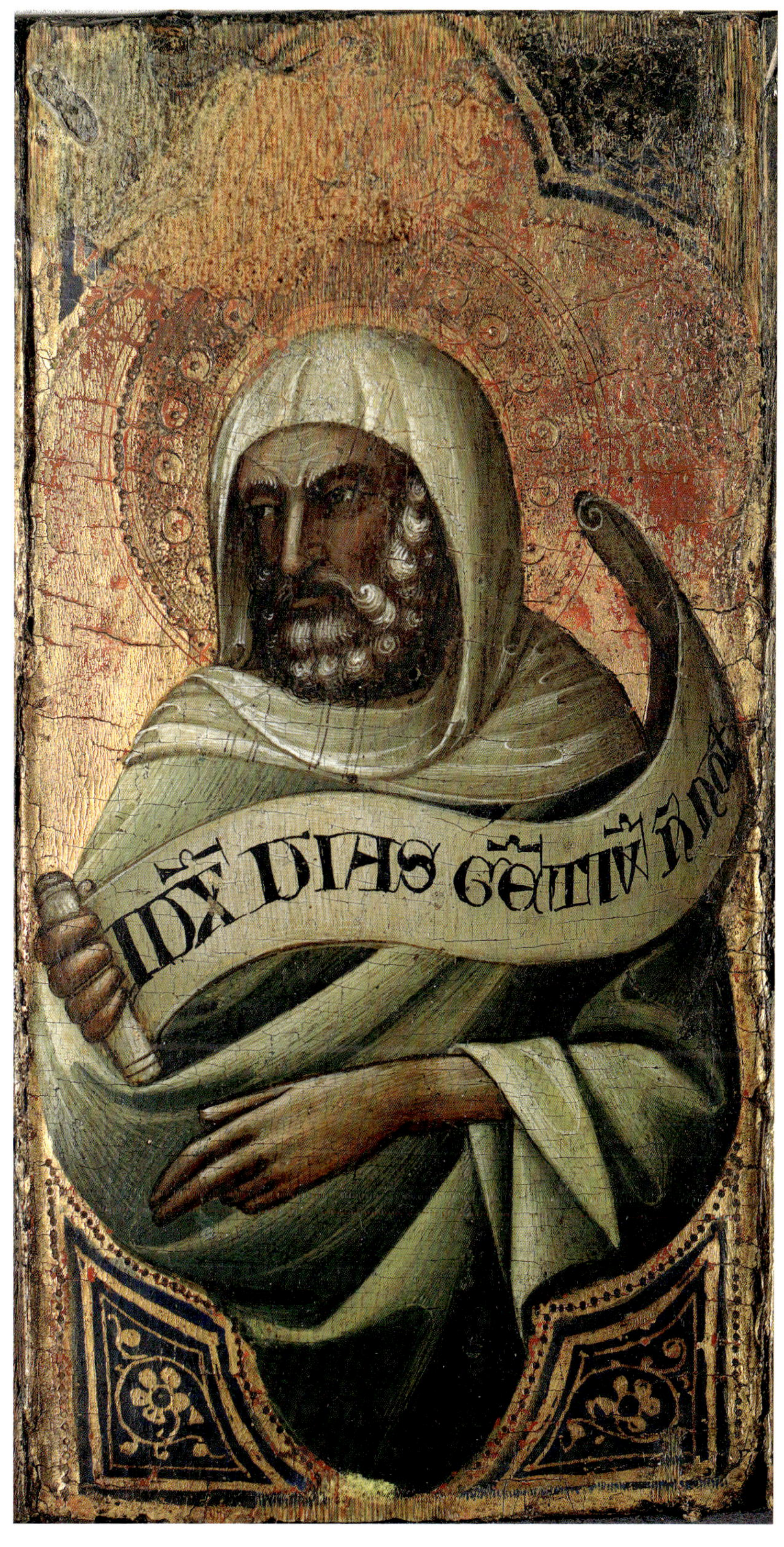

artist's masterpiece. Boskovits suggested that corroboratory evidence for this point of view might be the formal approval, at the Capitolo Generale of the Camaldolese order in 1407, for the foundation of San Benedetto—which he accepted as a *terminus ante quem* for the London altarpiece—while Kanter drew attention to an eighteenth-century notice claiming that the San Benedetto fuori della Porta Pinti altarpiece "fu fatta fare l'anno 1407" (was ordered to be made in the year 1407).[11] This issue was later clarified by Gordon, who, with Anabel Thomas, recovered the original of the document summarized in the eighteenth-century notice. According to this document, Luca di Piero di Rinieri Berri of Florence agreed in 1407 to support the entire cost of painting a high altarpiece for San Benedetto, less 50 florins that had previously been left to the monastery by Cristoforo da Barbarino for the embellishment of the high altar. While it is possible that

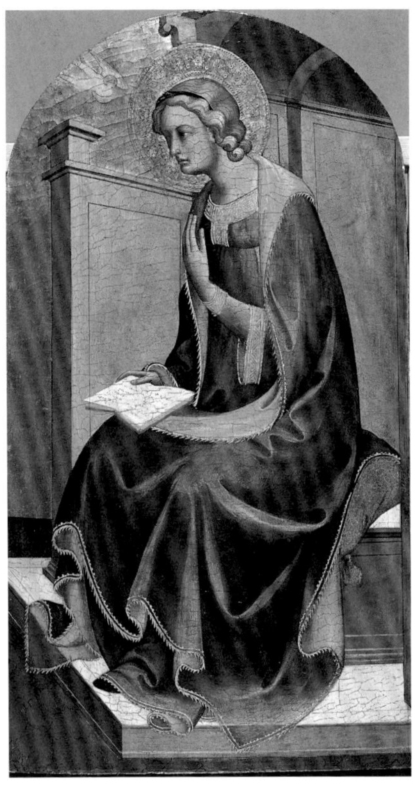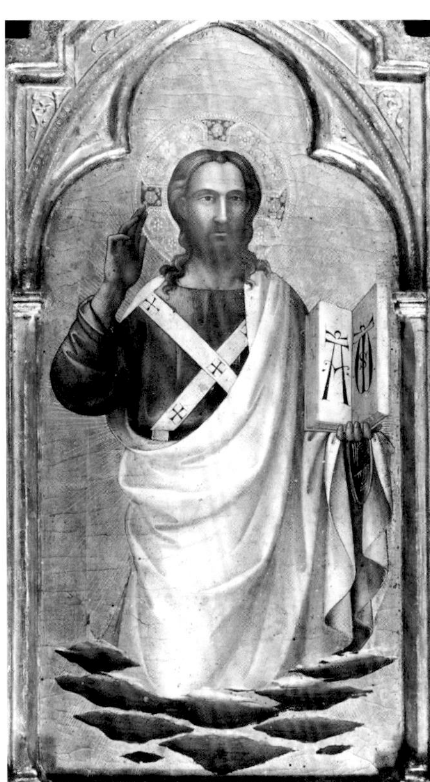

Fig. 2. Lorenzo Monaco, *The Virgin Annunciate*, ca. 1407. Tempera on panel, 80.3 x 44.5 cm (31⅛ x 17½ in.). Norton Simon Art Foundation, Pasadena, Calif., Gift of Mr. Norton Simon

Fig. 3. Lorenzo Monaco, *Blessing Redeemer*, ca. 1407. Tempera on panel, 81.3 x 41.4 cm (32 x 16⅛ in.). Galleria dell'Accademia, Florence

the altarpiece had been begun earlier, perhaps with receipt of the bequest of Cristoforo da Barbarino, it is referred to as complete and installed only in 1409. How long before this the painting may actually have been completed is unclear, but it is certain that a date for the London altarpiece of ca. 1407, and not substantially later, is accurate.

On the basis of these documentary notices and the stylistic comparisons adduced by Boskovits and Kanter, it seems inevitable to conclude that the *Jeremiah* was indeed once part of the framing structure of the San Benedetto altarpiece. Kanter's objection that the type of sgraffito decoration filling the spandrels of the gold ground in the present panel is more commonly encountered in Lorenzo Monaco's late works is valid. Such decoration does, however, occur in approximately this form in the pinnacles of the *Saint Lawrence* altarpiece now in the Musée du Petit Palais, Avignon, which is inscribed with the date 1407, and so must have been a part of the studio's decorative vocabulary from an early date even if it only came to be more consistently employed later.   L K

1. The painting occurs as no. 166 in the undated manuscript inventory of Tacoli-Canacci's collection (*Catalogo ragionato dei pittori della scuola toscana*, Biblioteca della Soprintendenza dei Beni Artistici e Storici di Parma, MS 145) with the following description: "Tavola. Piccolo quadro rappresentante in mezza figura dipinta sopra fondo d'oro un Santo con apparenza di Vecchio, coperto il capo e le spalle con un manto bianco, e che tiene nella mano destra un Cartello bianco con alcune parole in carattere Gottico. B[raccia] ⅓ – B[raccia] ¼ – Di Graffione Fiorentino – Di Alessio Baldovinetti – 2." It recurs in the dated manuscript inventory of 1792 (Archivio di Stato di Parma, MS 101) as no. 114 [*sic*]. See Vincenzo M. Buonocore, *Il marchese Alfonso Tacoli-Canacci: "Onesto gentiluomo smaniante per la pittura"* (Reggio Emilia, Italy, 2005), p. 224. This con-

forms to the manuscript notices pasted on the back of the panel (see Condition), where, however, the revised numeration of 1792 is given as 144, not 114. The painting is not identifiable in the 1789 inventory of Tacoli-Canacci's collection; see *Etruria pittrice o sia storia delli principi, risorsa de avanzamenti della pittura* (Florence, 1789) (Biblioteca Real di Madrid, MS II/574).

2. See Miklós Boskovits, "Su Don Lorenzo, pittore camaldolese," *Arte cristiana* 82 (1994): p. 353; Laurence Kanter, *Painting and Illumination in Early Renaissance Florence, 1300–1450*, exh. cat. (New York, 1994), pp. 261–62; and Marvin Eisenberg, conversation with Richard L. Feigen, August 8, 1994.

3. Kanter, *Painting and Illumination*, pp. 261–62.

4. See Dillian Gordon and Anabel Thomas, "A New Document for the High Altar-Piece for S. Benedetto fuori della Porta Pinti, Florence," *Burlington Magazine* 137 (1995): pp. 720–22; Dillian Gordon, *The Fifteenth Century: Italian Paintings*, National Gallery Catalogues (London, 2003), 1: pp. 177–79; and Angelo Tartuferi, in *Lorenzo Monaco: A Bridge from Giotto's Heritage to the Renaissance*, ed. Tartuferi and Daniela Parenti, exh. cat. (Florence, 2006), pp. 167–71.

5. Georg Pudelko, "The Stylistic Development of Lorenzo Monaco, I," *Burlington Magazine* 73 (1938): pp. 237–48; and Martin Davies, "Lorenzo Monaco's 'Coronation of the Virgin' in London," *Critica d'arte* 29 (1949): pp. 202–10.

6. See Kanter, *Painting and Illumination*, pp. 261–62; and Boskovits, "Su Don Lorenzo, pittore camaldolese," p. 353. See also Tartuferi, in Tartuferi and Parenti, *Lorenzo Monaco*, pp. 167–71.

7. Laurence Kanter, review of *Lorenzo Monaco*, by Marvin Eisenberg, *Burlington Magazine* 135 (1993): pp. 632–33.

8. See Gordon and Thomas, "A New Document for the High Altar-Piece," pp. 720–22; Gordon, *Fifteenth Century: Italian Paintings*, 1: pp. 177–79; and Tartuferi, in Tartuferi and Parenti, *Lorenzo Monaco*, pp. 167–71. On the four patriarchs and Saint Peter, see Laurence Kanter, in ibid., pp. 186–90.

9. Mirella Levi d'Ancona, "Matteo Torelli," *Commentari* 9 (1958): pp. 244–58.

10. Osvald Sirén, *Don Lorenzo Monaco* (Strasbourg, France, 1905), pp. 63–68; and see Marvin Eisenberg, *Lorenzo Monaco* (Princeton, N.J., 1989), pp. 138–45, with earlier bibliography.

11. M. L. Frawley, "Lorenzo Monaco and His Patrons" (M.PHIL. diss., Courtauld Gallery, London, 1975).

Lorenzo Monaco

Florence, ca. 1370–ca. 1422/23

20. *The Prophet Isaiah*, ca. 1414

Tempera on panel, 19.7 cm (7 ¾ in.), diameter

PROVENANCE: Alexis-François Artaud de Montor (1772–1849), Paris (his sale, Schroth, Paris, January 17, 1851, lot 51); private collection, Switzerland (sale, Sotheby's, London, July 8, 1987, lot 20)

BIBLIOGRAPHY: Alexis-François Artaud de Montor, *Peintres primitifs: Collection de tableaux rapportée d'Italie et publiée par M. le chevalier Artaud de Montor*, 3rd ed. (Paris, 1843), no. 51, pl. 17; August Schmarsow, "Maîtres italiens à la Galerie d'Altenburg," *Gazette des beaux-arts*, ser. 2, no. 20 (1898): p. 502; Osvald Sirén, *Don Lorenzo Monaco* (Strasbourg, France, 1905), p. 44; Georg Pudelko, "The Stylistic Development of Lorenzo Monaco, I," *Burlington Magazine* 73 (1938): p. 248n.3; Marvin Eisenberg, "The Origins and Development of the Early Style of Lorenzo Monaco" (PH.D. diss., Princeton University, 1954), pp. 283–88, 310–11; Marvin Eisenberg, "Un frammento smarrito dell'Annunciazione di Lorenzo Monaco nell'Accademia di Firenze," *Bolletino d'arte*, ser. 4, no. 41 (1956): pp. 333–35; Giovanni Previtali, *La fortuna dei primitivi: Dal Vasari ai neoclassici* (Rome, 1964), p. 232; Miklós Boskovits, *Pittura fiorentina alla vigilia del Rinascimento, 1370–1400* (Florence, 1975), p. 352; Marvin Eisenberg, *Lorenzo Monaco* (Princeton, N.J., 1989), pp. 149–50; Laurence Kanter, *Painting and Illumination in Early Renaissance Florence, 1300–1450*, exh. cat. (New York, 1994), pp. 270–71; Dillian Gordon, *The Fifteenth Century: Italian Paintings*, National Gallery Catalogues (London, 2003), 1: pp. 177, 186n.64; Daniela Parenti, in *Lorenzo Monaco: A Bridge from Giotto's Heritage to the Renaissance*, ed. Angelo Tartuferi and Parenti, exh. cat. (Florence, 2006), pp. 179 85

CONDITION: The panel, of a vertical wood grain, has been thinned to 11 mm but is not visibly warped. It has been trimmed within the picture field along its entire perimeter, but the treatment of the prophet's right shoulder, where pigment was never applied near the edge, and the lettering of the scroll, which seems to be complete, suggest that no considerable amount of image has been lost. The paint surface is unevenly stained from residues of old varnish but is very little abraded. Minor flaking losses in the blue immediately above the prophet's pointing finger and a percussion damage to the gold at the lower right have been repaired. Two scratches in the prophet's face and a shallow gouge above his left eyebrow have not been retouched.

The earliest notice of this tondo representing the prophet Isaiah—who may be identified by his scroll, lettered ECCE VI[R]GO CO[N]CIP[IET ET PARIET FILIUM] (Behold, a virgin shall conceive, and bear a son [Isa. 7:14])—is an engraving in the catalogue of the Artaud de Montor collection, where it is one of nine paintings attributed by the collector to Cimabue.[1] Alexis-François Artaud de Montor assembled his collection, consisting of 108 panels by the "primitives" of the thirteenth, fourteenth, and fifteenth centuries, in Italy before 1810, one of the pioneering collections of this material formed in Europe in the wake of the Leopoldine and Napoleonic suppressions of confraternal and monastic properties in Tuscany. His unrealistically generic attribution of this tondo to Cimabue was revised by August Schmarsow to Antonio Veneziano, before the panel was recognized by Osvald Sirén, still on the basis of the engraving in the Artaud de Montor catalogue, as a work by Lorenzo Monaco.[2] Georg Pudelko was the first to propose a reconstruction of the tondo's origins: identifying its subject as Saint Cyprianus (misreading the last letters of the inscription on the scroll as [S]CO CIP[RIANO]), he suggested that it may have decorated the right spandrel of the *Coronation of the Virgin* altarpiece by Lorenzo Monaco now in the National Gallery, London (no. 19, fig. 1).[3] This suggestion has been rejected by all later scholars, however, following Marvin Eisenberg's convincing reconstruction of the tondo as part of the pinnacle decoration of the *Annunciation* altarpiece from San Procolo in Florence, now in the Galleria dell'Accademia, Florence (fig 1)[4]

Of the three main panels that comprise the *Annunciation* altarpiece, only the central panel is preserved with its pinnacle intact, incorporating a large roundel representing the Blessing Redeemer sending the dove of the Holy Spirit down to the Annunciate Virgin below. The lateral panels, each portraying two standing saints, have been truncated at the level of the saints' haloes. Their missing upper portions were rebuilt prior to 1890 in imitation of the central panel and provided with painted tondi representing two angels that had been removed from Bernardo Daddi's San Pancrazio altarpiece and that were subsequently reunited in 1962 with the other fragments of that altarpiece in the Galleria degli Uffizi, Florence Eisenberg recognized the *Isaiah* roundel as one of the missing lateral pinnacles from the *Annunciation* altarpiece on the basis of stylistic conformity, iconography, and correspondence in size with the missing tondi of the frame. The present author observed that this last criterion is irrelevant as the frames in question are modern, but nonetheless accepted the reconstruction, which indeed appears to be correct.[5] Daniela Parenti

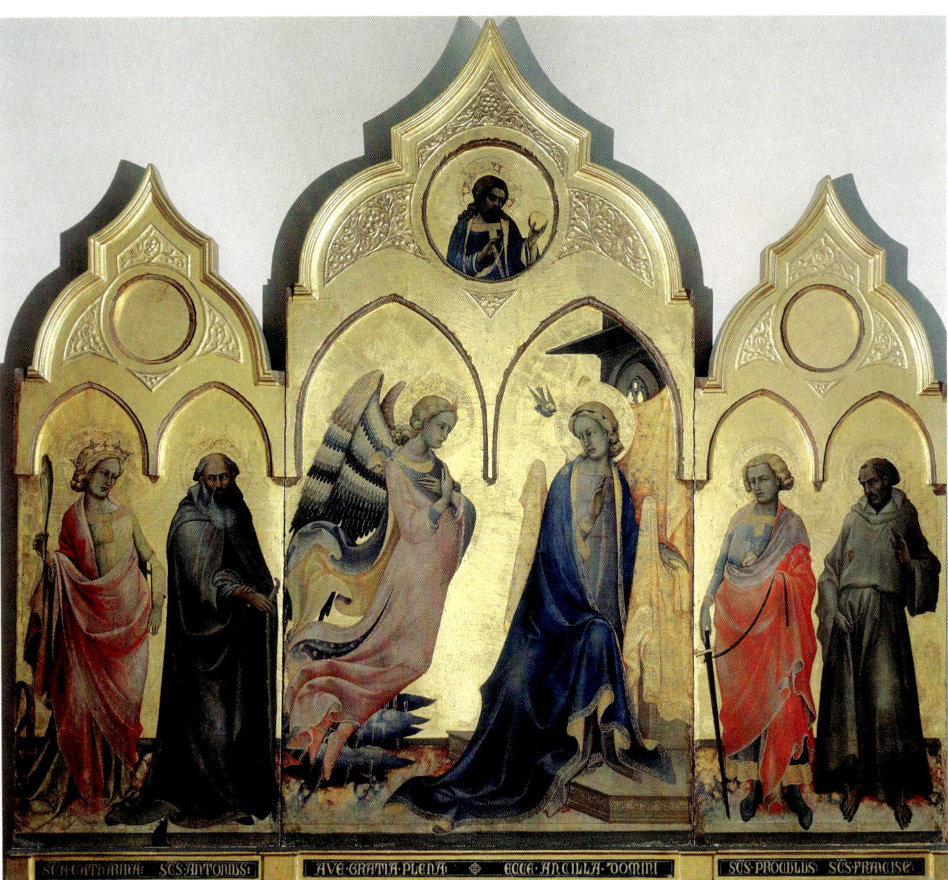

Fig. 1. Lorenzo Monaco, *The Annunciation*, ca. 1414. Tempera on panel, 210 x 229 cm (82¾ x 90⅛ in.). Galleria dell'Accademia, Florence

objected only to the positioning of the tondo in the reconstruction, preferring to situate it above the left lateral panel, following the direction of the prophet's gaze and his pointing finger, whereas Eisenberg had placed it above the right lateral panel.[6] This issue is difficult to resolve on internal evidence alone. The prophet's finger is pointing at his scroll, not at the scene below him. The turn of his head might indicate placement above the right lateral, whereas the direction of his gaze could argue the opposite, although his eyes would not focus on the central scene even if he were placed within the left pinnacle. While it is not conclusive evidence, it may be added that the fall of light from the left on the prophet's bust might also argue for placement in the right pinnacle, as the full-length figures of Saints Proculus and Francis in that panel are also lit from the left. Saints Catherine and Anthony Abbot in the left panel are not lit consistently from a single source: the light on Saint Anthony falls frontally and slightly from the left, while Saint Catherine is modeled with highlights predominantly on the right side.

The relevance of the prophet Isaiah to a scene of the Annunciation, symbolizing the Incarnation of Christ without insemination, is self-evident and is made explicit by the inscription on the prophet's scroll: "Behold a virgin shall conceive." In a later altarpiece of the *Annunciation* by Lorenzo Monaco, still in situ in the Bartolini-Salimbeni chapel in Santa Trinita in Florence, a figure of Isaiah fills the central pinnacle, and is accompanied in the lateral pinnacles by two other, unidentified prophets. The identity of the missing prophet from the San Procolo *Annunciation* is similarly unknown, although frequently in Renaissance painting Isaiah is paired with Ezekiel, another of the four major prophets, whose identifying inscription—PORTA HAEC CLAUSA ERIT; NON APERIETUR (This gate shall be shut, it shall not be opened [Ezek. 44:2])—was traditionally interpreted as another prophecy of the virgin birth.

The original provenance and date of the San Procolo *Annunciation* have been subjects of some debate. The altarpiece entered the collection of the Galleria dell'Accademia in 1812, and a label on its reverse states that it was found in 1810, at the time of the Napoleonic suppressions, in the Badia Fiorentina. Luigi Lanzi in 1795 described a painting of the Annunciation in the Badia that he believed was by Giotto and that has quite reasonably been identified with this altarpiece, which was, therefore, long known as the Badia *Annunciation*.[7] The inscription (which is modern but possibly reproduces a lost original) along the base of the altarpiece frame identifying the youthful warrior in the right panel as Saint Proculus led Walter and Elisabeth Paatz to suggest instead that this might be an altarpiece described in 1677 in the church of San Procolo: "una Nunziata dipinta da incerto sul legno nel 1409."[8] The church of San Procolo was suppressed in 1778, at which time its parochial rights were transferred to the Badia, and apparently works of art had been transferred from San Procolo to the Badia even earlier. An original provenance from San Procolo has been widely accepted in the modern literature concerning Lorenzo Monaco, though it was denied by Eisenberg on the basis of "a contradiction in hagiography," the Florentine

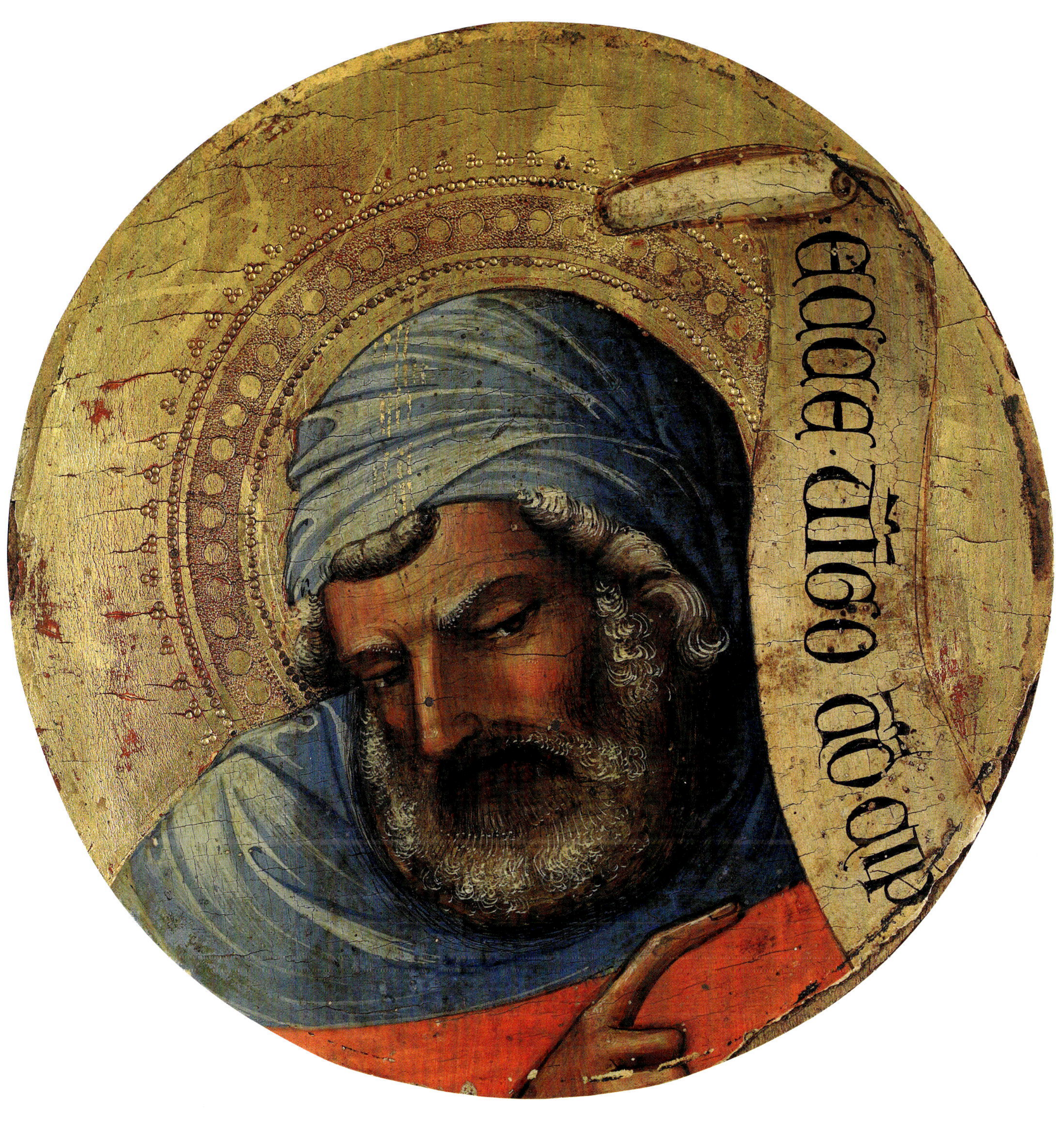

church being consecrated to the sixth-century bishop named Proculus, not to the fourth-century knight portrayed in the Accademia altarpiece.[9] It was pointed out by the present author, however, that the two Saints Proculus, the bishop and the knight, share a single feast day (June 1) and are believed to be buried in the same tomb in the Benedictine monastery of San Procolo in Bologna, and therefore that the coincidence of an altarpiece of the Annunciation containing a figure of either Saint Proculus—both of whom are extremely rare in Florentine hagiography—is too important to be dismissed.[10] Most

recently, Parenti has affirmed the provenance of the altarpiece from San Procolo and specifically from the altar in that church endowed by Antonio di Andrea del Pannocchia (d. 1412/13) with a dedication to Saint Anthony Abbott.[11]

Even those writers who acknowledge the identification of the Accademia *Annunciation* with the painting described in San Procolo in 1677 are divided in their opinions concerning its date. Paatz, Eisenberg initially, and the present author accept the reported date of 1409, for example; Mirella Levi d'Ancona, Luciano Bellosi initially, and Miklós Boskovits prefer to see it as a work of the first half of the following decade; while in a later moment Bellosi and Eisenberg consider it to have been painted probably between 1415 and 1420.[12] Parenti has advanced compelling arguments for grouping this work with paintings by Lorenzo Monaco close in date to the Santa Maria degli Angeli *Coronation of the Virgin* altarpiece (1413), and has suggested the possibility of the date having been misread in 1677: an inscription of MCCCCXIIII (1414) being confused with MCCCCVIIII (1409).[13] Whether such an error might have been a lapsus on the part of the writers or a result of damage to the original inscription, the argument is entirely plausible and may in fact, if accepted, assist with the identification of part of the altarpiece's now-missing predella.

Osvald Sirén first suggested that four quatrefoil panels representing the *Nativity* (Robert Lehman Collection, Metropolitan Museum of Art, New York), the *Visitation* and the *Adoration of the Magi* (Courtauld Gallery, London), and the *Flight into Egypt* (Lindenau-Museum, Altenburg, Germany) formed the predella to the San Procolo *Annunciation*, on the model of the predella to Lorenzo Monaco's later Bartolini-Salimbeni *Annunciation*, in which the same four scenes occur.[14] John Pope-Hennessy and Kanter rejected this proposal on the basis of an incongruency of dating and measurements, although Kanter later revised these arguments to accept Sirén's reconstruction.[15] Eisenberg and Parenti correctly rejected any connection between these four panels and the San Procolo *Annunciation* but proposed no alternative candidates for the altarpiece's predella.[16]

If the San Procolo *Annunciation* was once dated 1414 rather than 1409, one other predella panel by Lorenzo Monaco survives that might be associated with it on the grounds of style and iconography. Preserved in the Musée des Beaux-Arts in Nice (fig. 2), it represents the funeral of an unidentified bishop saint, and has recently been discussed by the present author as a probable work by the young Fra Angelico in Lorenzo Monaco's workshop.[17] Four paintings associated with it stylistically are all datable between 1411 and 1414, a date that seems generically appropriate for the Nice panel as well and that might now find circumstantial confirmation by relating it to the San Procolo altarpiece. While it is still not possible to identify "beyond the shadow of a doubt" the subject of the Nice panel, the fact that its iconography is nontraditional implies that the scene portrayed is drawn from the legend of a rarely represented saint. The possibility that this might be the bishop Saint Proculus to whom the Florentine church of that name was dedicated may be more than a tantalizing coincidence, especially since the remains of Saint Proculus are interred in a Benedictine monastery and the mourners in the Nice panel are apparently dressed in Camaldolese (a reformed Benedictine order) habits. L K

1. Alexis-François Artaud de Montor, *Peintres primitifs: Collection de tableaux rapportée d'Italie et publiée par M. le chevalier Artaud de Montor*, 3rd ed. (Paris, 1843), no. 51, pl. 17.
2. August Schmarsow, "Maîtres italiens à la Galerie d'Altenburg," *Gazette des beaux-arts*, ser. 2, no. 20 (1898): p. 502; and Osvald Sirén, *Don Lorenzo Monaco* (Strasbourg, France, 1905), p. 44.
3. Georg Pudelko, "The Stylistic Development of Lorenzo Monaco, I," *Burlington Magazine* 73 (1938): p. 248n.3.
4. Marvin Eisenberg, "The Origins and Development of the Early Style of Lorenzo Monaco" (PH.D. diss., Princeton University, 1954), pp. 283–88, 310–11; and Marvin Eisenberg, "Un frammento smarrito dell'Annunciazione di Lorenzo Monaco nell'Accademia di Firenze," *Bolletino d'arte*, ser. 4, no. 41 (1956): pp. 333–35.
5. Laurence Kanter, *Painting and Illumination in Early Renaissance Florence, 1300–1450*, exh. cat. (New York, 1994), pp. 270–71.
6. Daniela Parenti, in *Lorenzo Monaco: A Bridge from Giotto's Heritage to the Renaissance*, ed. Angelo Tartuferi and Parenti, exh. cat. (Florence, 2006), pp. 179–85.
7. Luigi Lanzi, *Storia pittorica dell'Italia* (Bassano, Italy, 1795), 1: p. 16.
8. Francesco Bocchi and Giovanni Cinelli, *Le bellezze della città di Firenze*

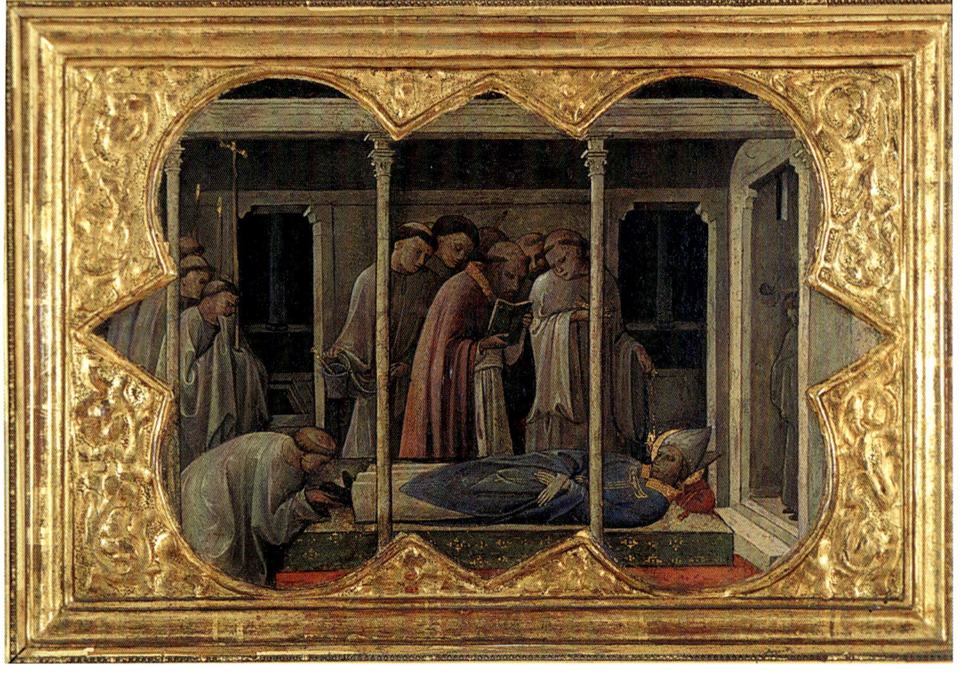

Fig. 2. Lorenzo Monaco (or Fra Angelico?), *The Funeral of an Unidentified Bishop Saint (Saint Proculus?)*, ca. 1414. Tempera on panel, 29 x 44 cm (11⅛ x 17⅛ in.). Musée des Beaux-Arts, Nice

(Florence, 1677), p. 389; and Walter and Elisabeth Valentiner Paatz, *Die Kirchen von Florenz* (Frankfurt-am-Main, Germany, 1940–54), 1: pp. 292, 315n.144, 316n.151; 4: pp. 694, 700n.31.

9. Marvin Eisenberg, *Lorenzo Monaco* (Princeton, N.J., 1989), pp. 149–50.

10. Kanter, *Painting and Illumination*, p. 269.

11. Daniela Parenti, "Qualche approfondimento su Lonrenzo Monaco e sulla chiesa di San Procolo a Firenze," in *Intorno a Lorenzo Monaco: Nuovi studi sulla pittura tardogotica*, ed. Parenti and Angelo Tartuferi (Florence, 2007), pp. 20–31.

12. See Paatz and Paatz, *Kirchen von Florenz*, p. 694; Eisenberg, "Frammento smarrito dell'Annunciazione," pp. 333–35; Kanter, *Painting and Illumination*, p. 269; Mirella Levi d'Ancona, "Bartolomeo di Fruosino," *Art Bulletin* 43 (1961): p. 93; Luciano Bellosi, *Lorenzo Monaco*, I Maestri di Colore (Milan, 1965), n.p.; Miklós Boskovits, *Pittura fiorentina alla vigilia del Rinascimento, 1370–1400* (Florence, 1975), p. 344; Luciano Bellosi, "Due note in margine a Lorenzo Monaco miniature: Il 'Maestro del Codice Squarcialupi' e il poco probabile Matteo Torelli," in *Studi di storia dell'arte in memoria di Mario Rotili* (Naples, 1984), 1: p. 313n.25; and Eisenberg, *Lorenzo Monaco*, pp. 103–4.

13. Parenti, in Tartuferi and Parenti, *Lorenzo Monaco*, pp. 179–85. In a later study, Parenti ("Qualche approfondimento su Lonrenzo Monaco," p. 25) tentatively withdrew this proposal, suggesting that the death of the altar's patron in or shortly after 1412 makes a date of 1409 for the altarpiece more likely. She did, however, leave open the possibility that the commission for the altarpiece might have been testamentary, in which case her original proposal to read its date as 1414 could still be valid.

14. Sirén, *Don Lorenzo Monaco*, pp. 53–56.

15. John Pope-Hennessy and Laurence Kanter, *Italian Paintings*, Robert Lehman Collection 1 (New York, 1987), pp. 170–72; and Kanter, *Painting and Illumination*, pp. 268–70.

16. Eisenberg, *Lorenzo Monaco*, p. 138; Daniela Parenti, in *Da Bernardo Daddi al Beato Angelico a Botticelli: Dipinti fiorentini del Lindenau-Museum di Altenburg*, ed. Miklós Boskovits and Parenti, exh. cat. (Florence, 2005), pp. 112–14; and Parenti, in Tartuferi and Parenti, *Lorenzo Monaco*, p. 182.

17. Laurence Kanter, in Kanter and Pia Palladino, *Fra Angelico*, exh. cat. (New York, 2005), pp. 8–9.

Fra Angelico
Florence, ca. 1395–1455

21. *Saint Joseph*(?), ca. 1418–20

Tempera on panel, 19.4 x 17.5 cm (7⅞ x 6⅞ in.)

PROVENANCE: private collection, England(?); Sotheby's, London, October 18, 1995, lot 50

BIBLIOGRAPHY: Laurence Kanter, in Kanter and Pia Palladino, *Fra Angelico*, exh. cat. (New York, 2005), pp. 24–25; William Hood, review of *Fra Angelico*, by Laurence Kanter and Pia Palladino, *Burlington Magazine* 148 (2006): p. 148

CONDITION: The panel, of a coarse, horizontal grain, has been thinned but not cradled. A knot at the lower left has broken the paint surface near the top of the halo cropped along the bottom edge but has not resulted in any appreciable losses. There are gilding repairs in Saint Joseph's(?) halo, and the flesh tones are evenly abraded.

This elegant and eloquent, though lightly abraded, panel first appeared at auction in 1995, with an attribution to Giovanni di Francesco Toscani, suggested by Everett Fahy. Previously it had been called Simone Martini, as is indicated by a label on the reverse of the panel: a telling reflection of its quality but unhelpful as an indication of its chronological or geographical origins. It was first recognized as an early work of Fra Angelico by Carl Strehlke and the present author, and subsequently accepted as his by Diane Cole Ahl and Michel Laclotte.[1] Kanter associated it chronologically with paintings by Fra Angelico such as the *Thebaid* in the Galleria degli Uffizi, Florence, or the *Griggs Crucifixion* in the Metropolitan Museum of Art, New York, implying a date for it around 1420. Strehlke went further in suggesting that it could have been a fragment of a documented altarpiece, of unknown subject, from the Gherardini chapel in Santo Stefano al Ponte, Florence, for which Angelico received residual payments in January and February 1418—the first documented reference to a painting by the young artist. For Cole Ahl, the painting "seems truly to be 'the missing link' between [Angelico's] lost, early works under Lorenzo Monaco's tutelage and those of the 1420s." Finally, William Hood described the *Saint Joseph*(?) as "a tiny miracle. . . . Its volumetric plasticity, which the painter fashioned by juxtaposing the planes of the head in distinct facets of light and dark effected by a single light source from behind, reveals pictorial intentions that otherwise had not appeared in Florence by this date."[2]

While an attribution to the young Fra Angelico for this panel may be defended on the basis of its palette, drawing, modeling, and decorative details, it is more difficult to determine the nature of the larger structure of which it must have formed part. Kanter initially presumed this to have been an altarpiece of the Lamentation over the Dead Christ, citing the panel's horizontal wood grain—appropriate to a large, horizontal composition—and the expression of pain or concern

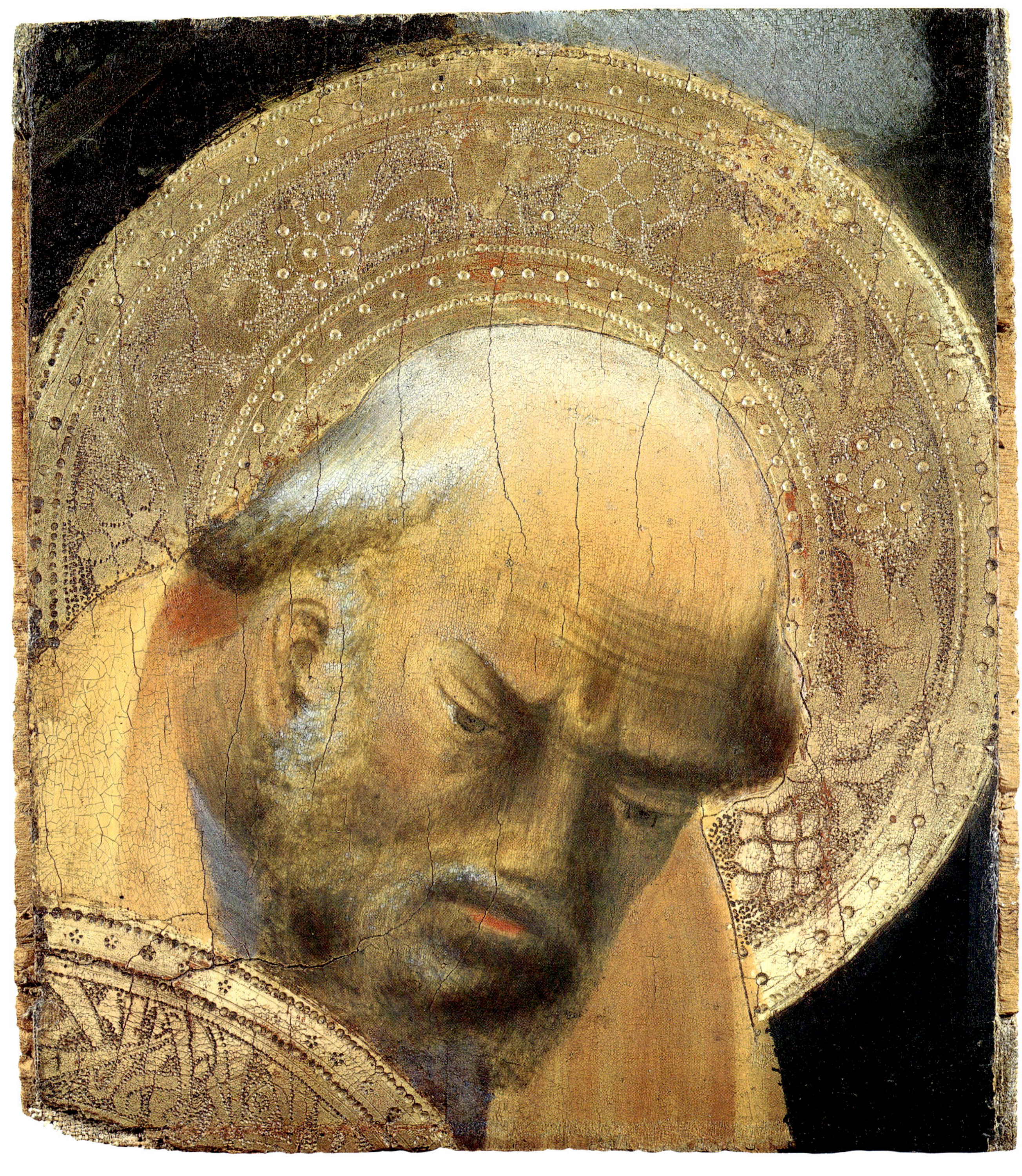

on the figure's face. In such a case the figure would probably represent Nicodemus or Joseph of Arimathea. Strehlke observed that what appears to be a fragment of a shed roof just visible across the background of the panel at the upper left implies instead that this was a fragment of an Adoration of the Magi and that the figure most likely portrays Saint Joseph, an observation supported by the pseudokufic decoration of the halo cropped at the bottom left edge of the panel: Angelico normally reserved this form of halo decoration for figures of the Virgin. Kanter subsequently concurred with this proposal, with the caveat that Angelico's composi-

tions of the Adoration of the Magi are usually oriented in the opposite direction.[3] It should be observed, however, that the supposed fragment of a shed roof, while clearly visible, is not clearly identifiable, and it could be interpreted as a rung of a ladder from a scene of the Deposition.

Though it still seems appropriate to date the Feigen *Saint Joseph*(?) to the last years of the second decade of the fifteenth century, the possibility that it might have formed part of the Gherardini altarpiece must be approached with extreme caution. Sonia Chiodo has advanced evidence for identifying this altarpiece with a polyptych by the Master of the Straus

Madonna—representing the Virgin and Child with Saints Stephen, Louis of France, Donatus, Nicholas, John the Baptist, Eufrosina, Michael Archangel, and Justus—that once bore the Gherardini arms and that may have been removed from their chapel in Santo Stefano al Ponte.[4] The decoration of the Gherardini chapel, including its altarpiece, was commissioned in the first instance from Ambrogio di Baldese (who would therefore be identifiable with the Straus Master), and Chiodo argues that Angelico was paid a relatively small sum merely for finishing and installing the altarpiece. The interpretation of these documents is not straightforward, as Angelico's hand is nowhere in evidence on the polyptych in question yet the amount he received, 12 florins, while not large, is more than he was offered for painting a complete altarpiece of the Annunciation for Alessandro Rondinelli in

1425. Nevertheless, Chiodo's observation that the Gherardini chapel in Santo Stefano al Ponte was dedicated to Saint John the Baptist does raise doubts about a painting either of the Adoration of the Magi or of the Deposition having stood on its altar.

LK

1. See Carl Brandon Strehlke and Laurence Kanter, unpublished notes, October 1995, Richard L. Feigen Co. files; Diane Cole Ahl, letter to Richard Feigen, July 2, 2001, Richard L. Feigen Co. files; and Michel Laclotte, unpublished note, May 1, 2002, Richard L. Feigen Co. files.
2. William Hood, review of *Fra Angelico*, by Laurence Kanter and Pia Palladino, *Burlington Magazine* 148 (2006): p. 148.
3. Laurence Kanter, in Kanter and Pia Palladino, *Fra Angelico*, exh. cat. (New York, 2005), pp. 24–25.
4. Sonia Chiodo, "Pittori attivi in Santo Stefano al Ponte a Firenze e un'ipotesi per l'identificazione del Maestro della Madonna Straus," *Paragone* 577 (1998): pp. 48–79.

Fra Angelico

Florence, ca. 1395–1455

22. *The Vision of Saint Lucy*, ca. 1427–29

Tempera on panel, 24.7 x 21.6 cm (9¾ x 8½ in.)

PROVENANCE: Ignazio Hugford(?), Florence (d. 1778); Marchese Alfonso Tacoli-Canacci(?), Florence, ca. 1787; Don Ferdinando di Borbone, Duke of Parma(?) (1751–1802); by descent to Princess Caroline of Parma(?) (1770–1804); by descent(?) to King Johann of Saxony (1801–1873); by descent to Prince Johann Georg of Saxony (1869–1938); Kurt Bauch (1898–1975), Freiburg-im-Breisgau, Germany (his sale, Sotheby's, London, July 9, 1998, lot 121)

BIBLIOGRAPHY: Staatsgalerie Stuttgart, *Frühe italienische Tafelmalerei*, exh. cat. (Stuttgart, Germany, 1950), no. 4; George Kaftal, *Iconography of the Saints in Tuscan Painting* (Florence, 1986), col. 645; Laurence Kanter, "A Rediscovered Panel by Fra Angelico," *Paragone* 599 (2000): pp. 3–13; Carl Brandon Strehlke, *Italian Paintings, 1250–1450, in the John G. Johnson Collection and the Philadelphia Museum of Art* (Philadelphia, 2004), pp. 45–51; Laurence Kanter, in Kanter and Pia Palladino, *Fra Angelico*, exh. cat. (New York, 2005), pp. 121–32; Diane Cole Ahl, *Fra Angelico* (London, 2008), p. 227; Laurence Kanter, *Reconstructing the Renaissance: "Saint James Freeing Hermogenes" by Fra Angelico* (Fort Worth, 2008), pp. 36ff

CONDITION: The panel, of a horizontal wood grain, has been thinned to 12 mm but is not cradled and exhibits a modest warp. The paint surface is extremely well preserved except for the figure of Saint Lucy in the right foreground, which has been repainted and its halo regilt, and the sarcophagus mounted on the wall in the center of the composition, which has been regilt and its moldings redrawn in black. Applied to the reverse of the panel are paper collector's stamps of Prince Johann Georg of Saxony (no. 295) and King Johann of Saxony (no. 189), and a paper label printed: "Sr. Maj. Des Konigs / Privat-vermogens-verwaltung / Familienwar[. . .]," and numbered "IX – 65." The first of these stamps is pasted over the second digit of a painted inventory number, "7[o]2 A," possibly belonging to Ignazio Hugford or his heir, Lamberto Gori.

This remarkable panel, unknown until recently to the general literature on Fra Angelico, was exhibited in Stuttgart, Germany, in 1950 with an attribution to the artist's workshop, and mentioned, though not illustrated, in 1986 by George Kaftal, presumably on the advice of Richard Offner, as an autograph work.[1] It represents an episode from the life of Saint Lucy as recounted in the *Legenda Aurea* of Jacobus da Varagine:

Lucy, the daughter of a noble family of Syracusa, saw how the fame of Saint Agatha was spreading throughout Sicily. She went to the tomb of this saint with her mother Euthicia, who for four years had suffered from an incurable flow of blood. . . . When all the people had left the church, the mother and her daughter stayed to pray at the tomb. Lucy then

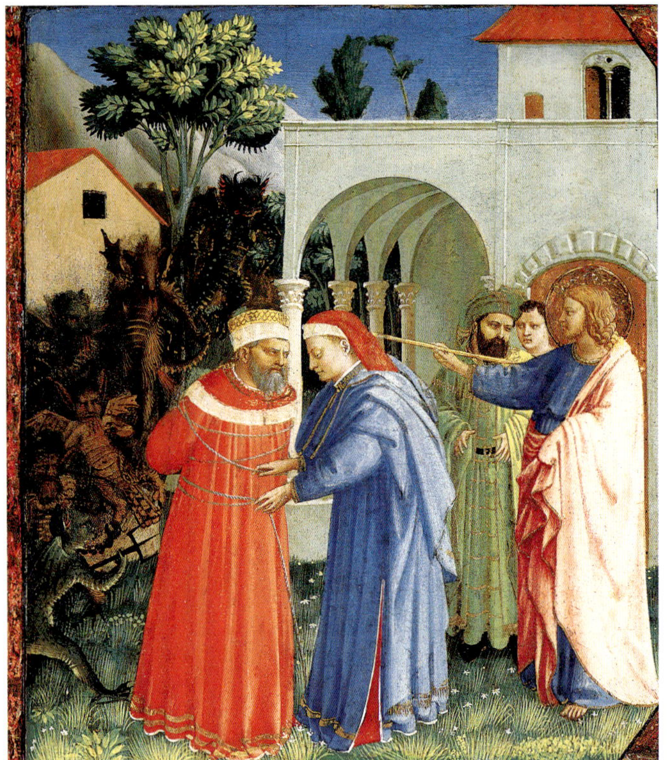

Fig. 1. Fra Angelico, *The Apostle Saint James the Greater Freeing the Magician Hermogenes*, ca. 1427–29. Tempera on panel, 26.8 x 23.8 cm (10⅝ x 9⅜ in.). Kimbell Art Museum, Kimbell Art Foundation, Fort Worth, 1986, inv. no. AP 1986.03

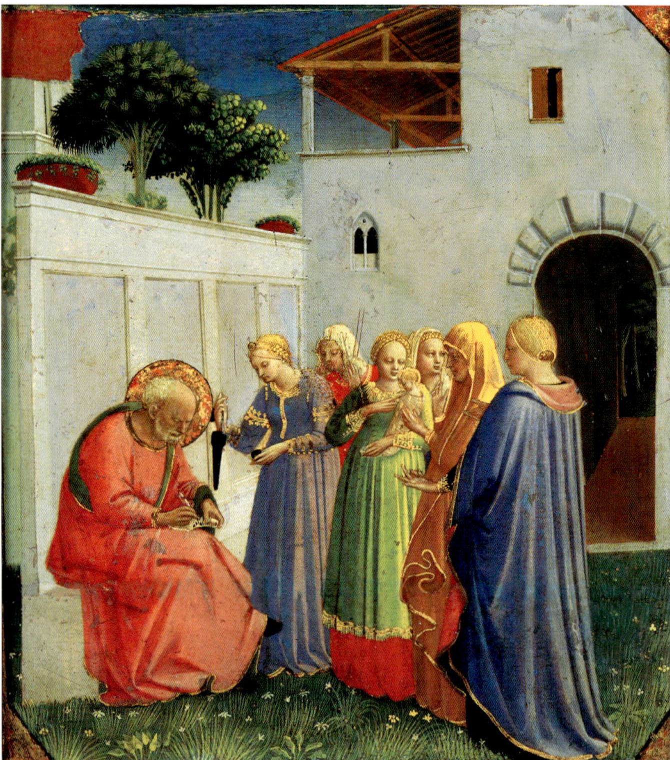

Fig. 2. Fra Angelico, *The Naming of Saint John the Baptist*, ca. 1427–29. Tempera on panel, 26 x 24 cm (10¼ x 9½ in.). Museo di San Marco, Florence

fell asleep, and had a vision of Agatha standing surrounded by angels and adorned with precious stones, and Agatha said to her: "My sister Lucy, virgin consecrated to God, why do you ask me for something that you yourself can do for your mother? Indeed, your faith has already cured her." Lucy, awakening, said to her mother: "Mother, you are healed!"[2]

Lucy and her mother are shown seated on the floor of a red stone chapel, leaning back asleep against low benches built along the lateral walls. Hovering above a gilded tomb mounted on the rear wall of the chapel is the vision of Saint Agatha granted to Lucy: the virgin saint, dressed in white, stands on a cloud with four blue-clad angels. An iron tie-rod, from which are suspended seven glass oil lamps, spans the chapel walls, while a wrought-iron candelabrum stands on the chapel floor before the tomb. Votive candles burnt to various lengths are mounted on the rim of the candelabrum, undoubtedly implying the crowd of worshippers who have just left the church. Additionally, the oil lamps and candles are probably intended as a visual pun playing on the Latin root of Lucy's name: *lux*, or light.

The *Vision of Saint Lucy* was recognized in 2000 as the missing panel from a famous predella by Fra Angelico, which also included the *Apostle Saint James the Greater Freeing the Magician Hermogenes* in the Kimbell Art Museum, Fort Worth (fig. 1), the *Naming of Saint John the Baptist* in the

Museo di San Marco, Florence (fig. 2), the *Dormition of the Virgin* in the John G. Johnson Collection at the Philadelphia Museum of Art (fig. 3), and the *Meeting of Saints Dominic and Francis* in the Fine Arts Museums of San Francisco (fig. 4).[3] A proposal that the first two of these were to be joined as a pair had been advanced by Roberto Longhi in 1940, and the San Francisco panel was added to them not long afterward by John Pope-Hennessy.[4] The Philadelphia *Dormition*, though long known to scholars, was not associated with this group until 1987.[5] These four panels were exhibited together at the Metropolitan Museum of Art, New York, in 1994, and all five panels were reassembled there in 2005, together with five other panels thought to be possible fragments from the framing pinnacles of the same altarpiece.[6]

On the occasion of the 2005 exhibition in New York, the five panels of the predella were arranged, in order from left to right, beginning with the Fort Worth *Saint James*, followed by the Florence *Naming of the Baptist* and the Philadelphia *Dormition*, concluding on the right side of the altarpiece with the Feigen *Saint Lucy* and the San Francisco *Meeting of Saints Dominic and Francis*. The sequence of the first three of these is demonstrably correct, but it was pointed out by Dora Sallay (verbally) that the order of the last two panels should be inverted, and this contention—that the *Vision of Saint Lucy* stood to the right of the *Meeting of Saints Dominic and Francis*—has now been borne out by reexamination of X-radiographs showing the wood grain of the

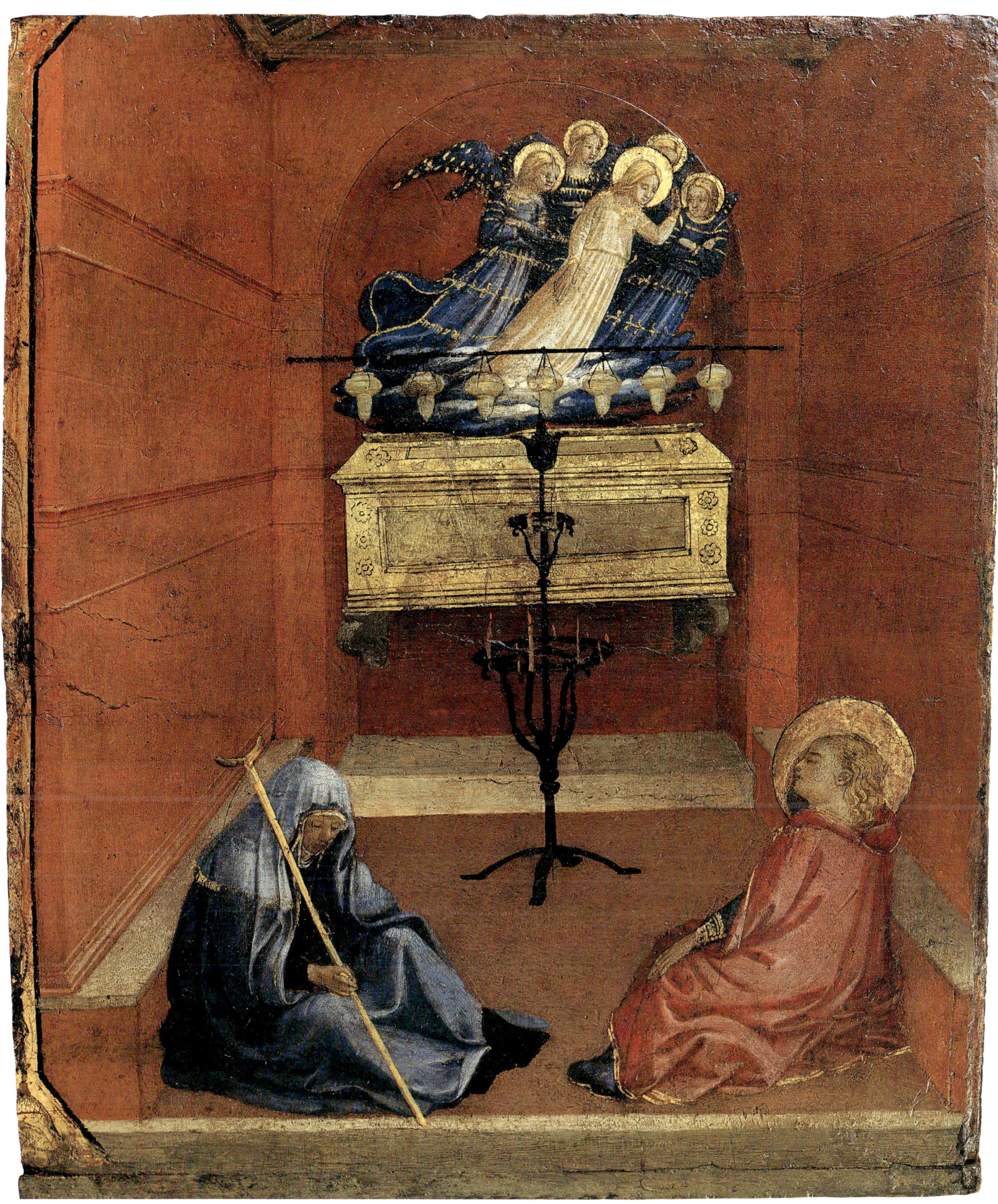

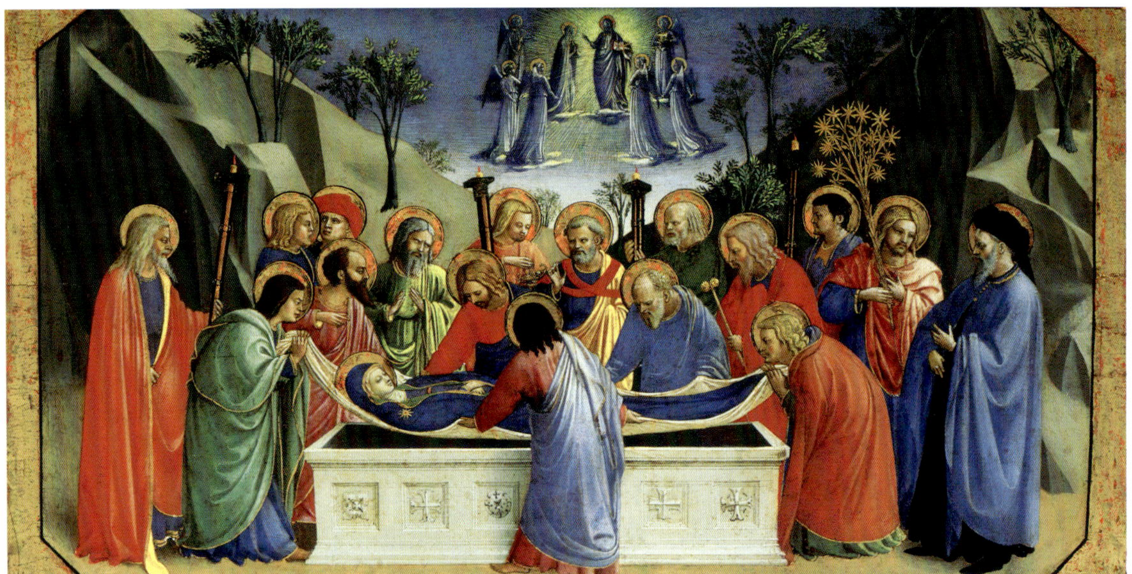

Fig. 3. Fra Angelico, *The Dormition of the Virgin*, ca. 1427–29. Tempera on panel, 26 x 52.9 cm (10¼ x 20⅞ in.). Philadelphia Museum of Art, John G. Johnson Collection, 1917

panels. Situating the Fort Worth and Feigen panels at the left and right ends, respectively, of the predella also suggests that while these two have always been presumed to have been cut along one vertical margin where they lack the gold framing band and chamfered corners that are present on all the other panels (the present left edge of the Fort Worth panel is a modern restoration), they may instead have been designed originally in this format.

X-radiographs of the panels not only confirm the sequence of their arrangement but also suggest that some not inconsiderable space originally separated the Philadelphia and San Francisco panels, and it is logical to assume that an equivalent gap also intervened between the Philadelphia and Florence panels. These spaces may have been filled by wider expanses of gilding, perhaps with superimposed coats of arms, or by projecting pilaster bases decorated either with heraldic devices or painted figures. The ends of the predella were undoubtedly closed off by projecting pilaster bases that may also have contained painted images. Proposals have been made to identify two small narrative panels in the Pinacoteca Civica at Forlì, Italy, representing the *Nativity* and the *Agony in the Garden*, and a full-length *Saint Peter Martyr* in the Royal Collection at Hampton Court, England, as possible candidates for three of these hypothetical bases, but such proposals must remain tentative as conclusive evidence is lacking.[7] Equally, the five pinnacle fragments proposed in 2005 as parts of the same altarpiece—two *Adoring Angels* in the Galleria Sabauda, Turin, Italy, the *Blessing Redeemer* in the British Royal Collection on loan to the National Gallery, London, and two *Annunciation* panels in the Detroit Institute of Arts—might well have originated from the same structure as the predella, but physical corroboration of this possibility is lacking.

Two suggestions have been advanced for identifying panels from the main tier of this altarpiece, which must be presumed to have represented (in order from left to right) Saint James, Saint John the Baptist, the Virgin (probably a Virgin and Child Enthroned), either Saint Dominic or Saint Francis, and Saint Lucy. In 1976 Miklós Boskovits attributed to Fra Angelico a full-length figure of Saint James standing in a meadow (formerly Minneapolis Museum of Art) and posited its association with the Kimbell predella panel.[8] The ex-Minneapolis *Saint James* is, judging from photographs, severely damaged and extensively repainted, so that it cannot be judged effectively on stylistic grounds. It is, furthermore, nearly twice as wide as the Kimbell predella panel, so that an arrangement incorporating both of them in a single

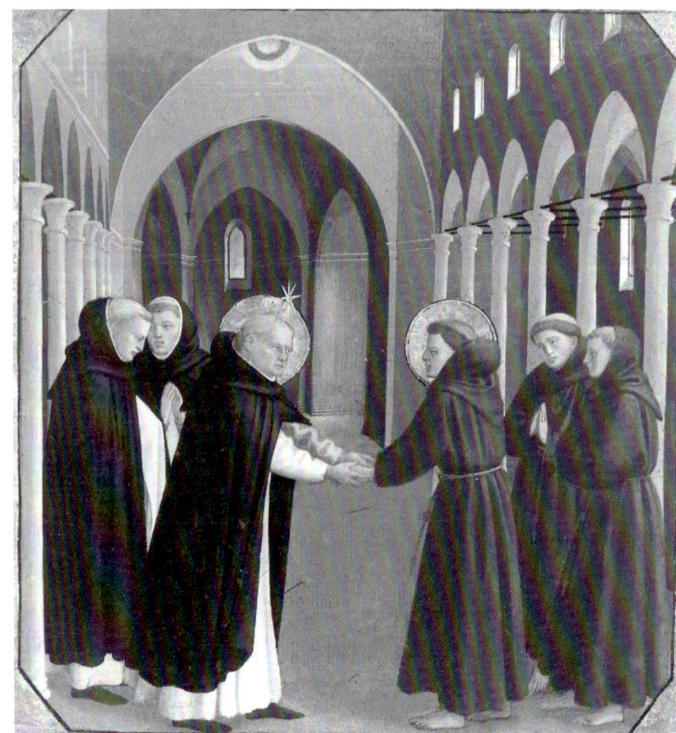

Fig. 4. Fra Angelico, *The Meeting of Saints Dominic and Francis*, ca. 1427–29. Tempera on panel, 26 x 26.7 cm (10¼ x 10½ in.). Fine Arts Museums of San Francisco, Gift of the Samuel H. Kress Foundation, inv. no. 61.44.7

structure is difficult to envision. In 2005 it was suggested, on stylistic and iconographic grounds, that a Virgin and Child Enthroned, known as the *Pontassieve Madonna*, in the Galleria degli Uffizi, Florence, might have been the central panel to this altarpiece, but the contention is erroneous. The direction of the light cast in this painting is reversed in relation to that in the five predella panels, and Alessandro Cecchi has argued, persuasively, that rather than any of the saints portrayed in the scenes of the predella, the *Pontassieve Madonna* is likely originally to have been accompanied by a figure of Saint Michael the Archangel.[9] Also erroneous is the proposal to identify a chapel "sotto le volte" in the church of Santa Croce in Florence as the original site of the altarpiece as reconstructed in 2005. Other suggestions advanced for the original provenance of the altarpiece include the church of Santa Lucia dei Magnoli in Florence, San Jacopo in Campo Corbolini in Florence, and the Dominican church of Santi Jacopo e Lucia in San Miniato al Tedesco.[10] All of these are based on iconographic considerations and cannot be verified as no secondary documentation of an altarpiece by Angelico in any of these places has yet been discovered.

Dates proposed for the individual panels of the predella have ranged widely over the course of Angelico's career, though an absolute *terminus ante quem* of 1435 is established by a dated altarpiece in Prato by Andrea di Giusto that incorporates in its predella a faithful copy of the San Marco *Naming of the Baptist*.[11] Roberto Longhi argued that the San Marco panel and the Kimbell *Saint James Freeing Hermogenes* could only have been painted by Angelico in response to direct contact with Masaccio, before 1428 (the year of Masaccio's death) therefore, and by inference before 1427, when Masaccio is presumed to have left Florence for Rome.[12] By the same argument, neither panel could predate the beginning of work in the Brancacci Chapel around 1425. No firmly dated works by Angelico in or around this period survive that can be used to anchor this contention to externally documentable factors, but it appears in substance to be correct. The present author has argued elsewhere that a date between 1427 and 1429 would most satisfactorily account for the internal development of Angelico's style in this decade.[13]   LK

1. See Staatsgalerie Stuttgart, *Frühe italienische Tafelmalerei*, exh. cat. (Stuttgart, Germany, 1950), no. 4; and George Kaftal, *Iconography of the Saints in Tuscan Painting* (Florence, 1986), col. 645.
2. Jacobus de Voragine, *The Golden Legend: Readings on the Saints*, trans. William Granger Ryan (Princeton, N.J., 1993), 1: pp. 27–28.
3. Laurence Kanter, "A Rediscovered Panel by Fra Angelico," *Paragone* 599 (2000): pp. 3–13.
4. Roberto Longhi, "Fatti di Masolino e di Masaccio," *Critica d'arte* 5 (1940): pp. 145–91; and John Pope-Hennessy, *Fra Angelico* (London, 1952), p. 170.
5. Everett Fahy, "The Kimbell Fra Angelico," *Apollo* 125 (1987): pp. 178–83.
6. Carl Brandon Strehlke, in Laurence Kanter, *Painting and Illumination in Early Renaissance Florence, 1300–1450*, exh. cat. (New York, 1994), pp. 326–32; and Laurence Kanter, in Kanter and Pia Palladino, *Fra Angelico*, exh. cat. (New York, 2005), pp. 121–32.
7. The association of the Forlì panels with those now in Fort Worth and at the Museo di San Marco was suggested by Roberto Longhi, in Longhi, "Fatti di Masolino e di Masaccio," but has been rejected by all subsequent authors. Discussion of possible additions to this predella is more fully developed in Laurence Kanter, *Reconstructing the Renaissance: "Saint James Freeing Hermogenes" by Fra Angelico* (Fort Worth, 2008), pp. 11–23, 38–48.
8. Miklós Boskovits, "Appunti sull'Angelico," *Paragone* 313 (1976): pp. 39–40.
9. Alessandro Cecchi, paper presented at the conference *Il Beato Angelico, il suo tempo, la sua eredità*, Palazzo della Cancelleria, Vatican, and University of Rome "La Sapienza," June 8–9, 2006.
10. Kanter, *Reconstructing the Renaissance*, pp. 38–56.
11. Giulio Datini, ed., *Musei di Prato* (Bologna, 1972), p. 17.
12. Longhi, "Fatti di Masolino e di Masaccio."
13. Kanter, *Reconstructing the Renaissance*, pp. 56–66.

Fra Angelico

Florence, ca. 1395–1455

23. *Saint Sixtus*, ca. 1453–54

Tempera on panel, 46.1 x 15.7 cm (18⅛ x 6¼ in.)

PROVENANCE: Alexis-François Artaud de Montor, Paris, by
1808; Georges Chalandon, Lyon, France; Mr. and Mrs. Deane
Johnson, Bel Air, Calif. (their sale, Sotheby's, London,
December 6, 1972, lot 7)

BIBLIOGRAPHY: Alexis-François Artaud de Montor, *Peintres
primitifs: Collection de tableaux rapportée d'Italie et publiée
par M. le chevalier Artaud de Montor*, 1st ed. (Paris, 1808),
no. 62; 2nd ed. (Paris, 1811), no. 85; 3rd ed. (Paris, 1843),
no. 82; August Schmarsow, "Maîtres italiens dans la collection A. de Montor," *Gazette des beaux-arts*, ser. 3, no. 20
(1898): p. 495; John Pope-Hennessy, *Fra Angelico*, 2nd ed.
(London, 1974), pp. 37, 218–19; Miklós Boskovits, "Appunti
sull'Angelico," *Paragone* 313 (1976): pp. 43, 45, 53nn.28, 32;
John T. Spike, *Fra Angelico* (New York, 1996), p. 195; Giorgio
Bonsanti, *Beato Angelico: Catalogo completo* (Florence, 1998),
p. 146; Carl Brandon Strehlke, *Angelico* (Milan, 1998), p. 51;
Gerardo De Simone, "L'ultimo Angelico: Le *Meditationes* del
cardinal Torquemada e il ciclo perduto nel chiostro di S. Maria
sopra Minerva," in *Ricerche di storia dell'arte 76, Presenze
cancellate: Capolavori perduti della pittura romana di metà
'400* (2002): pp. 59, 62; Pia Palladino, in Laurence Kanter and
Palladino, *Fra Angelico*, exh. cat. (New York, 2005), pp. 224–
25nn.3–5; Laurence Kanter, *Reconstructing the Renaissance:
"Saint James Freeing Hermogenes" by Fra Angelico* (Fort
Worth, 2008), p. 4; Gerardo De Simone, "Velut alter Apelles:
Il decennio romano del Beato Angelico," in *Beato Angelico:
L'alba del Rinascimento*, exh. cat. (Rome, 2009), pp. 139, 141

CONDITION: The panel support, of a vertical wood grain,
has been cropped on all four sides but is not thinned; its outer
edges have been gessoed and painted ochre. The paint surface,
other than losses along the bottom edge, is nearly perfectly
preserved and has suffered only mild abrasion, noticeable
especially in the loss of some of the mordant gilt decoration on
the left side of the saint's robe. The back of the panel has been
painted black with a thin, wood-colored stripe running its full
height along the center, perhaps meant to represent the shaft
of the Cross, the arms of which may have been cropped with
the loss of the demilunette at the panel's top. In the lower left
corner are painted the arms of Cardinal Juan de Torquemada.
In the lower right corner is the inventory number "H-7" in
black paint on the exposed wood of the panel.

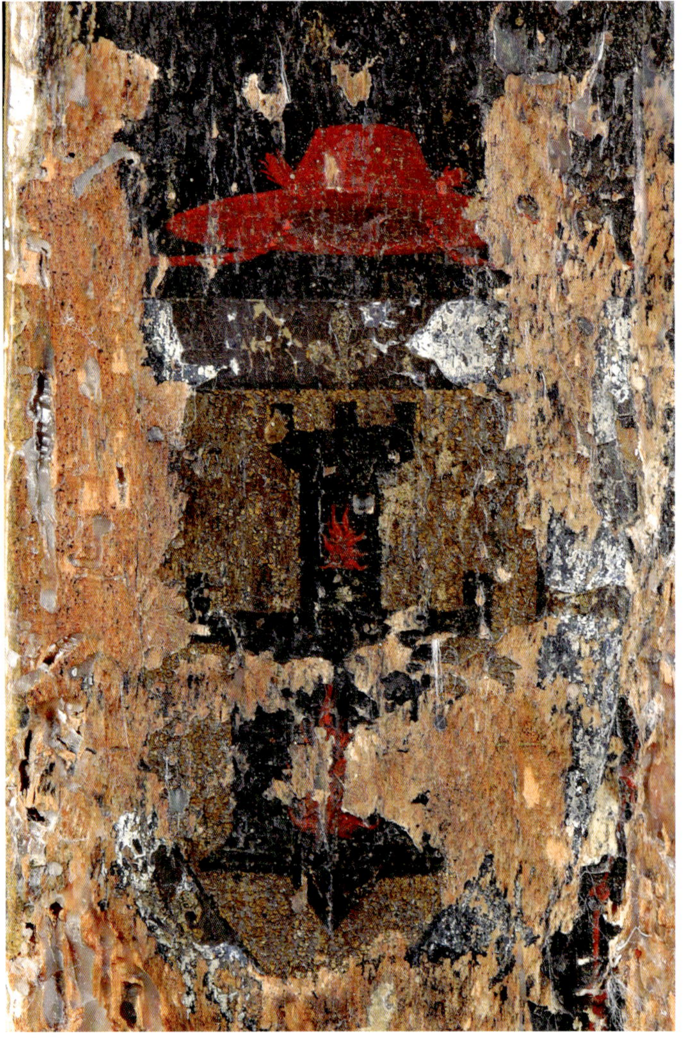

23 Detail of reverse

*S*aint Sixtus, then thought to be a portrayal of Saint Peter
as pope, was first recognized as the work of Fra Angelico
by Roberto Longhi, who assigned it to the artist's early maturity, between 1430 and 1435.[1] This dating was disputed by
John Pope-Hennessy, who related the panel to a *Crucifixion
with the Virgin, Saint John, and Cardinal Juan de Torquemada
as Donor* in the Fogg Art Museum, Cambridge, Massachusetts
(fig. 1), largely on the basis of the similar tooled decoration of
their gold grounds.[2] Pope-Hennessy considered both paintings
to be late works by Angelico, executed around the time of the
artist's second Roman sojourn in 1452 and the coincident inter-
ruption of work on the Silver Chest panels from Santissima
Annunziata in Florence. Reconstructing the probable original
height of the *Saint Sixtus*, Pope-Hennessy further proposed
that it once formed the wing of a triptych with the Fogg
Crucifixion, a suggestion that has been accepted in all the
subsequent literature and that can now be demonstrated
unequivocally with the recovery during cleaning of Cardinal
Torquemada's coat of arms on the reverse of the *Saint Sixtus*.[3]

While the association of these two paintings in a single
complex has not been, and is not to be, doubted, several
hypotheses regarding their dating have been put forward.
Miklós Boskovits—who first inferred the identity of the
papal saint not as Peter but as Sixtus II by correctly reading

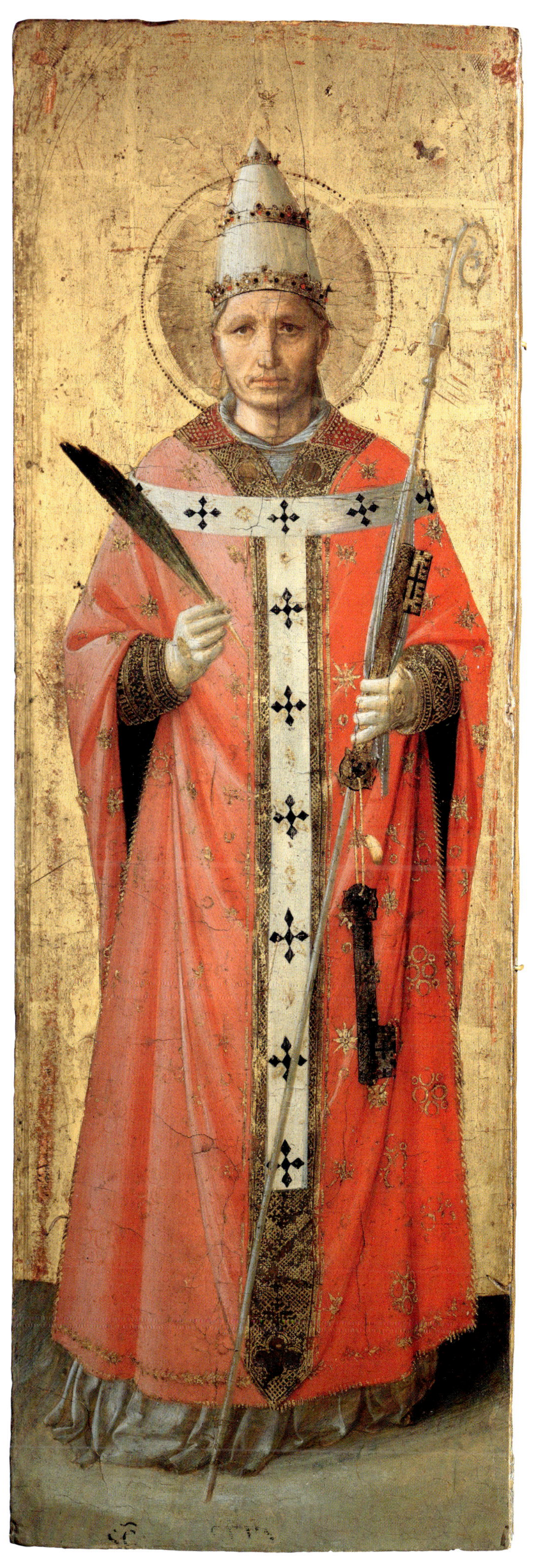

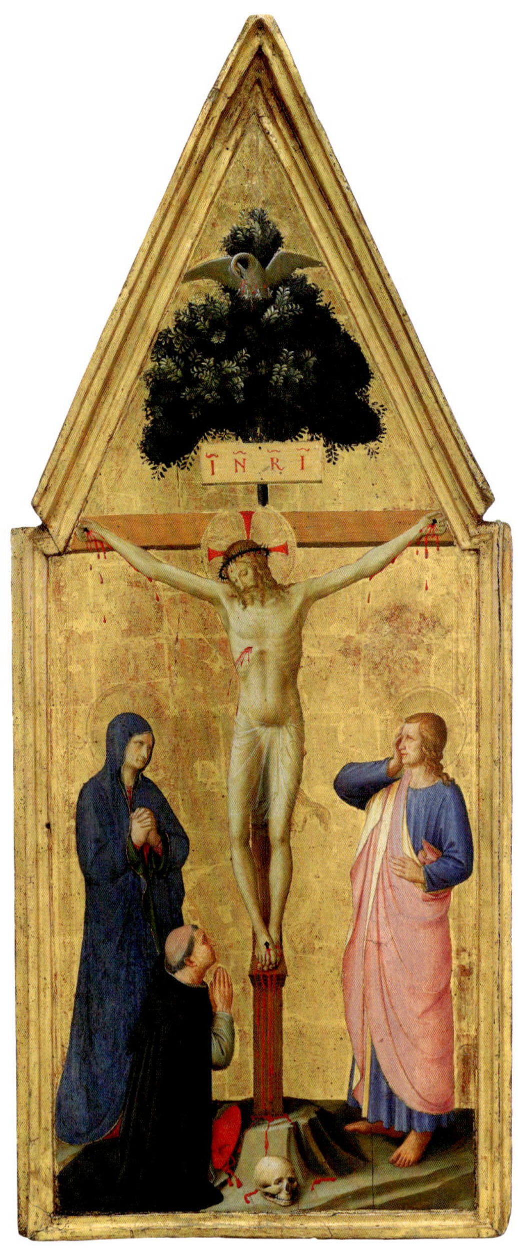

Fig. 1. Fra Angelico, *Crucifixion with the Virgin, Saint John, and Cardinal Juan de Torquemada as Donor*, ca. 1454–55. Tempera on panel, 96.6 x 42.5 cm (38 x 16¾ in.). Harvard University Art Museums, Fogg Art Museum, Cambridge, Mass., Hervey E. Wetzel Bequest Fund, inv. no. 1921.34

the fragmentary inscription at his feet as SC [. . .]STVS rather than SC [. . .]TRVS—suggested the possibility of interpreting the saint's features as a portrait of Pope Eugenius IV, and therefore of dating the work prior to the death of the pontiff in February 1447.[4] John Spike, Giorgio Bonsanti, Carl Strehlke, and Gerardo De Simone concur with this argument, placing the triptych within Angelico's first Roman sojourn as a work of either late 1445 or 1446.[5] Diane Cole Ahl, instead, contending that Torquemada and Eugenius were closely associated from at least 1439 in Florence, when the former was elevated by the pope to the dignity of Cardinal

(titular of San Sisto [i.e., Saint Sixtus]), advanced this date to 1441 or 1442, the period of work on the San Marco frescoes, based on suppositious resemblances to the various scenes of the Crucifixion there.[6] Comparisons between the San Marco frescoes and the Fogg *Crucifixion* are, however, generic and exclusively iconographic, and do not provide a sound basis for dating the latter.

Circumscribing a possible range of dates for the execution of the triptych based primarily on the details of the donor's biography is of relatively limited value in the present case. Juan de Torquemada was first summoned to the papal court in 1435 as theological advisor (Master of the Sacred Palace) to Eugenius, and so the commission for the Fogg triptych could theoretically date anytime between then (allowing for updating with the addition of a cardinal's beretta not earlier than 1439) and Angelico's death in 1455: two decades that comprise nearly the entirety of the painter's documented mature career. In addition, Pia Palladino has correctly observed that it is not possible to demonstrate that the image of Saint Sixtus was intended to be understood as a portrait or crypto-portrait of Pope Eugenius IV and that stylistic evidence contradicts the assertion.[7] Following Pope-Hennessy, she argues persuasively that the only acceptable date for this work is coincident with or following the Annunziata Silver Chest of ca. 1452, when Angelico had adopted the more attenuated figural canon, more nuanced realism of descriptive detail, and more subtle diffusion of color for atmospheric effects characteristic of both the Fogg and Feigen panels. According to William Hood, "There can be little doubt . . . that Fra Angelico painted this panel . . . while both [he and Torquemada] were in residence at Santa Maria sopra Minerva in Rome in the early 1450s."[8] As a probable work of 1453 or 1454, the Fogg *Crucifixion* and Feigen *Saint Sixtus* must be considered among the latest surviving paintings by Fra Angelico, the final expressions of his unique pictorial genius.

LK

1. Roberto Longhi, undated opinion, cited in Sotheby's, London, sale cat. (December 6, 1972), p. 8.
2. John Pope-Hennessy, *Fra Angelico*, 2nd ed. (London, 1974), pp. 37, 218–19.
3. The suggestion (made by Umbreto Baldini, *L'opera completa dell'Angelico* [Milan, 1970], p. 109) that "L'identificazione dell'effigie del committente non è del tutto accertata" is to be rejected. Torquemada was the only Dominican cardinal in the Curia at this date.
4. Miklós Boskovits, "Appunti sull'Angelico," *Paragone* 313 (1976): pp. 43, 45, 53nn.28, 32.
5. See John T. Spike, *Fra Angelico* (New York, 1996), p. 195; Giorgio Bonsanti, *Beato Angelico: Catalogo completo* (Florence, 1998), p. 146; Carl Brandon Strehlke, *Angelico* (Milan, 1998), p. 51; and Gerardo De Simone, "L'ultimo Angelico: Le *Meditationes* del cardinal Torquemada e il ciclo perduto nel chiostro di S. Maria sopra Minerva," in *Ricerche di storia dell'arte 76, Presenze cancellate: Capolavori perduti della pittura romana di metà '400* (2002): pp. 59, 62.
6. Diane Cole Ahl, *Fra Angelico* (London, 2008), p. 176.
7. Pia Palladino, in Laurence Kanter and Palladino, *Fra Angelico*, exh. cat. (New York, 2005), pp. 224–25nn.3–5.
8. William Hood, *Fra Angelico at San Marco* (New Haven, Conn., 1993), p. 173.

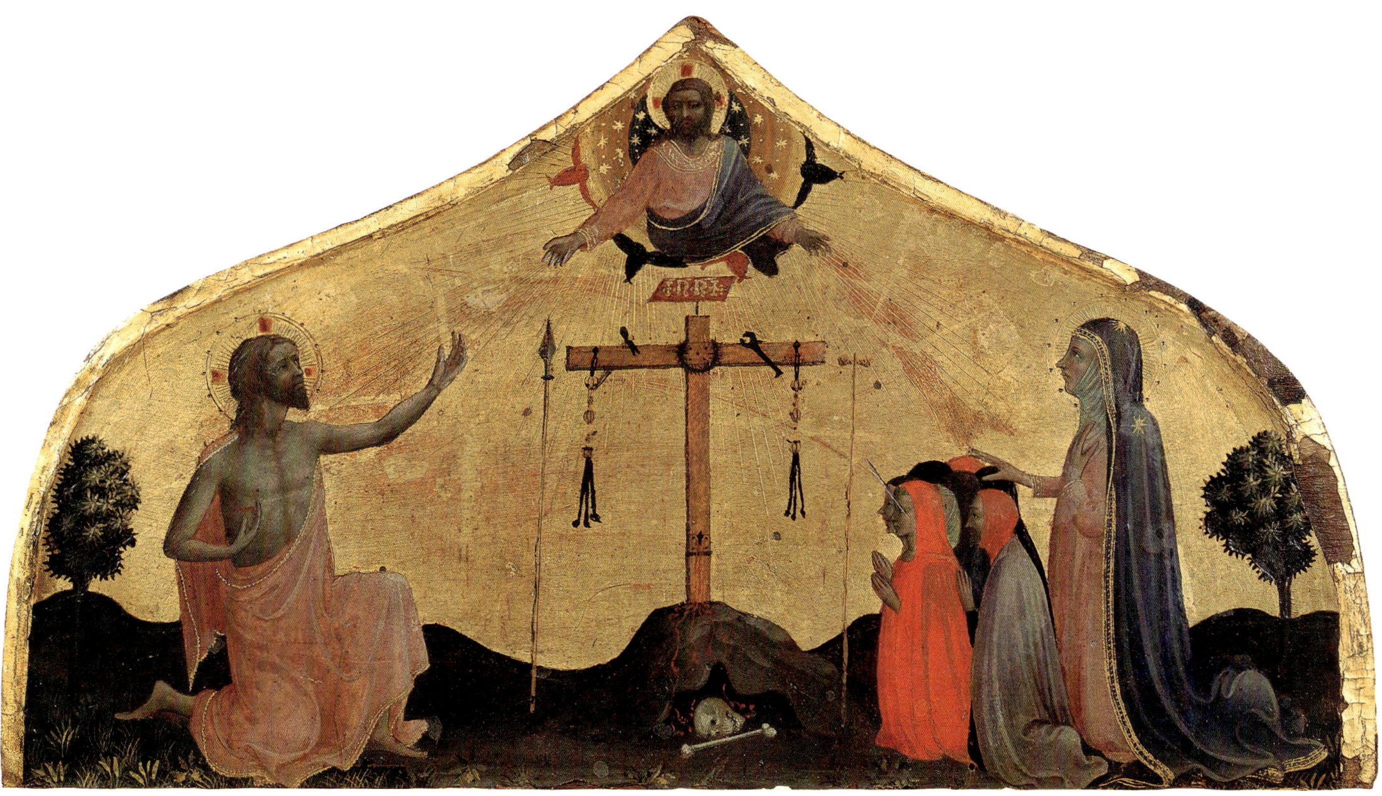

Master of the Sherman Predella

Florence, active 1430s

24. *The Intercession of Christ and the Virgin*, ca. 1435–38

Tempera on panel, 22.5 x 40.5 cm (8⅞ x 16 in.), overall; 21.6 x 38.8 cm (8½ x 15½ in.), picture surface

PROVENANCE: private collection, Florence, by 1948; Ernst Renan, Paris (his sale, Drouot Montaigne, Paris, May 31, 1988, lot 39)

BIBLIOGRAPHY: Roberto Longhi, "'Me pinxit': Il Maestro della Predella Sherman," *Proporzioni* 2 (1948): pp. 161–62; Roberto Longhi, "Un nuovo numero del 'Maestro della Predella Sherman,'" *Paragone* 211 (1967): p. 39; Frederico Zeri and Elizabeth E. Gardner, *Italian Paintings: A Catalogue of the Collection of the Metropolitan Museum of Art*, vol. 1, *Florentine School* (New York, 1971), p. 58n.2; Angelo Tartuferi, in *Miniatura del '400 a San Marco: Dalle suggestioni Avignonesi all'ambiente dell'Angelico*, ed. Magnolia Scudieri and Giovanna Rosario, exh. cat. (Florence, 2003), p. 81; Laurence Kanter, in Kanter and Pia Palladino, *Fra Angelico*, exh. cat. (New York, 2005), pp. 298–99; Luciano Bellosi, in *Lorenzo Monaco: A Bridge from Giotto's Heritage to the Renaissance*, ed. Angelo Tartuferi and Daniela Parenti, exh. cat. (Florence, 2006), p. 162; Keith Christiansen, in *Gentile da Fabriano and the Other Renaissance*, ed. Laura Laureati and Lorenza Mochi Onori, exh. cat. (Milan, 2006), pp. 286–87

CONDITION: The panel, of a horizontal wood grain, retains its original thickness of 34 mm. The top, bottom, and right edges are apparently original; the left edge seems to be trimmed slightly. Narrow engaged moldings around the upper edges have been removed and replaced by modern gesso and gilding. The gold ground is lightly worn, but the paint surface has suffered only scattered pinpoint flaking losses and incidental scratches.

The *Intercession of Christ and the Virgin* is the first, and smallest, of a series of fifteenth-century replicas of an altarpiece originally mounted, sometime before 1409, on the inner façade of Florence Cathedral and now in the Cloisters Collection at the Metropolitan Museum of Art, New York (fig. 1).[1] The altarpiece, unusual for the period in having been painted on canvas rather than panel, is a work by Lorenzo Monaco of the 1390s.[2] Its distinctive content is derived from a twelfth-century text composed by Ernaldus of Chartres, but believed in the fourteenth and fifteenth centuries to have been written by Saint Bernard of Clairvaux: "O man, you have a secure access to God when the Mother is before her Son, and the Son before His Father. The Mother showed

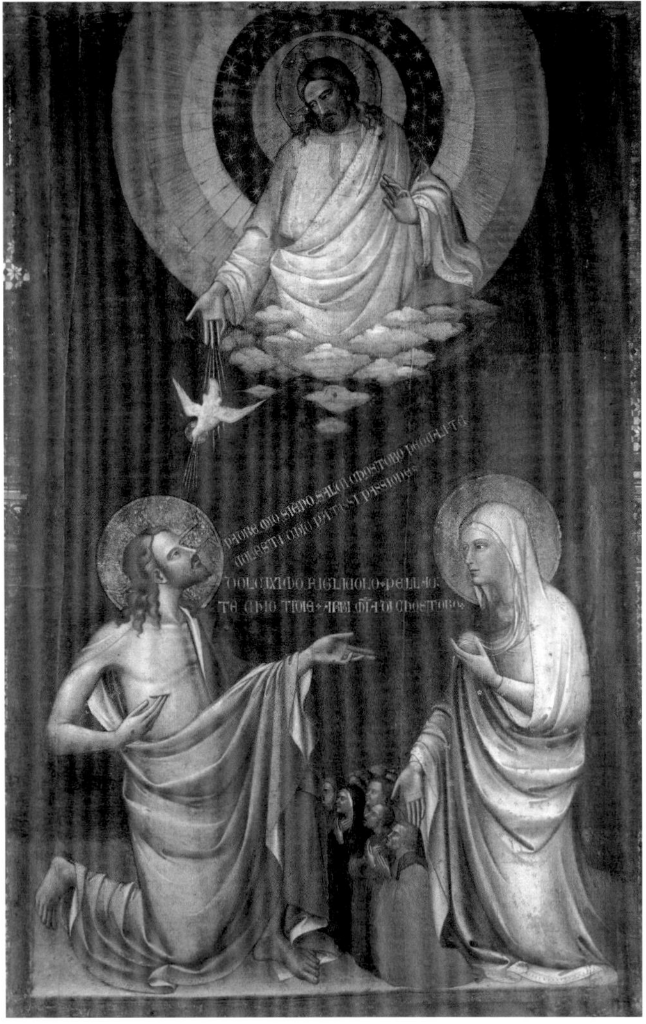

Fig. 1. Lorenzo Monaco, *The Intercession of Christ and the Virgin*, ca. 1395. Tempera on canvas, 239.4 x 153 cm (94¼ x 60¼ in.). Metropolitan Museum of Art, New York, Cloisters Collection, 1953, inv. no. 53.27

her breast to the Son, the Son showed His wounds to His Father. There where the proofs of love are so many no one can be denied." This text was widely disseminated as chapter 39 of the popular devotional treatise *Speculum humanae salvationis* (Mirror of Human Salvation). Lorenzo Monaco interpreted (or was instructed to interpret) the imagery of this text literally, providing inscriptions on his painting elucidating its meaning. The Virgin, baring her breast with her left hand and with her right hand indicating a group of supplicants, says, "Dearest Son, have mercy on them for the milk that I gave you." Christ, receiving His mother's message with His left hand and touching the wound in His side with His right hand, looks upward as He says, "My Father, let them be saved for whom you wished that I suffer the Passion." God the Father, appearing within the starred and gilt circles of Heaven at the top of the painting, returns the Dove of the Holy Spirit to Christ, completing the three-fold nature of the Trinity. These gestures, although not the inscriptions, have been retained almost exactly by the artist of the Feigen panel. Here, the Virgin reaches modestly toward her chest rather than baring her breast, and looks upward beseechingly

toward God the Father rather than across to her Son. Christ gestures upward and to His wound, as in the altarpiece, and God the Father shares His blessing with both Christ and the Virgin. Introduced into the center of the composition are the Arma Christi: the instruments of Christ's sacrifice atop an emblematic hill of Golgotha.

The *Intercession of Christ and the Virgin* now in the Feigen collection was first published by Roberto Longhi with an attribution to a painter who had been isolated and identified only a few years earlier by John Pope-Hennessy: the Master of the Sherman Predella.[3] Named after a painting in the Museum of Fine Arts, Boston, that had widely been considered a work by the Sienese master Sassetta, Pope-Hennessy emphasized the artist's exclusive dependence on the mature style of Fra Angelico, asserting that the painter must have been Florentine and active in the 1430s and 1440s. Longhi agreed that the artistic roots of the Master of the Sherman Predella were Florentine rather than Sienese, but averred that the Gothicizing archaisms of his style were not indications of a minor talent, as Pope-Hennessy had contended. He traced them instead to the influence of Lorenzo Monaco rather than Fra Angelico, moving the period of his activity back to the decade of the 1420s and claiming for him a historical stature comparable to that of Masolino. Although Longhi's vision of the artist as a progressive rather than derivative talent has gained fairly wide acceptance, it is difficult to see more than generic connections between his work and that of Lorenzo Monaco or other painters active in the first three decades of the fifteenth century. It is specifically with Fra Angelico's paintings of the early 1430s, and with Zanobi Strozzi's parallel efforts in the same years, that the *Intercession of Christ and the Virgin*, as well as the small number of other panels attributed to the Master of the Sherman Predella, evinces the most striking similarities, and it is no doubt to the later part of that decade that all these works are to be dated. A tentative proposal to attribute two frescoes in the Orange Cloister at the Badia Fiorentina to the Master of the Sherman Predella—and possibly thereby to uncover the artist's identity—has not met with critical approval but nonetheless seems possible.[4]

The shape and size of the *Intercession of Christ and the Virgin* suggest that it originally served as the pinnacle of a small devotional tabernacle, a parallel for the form of which is provided by a *Virgin and Child* by the Master of the Judgment of Paris (Giuliano d'Arrigo) in the Fogg Art Museum, Cambridge, Massachusetts. As the wood grain of the *Intercession* is horizontal, it is likely that it was glued onto the front of the main panel of the tabernacle and projected forward from the painted surface of the image below it. Such a structure implies that the tabernacle was a triptych whose wings folded flush below this panel, leaving the image of the *Intercession* exposed when the triptych was closed, although the thickness of the panel is exceptional for a tympanum in such circumstances, being two or three times that normally encountered in movable triptych shutters on this scale. As no further panels or fragments have yet been identified that might have completed such a triptych, the possibility must also be entertained that the panel served as the framing tympanum of a relief sculpture in stucco, terracotta, or marble. This might also explain the absence of an engaged molding along the bottom of the composition and the undistressed surface of the bottom edge of the panel. LK

1. Millard Meiss, "An Early Altarpiece from the Cathedral of Florence," *Metropolitan Museum of Art Bulletin*, n.s. 12, no. 10 (1954): pp. 302–12; and Charlotte Hale, "The Technique and Materials of the 'Intercession of Christ and the Virgin,' Attributed to Lorenzo Monaco," in *The Fabric of Images: European Paintings on Textile Supports in the Fourteenth and Fifteenth Centuries*, ed. Caroline Villers (London, 2000), pp. 31–41.

2. This (correct) attribution was first advanced by Everett Fahy, in Katharine Baetjer, *European Paintings in the Metropolitan Museum of Art, by Artists Born in or before 1865: A Summary Catalogue* (New York, 1995), 1: p. 13. Previously, the painting had been ascribed to Niccolò di Pietro Gerini, Mariotto di Nardo, Lorenzo di Niccolò, and Tommaso del Mazza; see Simona Pasquinucci and Barbara Deimling, *Tradition and Innovation in Florentine Trecento Painting: Giovanni Bonsi, Tommaso del Mazza*, A Critical and Historical Corpus of Florentine Painting, ed. Miklós Boskovits, sec. 4, vol. 8 (Florence, 2000), pp. 352–63, with full bibliography. Most recently, Lorenzo Monaco's authorship has been supported by Luciano Bellosi (in *Lorenzo Monaco: A Bridge from Giotto's Heritage to the Renaissance*, ed. Angelo Tartuferi and Daniela Parenti, exh. cat. [Florence, 2006], pp. 160–63) with a date of ca. 1400.

3. John Pope-Hennessy, *Sassetta* (London, 1939), p. 184.

4. Laurence Kanter, in Kanter and Pia Palladino, *Fra Angelico*, exh. cat. (New York, 2005), pp. 294–96.

Battista di Biagio Sanguigni

Florence, 1393–1451

25. *The Virgin of Humility*, ca. 1440

Tempera on panel, 77.5 x 44.5 cm (30½ x 17½ in.), overall; 77.5 x 41 cm (30½ x 16⅛ in.), picture surface

PROVENANCE: M. Conde, Château Biarge, Charente, France, by 1928;[1] Christie's, New York, May 25, 1999, lot 129

BIBLIOGRAPHY: Raimond van Marle, *The Development of the Italian Schools of Painting*, vol. 10 (The Hague, 1928), p. 190; Miklós Boskovits, "Ancora sul Maestro del 1419," *Arte cristiana* 90, no. 812 (2002): p. 340; Laurence Kanter, "Zanobi Strozzi miniatore and Battista di Biagio Sanguigni," *Arte cristiana* 90, no. 812 (2002): pp. 329, 331n.22; Laurence Kanter, in Kanter and Pia Palladino, *Fra Angelico*, exh. cat. (New York, 2005), pp. 240–41

CONDITION: The panel, approximately 1.8 cm thick, has been extended at the top by 6 cm and built into a modern engaged frame; the overall dimensions reported above do not include these additions and do not account for as much as 2 cm of original panel that may be covered by the frame at the bottom. A prominent vertical split runs the full height of the panel through the Christ Child's face but has resulted in only modest paint loss and repair. The paint surface is lightly and evenly abraded. The brown background is modern, and some of the engraving along the edges of the cloth of honor has been reworked to complete its extension beyond the profile of the original ogival arch of the picture field.

The original attribution of this painting, by Bernard Berenson and Raimond van Marle, to Domenico di Michelino was based on the assumption that he was the artist responsible for all or most of the paintings now recognized to be works by Zanobi Strozzi.[2] Everett Fahy correctly noted that this painting is among those mistakenly assigned to Domenico di Michelino rather than Strozzi, while Miklós Boskovits suggested that its damaged and repainted condition could permit the possibility of considering it instead to be an early work by Fra Angelico himself rather than by any minor artist in his entourage.[3] The painting, however, is neither considerably damaged nor repainted, and the attribution to Battista di Biagio Sanguigni proposed for it by the present author should be sustained.[4] While the drapery forms and the figure types and proportions are strongly reminiscent of those employed by Zanobi Strozzi in his numerous versions of the same subject, especially his *Virgin and Child Enthroned* in the Hermitage, Saint Petersburg, they are much more linear in their handling in the Feigen painting, less fleshy and less fully modeled, than in any work by that artist. They correspond in these particulars to the handling of Battista Sanguigni, and particularly to his documented work in the San Gaggio hymnal (Museo di San Marco, Florence, no. 10074, especially folio 143r) and his putative additions to Zanobi Strozzi's work in the marginal decorations of Corale 3 from Santa Maria degli Angeli, now in the Biblioteca Laurenziana, Florence.[5]

The personality of Battista Sanguigni, both as a panel painter and as a miniaturist, remains poorly defined despite the survival of an unusually large number of documents referring to him. It is probable that a significant portion and perhaps the majority of his paintings in any medium were executed in collaboration with other masters, primarily with Fra Angelico and with Zanobi Strozzi, and in this regard the alternative attributions to these painters proposed for the Feigen *Virgin of Humility* must be considered more carefully than might otherwise have been the case. The composition of the painting, for example, is loosely derived from the center panel of Angelico's Perugia altarpiece of 1437 and the slightly later triptych in Cortona executed in his studio, and it recalls the arrangement of figures in several domestic-scale works by Angelico, such as Madonnas now in the Gemäldegalerie, Berlin, and the Vatican Pinacoteca. While on the one hand this may suggest a *terminus post quem* of the late 1430s for the Feigen *Virgin*, it must also raise the question of whether the painting was conceived independently by Sanguigni in imitation of Angelico's example, or whether it might have been commissioned from Angelico himself and delegated to Sanguigni as executant of a general idea originating from the Dominican master. Even more compelling is the possibility that Zanobi Strozzi should be considered as the designer of the Feigen *Virgin* and perhaps a collaborator in its execution. While his own examples of the Madonna of Humility are equally influenced by Fra Angelico, if notably less statuesque and at the same time more freely inventive or even eccentric, the few known images of the Madonna Enthroned from his early career closely parallel the composition and handling of the Feigen painting. In either event, it is necessary to conclude that the Feigen painting dates only very shortly after Angelico's Guidalotti altarpiece of 1437, perhaps still during the period (until 1438) in which Strozzi and Sanguigni were living together at San Domenico, Fiesole. Almost certainly it was conceived and painted before the final dissolution of the studio relationships at San Domenico around 1445, when Angelico moved to Rome and Strozzi to Florence, while Sanguigni remained in Fiesole.

It is difficult to ascertain the original format and function of the Feigen *Virgin of Humility*, due to the repainting of its top edges outside the profile of the cloth of honor and the masking of its outer edges by the modern frame engaged to it. Its size and proportions are typical of the center panel of an altarpiece, while its subject is more commonly encountered in independent tabernacles. No related panels that might have stood alongside it in an altarpiece have yet been identified, although this consideration alone is not sufficient to discount the possibility that this was its original context. The portrayal of the Christ Child standing on His mother's right knee—the left side of the composition relative to the viewer—is unusual.

LK

1. This provenance is reported by Raimond van Marle. On the reverse of a photograph of the painting at Villa I Tatti, Bernard Berenson annotated that he received the image in 1923 from Wildenstein. According to the files at Wildenstein & Co., New York, the firm never owned the painting but had been considering its acquisition.
2. Berenson's publication of this thesis dates to 1932 (see "Quadri senza casa—Il quattrocento fiorentino, 1," *Dedalo* 12 [1932]: pp. 512–41), but his formulation clearly preceded this and must be the basis for van Marle's listing of works by Domenico di Michelino in 1928. The photograph of the Château Biarge painting at I Tatti is filed under Domenico di Michelino. Licia Collobi-Ragghianti, "Domenico di Michelino," *Critica d'arte* 8 (1950): pp. 363–78; "Zanobi Strozzi pittore," pts. 1–2, *Critica d'arte*, ser. 3, vol. 8 (1950): pp. 454–73; and ser. 3, vol. 9 (1950): pp. 17–27; and Mario Salmi, "Problemi dell'Angelico," *Commentari* 1 (1950): pp. 75–81, 146–56, first clarified the distinction between the two artists.
3. Everett Fahy, in Christie's, New York, sale cat. (May 25, 1999), p. 143; and Miklós Boskovits, "Ancora sul Maestro del 1419," *Arte cristiana* 90, no. 812 (2002): p. 340.
4. Laurence Kanter, "Zanobi Strozzi miniatore and Battista di Biagio Sanguigni," *Arte cristiana* 90, no. 812 (2002): pp. 329, 331n.22; and Laurence Kanter, in Kanter and Pia Palladino, *Fra Angelico* (New York, 2005), pp. 240–41.
5. Kanter, in Kanter and Palladino, *Fra Angelico*, pp. 240–41. The attribution to Sanguigni of two panel paintings included in the 2005 Fra Angelico exhibition in New York—a *Resurrection* from the Musée du Louvre, Paris, and a triptych in the Christ Church Picture Gallery, Oxford—is to be rejected, as is any relation of these two paintings to each other, but the other contentions advanced there still appear to be valid. For the San Gaggio hymnal, see Magnolia Scudieri and Sara Giacomelli, *Fra Giovanni Angelico: Pittore minatore o miniatore pittore?*, exh. cat. (Florence, 2007), pp. 117–19.

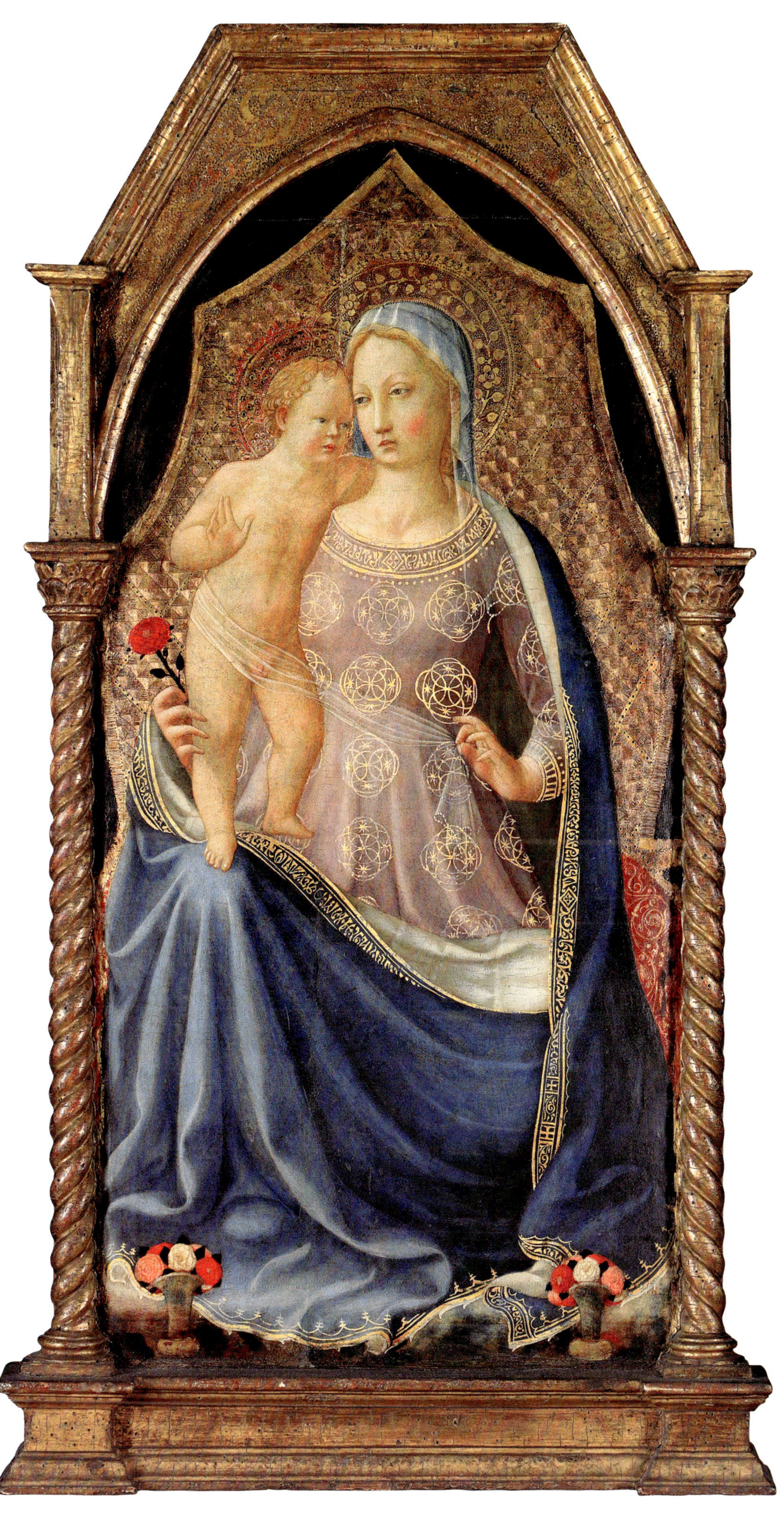

Benozzo di Lese di Sandro, called Benozzo Gozzoli

Florence, 1420/21–1497

26. *The Crucifixion with Saints Jerome and Dominic*, ca. 1448–49

Tempera on panel, 34.9 x 21.7 cm (13¾ x 8½ in.), overall;
30.4 x 17.6 cm (12 x 6⅞ in.), picture surface

PROVENANCE: William Drury-Lowe (1803–1877), Locko
Park, Derbyshire, England, acquired in Italy, 1862–65;
William Drury Nathaniel Drury-Lowe (d. 1906), Locko Park,
Derbyshire; William Drury-Lowe (d. 1916), Locko Park,
Derbyshire; J. A. E. Drury-Lowe, Locko Park, Derbyshire;
Lieut.-Col. J. Packe-Drury-Lowe, Locko Park, Derbyshire;
Capt. P. J. B. Drury-Lowe, Locko Park, Derbyshire (his sale,
Sotheby's, London, November 25, 1970, lot 11; Sotheby's,
London, July 2, 1986, lot 101)

BIBLIOGRAPHY: Bernard Berenson, *Florentine Painters
of the Renaissance*, 2nd ed. (London, 1900), p. 106; 3rd ed.
(London, 1909), p. 114; Jean Paul Richter, *Catalogue of the
Pictures at Locko Park* (London, 1901), p. 29; Adolfo Venturi,
Storia dell'arte italiana, vol. 7, *La pittura del quattrocento*,
pt. 1 (Milan, 1911), p. 430; Raimond van Marle, *The Develop-
ment of the Italian Schools of Painting*, vol. 11 (The Hague,
1929), pp. 142–43; G. J. Hoogewerff, *Benozzo Gozzoli* (Paris,
1930), p. 92; Bernard Berenson, *Italian Pictures of the Renais-
sance* (Oxford, 1932), p. 96; Birmingham City Museum and
Art Gallery, *Works of Art from Midland Houses*, exh. cat.
(Birmingham, England, 1953), no. 161; Bernard Berenson,
*Italian Pictures of the Renaissance: A List of the Principal
Artists and Their Works with an Index of Places: Florentine
School* (London, 1963), 1: p. 94; Alastair Smart, *Pictures
from Locko Park, Derbyshire*, exh. cat. (Nottingham, Eng-
land, 1968), no. 7; Luisa Vertova, "La raccolta di Locko Park,"
Antichità viva 7, no. 3 (1968): p. 23; Anna Padoa Rizzo,
Benozzo Gozzoli: Pittore fiorentino (Florence, 1972), p. 137;
Matthiesen Fine Art Ltd., *Early Italian Paintings and Works
of Art, 1300–1480*, exh. cat. (London, 1983), no. 31; Anna
Padoa Rizzo, *Benozzo Gozzoli: Catalogo completo dei dipinti*
(Florence, 1992), p. 81; Cristina Acidini Luchinat, *Benozzo
Gozzoli* (Milan, 1993), p. 41; Diane Cole Ahl, *Benozzo Gozzoli*
(New Haven, Conn., 1996), p. 223; Miklós Boskovits, *Italian
Paintings of the Fifteenth Century: The Collections of the
National Gallery of Art* (Washington, D.C., 2003), p. 345n.14;
Pia Palladino, in Laurence Kanter and Palladino, *Fra Angelico*,
exh. cat. (New York, 2005), pp. 304–6

CONDITION: The panel, of a vertical wood grain, has been
thinned to 1 cm but is not cradled. Two horizontal battens
have been inlaid in the back of the panel. Nail holes and miter
cuts from the attachment of the original engaged frame are
apparent along the margin and at the corners of the panel,
and the paint surface preserves its original barb along all four
sides. The painting has been lightly abraded throughout, but
losses are minor, and retouching is restricted to the area of
Christ's left arm and Saint Dominic's halo.

The Locko Park/Feigen *Crucifixion with Saints Jerome and
Dominic* has been well known as a work by Benozzo
Gozzoli for over a century, since it was first published under
that name by Bernard Berenson and Jean Paul Richter.[1] Although it is occasionally discussed as if it were a fragment
of a predella, it was correctly characterized by Diane Cole
Ahl, Miklós Boskovits, and Pia Palladino as an independent
devotional panel.[2] Cole Ahl suggested that the presence of
Saints Dominic and Jerome kneeling at the foot of the Cross
might imply an association with the Confraternity of the
Purification: both these saints appear in an altarpiece commissioned from Benozzo Gozzoli in 1461 by the members of
that confraternity for its chapel in the church of San Marco
in Florence. Palladino instead suggested a connection with
the Confraternity of Saint Jerome, which was established in
Fiesole in 1410 and was closely associated with the Dominican observant convent of San Domenico before moving to
the hospital of San Matteo in Florence, opposite the church of
San Marco. While it is possible that the substitution of these
two saints for figures of the Virgin and Saint John the Evangelist, more usually encountered in paintings of this subject
and format, is of strictly onomastic significance—referring to
the name saints of the painting's original owner—it is more
likely that they imply a devotional preference of the patron
and that one of the two confraternal suggestions mentioned
above is correct. A consideration of the painting's probable
date may make the second of these possibilities more likely.

Dates proposed for the Locko Park/Feigen *Crucifixion* have
ranged fairly widely over the first half of Benozzo Gozzoli's
career. Berenson indicated generically his opinion that it was
an early work; Raimond van Marle specified the Montefalco
period between 1453 and 1458; while Anna Padoa Rizzo suggested that it could be as late as 1466–67, when the artist was
active in San Gimignano.[3] Perhaps influenced by the evident
substitution of a view of Florence and the Arno valley behind
the Crucified Christ, in place of an idealized cityscape symbolizing Jerusalem, a majority of scholars believe the painting
to have been executed during Gozzoli's Florentine sojourn
between 1459 and 1463/64. Palladino, however, has correctly
observed that the painting, although in excellent condition,
lacks the incisive, linear forms and enamel-like surfaces of
works, both large and small scale, from this period, whereas
the soft modeling of the figures, the naturalistic atmospheric
effects, and the subdued palette of the painting correspond
more closely to works from the very beginning of the 1450s,
prior to Gozzoli's known activity at Montefalco in Umbria. A
more cogent understanding of Gozzoli's contribution within
Fra Angelico's workshop in the 1440s than was available to

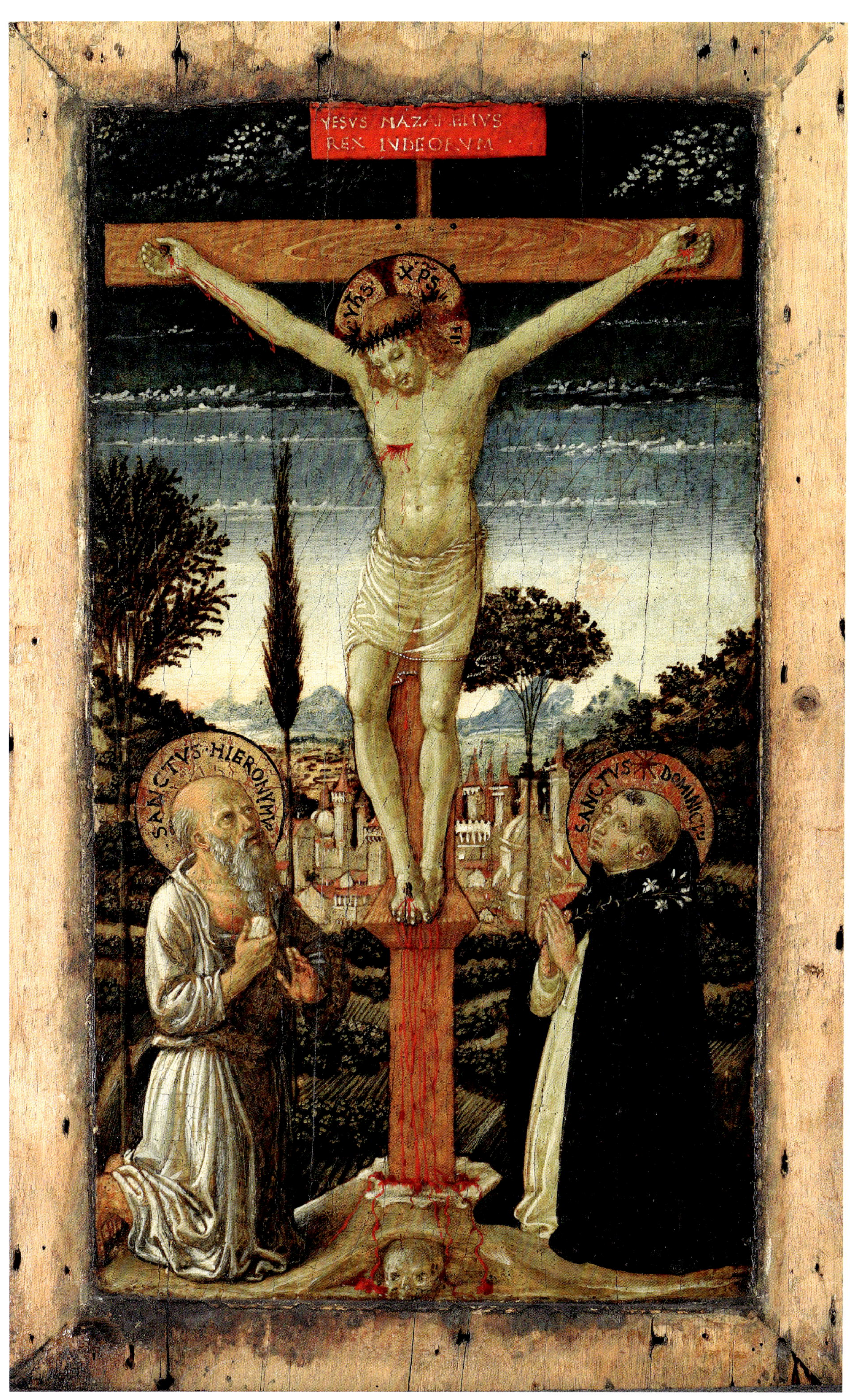
YESVS NAZARENVS
REX IVDEORVM
SANCTVS · HIERONYMVS
SANCTVS · DOMINICVS

earlier scholars, as well as of his independent work in Rome and Orvieto between 1446 and 1449, makes this earlier dating plausible. Palladino further presents evidence culled from a closer reading of well-known documents to suggest that Gozzoli (and Fra Angelico) had returned to Florence from Rome before the end of 1448 and may have remained there through the first half of 1449. This now seems the likeliest period in which to situate the commission for the Locko Park/ Feigen *Crucifixion*.   L K

1. Bernard Berenson, *Florentine Painters of the Renaissance*, 2nd ed. (London, 1900), p. 106; and Jean Paul Richter, *Catalogue of the Pictures at Locko Park* (London, 1901), p. 29.
2. Diane Cole Ahl, *Benozzo Gozzoli* (New Haven, Conn., 1996), p. 223; Miklós Boskovits, *Italian Paintings of the Fifteenth Century: The Collections of the National Gallery of Art* (Washington, D.C., 2003), p. 345n.14; and Pia Palladino, in Laurence Kanter and Palladino, *Fra Angelico*, exh. cat. (New York, 2005), pp. 304–6.
3. Berenson, *Florentine Painters*, p. 106; Raimond van Marle, *The Development of the Italian Schools of Painting*, vol. 11 (The Hague, 1929), pp. 142–43; Anna Padoa Rizzo, *Benozzo Gozzoli: Pittore fiorentino* (Florence, 1972), p. 137; and Anna Padoa Rizzo, *Benozzo Gozzoli: Catalogo completo dei dipinti* (Florence, 1992), p. 81.

Benozzo di Lese di Sandro, called Benozzo Gozzoli

Florence, 1420/21–1497

27. *The Adoration of the Christ Child*, ca. 1490

Tempera on panel, 50.6 x 33 cm (19⅞ x 13 in.)

PROVENANCE: private collection, France(?) (sale, Sotheby's, London, July 12, 2001, lot 60)

BIBLIOGRAPHY: Diane Cole Ahl, "Da Roma a Montefalco," in *Benozzo Gozzoli: Allievo a Roma, maestro in Umbria*, ed. Bruno Toscano and Giovanna Capitelli, exh. cat. (Milan, 2002), pp. 186–87; Pia Palladino, in Laurence Kanter and Palladino, *Fra Angelico*, exh. cat. (New York, 2005), pp. 309–11

CONDITION: The panel, of a vertical grain, is 8 mm thick and is gessoed on the reverse. A barb visible along all four edges of the paint surface implies the removal of an original engaged frame. The paint surface is only lightly abraded and exhibits no apparent paint losses. Written in ink (with a brush) across the back is "Benozzo Gozzoli / 1466 / N.o 53 / Ecole Lombarde / Fin du xv.e siecle / Vaux 200 fcs." Glue residue from a missing paper label surrounds (or covers) a faintly legible number, "293"(?).

This imposing panel was unknown to scholars until it appeared at auction in 2001 with an attribution to Benozzo Gozzoli's son, Alesso di Benozzo.[1] It is not mentioned, therefore, in any of the monographic literature on the artist, and it was first published under the correct attribution to Benozzo himself by Diane Cole Ahl, and then more fully by Pia Palladino on the occasion of the 2005 exhibition of Fra Angelico in New York.[2] Both scholars consider the painting a late work. Cole Ahl dates it to ca. 1495, at the very end of Gozzoli's life, while Palladino seems to imply the possibility of a slightly earlier date through comparisons to the last of the Camposanto frescoes in Pisa, finished in 1484, and to the tabernacle of the *Visitation* in Castelfiorentino, formerly inscribed with the date 1491. Palladino also aptly points out that at this stage of his career, Gozzoli's large and efficient workshop—in which his two sons,

Francesco (b. 1469) and Alesso (1473–1528) are documented as collaborators—must have participated in most aspects of his artistic production. She does not, however, discern any obvious traces of studio intervention in the Feigen *Adoration*.

The theme of the Adoration of the Christ Child as it is presented in this painting evolved over the course of the second half of the fifteenth century into one of the most popular devotional images in Florentine art. The genesis of the image, which focuses on the Virgin (and angels) adoring the naked Christ Child lying on the hem of her robes spread on the ground, may be traced to the late fourteenth-century account by Saint Bridget of Sweden of her mystical vision of the Nativity. Saint Bridget's vision was illustrated literally by an artist who undoubtedly knew her personally, Niccolò di Tommaso, and in more generalized form by numerous artists until several versions of the subject by Filippo Lippi and his followers in the mid-fifteenth century provided a more-or-less codified set of symbols for minor masters to follow. Gozzoli restored some of the narrative content to this mystical event by retaining details from conventional portrayals of the Nativity: the rustic shed roof of the manger, the ox and ass looking on at the left, Saint Joseph seated apart in the right middle distance, and a shepherd approaching over the shoulder of the hill in the left background. At the same time, he has dressed the Virgin in a blue, ermine-lined cloak denoting royalty. In the place of a radiant glory emanating from God the Father in the heavens, he has incorporated, cropped at the top edge of the composition, the eight-pointed star that guided the Magi to the scene of the Epiphany. A dotted gold line descends directly from the star to the Christ Child, its wavering, uncertain course possibly a testimony to the artist's extreme old age when he drew it.   L K

1. See Sotheby's, London, sale cat. (July 12, 2001), lot 60.
2. Diane Cole Ahl, "Da Roma a Montefalco," in *Benozzo Gozzoli: Allievo a Roma, maestro in Umbria*, ed. Bruno Toscano and Giovanna Capitelli, exh. cat. (Milan, 2002), pp. 186–87; and Pia Palladino, in Laurence Kanter and Palladino, *Fra Angelico*, exh. cat. (New York, 2005), pp. 309–11.

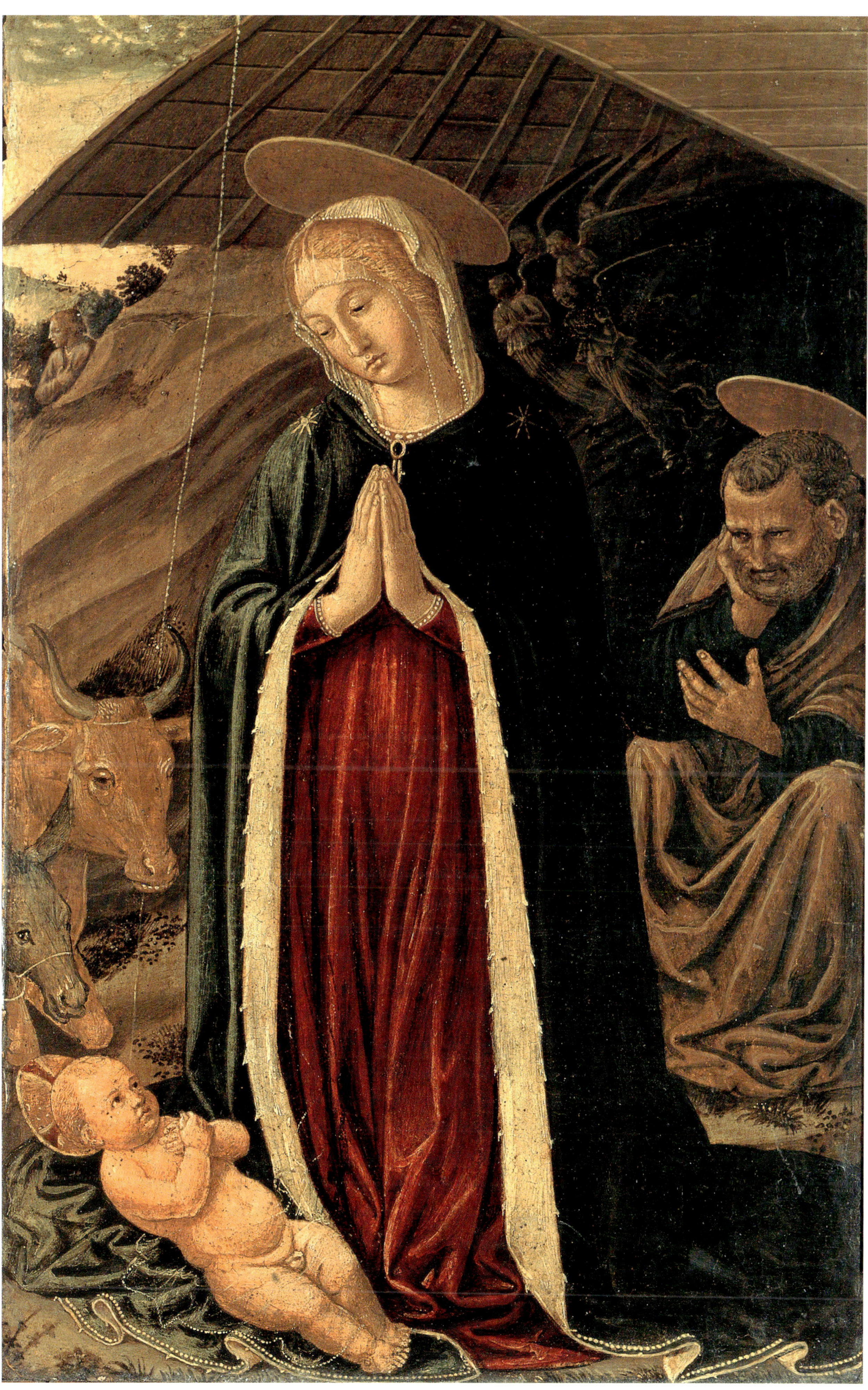

Follower of Paolo Uccello

Florence, ca. 1397–1475

28. *Virgin and Child with Two Angels,*
ca. 1460–70

Tempera and oil on panel, 23.5 x 16.7 cm (9¼ x 6⅝ in.)

PROVENANCE: Victor Hahn, Berlin (his sale, Ball & Graupe, Berlin, June 27, 1932, lot 5); Galerie van Diemen, Berlin; Hugo and Ruth Klotz, Monroe, N.Y. (their sale, Christie's, New York, April 6, 2006, lot 12)

BIBLIOGRAPHY: unpublished

CONDITION: The panel support has been thinned to 5 mm but is not cradled. The coarse wood grain is essentially vertical but veers to the diagonal around two conspicuous knots in the center (at the level of the Virgin's breast) and at the top right edge of the panel. A diagonal split rises 7.5 cm from the bottom edge through the Christ Child's right foot, which is repaired. The paint surface retains a barbe on all four sides. The flesh tones have been lightly abraded and scratches have been locally retouched. The mordant gilt decoration scattered across the Virgin's red dress—in the form of three gilt dots grouped as a triangle—is lost, as is a transparent veil covering the Christ Child that now appears only as a highlight draped over the Virgin's left wrist. The impasto of the rose hedge and of the angels' draperies is beautifully preserved.

This delicate panel is recorded in a photograph in the Richard Offner photo archive at New York University—a photograph sent to Offner from the Galerie van Diemen in Berlin—with an attribution to Alesso Baldovinetti, and this attribution was retained for it in the Klotz collection in Monroe, New York. When it appeared at sale in 2006, the work was described as by a follower of Paolo Uccello on the basis of an opinion expressed by Everett Fahy.[1] Keith Christiansen suggested shortly afterward switching its classification from Florentine to Ferrarese, specifically linking it to a *Virgin and Child* in the Cambò collection, Barcelona.[2] The Cambò *Madonna* has been the subject of a wide variety of opinion revolving around its disputed Florentine or Ferrarese origins. Most recently it has been attributed by Daniele Benati to an artist closely related to Francesco del Cossa, whom he christened the Master of the Boston Desco.[3] Benati has assigned a small number of panel paintings to this master, all of which reveal a complex blend of Florentine and Ferrarese cultural influences. His proposals, however, have not met with universal agreement.[4]

Closer examination of the Feigen *Virgin and Child with Two Angels* reveals that its evident similarities to the Cambò *Madonna* are iconographic rather than stylistic and that links between either of them and Ferrarese painting are tenuous. Both the Feigen and Cambò paintings, of distinctively high quality though not by the same hand, refer directly or obliquely to earlier Florentine compositions deriving from the studio of Domenico Veneziano, while their figure types, palette, and manner of handling paint and decorative gilding are clearly Florentine. Although Everett Fahy's creation of a "Master of the Cambò Madonna"—a Florentine, or at least Tuscan, artist—is perhaps not in its entirety convincing, it has the virtue of reuniting several panels generally related in style and composition to the Feigen *Virgin and Child* that unequivocally serve to establish a Florentine context for the latter.[5] Among the paintings grouped together by Fahy is a large and severely damaged panel portraying the Archangel Raphael and Tobias from a triptych in Santa Maria Novella in Florence that warrants further examination as possibly a work by the same hand as the Feigen *Virgin and Child*.[6] It is, however, less redolent of the influence of Paolo Uccello that is conspicuously characteristic of the Feigen *Virgin and Child*.

For the present it is prudent to conclude that no other works are known that are certainly by the same artist as the painting catalogued here, and to revert to the formula first articulated for it by Fahy as "follower of Paolo Uccello." The painting is certainly more closely related to the late style of Uccello than it is to any other known independent master in Florence or elsewhere.   LK

1. See Christie's, New York, sale cat. (April 6, 2006), lot 12.
2. Keith Christiansen, conversation with the author, 2006.
3. See Daniele Benati, in *Le muse e il principe: Arte di corte nel Rinascimento padano,* ed. Alessandra Mottola Molfino and Mauro Natale (Milan, 1991), pp. 300–305, for a discussion of the complicated attributional history of the Cambò *Madonna* and of the Museum of Fine Arts, Boston, *Solomon and the Queen of Sheba* desco, for whom the Master was named.
4. For recent discussion of Benati's Master of the Boston Desco, see Carolyn C. Wilson, *Italian Paintings, XIV–XVI Centuries, in the Museum of Fine Arts, Houston* (Houston, 1996), pp. 214–29; and Joseph Manca, in *Italian Paintings of the Fifteenth Century: The Collections of the National Gallery of Art,* ed. Miklós Boskovits (Washington, D.C., 2003), pp. 261–65.
5. Fahy's attributions, formulated in January 1985, are partially recorded in Benati, *Muse e il principe,* p. 300, and in Manca, *Italian Paintings of the Fifteenth Century,* p. 265n.10. See also Christopher Lloyd, *Italian Paintings before 1600 in the Art Institute of Chicago: A Catalogue of the Collection* (Chicago, 1993), pp. 65–67. I am grateful to Everett Fahy, the John Pope-Hennessy Chairman, Department of European Paintings, Metropolitan Museum of Art, New York, for generously sharing with me his thoughts on this painter and tentative revisions to his initial list of his works.
6. On this panel, see Luciano Bellosi, *Pittura di Luce: Giovanni di Francesco e l'arte fiorentina di metà quattrocento* (Florence, 1990), p. 25, who calls it unrelated to, and later than ("già di epoca pollaiolesca"), the other panels of the triptych (which portray Saints Catherine of Siena and Vincent Ferrer).

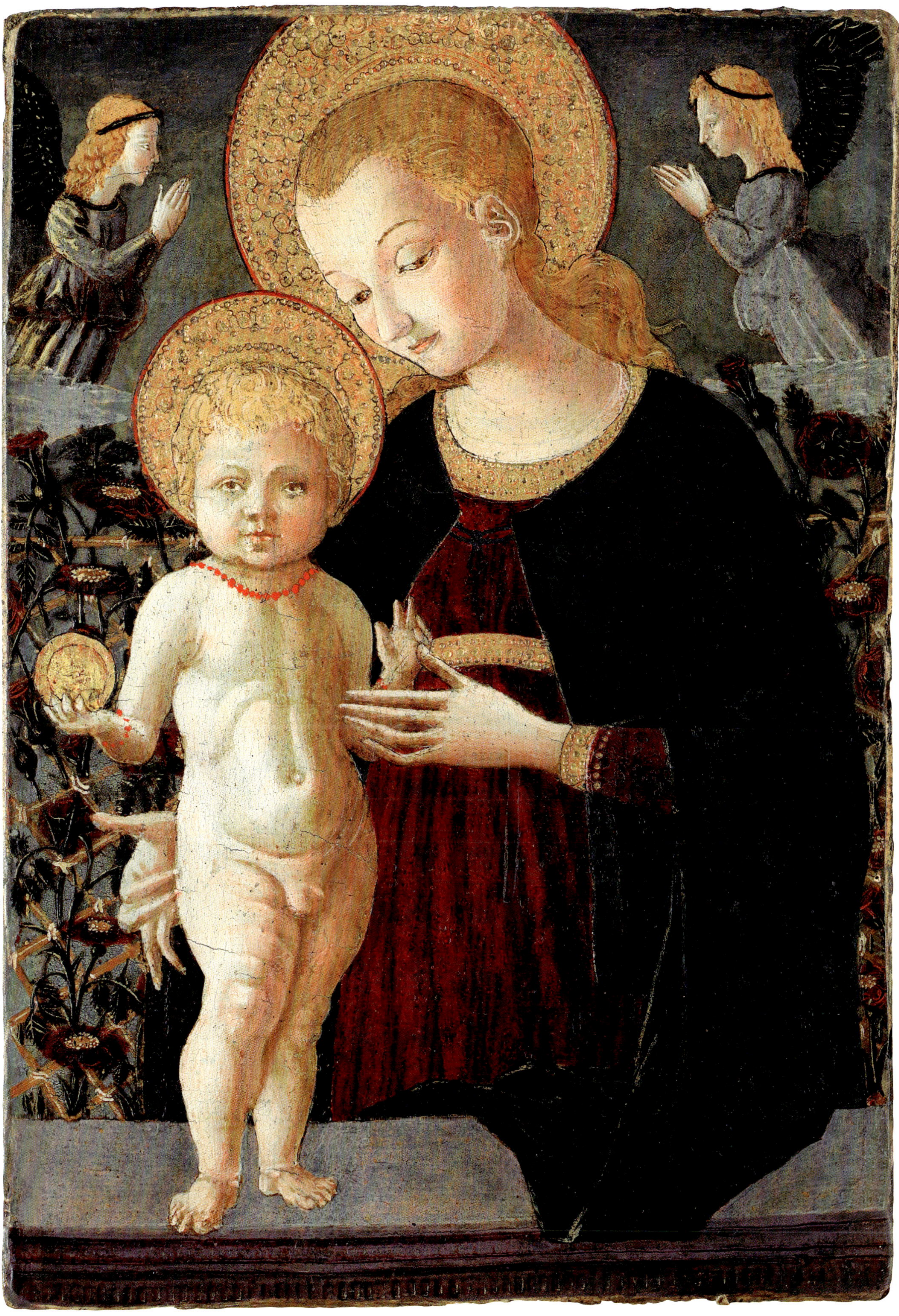

Polìto del Donzello

Florence, 1458–1490/94(?)

29. *The Archangel Raphael Prevents a Suicide*, 1471

Oil and tempera on panel, 20.8 x 48.3 cm (8¼ x 19 in.)

PROVENANCE: Eugène von Miller Aicholz, Vienna;[1] Albert Figdor, Vienna (his sale, Paul Cassirer, Berlin, September 29–30, 1930, lot 6); Jacques Goudstikker, Amsterdam (seized by Nazi authorities, July 1940; recovered by the Allies, 1945; assigned by the Dutch government to temporary exhibition at the Bonnefanten Museum, Maastricht, the Netherlands; restituted to the heir of Jacques Goudstikker, February 2006); Christie's, New York, April 19, 2007, lot 4

BIBLIOGRAPHY: Max J. Friedländer, *Die Sammlung Dr. Albert Figdor—Wien*, vol. 3, *Gemälde* (Berlin, 1930), no. 6; Bernard Berenson, *Italian Pictures of the Renaissance: A List of the Principal Artists and Their Works with an Index of Places: Florentine School* (London, 1963), 1: pp. 157–58; Allesandro Parronchi, "Due note para-uccellesche," *Arte antica e moderna* 30 (1965): p. 169; H. W. van Os, ed., *The Florentine Paintings in Holland, 1300–1500* (Maarssen, the Netherlands, 1974), pp. 92–93; Alessandro Parronchi, *Paolo Uccello* (Bologna, 1974), p. 64; Christopher Wright, *Paintings in Dutch Museums: An Index of Oil Paintings in Public Collections in the Netherlands by Artists Born before 1870* (London, 1980), p. 297; Charlotte Wiethoff, "De kunsthandelaar Jacques Goudstikker (1897–1940) en zijn betekenis voor het verzamelen van vroege Italiaanse kunst un Nederland," *Nederlands kunsthistorisch jaarboek* 32 (1981): pp. 260–61; Everett Fahy, "A predella panel by Neri di Bicci," *Burlington Magazine* 127 (1985): pp. 767–68; *Bulletin van de Vereeniging van Vrienden van het Bonnefantenmuseum* 5 (1989): pp. 3–6; C. E. de Jong-Janssen, in K. Schreuder, "De aartsengel Rafael op twee predellapanelen uit de school van Neri di Bicci," in *Restauratieverslag van twee predellapanelen uit de school van Neri di Bicci* (n.p., n.d.); Rijksdienst Beeldende Kunst, *Old Master Paintings: An Illustrated Summary Catalogue* (The Hague, 1992), p. 221; C. E. de Jong-Janssen and D. H. van Wegen, *Catalogue of the Italian Paintings in the Bonnefantenmuseum* (Maastricht, the Netherlands, 1995), p. 188; Carl Brandon Strehlke, *Italian Paintings, 1250–1450, in the John G. Johnson Collection and the Philadelphia Museum of Art* (Philadelphia, 2004), pp. 323–26

CONDITION: The panel, of a horizontal wood grain, has been thinned to 8 mm but is not cradled. The paint surface is in excellent state, with scattered small scratches but no appreciable losses and minimal abrasion. Architectural pentimenti are visible as incisions in the church apse at the left, in the building façade left of center, and in the bench and stool in the interior.

A textual source explaining the subject of this panel, or of any of its three companion panels (see below), has not yet been identified. In the center, in a sparsely furnished interior, an angel cuts the rope of a noose with which a young man has attempted suicide. The same two figures are seen again at the left, in the street outside the young man's house. The angel leads him by the hand into a church—identified as such by the exterior view of its apse—undoubtedly to confess his sin for attempting suicide, to undertake penance, and to pray for forgiveness. The young man's contrition is implied by his posture and downcast eyes.

This panel and another formerly together with it in the Eugène von Miller Aicholz, Albert Figdor, and Jacques Goudstikker collections, which represents the same angel leading two Dominican cardinals on horseback across a river (fig. 1), were believed by Max Friedländer to be *cassone* panels and were classified by him as Florentine, ca. 1450, in the style of Neri di Bicci.[2] They were first associated by Alessandro Parronchi with a third panel from the same series, now in a private collection, showing the same angel leading a woman through a town.[3] Parronchi identified the woman in the third panel as Saint Catherine of Siena, perhaps because of the Dominican habits worn by the two cardinals in the second Goudstikker panel, and proposed, on the basis of the unusually accomplished architectural forms and perspectival construction of space in all three scenes, an attribution for them to the workshop of Paolo Uccello. At a later date, he specified Uccello's son, Donato di Paolo, as the probable author of the panels.[4] H. W. van Os corrected the misreading of the subject of the panels to scenes from the legend of the Archangel Raphael rather than of Saint Catherine. Reverting to Bernard Berenson's opinion that they were works by Neri di Bicci, he noted that Neri's *Ricordanze* list two altarpieces with predellas dedicated to the archangel, both painted for the Augustinian church of Santo Spirito in Florence, one commissioned in 1462 and one in 1471.[5] Van Os declined to identify the panels directly with either of those commissions, citing the presence of the Dominican cardinals in the second Goudstikker panel, but Carl Strehlke correctly maintained that this is not necessarily relevant to the provenance of the panels, while Burton Fredericksen observed that the woman led through the streets depicted in the panel in a private collection appears to wear the habit of an Augustinian tertiary.[6] Everett Fahy reiterated the attribution to Neri di Bicci when he published a fourth panel from the same series in the John G. Johnson Collection at the Philadelphia Museum of Art,

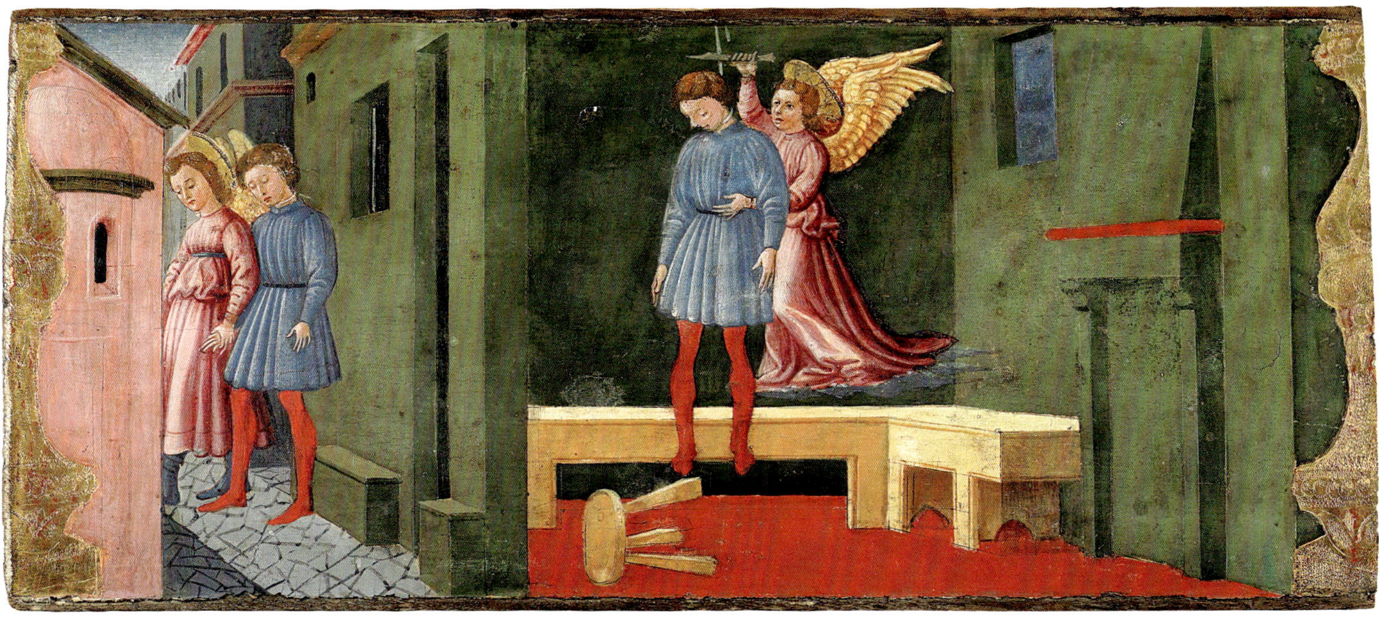

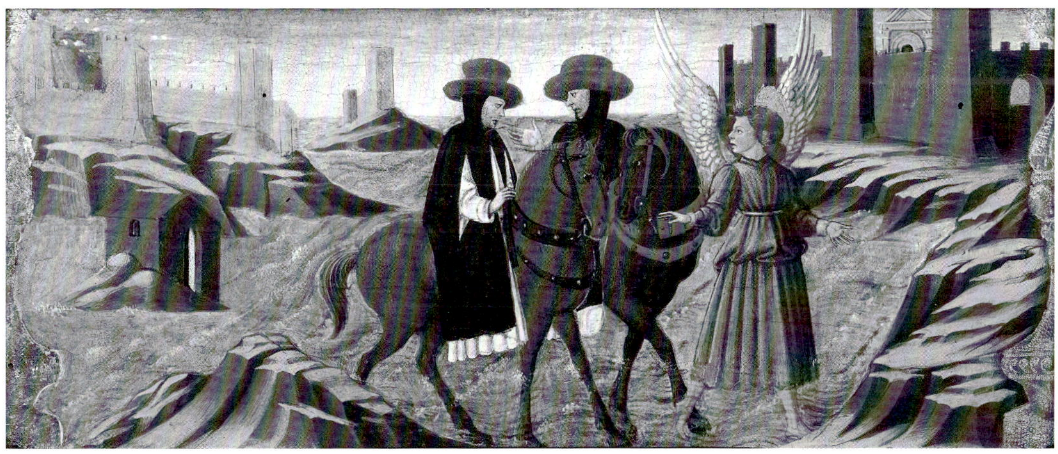

Fig. 1. Polìto del Donzello, *The Archangel Raphael Leading Two Dominican Cardinals across a River*, 1471. Tempera and oil on panel, 21 x 48.3 cm (8¼ x 19 in.). Private collection

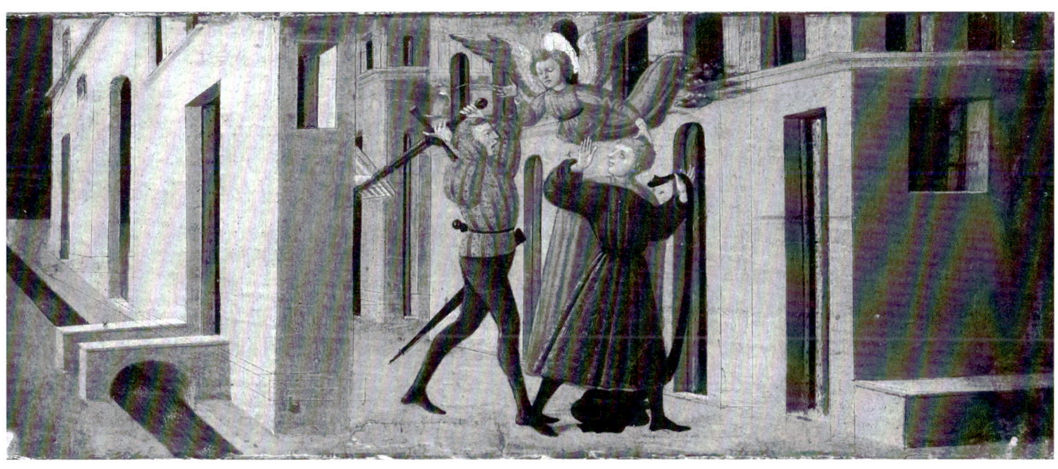

Fig. 2. Polìto del Donzello, *The Archangel Raphael Saving a Man from Attack on the Street*, 1471. Tempera and oil on panel, 21.3 x 48.6 cm (8⅜ x 19⅛ in.) Philadelphia Museum of Art, John G. Johnson Collection, 1917

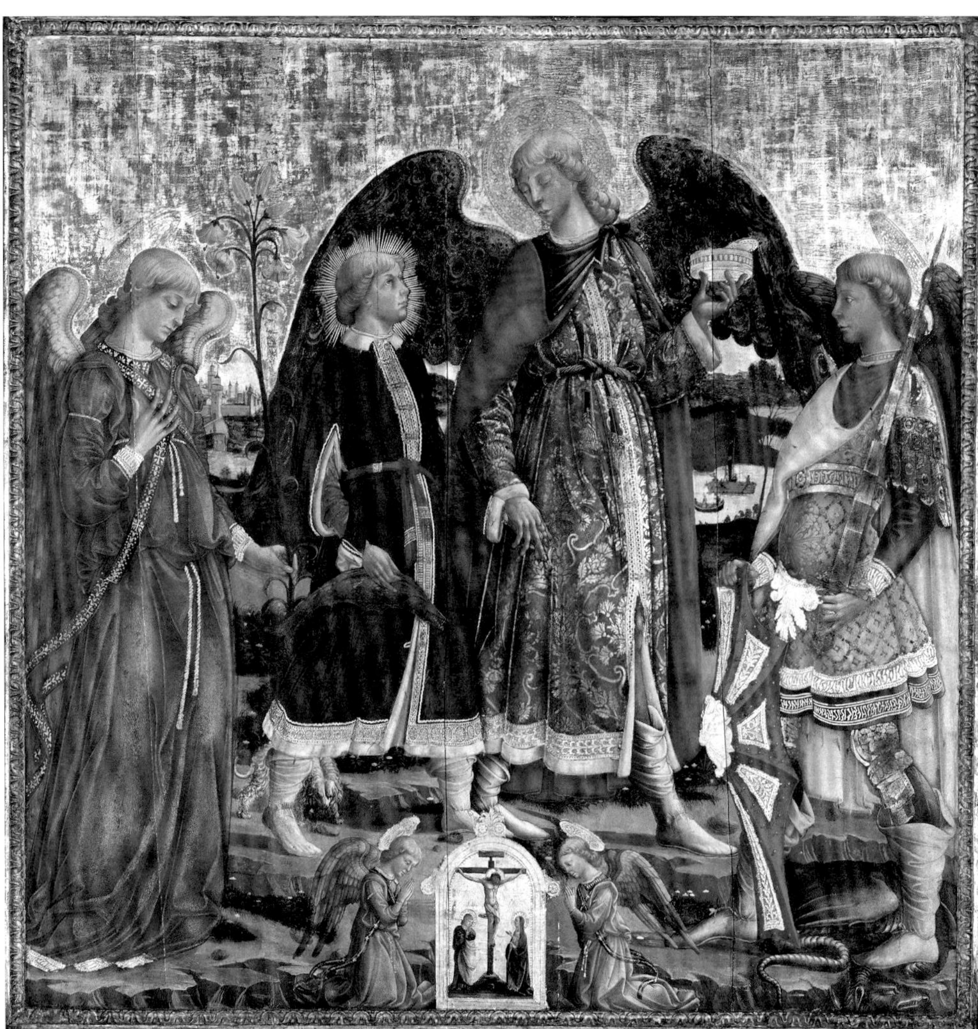

Fig. 3. Neri di Bicci, *Tobias and Three Archangels*, 1471. Tempera and oil on panel, 244.8 x 233.7 cm (96⅛ x 92 in.). Detroit Institute of Arts, City of Detroit Purchase, inv. no. 26.114

which he described as representing the Archangel Raphael saving a man from attack in a city street (fig. 2).[7] Fahy, too, hesitated to associate the panels with either of the Santo Spirito altarpieces by Neri di Bicci. Citing their exceptionally high quality, he suggested they may instead be early works by the artist, painted around 1450, before the initial date for entries in the *Ricordanze*.

In the absence of confirmation from a textual source corresponding to the narratives of these four panels, it must be acknowledged that van Os's identification of their subjects as scenes from the legend of the Archangel Raphael is, logically, a circular argument derived from the references in Neri di Bicci's *Ricordanze*. It nevertheless begs the question of rejecting any specific association with those references, especially since the only commonly acknowledged scene from the legend of the Archangel Raphael—his encounter with the young Tobias—is conspicuously lacking from the series, precisely because it is included emblematically in the main panel of the altarpiece from Santo Spirito commissioned from Neri di Bicci on May 7, 1471, by the apothecary Mariotto di Marco della Palla. The entry in Neri's account book referring to this painting describes it as "una tavola d'altare . . . quadra, chogli sghuanci e cholonne tonde a chanali e da piè la predella e di sopra isghuanc[i]o, architrave, freg[i]o, chornic[i]one e foglia;

. . . nella quale ò a fare l'angelo Rafaello e Tubia e da mano destra Santo Michele agniolo; da mano sinistra l'angelo Ghabriello, da piè l'angelo Rafaello, una tavoluza chontrafatta drentovi el Crocifisso, la Vergine Maria e Santo Giovanni e da lato dua ang[i]oletti e nella predella da piè miracholi dell'a[n]gelo Rafaello . . ." (an altarpiece . . . square, with capitals and round fluted columns, with a predella below, and above the capitals an architrave, frieze, and cornice with leaves; . . . in which I have to make the archangel Raphael with Tobias and on the right side Saint Michael the archangel and on the left side the archangel Gabriel, and beneath the archangel Raphael a fictive tabernacle in which is the Crucifixion with the Virgin Mary, Saint John the Evangelist and two angels at the sides, and in the predella below, miracles of the archangel Raphael).[8] The entry specifies that Mariotto della Palla was to install this painting in his chapel in Santo Spirito "overo dove a lui parà" (or wherever else he wishes), and it is a reasonable assumption that it was intended to replace the earlier altarpiece of the same subject painted by Neri di Bicci for the same church, which appears to have been destroyed in the fire of March 21, 1471.[9] Following its detailed description in the *Ricordanze*, the altarpiece for Mariotto della Palla was identified by William Valentiner with a painting now in the Detroit Institute of Arts (fig. 3), and this identification appears to be correct.[10]

In the spring and summer of 1471, when Neri di Bicci was engaged in painting the della Palla altarpiece (final payment for which is registered in the *Ricordanze* on October 2, 1471), the principal assistant in his workshop was Ippolito di Francesco del Donzello, whom Giorgio Vasari called Polìto del Donzello. Although Polìto del Donzello went on to a distinguished career working with the architect and wood carver Giuliano da Majano in Florence and Naples, his artistic legacy was lost to modern scholarship until recently.[11] Donzello's career can be reconstructed on the basis of a partially documented altarpiece of the *Annunciation*, painted in 1485 on the commission of the heirs of Stoldo di Lionardo Frescobaldi for another chapel in Santo Spirito; a *spalliera* panel painted in 1487 as part of the apparatus celebrating the Tornabuoni–Albizzi wedding of the previous year; and certain painterly characteristics common to the altarpieces painted in Neri di Bicci's studio during his four-year residence there. An examination of these works reveals Polìto del Donzello to have been an important, if previously unrecognized, exponent of a vein of highly imaginative, naturalist painting in Florence in the eighth and ninth decades of the fifteenth century and a singular influence on younger but much better-known masters such as Filippino Lippi and Piero di Cosimo. Much of the execution of the Detroit altarpiece can be ascribed to Polìto del Donzello. Given the uniformity of conception and handling between it and the four panels of its putative predella, it is reasonable to assign the entirety of their design and execution to him as well. Parronchi was correct to observe that the architectural forms and perspectival structure of these four predella panels are far more sophisticated than in any other work by Neri di Bicci, and the same observation could be extended to the finer and more emotive figure types, to the subtle deployment of light and shade to render volumes, and to the fluidity of the paint medium persuasively rendering surfaces and textures. Even the gilt balusters closing off each scene at either end, although outlined with the use of a standard pattern or *patrono* available in Neri di Bicci's studio,

are stippled to suggest the projecting volumes of knops and foliation seen in raking light, and with a sensitivity to establishing a controlled, uniform direction for the light source unparalleled in Neri di Bicci's output—indeed, scarcely equaled in all of Florentine painting at the time outside the studio of Antonio del Pollaiuolo. The extraordinary accomplishment of these effects, achieved by a fifteen-year-old apprentice working within the most conservative studio in Florence in 1471, is a partial indication of the remarkable quality of Polìto del Donzello's mature works in the next decade and contributes to explaining the high esteem in which he was held by Giuliano da Majano, as well as accounting for the survival of his reputation down to the time of Vasari in the mid-sixteenth century if not, unfortunately, down to the present.   LK

1. This provenance is reported in the sale catalogue of the Figdor collection; see Paul Cassirer, Berlin, sale cat. (September 29–30, 1930), lot 6. The painting does not appear in the sale catalogue of the Eugène von Miller Aicholz collection at the Galerie Georges Petit, Paris, May 18–22, 1900.
2. Max J. Friedländer, *Die Sammlung Dr. Albert Figdor—Wien*, vol. 3, *Gemälde* (Berlin, 1930), no. 6.
3. Alessandro Parronchi, "Due note para-uccellesche," *Arte antica e moderna* 30 (1965): p. 169.
4. Alessandro Parronchi, *Paolo Uccello* (Bologna, 1974), p. 64.
5. H. W. van Os, ed., *The Florentine Paintings in Holland, 1300–1500* (Maarssen, the Netherlands, 1974), pp. 92–93; and Bernard Berenson, *Italian Pictures of the Renaissance: A List of the Principal Artists and Their Works with an Index of Places: Florentine School* (London, 1963), 1: pp. 157–58.
6. Carl Brandon Strehlke, *Italian Paintings, 1250–1450, in the John G. Johnson Collection and the Philadelphia Museum of Art* (Philadelphia, 2004), pp. 323–26. For Burton Fredericksen's observation, see ibid., p. 326n.1.
7. Everett Fahy, "A Predella Panel by Neri di Bicci," *Burlington Magazine* 127 (1985): pp. 767–68.
8. Bruno Santi, ed., *Neri di Bicci: Le Ricordanze* (Pisa, 1976), p. 372, no. 698.
9. Ibid., and pp. 176–77, nos. 347, 350, commissioned by "maestro Francescho zopo frate di Santo Spirito" on February 17, 1462 [n.s.].
10. William R. Valentiner, "The Three Archangels by Neri di Bicci," *Bulletin of the Detroit Institute of Arts* 8 (1926): pp. 14–15, no. 2.
11. Laurence Kanter, "Polìto del Donzello," forthcoming. For the final payment of the della Palla altarpiece, see Santi, *Neri di Bicci*, p. 373.

Giovanni di Paolo
Siena, 1398–1482

30. *The Virgin Annunciate*, ca. 1425–26

Tempera on panel, 12.5 x 9.3 cm (4⅞ x 3⅝ in.)

PROVENANCE: anonymous sale, Kunsthaus Lempertz,
Cologne, November 25, 2000, lot 1264a; anonymous sale,
Sotheby's, London, April 26, 2001, lot 18; Edwin L. Weisl, Jr.,
New York (his sale, Christie's, New York, April 6, 2006, lot 32)

BIBLIOGRAPHY: Michel Laclotte and Esther Moench, *Peinture italienne: Musée du Petit Palais, Avignon* (Paris, 2005),
pp. 110, 236; Andrea de Marchi, in Giovanni Sarti, *Entre tradition et modernité: Peinture italienne des XIVe et XVe siècles/
From Gothic Tradition to the Renaissance: Italian Painting
from the 14th and 15th Centuries*, exh. cat. (Paris, 2008),
pp. 131, 133n.6

CONDITION: The panel has been thinned to 5 mm but is not
cradled. The removal of an engaged frame has exposed the
wood of the panel in the upper left corner, and small fills cover
minor losses at the top right corner and along the bottom edge
of the panel. The paint surface is in excellent condition.

This delicate panel was unknown before its appearance at
public auction in Cologne in 2000, catalogued as "Tuscan
Master ca. 1400," and in London in 2001, catalogued as "follower of Lorenzo di Bicci." It shows the Virgin standing in
slightly more than half-length and turned three-quarters to
the left. Her head is gently bowed and her right hand is crossed
over her breast—both gestures of humility in receipt of the
Angelic salutation—while with her left hand she gathers a
fold of her blue cloak. The painting was first recognized by
Pia Palladino, at the time of the London sale of 2001, as an
early work by Giovanni di Paolo. Specifically, it was associated by her, on the basis of its size and shape, the tooling of
its gold ground, and the luminous glazing of the Virgin's red
draperies, with a related panel of the *Annunciatory Angel* in
the collection of the Musée du Petit Palais, Avignon (fig. 1),
an association that was subsequently acknowledged by Keith
Christiansen, Everett Fahy, and Michel Laclotte.[1]

The Avignon *Angel*, which measures 13 x 10 cm, was initially identified by Federico Zeri as the pinnacle to the left wing
of a portable triptych, where it would have surmounted a
half-length figure of *Saint James* now in the Perkins Collection at the Museo-Tesoro della Basilica di San Francesco, Assisi
(fig. 2).[2] Zeri cited a similar figure of Saint Christopher, formerly in the collection of M. Moratilla, Paris, as a fragment
of the corresponding right wing of the triptych, noting that
this panel would have been surmounted by a pinnacle showing the Virgin Annunciate, which may now be recognized as
the present painting.[3] Both the *Saint James* and the *Saint
Christopher* have been cut to their present sizes (15.2 x 11.5
cm and 16 x 13 cm, respectively) from full-length figures,

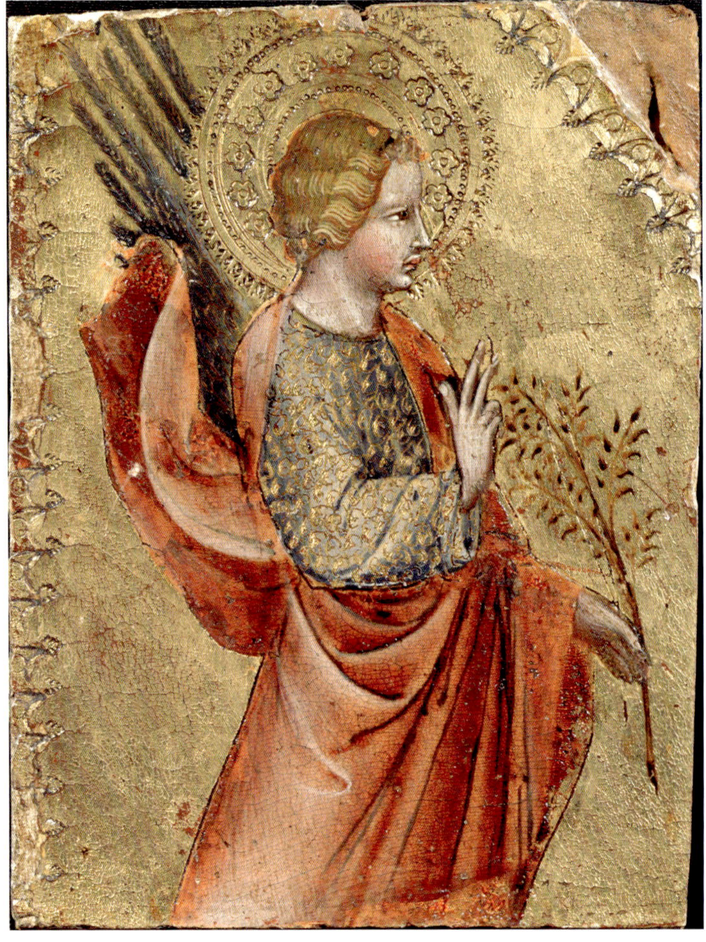

Fig. 1. Giovanni di Paolo, *The Annunciatory Angel*, ca. 1425–26.
Tempera on panel, 13 x 10 cm (5⅛ x 4 in.). Musée du Petit Palais,
Avignon

which were probably shown standing on tiled or marbleized
pavements and beneath ogival or trilobe arches of pastiglia
lined with punched decoration along the margins of the gold
ground. Allowing for completion of these pastiglia arches and
of the truncated gables of the Avignon *Angel* and the Feigen
Virgin, an original height for these wings may be estimated
at between 55 and 60 cm, and a width at approximately 13 to
15 cm (the right wing may have been as much as 2 cm wider
than the left, a difference not infrequently encountered between
the wings of intact fifteenth-century triptychs). The missing
center panel would then have measured roughly 58 x 28 cm
overall, and probably represented either the Crucifixion or
the Virgin and Child Enthroned. No likely candidates for this
center panel have yet been identified among the surviving
works of Giovanni di Paolo, but comparable, complete triptychs from his early career are to be found at the Los Angeles

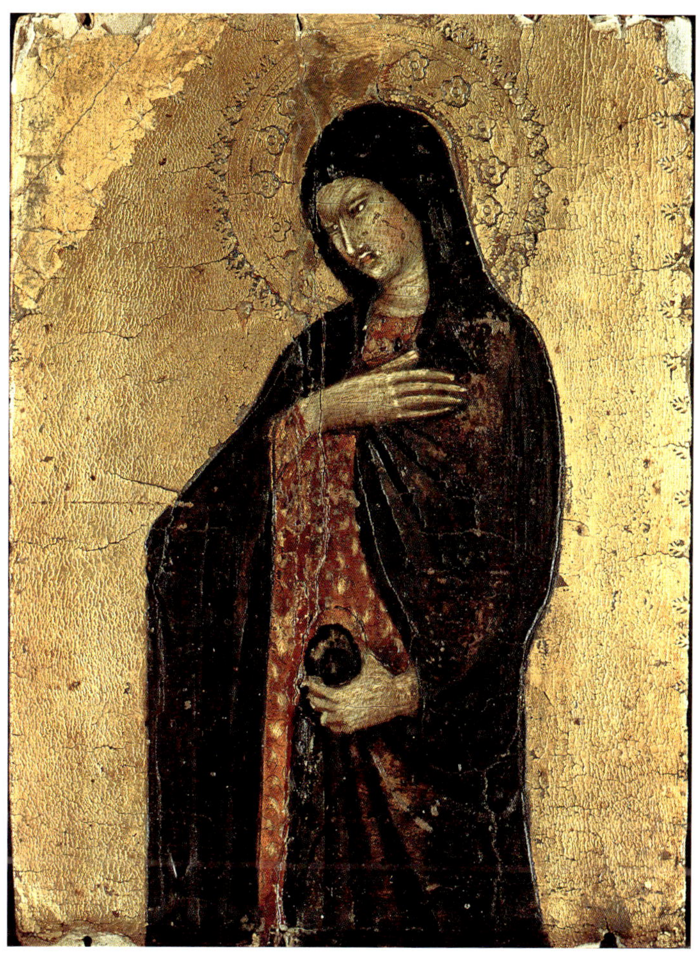

County Museum of Art and formerly at the Kimbell Art Museum, Fort Worth.[4]

Discussing the Avignon, Paris, and Assisi fragments, Zeri suggested that a date of ca. 1430 or even a few years earlier—that is, at the very beginning of Giovanni di Paolo's known career—would not be inappropriate. Laclotte pointed out convincing analogies between these paintings and a group of narrative panels in Siena and Otterlo generally thought to have formed the predella to the Fondi altarpiece of 1436. Palladino accepted both Zeri's and Laclotte's observations, noting correctly that the Siena and Otterlo panels must originate from a different commission than that for the Fondi altarpiece, as they also date from the second half of the 1420s.[5] For Palladino, the Avignon/Paris/Assisi triptych (and by logical extension the Feigen *Virgin*) most closely resembles the surviving fragments of Giovanni di Paolo's first public commission in Siena, the Pecci altarpiece of 1426, now divided among the Prepositura at Castelnuovo Berardenga; the Pinacoteca Nazionale, Siena; the Walters Art Museum, Baltimore; and the Lindenau Museum, Altenburg, Germany, an opinion seconded recently by Laclotte and Esther Moench.[6]

An inordinate number of portable triptychs from the last third of the trecento and the opening decades of the quattrocento in Siena contained an image of Saint Christopher on one wing, though most often paired not with an image of Saint James but rather of Saint Anthony Abbot on the other wing. Both Christopher and Anthony Abbot were commonly invoked for protection against disease: the latter was known as the healer of men and animals and was the patron of an order of hospitalers, while an inscription beneath the image of Saint Christopher on a fourteenth-century triptych in the Walters Art Museum, where he is not coincidentally paired

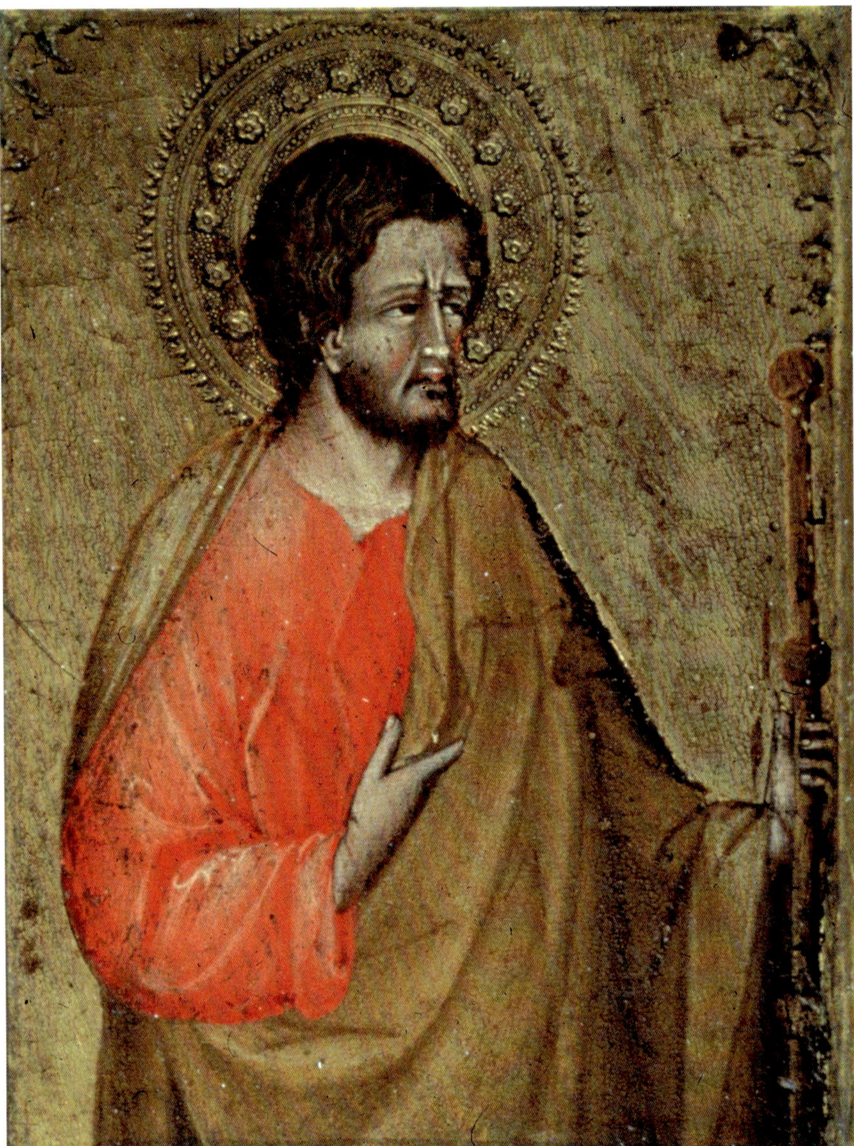

Fig. 2. Giovanni di Paolo, *Saint James*, ca. 1425–26. Tempera on panel, 15.2 x 11.5 cm (6 x 4½ in.). F. M. Perkins Collection, Treasury of the Basilica of Saint Francis, Assisi

with a figure of Anthony Abbot, reads XPOFORI SANCTI SPETIEM QUICUMQUE TUETUR ILLO NAMQUE DIE NULLO LANGUORE TENETUR (Whoever contemplates the image of Saint Christopher will not be taken by any illness during that same day).[7] Christopher was also invoked for protection against sudden death and was known as the patron saint of travelers. It is undoubtedly in this guise that he appears in the triptych of which the present panel formed part. Saint James, the elder brother of Saint John the Evangelist, is shown in the Assisi panel with his standard attribute of a pilgrim's staff, in reference to the popularity, since at least the eleventh century, of his shrine at Compostela in Spain as one of the principal pilgrimage centers of Europe and consequently to the saint's role as patron and protector of pilgrims and of travelers in general.   LK

1. Keith Christiansen, Everett Fahy, and Michel Laclotte, conversation with Richard L. Feigen. On the Avignon *Annunciatory Angel*, see Michel Laclotte and Esther Moench, *Peinture italienne: Musée du Petit Palais, Avignon* (Paris, 2005), no. 101.
2. Federico Zeri, cited in Michel Laclotte and Elisabeth Mognetti, *Avignon, Musée du Petit Palais: Peinture italienne* (Paris, 1976), no. 88; and Federico Zeri, *La collezione Federico Mason Perkins* (Turin, 1988), p. 106.
3. See Laclotte and Moench, *Peinture italienne*, p. 236, for a graphic reconstruction.
4. Frank Dabell, in Matthiesen Fine Art Ltd., *Gold Backs, 1250–1480* (London, 1996), pp. 111–17.
5. Pia Palladino, in *The Treasury of Saint Francis of Assisi*, ed. Giovanni Morello and Laurence Kanter, exh. cat. (Milan, 1999), p. 114.
6. Laclotte and Moench, *Peinture italienne*, p. 110. For the most recent study of the Pecci altarpiece, see Ada Labriola, in *Maestri senesi e toscani nel Lindenau-Museum di Altenburg*, ed. Miklós Boskovits, exh. cat. (Siena, 2008), pp. 145–50.
7. Federico Zeri, *Italian Paintings in the Walters Art Gallery* (Baltimore, 1976), p. 16.

Giovanni di Paolo

Siena, 1398–1482

31. *Christ as the Man of Sorrows*, ca. 1460–65

Tempera on panel, 26 x 38.7 cm (10⅛ x 15¼ in.)

PROVENANCE: Silvano Lodi, Switzerland, by 1983; E. V. Thaw & Co., New York; Peter Jay Sharp, New York, by 1988 (his sale, Sotheby's, New York, January 13, 1994, lot 61); private collection until 2003

BIBLIOGRAPHY: Carlo Volpe, in Matthiesen Fine Art, Ltd., *Early Italian Paintings and Works of Art, 1300–1480*, exh. cat. (London, 1983), p. 54; John Pope-Hennessy and Laurence Kanter, *Italian Paintings*, Robert Lehman Collection 1 (New York, 1987), p. 120; John Pope-Hennessy, *Giovanni di Paolo* (New York, 1988), p. 44; Carl Brandon Strehlke, in *Painting in Renaissance Siena, 1420–1500*, ed. Keith Christiansen, Laurence Kanter, and Strehlke, exh. cat. (New York, 1988), pp. 200–204; Keith Christiansen, "Notes on 'Painting in Renaissance Siena,'" *Burlington Magazine* 132 (1990): p. 210; Mojmír S. Frinta, *Punched Decoration on Late Medieval Panel and Miniature Painting* (Prague, 1998), 1: p. 193; Andrea de Marchi, in de Marchi and Alberto Fiz, *Gold: Gothic Masters and Lucio Fontana*, ed. Marco Voena, exh. cat. (Milan, 1999), p. 49

CONDITION: The gilding and paint surface are exceptionally well preserved, exhibiting negligible abrasion, minimal local flaking loss, and only minor scratches and nicks, principally across the chest of Christ, through His left forearm, and in the rocky background in the right half of the panel. Two prominent losses approximately 15 cm apart on the left edge of the panel, and two more approximately 14 cm apart on the right edge, were caused by large nails driven obliquely into the panel at those points: their exit holes are clearly visible on the back of the panel—which has not been thinned—with no evidence of splayed channels typical of the flattened ends of hinges. Probably these nail holes are to be associated with a later addition of frame moldings along the lateral edges (see below). The bottom left nail generated a modest split in the panel. Two holes on the back of the panel near the center of the top edge retain remnants of a rope hanging-strap of some considerable but indeterminate age.

The Eucharistic Man of Sorrows is an image that recurs with some frequency in Giovanni di Paolo's art. It appears, for example, in the pinnacle of a small devotional triptych in the Pinacoteca Nazionale, Siena (inv. no. 178), and in an unusual private devotional panel recently on the art market, both probably painted in the late 1450s, and again in a form even closer to that of the present painting—differing only in the projection of the haloes: flat in the one and in a coarse simulation of perspective foreshortening in the other—in the predella to the so-called Staggia altarpiece of ca. 1475, also in the Pinacoteca Nazionale, Siena (fig. 1).[1] The tomb, pebble-strewn ground, and fantastic rocks silhouetted against the gold background in the Staggia and Feigen panels are also closely similar, except that in the Staggia predella, they are stretched to fill a more horizontal format. The composition of the Staggia predella is closed off at either side by mourning figures of the Virgin and Saint John the Evangelist, the Virgin separated from Christ by a greater distance than is the Evangelist in order to accommodate a cutout tabernacle-door opening in the panel between them. The Feigen *Man of Sorrows* must originally have been the center of a predella as well, where it would have been accompanied by mourning figures of the Virgin and Saint John the Evangelist, though in this case separated from the central figure by bands of decorative punch tooling—preserved intact at the left and right edges of the Feigen panel—and thus isolated within their own compartments. The presence of a beard of gilding at the top edge and of paint at the bottom edge of the Feigen panel, indicative of the attachment of engaged moldings along these sides only, is also typical of predella construction in the fifteenth century. No beard is evident at either the left or right edge, as would have been the case with an independent devotional panel, in which the decorative punch tooling would have continued along the top edge as well. Four semicircular damages visible at the left and right edges of the Feigen panel are similar to those sometimes associated with the presence (and subsequent removal) of hinges, but in this case they undoubtedly indicate instead the attachment of vertical frame moldings along these edges when the panel was first cut out of its predella. At that time, the top edge of the frame (i.e., the original engaged upper molding, which was then still intact) was pierced to accommodate a rope hanging-strap, traces of which are still visible on the reverse of the panel.

Assuming that the Feigen *Man of Sorrows* (then in the collection of Peter Jay Sharp) was indeed the center panel of a predella, John Pope-Hennessy identified two further panels that he felt might have originated from the same structure.[2] One, representing a half-length Saint Bartholomew, a scene of the Entombment of the Virgin, and a half-length figure of the Mourning Virgin (Fitzwilliam Museum, Cambridge) would have stood adjacent to the *Man of Sorrows* on the left; the other panel, representing the Mourning Saint John the Evangelist, the Assumption of the Virgin, and Saint Ansanus (Kress Collection, El Paso), would have stood on the right of the *Man of Sorrows*. Both panels, which came from the collection of Johann Anton Ramboux in Cologne in the early nineteenth century, exhibit similar though not identical punch

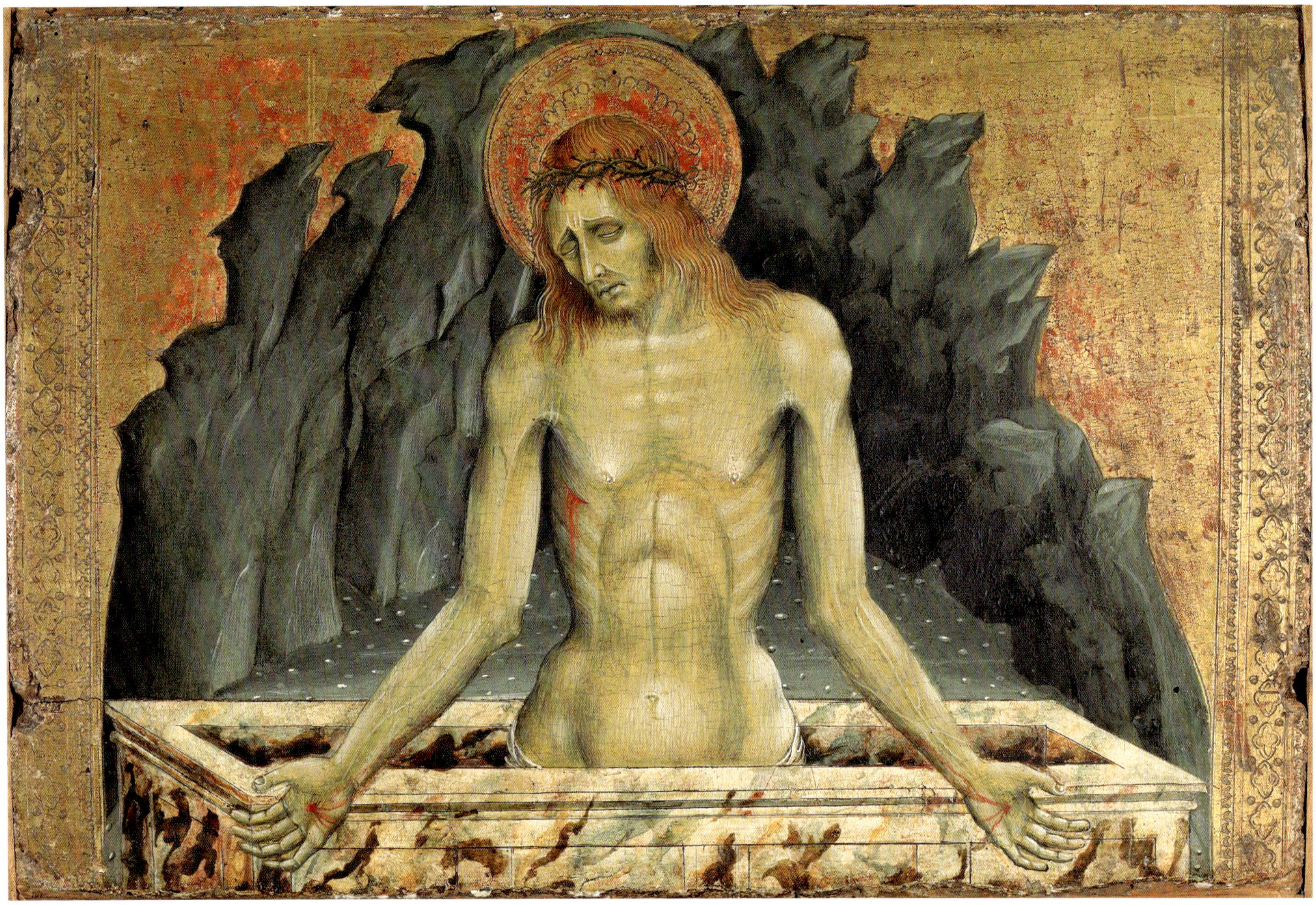

tooling as the Feigen panel, decorating both the haloes and
the vertical bands separating the figures from the narrative
compartments. They presuppose a Man of Sorrows as the
subject of the panel that once separated them, and they
generally agree in style with the Feigen panel, being works of
Giovanni di Paolo's maturity, painted after 1450. Pope-
Hennessy further observed that the aggregate width of the
three panels is only 2 cm greater than that of an altarpiece of
the *Coronation of the Virgin* in the Robert Lehman Collection at the Metropolitan Museum of Art, New York, and as
that altarpiece complements both the style of the predella
and its iconography—representing the conclusion of the two
narrative scenes in Cambridge and El Paso—it might be the
main panel beneath which this predella once stood. All four
panels were then reunited in the exhibition of Sienese Renaissance painting held at the Metropolitan Museum in 1988, but
it was recognized on that occasion that the Feigen panel is
significantly taller than the Cambridge and El Paso panels
(the Cambridge panel, which retains its original upper and
lower moldings, measures 25.5 cm in height, overall, but its

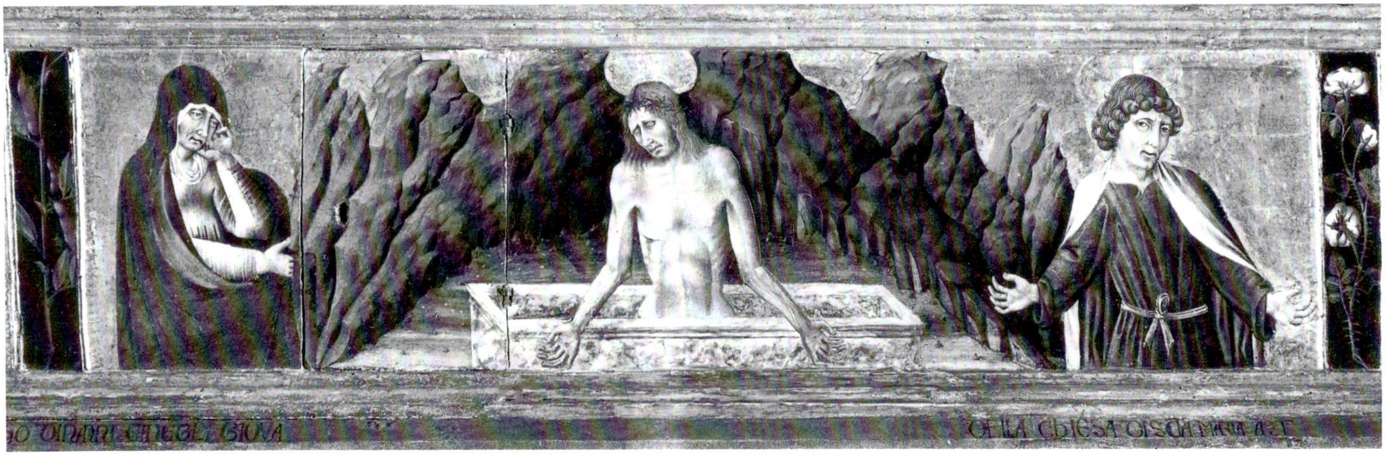

Fig. 1. Giovanni di Paolo, *Christ as the Man of Sorrows* (detail of predella from the Staggia altarpiece), ca. 1475. Tempera on panel, 41 x 260 cm
(16⅛ x 102⅜ in.), predella. Pinacoteca Nazionale, Siena

picture surface is only 18.9 cm tall) and that it differs from them in having a gold rather than silver ground.[3] Keith Christiansen concluded afterward that while it is probable that the Cambridge and El Paso predella panels did originate with the Lehman *Coronation of the Virgin*, the Feigen *Man of Sorrows* must have been part of a different altarpiece.[4] Andrea de Marchi, mistakenly assuming that the ex-Sharp *Man of Sorrows* was also in the Fitzwilliam Museum, accepted its identification as part of the predella to the Lehman *Coronation of the Virgin*.[5]

Giovanni di Paolo's habit of repeating figural motifs—or even entire compositions—from painting to painting makes it necessary to agree with Christiansen's conclusion. The Cambridge/El Paso predella must have been completed by a panel identical in all respects (except height) to the Feigen *Man of Sorrows*, but the latter must have been the center of a different predella. Unusually for Giovanni di Paolo, no other predella panels survive with the same height measurement as the Feigen panel, and it is therefore not possible to identify the rest of this predella except to say that at a minimum it must have included figures of the Mourning Virgin and Saint John the Evangelist, probably in most respects identical to those in the Cambridge and El Paso panels. It may, however, be possible to propose a candidate for the altarpiece beneath which this predella might have stood.

If the Cambridge/El Paso predella served as an iconographic precedent for the Feigen predella—which it seems slightly to predate on stylistic grounds—the latter could similarly have been intended to complete an altarpiece of the Coronation of the Virgin. Only one other such altarpiece by Giovanni di Paolo is known. Still in situ in the church of Sant'Andrea in Siena and reputedly dated by inscription 1445 on its now missing frame, this *Coronation of the Virgin* altarpiece is demonstrably earlier than either the Cambridge/El Paso predella or the Feigen predella. On the other hand, if the Feigen predella itself served as an iconographic precedent for the Staggia predella, it could have completed an altarpiece not of the Coronation but of the Assumption of the Virgin. One such altarpiece, now in the Museo d'Arte Sacra in the Palazzo Corboli, Asciano (fig. 2), has long been discussed in relation to the Staggia altarpiece, with scholarship divided over which might have been a prototype for the other. Janneke Panders has recently confirmed, on the basis of its underdrawing, that the Asciano *Assumption of the Virgin* preceded the Staggia version of the subject, and comparison to the only firmly dated work of this period, the Pienza *Lamentation* altarpiece of 1463, would suggest a date in the early or mid 1460s for the Asciano *Assumption* as well.[6]

It is difficult to establish with any precision a relative chronology for Giovanni di Paolo's late works, but suggesting a date in the early 1460s for the Feigen *Man of Sorrows* is entirely reasonable and is endorsed by de Marchi. Like the Staggia *Assumption*, the Feigen panel exhibits marked similarities in detail and in overall tenor to the Pienza altarpiece

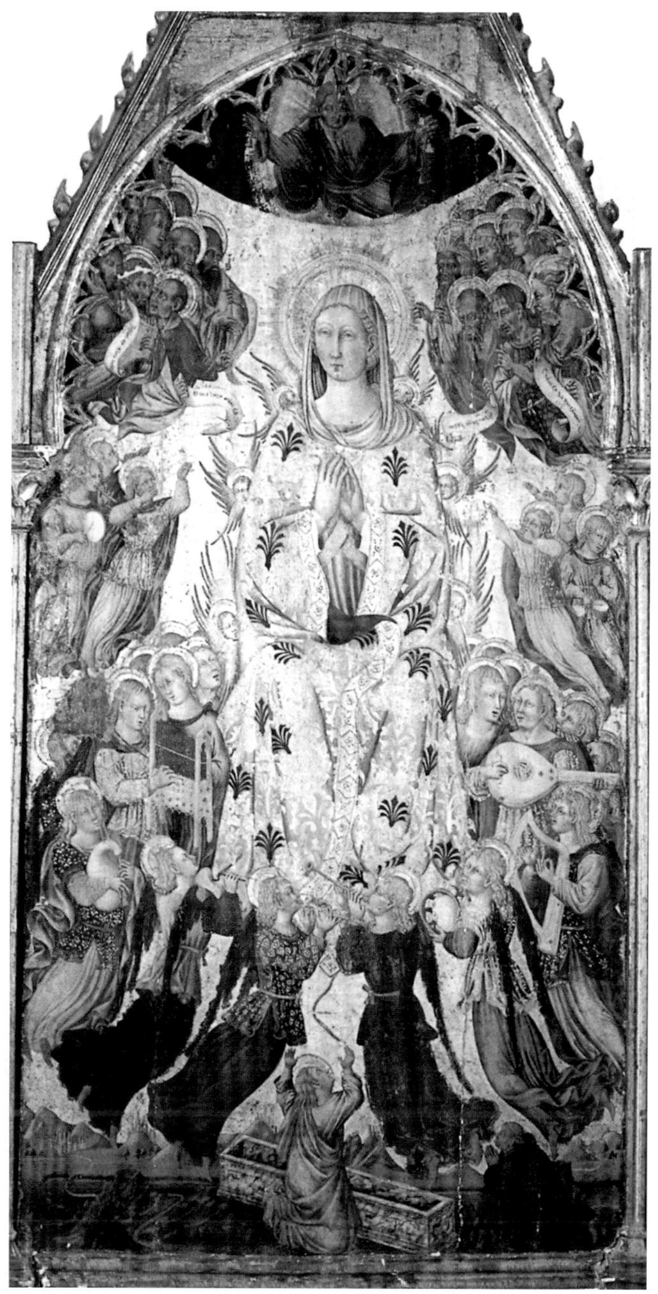

Fig. 2. Giovanni di Paolo, *Assumption of the Virgin*, ca. 1460–65. Tempera on panel, 240 x 101 cm (94½ x 39¾ in.). Palazzo Corboli, Asciano

of 1463, making an association between these works if not a likelihood at least a strong possibility.   L K

1. Andrea de Marchi, in de Marchi and Alberto Fiz, *Gold: Gothic Masters and Lucio Fontana*, ed. Marco Voena, exh. cat. (Milan, 1999), p. 49.
2. John Pope-Hennessy and Laurence Kanter, *Italian Paintings*, Robert Lehman Collection 1 (New York, 1987), p. 120; and John Pope-Hennessy, *Giovanni di Paolo* (New York, 1988), p. 44.
3. Carl Brandon Strehlke, in *Painting in Renaissance Siena, 1420–1500*, ed. Keith Christiansen, Laurence Kanter, and Strehlke, exh. cat. (New York, 1988), pp. 200–204.
4. Keith Christiansen, "Notes on 'Painting in Renaissance Siena,'" *Burlington Magazine* 132 (1990): p. 210.
5. De Marchi, *Gold*, p. 49.
6. Janneke Panders, *The Underdrawing of Giovanni di Paolo: Characteristics and Development* (Berlin, 1997), pp. 81–89.

Pietro di Francesco degli Orioli

Siena, 1458–1496

32. *David, Moses, and Two Prophets,*
ca. 1480–85

Oil on panel, 40.8 x 36.6 cm (16 x 14⅜ in.)

PROVENANCE: William Graham, M. P. (1817–1885),
London; Sir Kenneth Muir Mackenzie, London; Lady Muir
Mackenzie, London; Mrs. Donnell Post, London, by 1936;
Anthony Post, London

BIBLIOGRAPHY: Bernard Berenson, *Central Italian Painters
of the Renaissance* (London, 1899), p. 160; 2nd ed. (London,
1911), p. 213; Bernard Berenson, *Pitture italiane del Rinascimento* (Milan, 1936), p. 349; Luisa Vertova, "On Pacchiarotto's Dismembered Assumption," *Gazette des beaux-arts* 69
(1967): pp. 159–63; Bernard Berenson, *Italian Pictures of the
Renaissance: A List of the Principal Artists and Their Works
with an Index of Places: Central and North Italian Schools*
(London, 1968), 1: p. 309; Fern Rusk Shapley, *Paintings from
the Samuel H. Kress Collection: Italian Schools*, vol. 2, *XV-
XVI Century* (London, 1968), p. 111; Gertrude Rosenthal, ed.,
*Italian Paintings, XIV–XVIIIth Centuries, from the Collection
of the Baltimore Museum of Art* (Baltimore, 1981), pp. 116–
26; Oliver Garnett, "The Letters and Collection of William
Graham—Pre-Raphaelite Patron and Pre-Raphael Collector,"
The Walpole Society 62 (2000): p. 327

CONDITION: The panel has been thinned to 17 mm,
reoriented approximately 30 degrees off the vertical axis,
cut to an arched top, and inlaid in a larger rectangular panel,
the spandrels of which have been painted olive-brown. A
12 cm long dowel channel is cut into the right edge and is
now exposed to half its original depth. The paint surface is in
excellent state, with negligible and localized retouches only
along the right edge and the lower right corner.

This fragmentary panel was recognized by Bernard Beren-
son as a typical work by the Sienese artist then known as
Giacomo Pacchiarotto.[1] It was grouped by him with another,
similar fragment in the Murnaghan collection, Dublin (most
recently with Fabrizio Moretti, Florence), which shows four
bust-length figures of saints(?), including Saint John the
Baptist, facing in the opposite direction to the prophets in the
Feigen panel (fig. 1). These in turn were identified by Luisa
Vertova as two further fragments of an altarpiece of the
Assumption of the Virgin, four pieces of which had previously been reassembled by Gertrude Coor.[2] These comprise: a
full-length *Virgin* formerly in the Speyer, W. W. Burrell, and
Charles Butler collections and subsequently belonging to John
Pope-Hennessy (fig. 2); two panels with music-making angels
in the Kress Collection, now in the El Paso Museum of Art
(figs. 3–4); and a lute-playing angel given in 1962 to the Baltimore Museum of Art (fig. 5).[3] Vertova situated the prophets

on either side of the Virgin, assuming that the direction of
the gilt rays entering the Feigen panel from the left edge pre-
supposed a position roughly in the center of the completed
composition. She further presumed that such a position
confirmed Coor's intuition that the composition foreshad-
owed that of Pietro Orioli's later *Ascension* altarpiece in the
Pinacoteca Nazionale, Siena. Coor, however, had only intended
to compare the posture of the standing Virgin in the Speyer/
Pope-Hennessy fragment, unusual in Sienese representations of the Assumption, to that of Christ in the *Ascension,*
not to use the latter as a prototype for the grouping of subsid-
iary figures in the former. Inexplicably, Fern Rusk Shapley
assumed that the bust-length prophets were situated at the
lower corners of the completed altarpiece.[4]

While there is no reason to doubt that these six fragments
were all parts of a single altarpiece, detailed suggestions for
their reconstruction have until now been unsatisfactory. One
important factor not previously taken into consideration is
the direction of the wood grain in each panel. Only that in the
Speyer/Pope-Hennessy and Baltimore fragments runs truly
vertical. The two sets of angels now in El Paso have been
transferred from panel to canvas, but the direction of the

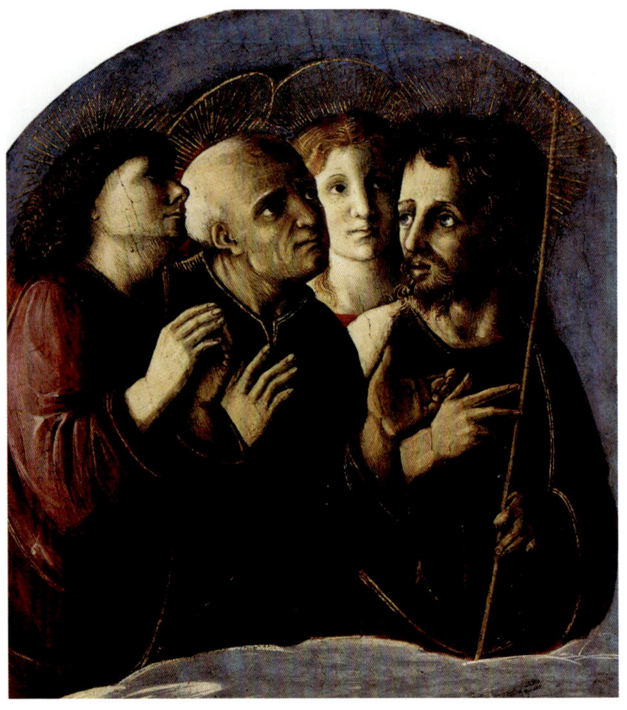

Fig. 1. Pietro di Francesco degli Orioli, *Four Saints*, ca. 1480–
85. Tempera and oil on panel, 38.5 x 41.5 cm (15⅛ x 16⅜ in.).
Private collection

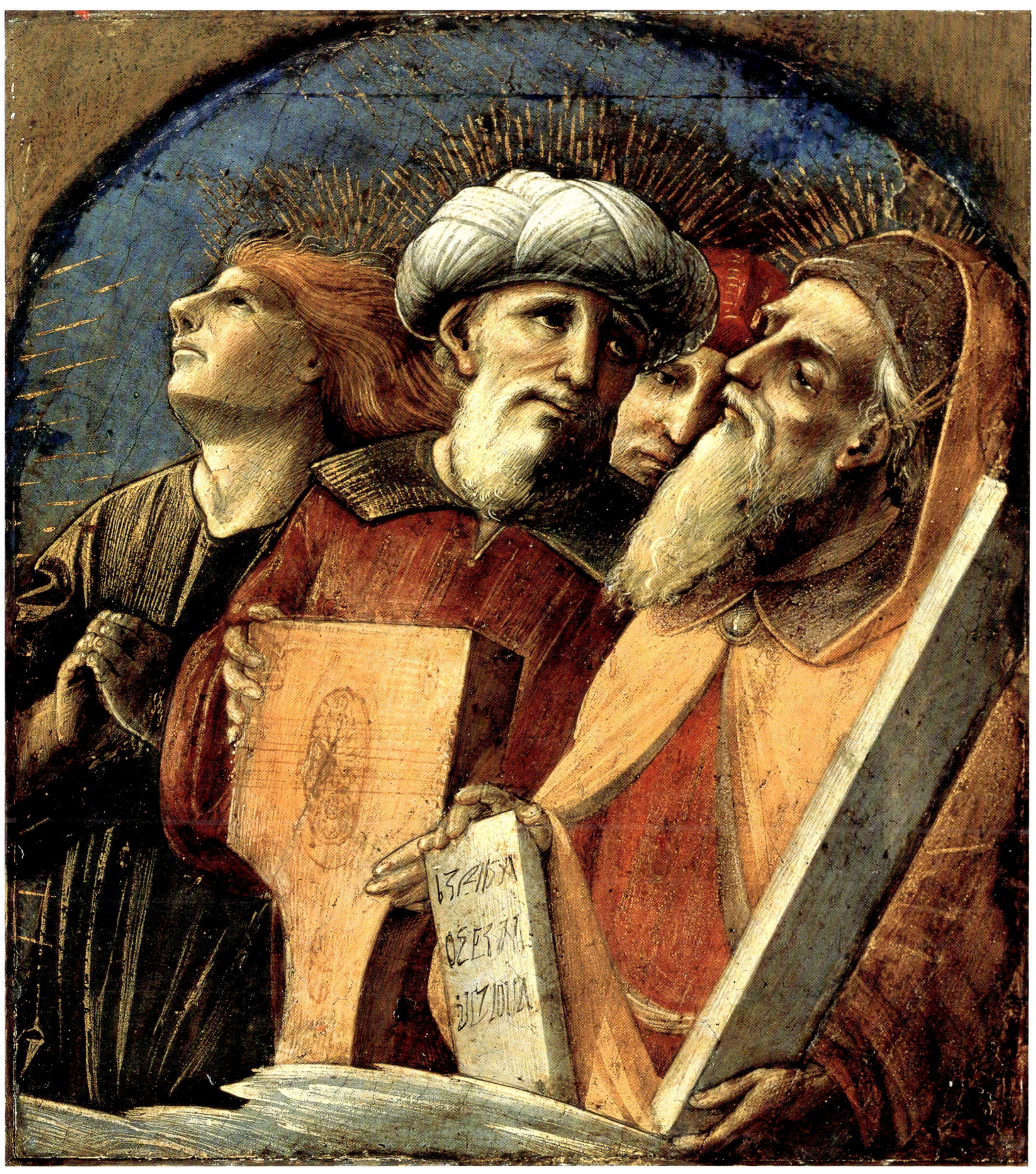

wood grain of their original support can be inferred from the pattern of splits and craquelure in the paint surface. These run at pronounced angles—approximately 30 degrees off the vertical—in opposite directions to each other, which is impossible for the construction of an Italian Renaissance altarpiece. The same is true of the two sets of bust-length prophets, and it must be concluded that all four of these panels were not originally oriented as they are now but were tilted upward at their "outer" edges. In this orientation, the figures would have appeared to be moving in toward the center and forward, and they would have described more strongly foreshortened arcs in space around the central figure. Adjusting the angle of the rays entering the Feigen panel at the left edge to account for this reorientation indicates that the prophets could only have been set above rather than alongside the Virgin, as is in any event suggested by the second set

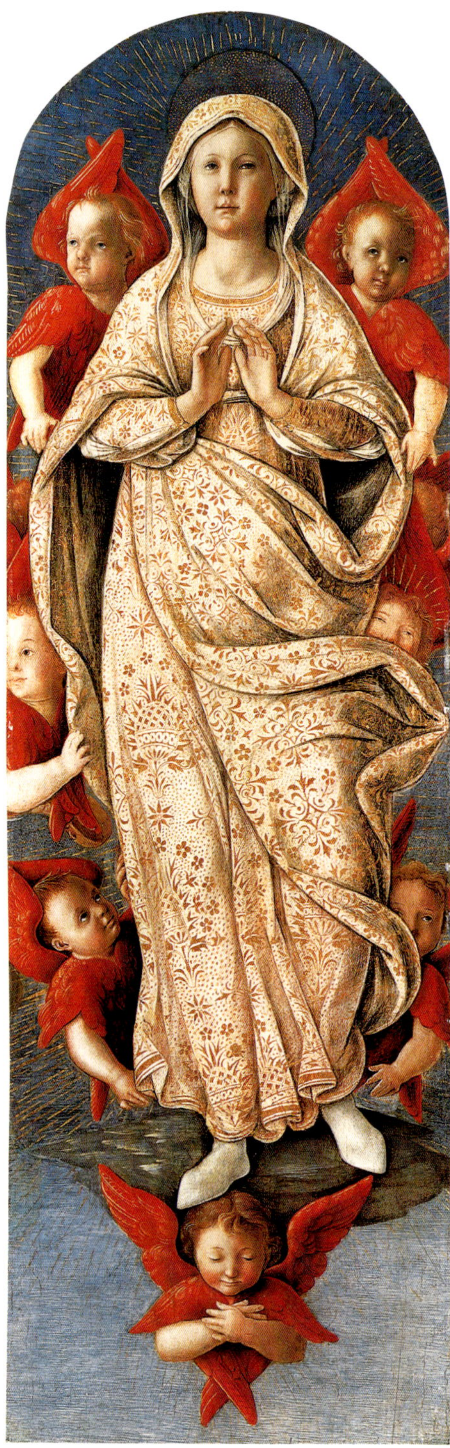

Fig. 2. Pietro di Francesco degli Orioli, *The Assumption of the Virgin*, ca. 1480–85. Tempera and oil on panel, 144.2 x 45.7 cm (56¼ x 18 in.). Formerly collection of John Pope-Hennessy

The El Paso angels were originally situated alongside the Virgin at the level of her waist, approximately the position thought by Vertova to have been occupied by the Feigen and ex-Murnaghan fragments. The red cherub wings cropped at the upper right corner of figure 3 in El Paso are the remnants of the center cherub cropped at the left edge of the Speyer/Pope-Hennessy panel. Directly beneath the arm of that cherub (all but invisible in the indifferent black-and-white photographs of the panel published by Coor and Gertrude Rosenthal) is the head and neck of the viol played by the angel on the right in figure 3 and cropped at the edge of that panel. The lute-playing angel in Baltimore was clearly cut from a lower register of the composition. The wood grain of this panel is vertical and the position of the angel's body correctly implies the flying motion implicit in the other figures when properly reoriented.[5] The fragmentary bishop's crozier cropped at the lower edge of this panel indicates that the foreground of the painting, when complete, was occupied by several figures of saints standing or kneeling in a landscape. If any of these have survived they have not yet been convincingly identified.[6] Also missing are a figure of Christ, which must have filled the uppermost level of the painting, an indeterminate number of angels once painted alongside the fragment now in Baltimore, and one further angel cropped at the left ends of each panel in El Paso. The latter have been identified by Eliot Rowlands in two fragmentary heads, cut to an oval shape, formerly in the collection of Mr. and Mrs. Fielding Lewis Marshall (present whereabouts unknown).[7] That the Feigen and ex-Murnaghan panels of prophets and saints are substantially complete in width, cropping no further figures at their outer edges, is implied by the dowel channel cut into the back of the former. This must have been intended to affix the altarpiece panel to an adjacent structural support, probably the painted pilaster of a heavy architectural frame (see below).

As reconstructed here, the altarpiece of which the Feigen *Prophets* formed part follows one of the two most common formats for representations of the Assumption of the Virgin in fifteenth-century Siena. Both of these supposedly refer to a much-venerated prototype thought to have been painted by Simone Martini in the 1320s or 1330s, the closest-surviving reflection of which is believed to be a small panel in the Alte Pinakothek, Munich, attributed to Lippo Memmi or his circle. In this painting, the Virgin is seated on a bank of cloud held up by cherubim and encircled by a ring of music-making angels. Above her, a half-length figure of Christ, flanked by prophets and patriarchs flying in from the edges of the composition, waits to receive her into Heaven. The Munich painting, or its prototype, was copied numerous times in the late fourteenth and early fifteenth centuries. A monumental version of this image was apparently frescoed above the Antiporto di Camollia in Siena, one of the gates of the city, which inspired Saint Bernardino's *ekphrasis* on the Assumption in one of his famous sermons of 1427. The words of Saint Bernardino in turn informed the content and format of the second type

of rays entering the Feigen panel from the top. These must have emanated from a figure of Christ receiving His mother into Paradise at the top center of the original composition, and it must be toward this figure rather than toward the Virgin that several of the prophets look. The cherub at the upper left corner of the Speyer/Pope-Hennessy fragment is looking out to the left and slightly upward, undoubtedly focusing on the saints and prophets once there and now included in the ex-Murnaghan panel.

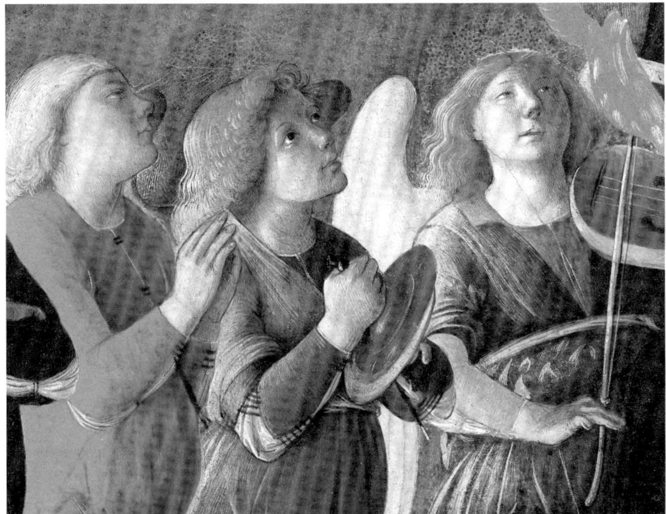

Fig. 3. Pietro di Francesco degli Orioli, *Music-Making Angels,*
ca. 1500. Tempera on panel, 35.6 x 43.8 cm (14 x 17¼ in.). El
Paso Museum of Art, Gift of the Samuel H. Kress Foundation,
inv. no. 1961.1.10a

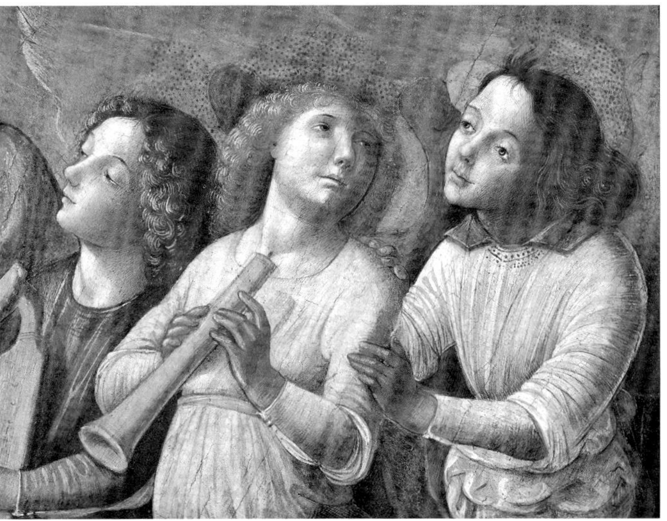

Fig. 4. Pietro di Francesco degli Orioli, *Music-Making Angels,*
ca. 1500. Tempera on panel, 35.6 x 43.8 cm (14 x 17¼ in.). El
Paso Museum of Art, Gift of the Samuel H. Kress Foundation,
inv. no. 1961.1.10b

of Sienese Assumption. An altarpiece by Sassetta (formerly
in Berlin, destroyed in 1945) that follows closely the text of
Bernardino's description is said to have been ordered by the
saint for the high altar of his church at the Osservanza in
Siena and served as the model for several faithful replicas. In
this painting, the circles of angels are multiplied and made
more specific, as Bernardino described the Virgin's ecstatic
ascent through all nine angelic orders as well as the planetary
heavens before reaching the presence of God and the saints.
Orioli chose, or was directed, to follow the more simplified,
earlier version of the composition, deviating from his model
almost exclusively by showing the Virgin standing rather
than seated. Presumably, the figures represented in the Feigen
and ex-Murnaghan fragments are the patriarchs and prophets
liberated from Purgatory by Christ in the Harrowing of Hell,
as few saints actually predeceased the Virgin. The fact that
two figures in the ex-Murnaghan panel are portrayed with
haloes rather than simple rays is misleading, as Saint John
the Baptist in that panel has only rays, not a halo.

As long as the artistic personality of Pietro Orioli was
confused with that of Giacomo Pacchiarotto (1474–ca. 1540),
the complete body of works now recognized as having been
painted by the former was assigned to the early career of the
latter and was somewhat unrealistically collapsed into a short
period of time stretching roughly from 1495 to 1500. Following the research of Alessandro Angelini, however, it is
now apparent that these paintings are not precocious efforts
by a modest and *retardataire* talent primarily active in the
first third of the sixteenth century but rather innovative and
influential works by Siena's leading master of an earlier generation, datable from the late 1470s through to the artist's
death in 1496.[8] The *Assumption* altarpiece of which the Feigen
panel formed part must have been executed toward the beginning of this span, in the early or mid-1480s. Not as closely
indebted to the example of his master, Matteo di Giovanni, as

Orioli's first creations, it also shows little of the impression
made on him by his contemporaries Francesco di Giorgio and
Luca Signorelli toward the end of that decade and none of
the dark and somber atmosphere of his last paintings from
the mid-1490s. The technique of the *Assumption* fragments
also points to an early date for them. As his career advanced,
Orioli appears to have grown increasingly comfortable in his
mastery of an oil medium that is not yet in evidence here.

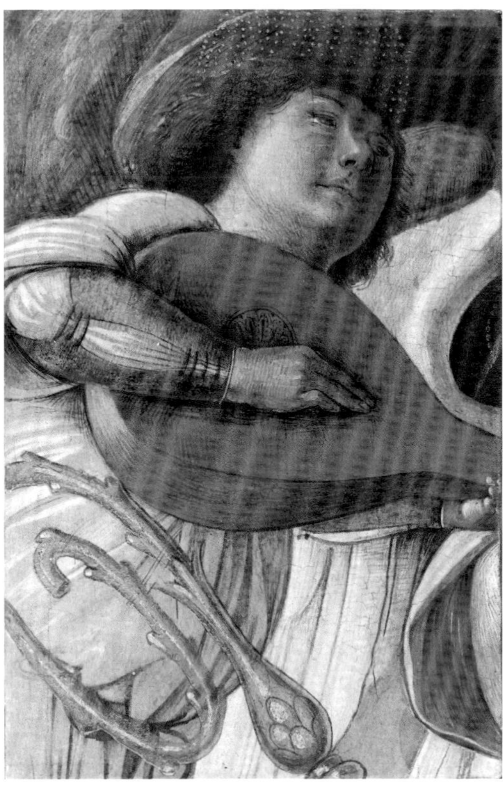

Fig. 5. Pietro di Francesco degli Orioli, *Lute-Playing
Angel,* ca. 1493–95. Tempera and oil on panel, 32.4 x
21.6 cm (12¾ x 8½ in.). Baltimore Museum of Art,
Gift of M. Knoedler & Co. in honor of Adelyn D.
Breeskin, inv. no. BMA 1962.1

No archival documentation for a commission that might
be related to this painting has been uncovered, nor have ancillary parts of the altarpiece (predella, pilasters), if they existed,
been identified. Vertova's proposal that a set of predella
panels in the Fitzwilliam Museum, Cambridge, the Walters
Art Museum, Baltimore, and elsewhere, as well as three
pilaster figures in the Courtauld Gallery, London, might have
been joined to this altarpiece is inherently improbable. On
the grounds of iconography and style, these are more likely
to have been part of the later altarpiece of the *Ascension of
Christ* painted by Orioli for the Basilica dell'Osservanza and
now in the Pinacoteca Nazionale, Siena.   LK

1. See Bernard Berenson, *Central Italian Painters of the Renaissance*
   (London, 1899), p. 160.
2. Luisa Vertova, "On Pacchiarotto's Dismembered Assumption," *Gazette
   des beaux-arts* 69 (1967): pp. 159–63; and Gertrude Coor, "Notes on Six
   Parts of Two Dismembered Sienese Altarpieces," *Gazette des beaux-arts*
   65 (1965): pp. 129–36.
3. For the full-length *Virgin,* see Christie's, New York, sale cat. (January 10,
   1996), lot 102.
4. Fern Rusk Shapley, *Paintings from the Samuel H. Kress Collection:
   Italian Schools,* vol. 2, *XV–XVI Century* (London, 1968), p. 111.
5. The lute-playing angel in Baltimore has been transferred to a new
   wooden support, but the grain direction of its original support is easily
   inferred from vertical splits in the paint surface.
6. It is tempting to agree with Luisa Vertova that a "Saint Onophrius
   kneeling in a landscape" by "Pacchiarotto" indicated in a handwritten
   note by Bernard Berenson as accompanying the Feigen panel in the
   collection of Sir Kenneth Muir Mackenzie might be a fragment of this
   painting. In the absence of any further record of such a painting, or
   even of its size, such a proposal cannot be advanced beyond pure
   speculation.
7. See Bonham's, London, sale cat. (March 28, 1974). The two *Angels*
   also figured in an exhibition of the Fielding Lewis Marshall collection
   held at Sotheby's, London, *Exhibition of the Marshall Collection . . .*
   (December 31, 1973–January 8, 1974), p. 62, no. 85, where they were
   already identified as fragments of this dispersed altarpiece. Previously,
   they had been offered at Christie's, London (February 23, 1968, lot 21), as
   by Francesco Botticini. I am grateful to Eliot Rowlands for this reference.
8. Alessandro Angelini, "Pietro Orioli e il momento 'Urbinate' della pittura
   senese del quattrocento," *Prospettiva* 30 (1982): pp. 30–43.

Ambrogio da Fossano, called il Bergognone
Milan, ca. 1453–1523

33. *Three Singing Angels,* ca. 1485

Tempera and oil(?) on panel, 14 x 19.8 cm (5½ x 7⅞ in.)

PROVENANCE: Albert Lehmann, Paris (his sale, Galerie
Georges Petit, Paris, June 12–13, 1925, lot 224 [as "School of
Fra Angelico"]); private collection, France; Sotheby's, Munich,
June 16, 1989, lot 301

BIBLIOGRAPHY: Mauro Natale, ed., *Pittura italiana dal '300
al '500* (Milan, 1991), pp. 119–20; Maria Grazia Balzarini,
Vincenzo Foppa: La formazione e l'attività giovanile (Florence,
1996), pp. 71–72; Nadia Righi, in *Ambrogio da Fossano detto
il Bergognone: Un pittore per la Certosa,* ed. Gianni Carlo
Sciolla, exh. cat. (Milan, 1998), pp. 132, 136n.80; Mauro
Natale, ed., *El Renacimiento mediterráneo: Viajes de artistas
e itinerarios de obras entre Italia, Francia, y España en el
siglo XV,* exh. cat. (Madrid, 2001), no. 69; Federica Armiraglio,
Museo Poldi Pezzoli Milano (Milan, 2006), p. 70

CONDITION: The strong vertical craquelure of the surface
results from the warping of the wooden panel, which was corrected at an unknown date. The panel has been thinned, and
although the painted surface of the lunette is more or less
intact, the panel has clearly been trimmed at the sides, which
would originally have been covered by moldings. Two battens
have been attached to the back. The paint surface is well preserved, but the bottom edge of the shelf is repainted.

Ambrogio Bergognone, active in Milan, Pavia, and elsewhere, was among the leading artists in Lombardy during his lifetime. He probably received his primary training
from Vincenzo Foppa, to whose works his bear the closest
comparison, but Bergognone's painting also betrays the
strong influence of Northern European art. What is still not
clear is whether Bergognone had direct contact with Netherlandish artists or only with Netherlandish paintings; certainly, there were many Northern paintings in Milan by
the later quattrocento, and also in Liguria, where the young
Bergognone perhaps accompanied Foppa during the latter's
periods there in the 1470s and 1480s. The influence on both
Foppa and Bergognone of Donato de' Bardi, whose synthesis
of Flemish and Lombard painting was the model for many
Italians, was also considerable, and likewise, Bergognone's
French stylistic touches might come via an artist like the
Master of the Cagnola Madonna, rather than through direct
contact with Provençal painting. Whatever their sources,
Bergognone's works are characterized by the gray tonalities
and ropy musculature inherited from Foppa, by a fineness of
detail usually linked to Northern painting, and—especially in
the 1490s and after—by a reflection of the perspectival lessons
and spatial constructions of Donato Bramante.

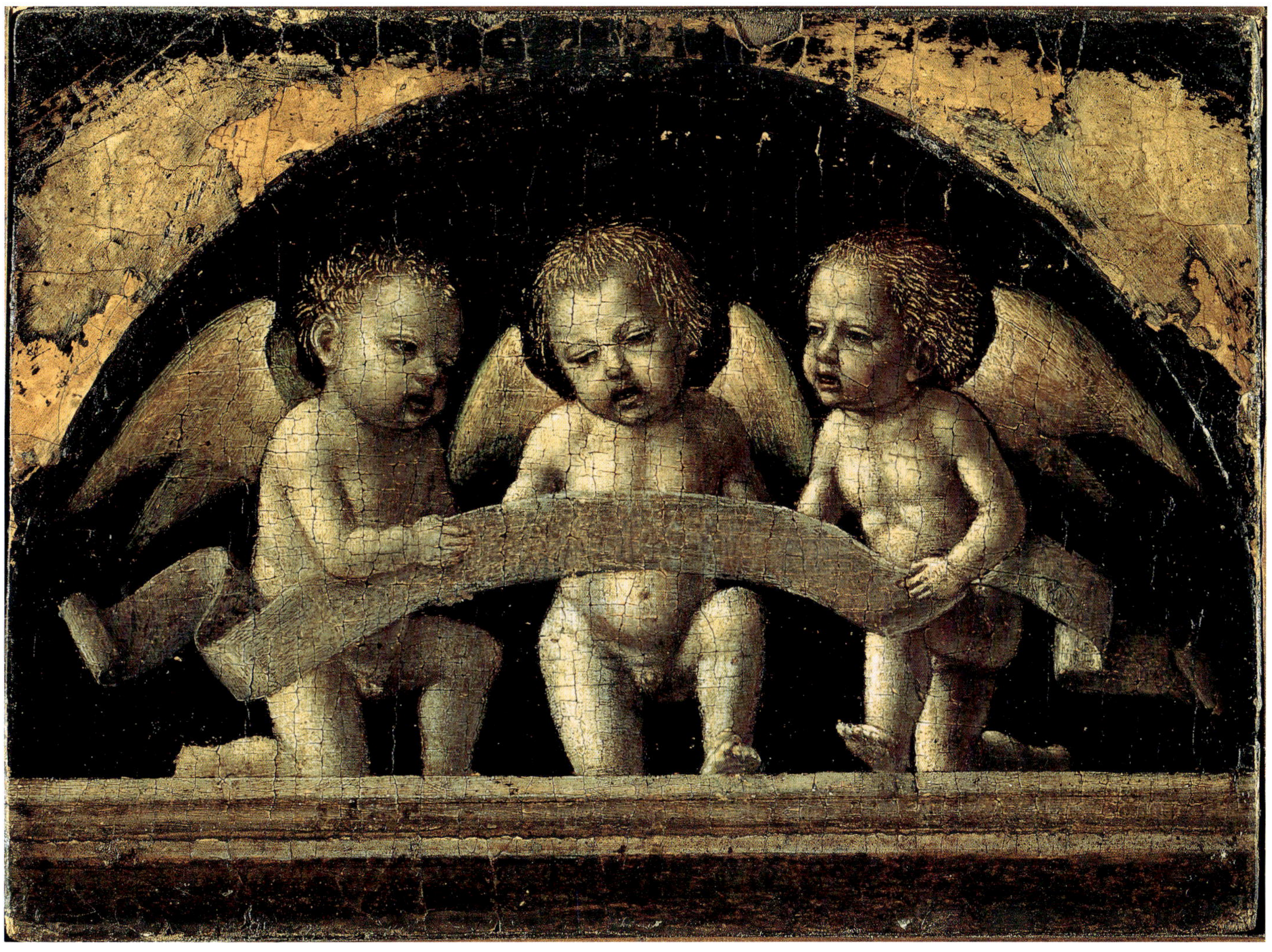

When it appeared at auction in 1989, the present work was attributed not implausibly to Foppa, but it has since been identified as the work of Bergognone by Mauro Natale, Maria Grazia Balzarini, Nadia Righi, and others. The panel, clearly a fragment of a larger work, is not signed or dated, but Bergognone's earliest surviving dated work was completed in 1488, fifteen years into his activity as a painter. Balzarini placed the painting in the 1470s, but in a convincing reconstruction of Bergognone's early career, Righi argued instead that the *Three Singing Angels* dates to around the year 1485.[1] One benchmark for this date is Bergognone's *Virgin and Child Enthroned with Saints* altarpiece, now in the Pinacoteca Ambrosiana, Milan. That painting, his first important commission of which we are aware, was commissioned for Sant'Epifano, Pavia, by Gerolamo Calagrani, who probably did so in 1484 when his own principal patron, Giovanni Angelo Cybo, was chosen as Pope Innocent VIII. At this moment, Bergognone was still close to Foppa (whose Bottigella altarpiece now in the Pinacoteca Malaspina, Pavia, is an immediate model) and although aware of Bramante's lessons in monumentality, he was still more interested in minute description of the sort common in Flemish painting. All of these traits are seen equally in the Feigen panel and the Ambrosiana altarpiece, despite their widely varying scale. As noted by Righi, the angels in both paintings not only share the same typology and the same sorts of expressions but are also executed in the same technique, with the highlights of the hair created by touches of color applied with the tip of the brush. Righi's second benchmark for dating the Feigen *Angels* is the Villa di Caselle Lomellina, near Pavia, where Bergognone's frescoes were commissioned by Francesco degli Eustachi around 1484. Finally, the Feigen *Angels* can be compared to those in the *Sacra Conversazione* altarpiece in the church of Santi Gratiniano e Felino at Arona, which was also commissioned by Gerolamo Calagrani and is datable to ca. 1487–88.[2] Although all three of the aforementioned benchmarks are able to be dated only approximately, they fit together as a set and seem, on the basis of probable if not certain evidence, all to fall within a few years of 1485, where the *Three Singing Angels* should also be placed. Compositionally, the low viewpoint and the treatment of the lunette's lower edge as a cornice onto which step the angels are similar to those in Bergognone's ca. 1490 *Pietà with Angels* lunette at the Castello Sforzesco, Milan; as has been noted before, that work seems to reflect Foppa's *Virgin and Child with Saints John the Baptist and John the Evangelist* (Milan, Brera), dated 1485.[3]

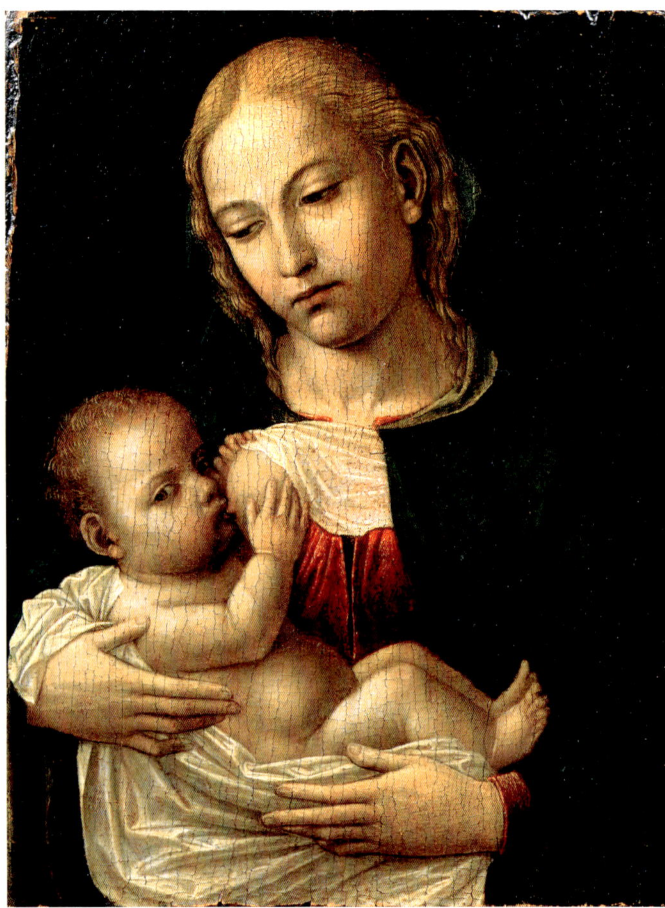

Fig. 1. Ambrogio da Fossano, called il Bergognone, *Madonna del Latte*, ca. 1485. Tempera and oil on panel, 29.5 x 22.5 cm (11⅝ x 8⅞ in.). Museo Poldi Pezzoli, Milan

a modern cradle and preserves fictive marble painting on its back face, but the Feigen panel has been thinned.[4]

The Milan panel has itself been variously attributed over the past decades. Ascribed to Bergognone when acquired by Gian Giacomo Poldi Pezzoli, and so catalogued by Giuseppe Bertini and Evelyn Sandberg Vavalà, the *Madonna del Latte* was alternately attributed to Foppa by Roberto Longhi or to Donato de' Bardi by Federico Zeri, Mauro Natale, and Frangi.[5] Franco Russoli, C. L. Ragghianti, Bernard Berenson, and, more recently, Giovanni Romano and Roberto Battaglia have all instead maintained an attribution to the young Bergognone.[6] In light of the persuasive argument that the Feigen lunette, so clearly by Bergognone, was connected to the Milan panel, Natale and others have now accepted the reattribution of the latter painting to Bergognone as well, despite its slightly *retardataire* style. The frequent collaborations of Lombard artists remain to be unraveled, and the portable altar could have been a collaboration between Bergognone and one of his older contemporaries, but the fairly secure dating of the lunette—and therefore also the *Virgin and Child*—to ca. 1485 would rule out any intervention by Donato de' Bardi, who had died long before.[7] The most probable conclusion is that both the lunette and main panel are by Bergognone, and that taken together, they will figure in the continuing attempts to understand the artist's synthesis of Lombard, Flemish, and French influences.

JJM

Following the suggestion of Francesco Frangi, Righi also asserted that the *Three Singing Angels* originally constituted the lunette top of a portable altar of which the *Madonna del Latte* in the Museo Poldi Pezzoli, Milan, was the main panel (fig. 1). This suggestion is compelling, for not only are the panels essentially the same width (the minor discrepancies can be accounted for by the trimming of the Feigen panel), but also the black backgrounds of both paintings are unusual and otherwise unknown in Bergognone's oeuvre. X-radiographs have not been taken to compare the grain of the wood, which would confirm that the pieces were cut from a single panel, but the pronounced craquelure of both pictures is consistent. This craquelure resulted from the warping of the wood support, but the *Angels* and *Virgin and Child* were separated (perhaps following damage to the original frame that resulted from the curvature of the wood) long ago, and they were flattened in different restorations: the Milan panel, which entered the Poldi Pezzoli collection in the mid-nineteenth century, has

1. See Maria Grazia Balzarini, *Vincenzo Foppa: La formazione e l'attività giovanile* (Florence, 1996), pp. 71–72; and Nadia Righi, in *Ambrogio da Fossano detto il Bergognone: Un pittore per la Certosa*, ed. Gianni Carlo Sciolla, exh. cat. (Milan, 1998), p. 132.

2. Righi, in Sciolla, *Ambrogio da Fossano*, pp. 130–33.

3. On the Castello Sforzesco lunette, see ibid., p. 206, no. 25.

4. Notes on the Milan panel's conservation history are found in Mauro Natale, *Museo Poldi Pezzoli: Dipinti* (Milan, 1982), p. 71.

5. See Giuseppe Bertini, *Catalogo generale della Fondazione Artistica Poldi Pezzoli* (Milan, 1881), p. 37; Evelyn Sandberg Vavalà, "Ambrogio Bergognone in a Recent Publication," *Burlington Magazine* 89 (1947): p. 306; Roberto Longhi, in Franco Russoli, *Catalogo della Pinacoteca Poldi Pezzoli* (Milan, 1955), p. 156; Natale, *Museo Poldi Pezzoli*, pp. 71–72; and Francesco Frangi, in Mina Gregori, ed., *Pittura a Pavia dal romanico al settecento* (Milan, 1988), p. 207.

6. C. L. Ragghianti, review of *Catalogo della Pinacoteca Poldi Pezzoli*, by Franco Russoli, *Critica d'arte*, n.s. 2 (1955): p. 195; Bernard Berenson, *Italian Pictures of the Renaissance: A List of the Principal Artists and Their Works with an Index of Places: Central Italian and North Italian Schools* (London, 1968), p. 44; Giovanni Romano, "Sur Antoine de Lonhy en Piémont," *Revue de l'art* 85 (1989): p. 42n.5; and Roberto Battaglia, review of *Ambrogio Bergognone: Acquisizioni, scoperte e restauri*, by Pietro C. Marani and Janice Shell, *Osservatorio delle arti* 4 (1990): pp. 109–13.

7. The complicated matter of collaboration among artists of the Lombard school is noted by Luke Syson, review of *Ambrogio da Fossano detto il Bergognone: Un pittore per la Certosa*, ed. Gianni Carlo Sciolla, *Burlington Magazine* 140 (1998): p. 575.

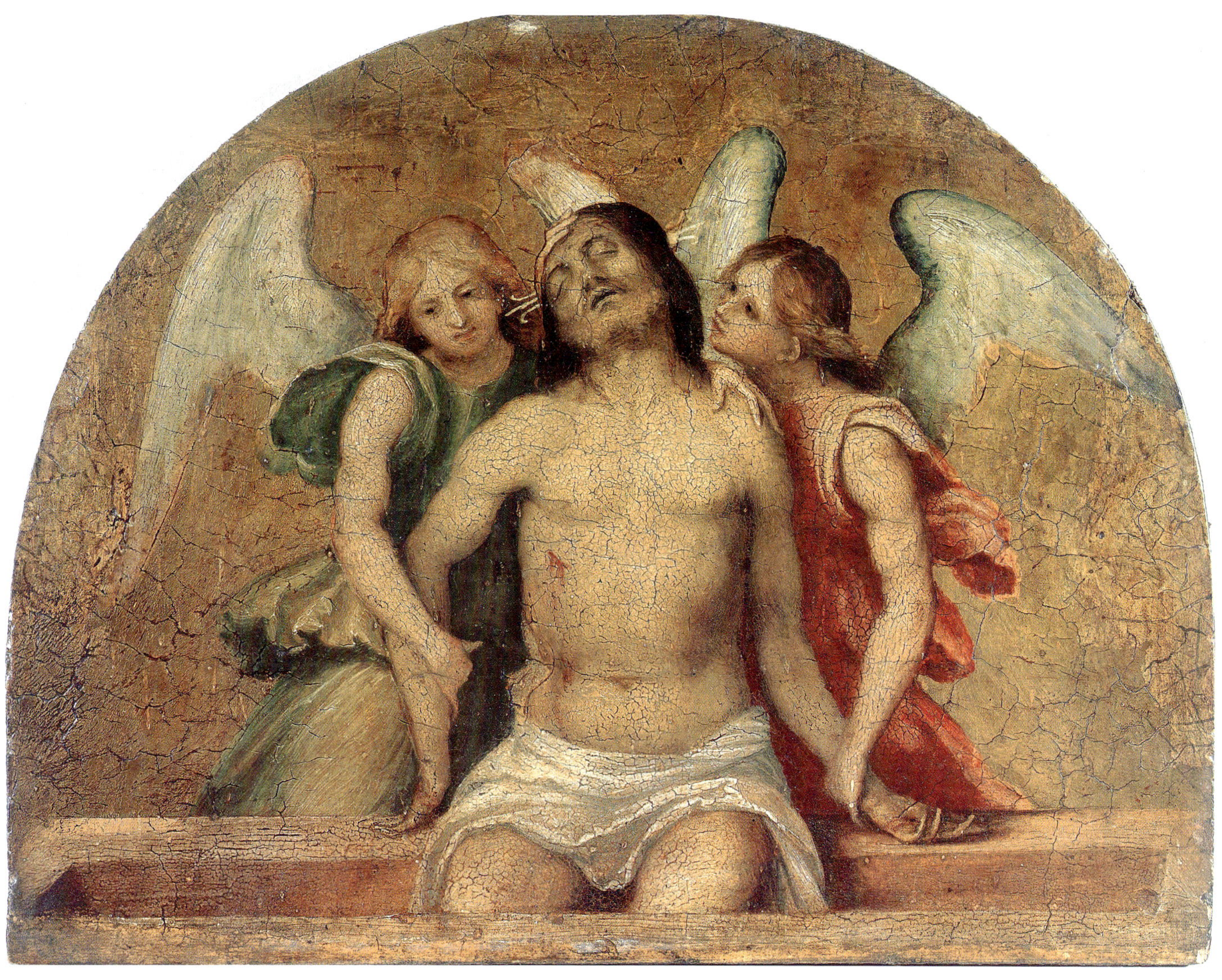

Lorenzo Lotto

Venice, ca. 1480–1556

34. *Pietà*, ca. 1516–17

Oil on panel, 16 x 20 cm (6¼ x 8 in.), lunette

PROVENANCE: probably collection of Robert Stayner Holford (1808–1892), London and Westonbirt, Gloucestershire, England; Sir George Lindsay Holford (1860–1926), London; Robert Henry Benson (1850–1929) and Evelyn Mary Holford Benson (1856–1943), London and Buckhurst Park, Sussex, England, by 1925; by descent to Lt. Col. Sir Reginald Lindsay (Rex) Benson (1889–1968), Chichester, Sussex; Sotheby's, London, June 21, 1978, lot 1 (sold as "Property of a Lady" and likely to have come directly from Leslie Foster Benson, widow of Rex Benson).

The panel was not included in the sale of the Benson collection to Duveen in 1927, perhaps because it had been passed down from the Holford family, in contrast to those works that had been purchased by Robert Henry and Evelyn Benson.

BIBLIOGRAPHY: Adolfo Venturi, *Grandi artisti italiani* (Bologna, 1925), p. 114; Manchester City Art Gallery, *Loan Exhibition of the Benson Collection of Italian Masters*, exh. cat. (Manchester, England, 1927), no. 91; Adolfo Venturi, *Storia dell'arte italiana*, vol. 9, *La pittura del cinquecento*, pt. 4 (Milan, 1929), p. 30; Anna Banti and Antonio Boschetto, *Lorenzo Lotto* (Florence, 1953), p. 71, no. 35; Bernard Berenson, *Lotto*, trans. Luisa Vertova (Milan, 1955), p. 215; Piero Bianconi, *Tutta la pittura di Lorenzo Lotto* (Milan, 1955), p. 43; Bernard Berenson, *Lorenzo Lotto* (London, 1956), pp. 27, 465; Bernard Berenson, *Italian Pictures of the Renaissance: A List of the Principal Artists and Their Works with an Index of Places: Venetian School* (London, 1957), 1: p. 103; Rodolfo Pallucchini and Giordana Maria Canova, *L'opera completa del Lotto*,

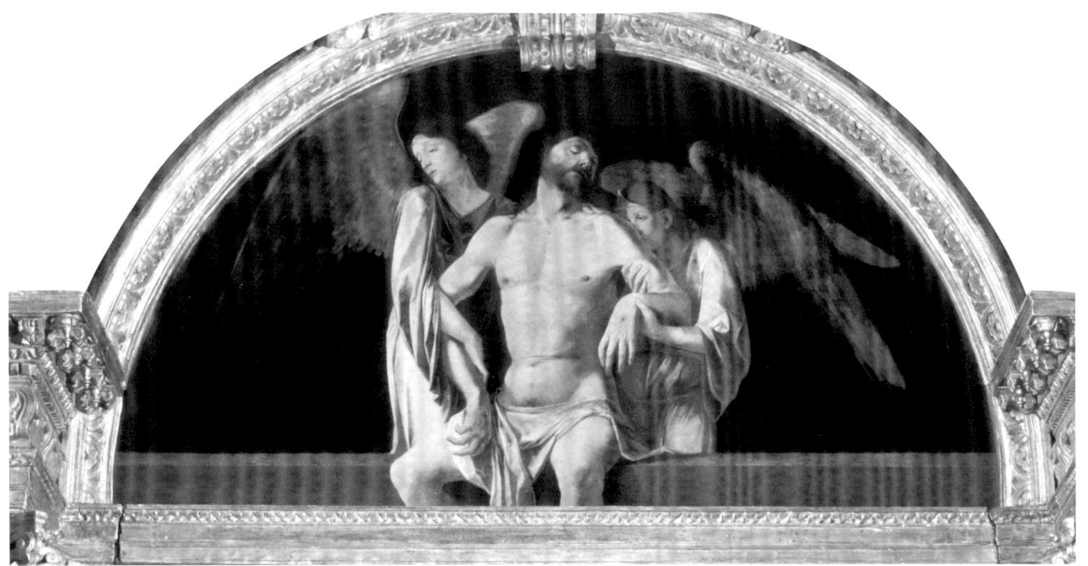

Fig. 1. Lorenzo Lotto, *Pietà*, 1505. Oil on panel, 90 x 179 cm (35 ½ x 70½ in.). Santa Cristina, Treviso

Classici dell'arte 79 (Milan, 1975), p. 95, no. 51; Flavio Caroli, *Lorenzo Lotto e la nascita della psicologia moderna* (Milan, 1980), pp. 254–55; Tamara D. Fomichova, *Venetian Painting, Fourteenth to Eighteenth Centuries,* The Hermitage Catalogue of Western European Painting 2 (Florence, 1992), p. 194

CONDITION: The earliest photographs of the panel show it as a rectangle, and the first descriptions correspondingly note that much of the gold was not original. The first photograph to show the panel trimmed to its original lunette shape appears in Bernard Berenson's 1955 book on Lorenzo Lotto, although there is no record of when, or by whom, this work was done.[1] The background is silver gilt with a gamboge glaze and is largely original. Irregular repairs to the gilding are applied across the top of the panel and outside the angels' wings at both sides. A broad traction crackle interrupts the red draperies of the angel at the right, but the paint surface otherwise is well preserved.

Depicting two angels supporting the dead body of Christ above the tomb, this intimate lunette of the *Pietà* was presumably the top of a small private altarpiece, and its delicate touches—the hand of the angel gently cradling Christ's head, for example—are best appreciated at close view. It is the only known painting by Lorenzo Lotto on a gold ground, a choice of medium perhaps related to its original function as a small private altar (an unusual format for the artist) or perhaps reflecting the wishes of a conservative patron.

The *Pietà* is an early work by Lotto, surely from the first third of his career. It still evokes the paintings of Giovanni Bellini and others of Lotto's earliest models, and there is an obvious similarity to the *Pietà* atop Lotto's early altarpiece in Santa Cristina in Treviso, completed in 1505 (fig. 1), and to the *Pietà* atop Lotto's polyptych in the Pinacoteca Civica, Recanati, completed in 1508. Yet, the manner of organizing draperies around the body, as seen, for example, in the folds bunched at the waist and hips of the angels, is not consistent with the

harder, planar draperies of Lotto's pre-Roman paintings. Bernard Berenson, noting that the "face of the angel on the right is Raphaelesque," accordingly dated the work to ca. 1512, the period just after Lotto's Roman sojourn.[2] The lyrical painting is indeed among the least eccentric of Lotto's works, and its classicism might well be Lotto's immediate response to seeing the style of Raphael and others in Rome. Yet, Adolfo Venturi, who was responsible for reattributing the panel from Correggio to Lotto, argued that the work demonstrates the "full maturity" of Lotto and placed it slightly later still, dating it to ca. 1515, a date echoed by Antonio Boschetto and Piero Bianconi.[3] This date does seem closer to the mark. The typology of the angels, notwithstanding the shift of scale, is closest to those in Lotto's enormous Martinengo altarpiece of 1516 for Santo Stefano in Bergamo (now San Bartolomeo, Bergamo), while the slightly miniaturist aspect of the anatomy can be compared to that in a number of Lotto's paintings of that time, including the *Saint Dominic Reviving Napoleone Orsini, Deposition,* and *Stoning of Saint Stephen* from the predella of that altarpiece (now Accademia Carrara, Bergamo). Whatever its precise date, the *Pietà* was presumably painted during Lotto's first years at Bergamo, a time when he executed a number of works on a similarly small scale. These include the *Saint James the Greater* (Pinacoteca Comunale, Recanati), which seems to have been painted in Bergamo and then sent back to Recanati,[4] the *Penitent Saint Jerome* now in Bucharest (Muzeul National de'Arta al Romaniei[5]), and the small roundels in Raleigh (North Carolina Museum of Art), which, with the Dominican saints from the Fondazione Roberto Longhi, Florence, are sometimes said to have been from the original frame of the Martinengo altarpiece.[6] Although the Lotto bibliography is enormous and ever expanding, the discrepancies in previous datings of the Feigen panel might be said to emphasize the need for a new catalogue raisonné of the painter's work.

Accepted as the work of Lotto since it was attributed to him by Venturi, the panel has nonetheless received little critical comment from the present generation of Lotto scholars. Flavio Caroli ended his brief comment on the painting in his 1980 Lotto publication by writing that "the refacing of the gold ground does not permit a secure attribution."[7] While the margins of the panel have been retouched where it had previously been extended to make a rectangle, the glazed silver gilt background is original and the paint surface is well preserved. It is unlikely, moreover, that Caroli actually saw this panel in person, for he cites the location as formerly in the Holford collection, which it left in the first decades of the twentieth century, and his published image is reversed.

The Feigen panel has sometimes been linked with the "figura di Cristo morto sopra il Sepolcro sostenuto da due angeli" (figure of the dead Christ over the Sepulcher, held by two angels) described by Carlo Ridolfi in 1648 as then in the collection of Jan and Jacob Van Buren (or Van Boeren) of Antwerp, although, as noted by Berenson, the Van Buren painting was probably a larger picture.[8] After the "Dead Christ," Ridolfi next describes a "piccolo ritratto d'una Monaca" (small portrait of a Nun), and one might expect that the notably modest Feigen panel would also have been described as small had it been the *Pietà* in the Van Buren collection. Following the same logic, the Van Buren *Pietà* might be the work of that subject that Marcantonio Michiel saw in the house of Domenico Tassi dal Cornello at Bergamo, described as a "quadro" and therefore presumably larger than the "quadretto de S. Hieronimo" that follows in Michiel's list; the latter work is alternately identified as the aforementioned *Saint Jerome* in Bucharest or the *Saint Jerome* dated 1515 from the Kress Collection, now in the Allentown Art Museum, Pennsylvania, each of which is over twice the width of the Feigen panel.[9] The Tassi dal Cornello *Pietà* is thereafter untraced and could be that which went to Antwerp. Alternately, the Van Buren *Pietà* could be another work painted in Bergamo. Lotto charged Giovanni Cassotti 12 lire in 1523 "per refar el quadro de la pieta tuto de novo che se era guasto" (to remake entirely anew the panel of the *Pietà* which was ruined).[10] It is not clear whether that 12-lire sum (half of what Lotto charged for a half-length *Virgin and Child*) was so modest because the *Pietà* was small—in which case it might have been the Feigen picture—or because it was simply being remade. Another of Giovanni Cassotti's pictures, the *Portrait of a Married Couple*, now in the Hermitage, Saint Petersburg, was also later in the Van Buren collection, and the Cassotti *Pietà* could have gone along with it.[11] In sum, though, these references probably do not relate to the Feigen *Pietà*; the damaged and little-studied *Pietà* in the Hermitage is more likely to have been the work in the Van Buren, Tassi dal Cornello, and/or Cassotti collections.[12]

Rather than an independent work like those just mentioned, the present small panel was almost certainly part of a portable altar, like the similarly scaled *Three Singing Angels* by Bergognone in the Feigen collection (no. 33). The central subject of such an ensemble was most likely to be the Virgin and Child, and the *Pietà* would have served as a crowning

lunette, as an image of the subject does in several of Lotto's full-scale altarpieces. No reconstruction has ever been suggested for the Feigen *Pietà*, but it is here proposed that it could have been part of a portable altar with the *Madonna del Latte* in the Pushkin Museum, Moscow (fig. 2). Repeatedly catalogued as located in the Hermitage, although since 1928 in Moscow, the *Madonna del Latte* is as little studied by Lotto scholars as is the Feigen *Pietà*.[13] The subject is one commonly found in portable altars, and the panel (32.5 x 28.5 cm) is only slightly wider than the Feigen lunette (20 cm), which has been cut at the sides. In 1981 the Moscow panel was cleaned, revealing two angels that had been overpainted long ago.[14] Matching the angels in the Feigen *Pietà* in virtually every detail—the style of drapery, their physiognomy, and the manner in which they are painted—the unveiled angels seem to emphasize the likely connections between the Feigen and Pushkin Museum compositions. As Vittoria Markova notes, the rediscovered angels make the Moscow composition more interesting from an iconographic point of view, and indeed, if the Moscow and Feigen panels were part of the same composition, the juxtaposition of the angels in the lower panel, where they are merely attendant on the Virgin and Child, with the active angels in the lunette, who are supporting the dead body of Christ, does bring the entire work in line with our usual image of Lotto as an iconographically innovative painter. Although the two panels do not have a unified space or ground color to unite them (as is the case, for example,

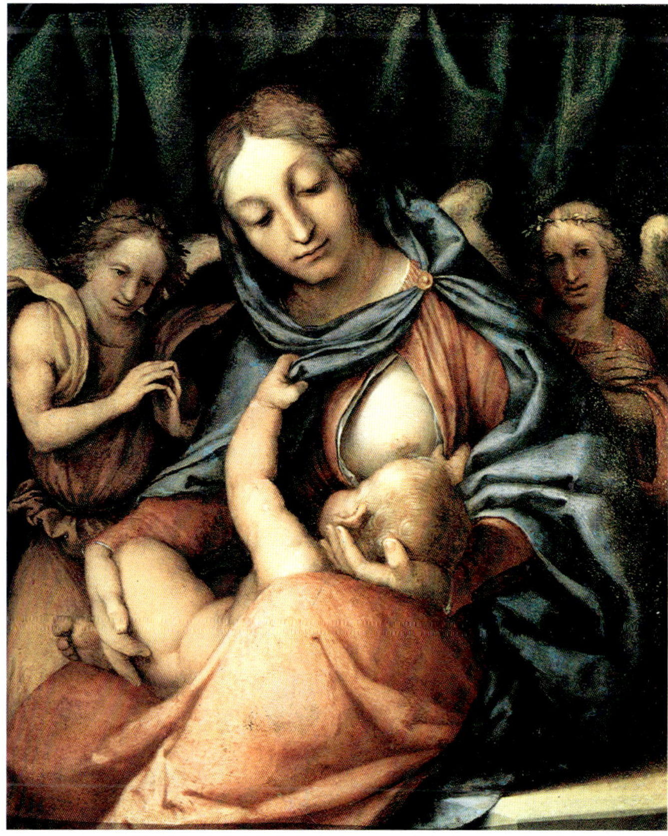

Fig. 2. Lorenzo Lotto, *Madonna del Latte*, ca. 1516–17. Oil on panel, 32.5 x 28.5 cm (12⅞ x 11¼ in.). Pushkin Museum, Moscow

with the Feigen Bergognone *Angels* and its related panel in Milan [see no. 33]), this ought not be surprising, for such unities are absent in Lotto's earlier depictions of the Pietà atop the Treviso and Recanati altarpieces.

Prior to its cleaning, the Moscow *Madonna del Latte* was dated, with some minor variation, to the period ca. 1515–20, most often to ca. 1516–18. Although Markova argues for a later date of 1521–22 on the basis of the newly revealed angels, the present author believes that the older idea was closer to the mark, and that both the Moscow and Feigen panels fit, stylistically, to the first years after Lotto's arrival in Bergamo, ca. 1516–17. Whether the two works were indeed part of a single portable altar remains to be confirmed, although X-radiographs could reveal that they were indeed once a single panel.

An inscription on the back of the Moscow panel, in English, is dated 1779 and identifies the work as a Madonna and Child by Leonardo da Vinci. The mistaken attribution aside, the inscription implies that the angels had already been over-painted by that time, as is also suggested by the old copy of the composition, without angels, in the John G. Johnson Collection at the Philadelphia Museum of Art.[15] Regardless of when the angels were overpainted, the inscription also suggests an English provenance for the Russian panel, which likewise lends support to the hypothesis that it was once joined to the Feigen panel, which too is first recorded in England.   JJM

1. Bernard Berenson, *Lotto*, trans. Luisa Vertova (Milan, 1955), p. 215.
2. Ibid.
3. See Adolfo Venturi, *Grandi artisti italiani* (Bologna, 1925), p. 114; Anna Banti and Antonio Boschetto, *Lorenzo Lotto* (Florence, 1953), p. 71, no. 35; and Piero Bianconi, *Tutta la pittura di Lorenzo Lotto* (Milan, 1955), p. 42.
4. As argued by Mauro Lucco in Lucco, ed., *Lorenzo Lotto a Recanati: "Nel cor profondo un amoroso affetto,"* exh. cat. (Venice, 1998), no. 10.
5. See David Alan Brown et al., *Lorenzo Lotto: Rediscovered Master of the Renaissance*, exh. cat. (Washington, D.C., 1997), no. 10.
6. For a contrary argument, see Giorgio Mascherpa, in Gian Alberto Dell'Acqua, *La pala Martinengo di Lorenzo Lotto: Studi e ricerche in occasione del restauro* (Bergamo, 1978).
7. Flavio Caroli, *Lorenzo Lotto e la nascita della psicologia moderna* (Milan, 1980), p. 254.
8. Carlo Ridolfi, *Le maraviglie dell'arte*, ed. Detlev Freiherrn von Hadeln (Rome, 1965), p. 146; echoed in Francesco Maria Tassi, *Vite de' pittori, scultori, e architetti bergamaschi*, ed. Franco Mazzini (Milan, 1969), 1: p. 11.
9. For Michiel's comments, see Marcantonio Michiel, *Der Anonimo Morel-liano: Marcanton Michiel's notizie d'opere del disegno*, ed. Theodor von Frimmel (Vienna, 1888), p. 69.
10. Lorenzo Lotto, *Libro di spese diverse*, ed. Pietro Zampetti (Venice, 1969), pp. 259–60.
11. For the Hermitage painting, see Brown, *Lorenzo Lotto*, no. 35.
12. Tamara D. Fomichova, *Venetian Painting, Fourteenth to Eighteenth Centuries*, The Hermitage Catalogue of Western European Painting 2 (Florence, 1992), pp. 194–95.
13. For the work as catalogued in the Hermitage, see Caroli, *Lorenzo Lotto*, p. 258.
14. Vittoria Markova, "Un nuovo aspetto della 'Madonna del Latte' di Lorenzo Lotto," *Arte veneta* 35 (1981): pp. 146–49.
15. Bernard Berenson, *Lorenzo Lotto* (London, 1956), pp. 27–28.

"Capanna Senese"

Siena, active ca. 1515–30

35. *The Adoration of the Christ Child,* ca. 1515–20

Oil on panel, 55.9 x 37.5 cm (22 x 14¾ in.)

PROVENANCE: Leon de Somzée, Brussels (his sale, Galerie Fievez, Brussels, May 24, 1904, lot 449); Prince Golinicheff-Koutousoff, Saint Petersburg; N. Raibouchinsky (his sale, Plaza Hotel, New York, April 26, 1916, lot 15); Jules Bache, New York (his sale, Sotheby's, New York, April 23, 1945, lot 22); Julius H. Weitzner, London

BIBLIOGRAPHY: Andrea de Marchi, "Maestro delle Eroine Chigi-Saracini," in *Da Sodoma a Marco Pino: Pittori a Siena nella prima metà del cinquecento*, ed. Fiorella Sricchia Santoro (Siena, 1988), p. 87; Fiorella Sricchia Santoro, in *Domenico Beccafumi e il suo tempo*, exh. cat. (Siena, 1990), pp. 270–71; Gabriele Fattorini, "Alcune questioni di ambito beccafumiano: Il 'Maestro delle Eroine Chigi Saracini' e il 'Capanna Senese,'" in *Beccafumi*, ed. Piero Torriti (Milan, 1998), p. 50n.8; Laurence Kanter, "Luca Signorelli and Girolamo Genga in Princeton," *Record of the Art Museum, Princeton University* 62 (2003): p. 83nn.38–39

CONDITION: The panel, of a vertical wood grain, has been thinned to 13 mm and cradled. The paint surface is well pre-served but exhibits a pronounced tenting to the craquelure, the result of cradling, and pinpoint losses along these raised surfaces have been inpainted.

The Feigen *Adoration of the Christ Child* was first known as a work by Sodoma, the attribution under which it appeared in the Leon de Somzée sale catalogue.[1] It was pur-chased by the New York financier Jules Bache as a work by that artist, but in the sale of the portion of his property not donated to the Metropolitan Museum of Art, New York, it appeared instead under the name of Girolamo del Pacchia.[2] Roberto Longhi annotated his photograph of the painting with an ascription to Girolamo Genga, and it was on this basis that Anna Maria Petrioli Tofani extended that attribution to a nearly exact replica of the painting in a private collection in

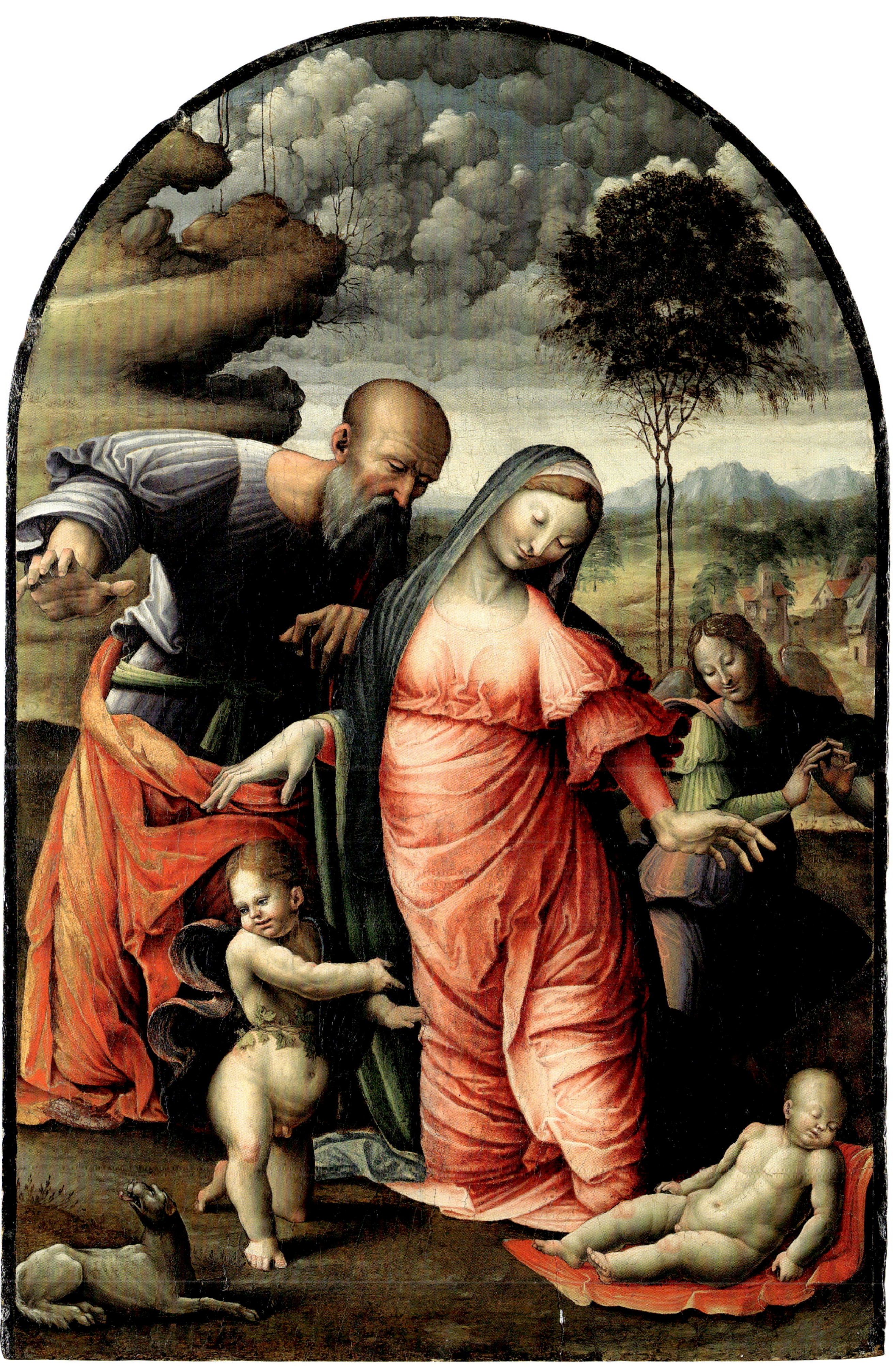

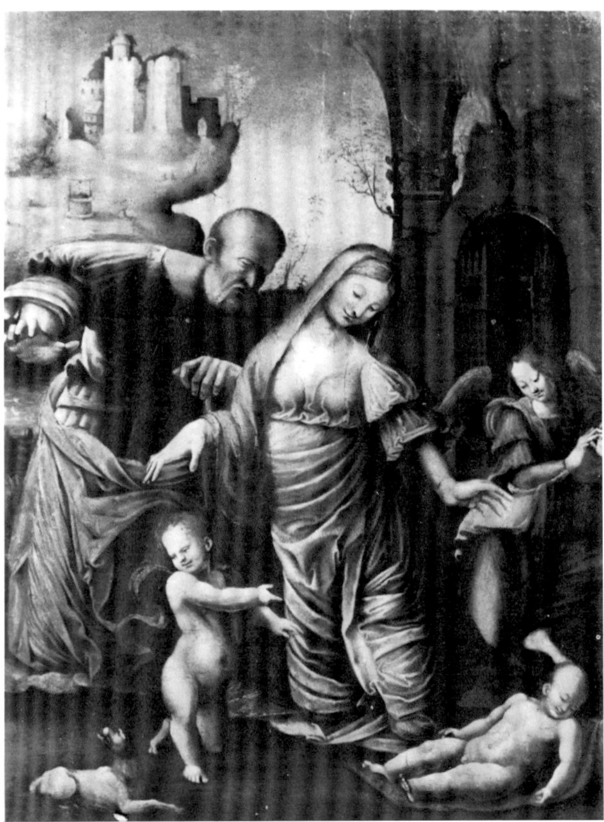

Fig. 1. "Capanna Senese," *The Adoration of the Christ Child,*
ca. 1515–20. Oil on panel, 438 x 290 cm (172½ x 114¼ in.).
Private collection

The confusion of names given to these works and of opinions expressed about their relation to each other is indicative of a complex set of workshop relationships in Siena in the second and third decades of the sixteenth century. The three Chigi Saracini Heroines, for example, clearly formed part of a single commission, but just as clearly they are the work of two distinct painters not, as asserted by de Marchi, of one painter maturing over a protracted period of time. On the other hand, neither of these two painters was involved in any way in the decoration of the Palazzo Petrucci, as maintained by Sricchia Santoro: the Petrucci frescoes mentioned above, now in Princeton, were painted by Girolamo Genga, probably as early as 1506, whereas all the other paintings in the group make reference to the style of both Genga and Beccafumi of a decade later.[9] Two of the Chigi Saracini Heroines—*Artemisia* and *Cleopatra*—in fact seem to have been painted by an artist who either apprenticed with or was employed by Domenico Beccafumi at the end of the second decade of the century: their palette, impossibly out-scaled feet and hands, and landscape style are all to be found in three similar panels (National Gallery, London; Galleria Doria-Pamphilj, Rome) believed to have been provided by Beccafumi's workshop in 1519 or 1520 for the bedchamber of Francesco di Camillo Petrucci.[10] Whether either of these artists may be identifiable as a stage in the career of another, better-known master has yet to be determined.

A significant contribution in this regard was advanced by Fattorini, who proposed recognizing many of the paintings once assigned to Giorgio di Giovanni (doc. 1538–59) as probably painted instead by "Capanna Senese," an artist unknown from archival documents but said by Giorgio Vasari to have been "ragionevol maestro, . . . se fusse ito per vita, si faceva molto onore nell'arte, secondo che da quell poco che aveva fatto si può giudicare" (A meritorious master, . . . If he had lived he would have won great honor in the art, to judge from the little which he did accomplish).[11] According to Vasari, Capanna Senese finished an altarpiece for the Marinelli chapel in the cathedral at Arezzo that had been begun by the Aretine painter Domenico Pecori, and this altarpiece is preserved today in the Galleria Nazionale d'Arte Antica in Arezzo. Fattorini proposed dating the altarpiece around 1527, the year of Pecori's death, and correctly established a link between it and the paintings that had previously been thought to have been the work of Giorgio di Giovanni. Without commenting on the validity of these attributions, Nicoletta Baldini argued that the date of 1527 conventionally assigned to the Marinelli altarpiece is entirely inferential, and she published documents suggesting that work on the painting may have begun as much as a decade earlier.[12] On March 30, 1519, the heirs of Donato di Tommaso Marinelli agreed to subsidize the completion of work on the altarpiece that had been commissioned by the latter before his death. While this document mentions no artists by name, it is reasonable to suppose that Capanna may have been called to Arezzo to contribute to this project in 1519 or 1520.

Turin (fig. 1).[3] All subsequent discussion of the picture refers to it and the Turin version as a pair, and seeks to clarify their place within a discreet group of works sometimes generically referred to as by the "Sienese eccentrics."[4] Andrea de Marchi first grouped the two paintings together with eleven others under the name "Master of the Chigi Saracini Heroines"—after a set of three virtuous women of antiquity in the Chigi Saracini Collection, Siena—an artist he believed to be a follower of Girolamo Genga and of Domenico Beccafumi active in the middle years of the 1510s.[5] Fiorella Sricchia Santoro contended that this group was not entirely homogeneous. She identified two principal artists at work on these paintings (along with three other paintings that she added), whom she rechristened the first and second "Painters of Pandolfo Petrucci," assuming the key works in the group to be not the Chigi Saracini Heroines but a set of frescoes from the Palazzo Petrucci in Siena, now in the Princeton University Art Museum, New Jersey.[6] The Feigen and Turin panels she felt to be extraneous to the others in the group, and she included the former in the 1990 Beccafumi exhibition in Siena with an uninformative attribution to a "Master of the Feigen Adoration," author of no other works but these.[7] Gabriele Fattorini, finally, asserted that the paintings initially identified by de Marchi were indeed homogeneous, rejecting the rubric "Painters of Pandolfo Petrucci."[8] He agreed with Sricchia Santoro only in isolating the Feigen and Turin panels as by a different, more "eccentric" hand.

Although not suggested by Fattorini, the Feigen *Adoration of the Christ Child*, along with its replica in Turin, is entirely consonant with the passages he isolated in the Marinelli altarpiece as attributable to Capanna Senese, and they should be appended to his discussion as earlier, slightly less mature works by the same hand. Morphological details, especially of figure types and attitudes, are recognizably related between them and all the works discussed by Fattorini, but the Feigen and Turin panels show more clearly the influence of Pacchia and Sodoma than do the calmer, more classicizing compositions that apparently follow the Marinelli altarpiece. The only material difference between the Feigen and Turin panels, other than their shape, is the substitution in the latter of two architectural vignettes in the middle distance for the landscape background present in the Feigen version. The vignette at the right is borrowed exactly from an early work by Domenico Beccafumi, a small panel of the *Nativity* in the Museo Civico, Pesaro, on which Capanna may even have collaborated as an apprentice. It is unlikely (though not impossible) that the motif would have been reemployed in this composition too many years after its invention, suggesting a date in the middle of the second decade of the century for the Feigen and Turin panels.   LK

1. Galerie Fievez, Brussels, sale cat. (May 24, 1904), lot 449.
2. Sotheby's, New York, sale cat. (April 23, 1945), lot 22.
3. Anna Maria Petrioli Tofani, in *Urbino e le Marche prima e dopo Raffaello*, ed. Maria Grazia Ciardi Duprè Dal Poggetto and Paolo Dal Poggetto, exh. cat. (Urbino, Italy, 1983), p. 363.
4. The reference is a paraphrase of Federico Zeri's isolation of a group of early sixteenth-century painters that he dubbed the "Florentine eccentrics"; see Federico Zeri, "Gli eccentrici Fiorentini," in *Bollettino d'arte* 47 (1962): pp. 216–31.
5. Andrea de Marchi, "Maestro delle Eroine Chigi-Saracini," in *Da Sodoma a Marco Pino: Pittori a Siena nella prima metà del cinquecento*, ed. Fiorella Sricchia Santoro (Siena, 1988), pp. 83–90.
6. Fiorella Sricchia Santoro, in *Domenico Beccafumi e il suo tempo*, exh. cat. (Siena, 1990), pp. 266–69.
7. Ibid., pp. 270–71.
8. Gabriele Fattorini, "Alcune questioni di ambito beccafumiano: Il 'Maestro delle Eroine Chigi Saracini' e il 'Capanna Senese,'" in *Beccafumi*, ed. Piero Torriti (Milan, 1998), pp. 37–45.
9. See Laurence Kanter, "Luca Signorelli and Girolamo Genga in Princeton," *Record of the Art Museum, Princeton University* 62 (2003): pp. 73–80. Notwithstanding the severely damaged and heavily restored condition of the Princeton frescoes, most scholars concur in their attribution to Genga— deriving ultimately from Vasarian tradition—though a date for them in 1509 rather than 1506 is generally assumed. It is impossible to concur with the contention of Nicole Dacos (see Riccardo Massagli, "Michele Angelo da Lucca nella Roma di Pintoricchio," in *Pintoricchio*, ed. Vittoria Garibaldi and Francesco Federico Mancini, exh. cat. [Milan, 2008], pp. 74–91; and Fabio Marcelli, in ibid., pp. 282–83) that one of the Princeton frescoes, *Minerva*, is the work of Michelangelo di Pietro Membrini da Lucca.
10. Carol Plazzotta, in *Renaissance Siena: Art for a City*, ed. Luke Syson, exh. cat. (London, 2007), pp. 323–33.
11. Giorgio Vasari, *Le vite dei piu eccelenti pittor, scultori, e architetti*, ed. Gaetano Milanesi (Florence, 1878), 3: p. 223. Fattorini, "Alcune questioni di ambito beccafumiano," p. 51n.14, rejects Milanesi's contention that this citation refers to Jacopo di Lorenzo Capanna as well as Ettore Romagnoli's suggestion of Jacopo's son, Giovanbattista Capanna. He admits the possibility that it may refer to a certain "Angnolo Chappanna" who was paid two lire on March 22, 1518, for painting a Pietà on the altar of the sacristy in the hospital of Santa Maria della Scala in Siena, though neither this painting nor any other notice of this artist has been found.
12. Nicoletta Baldini, *La bottega di Bartolomeo della Gatta: Domenico Pecori e l'arte in terra d'Arezzo tra quattro e cinquecento* (Florence, 2004), pp. 259–65.

Tommaso Manzuoli, called Maso da San Friano

Florence, 1531–1571

36. *The Resurrection of Christ*, ca. 1560

Oil on panel, 31 x 16 cm (12¼ x 6¼ in.)

PROVENANCE: Prince George, Duke of Cambridge(?); private collection, England; Phillips, London, July 7, 1992, lot 7

BIBLIOGRAPHY: Alexander Wied, in Sylvia Ferino-Pagden, *Vittoria Colonna: Dichterin und Muse Michelangelos,* exh. cat. (Vienna, 1997), p. 477; Philippe Costamagna, "Continuity and Innovation: The Art of Maso da San Friano," in *Continuity, Innovation, and Connoisseurship: Old Master Paintings at the Palmer Museum of Art*, ed. Mary Jane Harris, exh. cat. (University Park, Pa., 2003), p. 41

CONDITION: The panel support is 2.8 cm thick and all of its present moldings are original except for that along the bottom edge, which is a modern repair. The paint surface is exceptionally well preserved.

This small panel depicting the Resurrection of Christ, formerly attributed to Marcello Venusti, was independently reattributed to Maso da San Friano by Robert Simon, Larry Feinberg, and Philippe Costamagna. During his relatively short career, Maso vacillated from his initial style based on the works of his masters Pier Francesco Foschi and Carlo Portelli, to a second period under the influence of the Romanizing works of Giorgio Vasari and Francesco Salviati, and finally to a style that grew from a revived interest in Andrea del Sarto and Jacopo Pontormo. The shift in Maso's manner is often associated with the concerns of the Counter-Reformation, but it might be better tied to the politics of the art world in mid-cinquecento Florence. During the later 1550s and 1560s, that is, Vasari's influence on Florentine art cannot be overestimated, for Vasari controlled the most important secular and sacred commissions in the city and required that the artists working

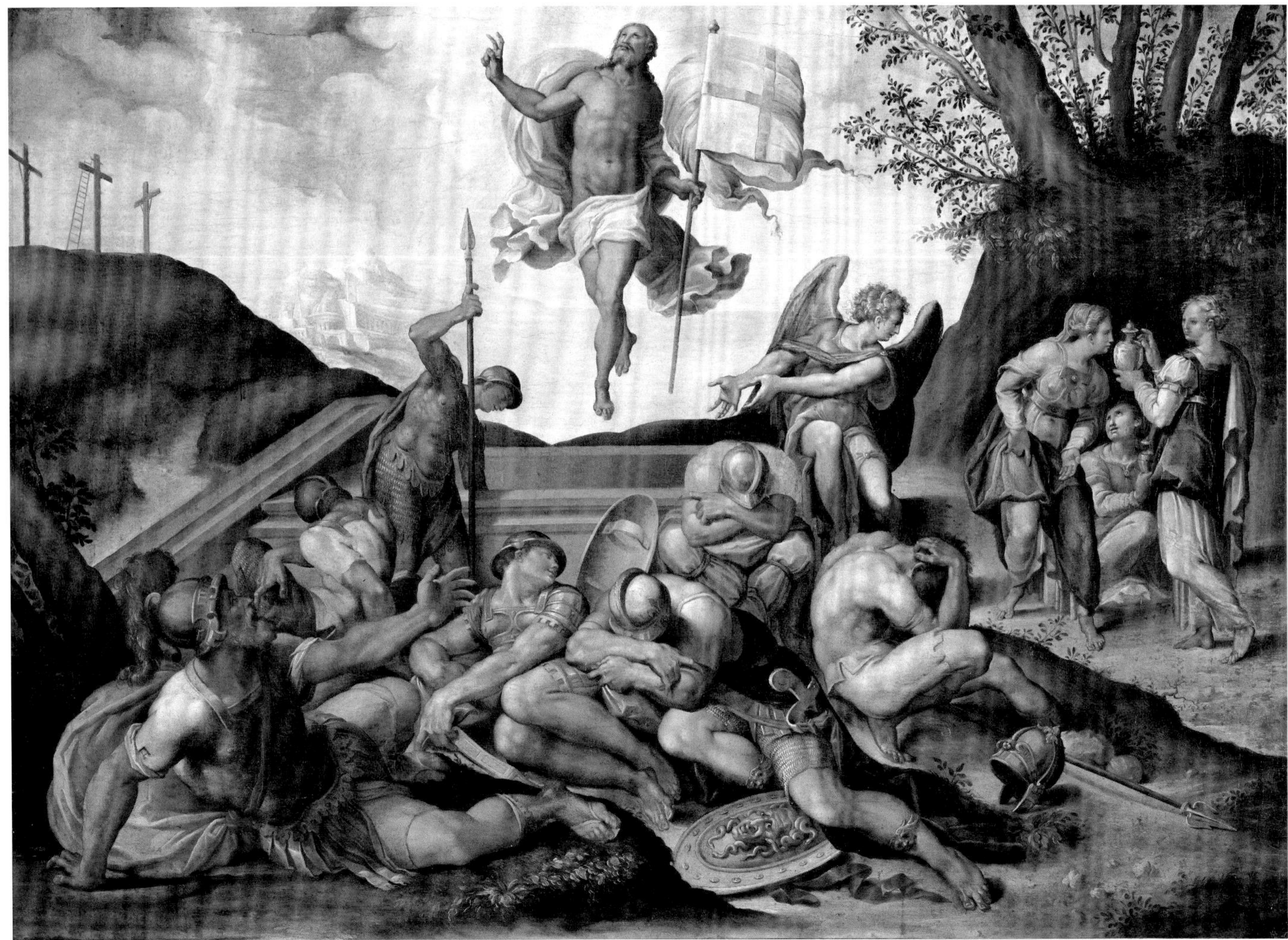

Fig. 1. Tommaso Manzuoli, called Maso da San Friano, *The Resurrection*, ca. 1560. Oil on panel, 60 x 84 cm (23⅝ x 33⅛ in.). Kunsthistorisches Museum, Vienna, inv. no. 215

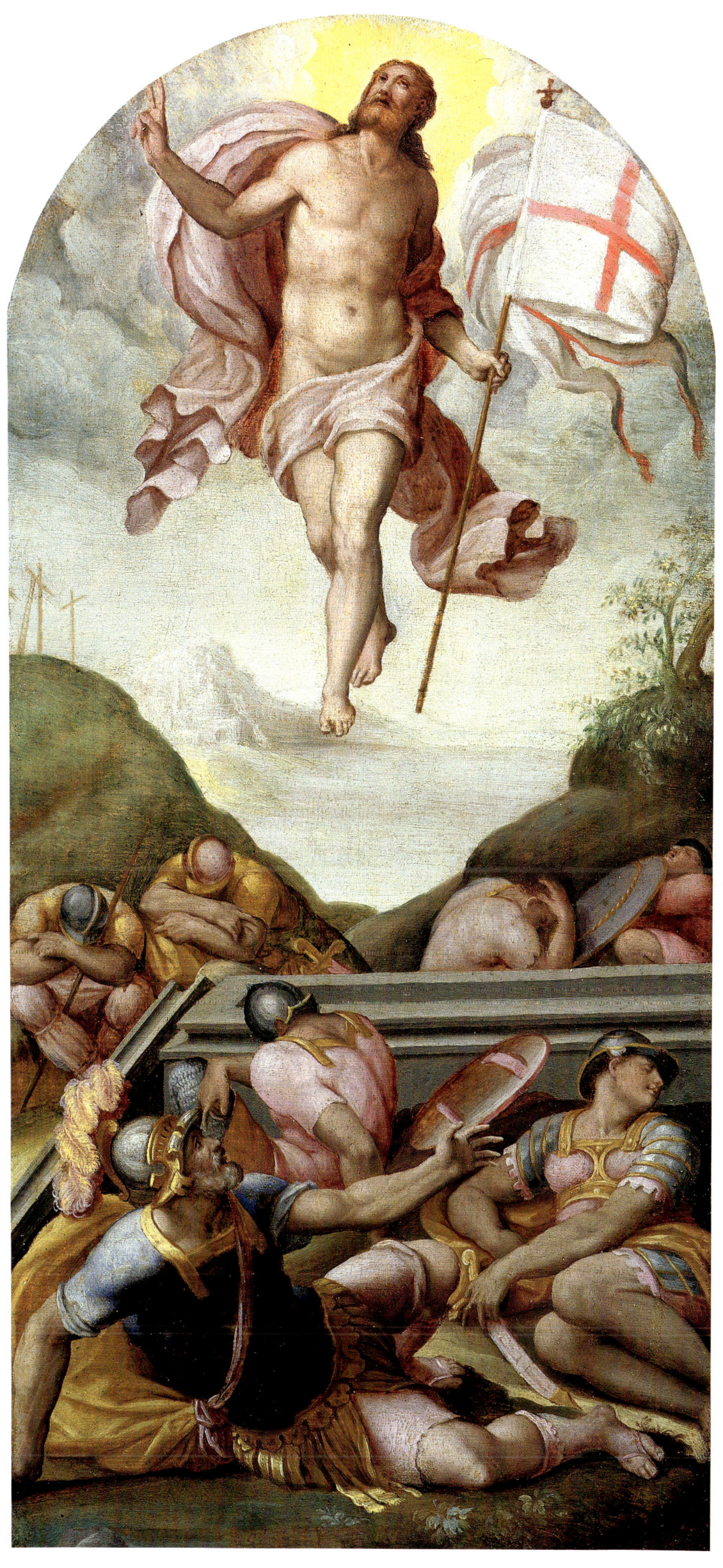

under him paint in a style that mimicked his own; even those artists not working for him fell under his sway. In the latter half of the 1560s, however, a younger generation of artists associated with the Accademia del Disegno turned back to the models of Sarto, Rosso Fiorentino, and Pontormo. Maso's works fit into these stylistic trends, which can be linked to Tridentine concerns in only the most insubstantial way.

The general trends of Maso's stylistic development, however, do aid in dating the present work, for the Michelangelesque qualities that underlie the old attribution to Venusti would put the panel in the middle of Maso's career, around 1560, rather than among the works from his last years, where the *Resurrection of Christ* has hitherto been placed. The foreground figure is adapted from the principal figure in Michelangelo's *Conversion of Saul* (Cappella Paolina, Vatican Palace, Vatican City), for example, while the sleeping soldier at left in the background is based on a figure in Michelangelo's much-copied *Dream of Human Life* drawing (Courtauld Gallery, London). There is, furthermore, a monumentality to both anatomy and drapery in the *Resurrection* that stands in contrast to the more delicate figures and faceted draperies of Maso's later works, such as the ca. 1570 *Diamond Mine* for the *studiolo* of Francesco I (Palazzo Vecchio, Florence). Parallels might be drawn between the *Resurrection* and two other paintings done by Maso for Florentine churches, the 1560 *Visitation* from San Pier Maggiore (Fitzwilliam Museum, Cambridge, on loan to Trinity Hall) and his *Pietà* for Santa Maria dei Candeli (recently with Gallery Gismondi, Paris) of similar date.

The Feigen *Resurrection* is closely related to a larger panel in Vienna (fig. 1). Always considered a Florentine painting of around 1560, the Vienna *Resurrection* was sometimes attributed to Salviati and has recently been reattributed to Giulio Clovio by Costamagna, although that suggestion has found little acceptance.[1] Costamagna's argument that the Vienna and Feigen panels must be by different hands must likewise be questioned, for the differences in facture are minor indeed. The panels share a thin, dry application of paint, for example. Some details of the Vienna version are more precisely resolved (the landscape in the distance at left or the drapery of Christ, for example), but these differences might be attributed to the larger scale of the Vienna painting; moreover, other details—the helmet and plume of the foreground soldier, for example—are more carefully rendered in the Feigen painting. The differences do not admit the work of a mere copyist, and the two should be considered the work of the same artist, a view consistent with Alessandro Cecchi's recent attribution of the Vienna painting to Maso himself.[2] As noted above, Maso's *michelangelismo* derives from the works of Salviati and Vasari, whose Roman stylistic orientation has recently been explored by David Franklin, and the *Resurrection* would seem to have been created with a composition by Salviati in mind.[3] A drawing by Maso is apparently preparatory for a frescoed altarpiece of the subject, although

no such work is known to have been executed by the artist.[4] Regardless, the drawing would seem to document an earlier stage in the evolution of Maso's painted Resurrections.

The format and subject matter of the Feigen panel indicate that the painting was made as the door of a Eucharistic tabernacle or ciborium. Although tabernacles had occasionally decorated altars before the mid-sixteenth century, contemporary theological concerns brought about a new wave of construction in the later sixteenth and early seventeenth centuries. Presenting the consecrated Host on the altar, the tabernacles were a response to Protestant challenges to transubstantiation and other Eucharistic doctrine and are analogous to the Forty Hours devotional practice, which likewise developed in the mid-sixteenth century. The thirteenth session of the Council of Trent addressed such matters in 1551, and the installation of many ciboria on the high altars of churches must be a response to the Tridentine call for the reservation of the Eucharist in a sacred place in the church.[5] The large tabernacles placed on the high altars of the Duomo and of San Domenico in Siena are evidence, though, of the practice developing in Tuscany even before its codification by the Council of Trent.[6] A tabernacle door showing the Dead Christ with Angels, apparently by Bartolomeo Neroni, il Riccio, is dated 1548, likewise pre-Tridentine.[7]

Given the function and theological concerns associated with the tabernacles, the body of Christ was the most common subject chosen for their painted decoration. In the Feigen painting, the radiant white body of the Resurrected Christ rises above the tomb, a parallel to the practice of elevating the Host above the altar at the climax of the Mass. A Resurrected Christ by an anonymous Sienese painter likewise decorates the door of the largely intact tabernacle in the Patrizi collection, Rome, and in addition to the aforementioned door by Riccio, another Sienese tabernacle dated 1601, from the workshop of Francesco Vanni or Ventura Salimbeni, similarly shows an angel holding the dead body of Christ above the tomb.[8] The latter examples serve, too, as a reminder that such iconography is not limited to tabernacles, for they bring to mind Rosso Fiorentino's *Dead Christ* of 1525–26 (Museum of Fine Arts, Boston), about which similar arguments have been made.[9] Returning to Maso, another tabernacle door showing the ethereal body of a Resurrected Christ is in the Musée des Beaux-Arts de Chambéry, France.[10] Where the Feigen panel is related to the Vienna picture, the Chambéry tabernacle door adapts the figure of Christ from Maso's later *Ascension* design of 1564–66, demonstrating a parallel practice. The *Ascension* was intended for the Church of the Carmine in Florence, but the altarpiece commission was suspended while the entire church was rebuilt, and the altarpiece was eventually painted by Battista Naldini after Maso's death. Maso's design, however, is recorded in a compositional *modello* and other drawings in the Galleria degli Uffizi, Florence.[11]

A variant formulation also often used for the tabernacle paintings shows the nearly nude Resurrected Christ holding his Cross and dripping blood from his wounds into a chalice, an iconographical motif that draws an even clearer connection between the function of the tabernacles and the theology of transubstantiation. Examples of this type include a panel in the Museum of Fine Arts, Boston (inv. no. 74.22), alternately attributed to Bartolomeo Passarotti or to Pellegrino Tibaldi; a ciborium in Sant'Egidio, Montalcino, tentatively attributed to Alessandro Casolani but perhaps instead by the same Sienese workshop as the aforementioned Patrizi tabernacle; and a panel improbably attributed to the circle of Sebastiano Conca in a recent sale but probably painted by a Bolognese artist of the later cinquecento.[12] A print by Giovanni Maggi celebrating the Vatican basilica also shows a tabernacle decorated with the Wounds of Christ motif on the principal altar of the Gregorian chapel.[13] There is no trace today of the Gregoriana tabernacle, made under the patronage of Pope Gregory XIII, who employed many artists from his native Bologna, but the painting in Boston is perhaps closely related. The figure of Christ in all of the preceding examples is related to Michelangelo's *Risen Christ* in Santa Maria sopra Minerva, Rome, itself a work evoking Eucharistic themes with its nudity and with its instruments of the passion. An additional tabernacle door of this type, convincingly attributed to Maso da San Friano, would seem to predate the Gregorian chapel tabernacle as well as the Sienese examples.[14]

While thus among the earliest surviving examples of the genre from central Italy, it would be hard to substantiate a claim that tabernacle doors by Maso were the model for all the later examples, although Vasari perhaps had them in mind when he noted that Maso had shown "quanto sa e quanto si può di lui sperare in molti quadri e pitture minore" (how much he knew, and how much one could hope for from him, in many paintings and small pictures).[15] The Feigen panel is of a fineness and a compositional complexity otherwise unknown in works of this type, even in the panels for Vasari's own ciboria of 1565–67 for Pistoia and for Santa Croce in Florence.[16] Although it cannot be linked to any known commission, Maso's tabernacle must have been destined for a privileged place in some Florentine church; the related *Resurrection* in Vienna was in the Medici collection until 1792, and it is tempting to suggest that the Feigen panel might likewise have been a Medici commission.   JJM

1. See Luisa Mortari, *Francesco Salviati* (Rome, 1992), no. 90; and Philippe Costamagna, "À propos du séjour florentin de Giulio Clovio," in *Kunst des Cinquecento in der Toskana*, ed. Monica Cämmerer (Munich, 1992), p. 170.
2. Alessandro Cecchi, "Addenda a Maso da San Friano," in *Scritti di storia dell'arte in onore di Sylvie Béguin*, ed. Mario di Giampaolo and Elisabetta Saccomani (Naples, 2001), pp. 276–77.
3. On Roman style, see David Franklin, *Painting in Renaissance Florence, 1500–1550* (New Haven, Conn., 2001), chaps. 11–12. For the Salviati, see Catherine Monbeig Goguel, ed., *Francesco Salviati o la Bella Maniera*, exh. cat. (Milan, 1998), no. 118.
4. See Christie's, New York, sale cat. (January 28, 2000), lot 1.
5. H. J. Schroeder, ed. and trans., *Canons and Decrees of the Council of Trent* (Rockford, Ill., 1978), pp. 72–80; see also Maurice E. Cope, *The Venetian Tabernacle of the Sacrament in the Sixteenth Century* (New York, 1997).
6. The Duomo tabernacle was made by Vecchietta in 1467–72 for Santa Maria della Scala but was transferred to the Duomo in 1506; the San Domenico tabernacle was made by Benedetto da Maiano in the 1480s.
7. See Christie's, London, sale cat. (July 8, 2005), lot 9.
8. For the Patrizi collection, see Anna Maria Pedrocchi, *Le stanze del tesoriere, la quadreria Patrizi: Cultura senese nella storia del collezionismo romano del seicento* (Milan, 2000), no. 183. For the Vanni/Salimbeni workshop tabernacle, see *Mostra di opere d'arte restaurate nelle province di Siena e Grosseto*, exh. cat. (Genoa, 1979), no. 85.
9. Regina Stefaniak, "Replicating Mysteries of the Passion: Rosso's Dead Christ with Angels," *Renaissance Quarterly* 45 (1992): pp. 677–738, provides a good summary of the debate over the Eucharist in the cinquecento.
10. Véronique Damian, *Collections du musée de Chambéry: Peintures florentines* (Chambéry, France, 1990), no. 26.
11. Peter Cannon-Brookes, "Three Notes on Maso da San Friano," *Burlington Magazine* 107 (1965): pp. 195–96; Valentino Pace, "Maso da San Friano," *Bollettino d'arte* 61 (1976): pp. 77, 84; and Catherine Clover, "Documentation on Naldini's Ascension for S. Maria del Carmine in Florence," *Burlington Magazine* 141 (1999): pp. 615–17.
12. The Boston panel, according to notes in the curatorial file, was attributed to Passarotti by Scott Schaefer and then reattributed to Tibaldi by Laurence Kanter. On the Montalcino panel, see Fiorella Sricchia Santoro, ed., *L'arte a Siena sotto i Medici, 1555–1609*, exh. cat. (Rome, 1980), no. 25. On the Bolognese panel, see Christie's, South Kensington, sale cat. (February 23, 2005), lot 245.
13. Antonio Vannugli, "Per Jacopo Zucchi: Un'Annunciazione a Bagnoregio ed altre opere," *Prospettiva* 75/76 (1994): p. 168, fig. 7.
14. Formerly in the collection of Barbara Piasecka Johnson, the work was sold at Sotheby's, London, sale cat. (July 9, 2009), lot 5.
15. Giorgio Vasari, *Le vite de' più eccelenti pittori, scultori, et architettori*, ed. Gaetano Milanesi, vol. 7 (Florence, 1889), pp. 611–12.
16. See Antonio Paolucci, "L'arredamento ecclesiale nell'età della Riforma," in *Arte e religione nella Firenze de' Medici* (Florence, 1980), pp. 95–110.

Jacopo Zucchi

Florence, ca. 1540–1596

37. *The Crucifixion*, ca. 1583

Oil on copper, 29.2 x 22.9 cm (11½ x 9 in.)

PROVENANCE: acquired Sotheby's, London, July 10, 2003, lot 160 (as "Attributed to Zucchi")

BIBLIOGRAPHY: unpublished

CONDITION: The painting was restored in 2003, at which time a discolored varnish was removed, along with old retouching. The paint surface is well preserved. There are small losses by the mouth of Christ, in the sleeve of Saint John, in the drapery of the Virgin, and at the margins of the panel.

This small painting is one of a large number by Jacopo Zucchi on copper panels, a technique that came into vogue in the later cinquecento and found an even greater popularity in the seventeenth century, to which a number of works in the present exhibition can attest. The use of thin oil glazes on unprimed copper plates enabled unusually precise brushwork, often juxtaposed with passages of sketchy handling, as well as luminous lighting effects, all of which are evident in the present work. The earliest of Zucchi's coppers, including the *Assembly of the Gods* now at the Yale University Art Gallery, date to 1575–76 and were intended to be built into the *studiolo di noce* at the Villa Medici in Rome.[1] Other small allegorical paintings on copper might have served as the covers for painted portraits or mirrors, but by the time that Zucchi painted his *Fishing for Coral* and *Allegory of Creation* of ca. 1585 (Galleria Borghese, Rome)—as well as the present work—the copper panels constituted an independent painting genre of their own. It is unclear exactly how the copper technique developed; Sebastiano del Piombo, Correggio, and Parmigianino are all said to have experimented with the support, but the first regular use of it seems to have had its roots in Florence and Rome in the 1560s and 1570s.[2] The earliest Florentine examples were by Giorgio Vasari, Alessandro Allori, and others, who used copper panels for a number of small pictures made for Francesco de' Medici in the late 1560s (for a later copper by Allori, see no. 38). In Rome, the Venetian-trained Girolamo Muziano, who was responsible for other experiments intended to exploit color (including painting on slate and other stone, in oil directly on prepared walls, and in using large canvases rather than frescoes to decorate the lateral walls of chapels), was among the first to use copper supports, as he did for some of his paintings in the Ruiz chapel at Santa Caterina dei Funari, painted ca. 1570,[3] but Zucchi's first copper plates were done soon after. Regardless of which artist is to be credited with inventing or promoting the technique, Zucchi was among its earliest and most successful practitioners in the sixteenth century.

The Feigen *Crucifixion* is one of a number of coppers painted by Zucchi around 1580. These include the *Hercules Musagete* (or *Reign of Jupiter*) also made for the Villa Medici and now in the Galleria degli Uffizi, Florence, but an even better comparison might be drawn between the *Crucifixion* and another work of religious subject matter, the *Holy Family with Saint John the Baptist in a Landscape*, which exists in two versions (Musée des Augustins, Toulouse, and a private collection). The *Holy Family* has been dated to 1584 on the basis of a payment for "two small panels in copper, one about 1 palm in height, for a picture of Our Lady with Christ in her arms, dressed in the costume of a gypsy, and one with her dressed in the ordinary manner, after one by Michelangelo," which Zucchi received in February 1584.[4] Yet, the copper panels in the document are described as being 1 palm tall (about 20 or 22 cm), which is precisely the size of the *Crucifixion*, while the Toulouse painting, the related work in a private collection, and all of Zucchi's other coppers are actually twice that size. The discrepancies of size and of description have led Alessandro Cecchi to question the link between the Toulouse painting and the document, but the dating of the *Holy Family* to the early 1580s has been confirmed by all.[5] As in the Toulouse painting, the Feigen panel demonstrates a palette keyed to the primary colors, an impressionistic landscape in the background, and draperies that surround the body in stiff arching folds. The figures in these compositions from the early 1580s lack the more extreme mannerism of Zucchi's early work under Vasari but do not yet show evidence of the naturalism that Zucchi adopted later in the decade, presumably under the influence of Scipione Pulzone, his colleague in the service of Cardinal Ferdinando de' Medici. Among Zucchi's larger paintings from the same moment, his altarpiece of ca. 1580 for the Patrizi chapel in San Francesco in Siena, and his paintings in the Sagrestia dei Canonici in the Vatican show the same characteristics.[6] Previously attributed to Cigoli and to Francesco Vanni before being definitively ascribed to Zucchi by Edmund Pillsbury in 2003, the Feigen *Crucifixion* looks ahead to the relatively straightforward manner that would characterize art in the last two decades of the cinquecento, in contrast to the extravagant stylization of midcentury Mannerism. The old attribution to Vanni, in fact, is not far from the mark, for Zucchi's aforementioned altarpiece in Siena was a distinct influence on Vanni's earliest works.

Zucchi's *Crucifixion* at San Giovanni Decollato in Rome (fig. 1) and a related drawing in Vienna (fig. 2) provide additional reference points for the composition. The painting was first identified and published by Pillsbury when it was in the

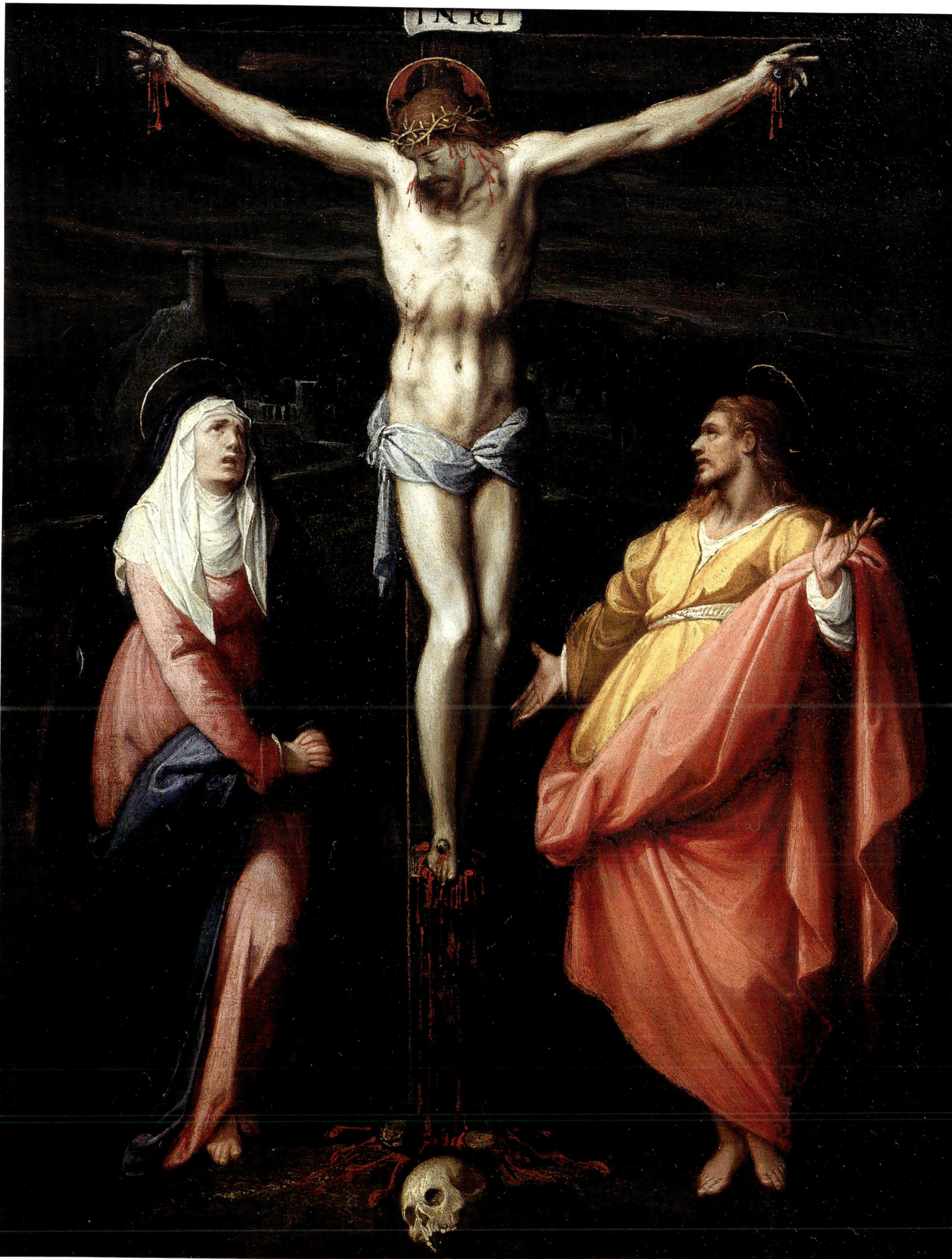

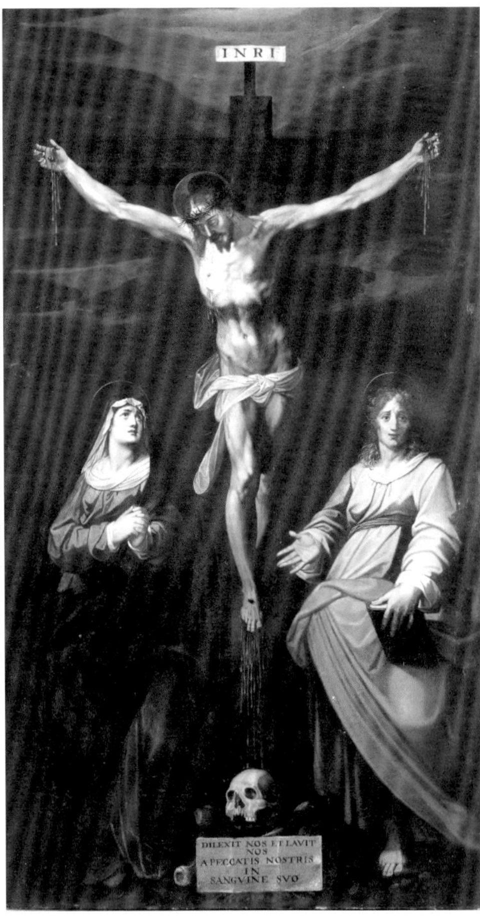

Fig. 1. Jacopo Zucchi, *The Crucifixion*, 1584. Oil on canvas, 260 x 137 cm (102⅛ x 53⅞ in.). San Giovanni Decollato, Rome

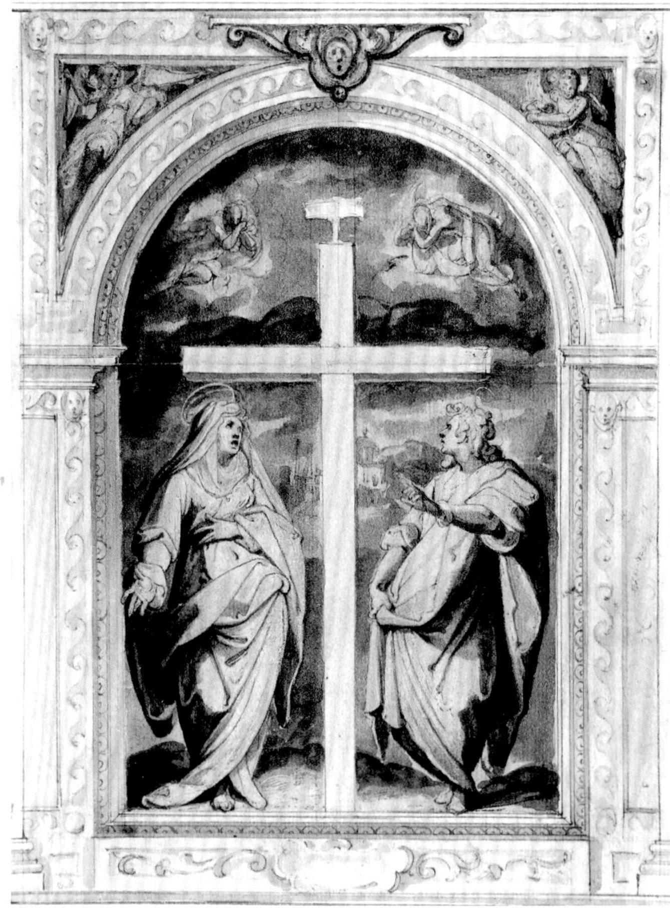

Fig. 2. Jacopo Zucchi, *Design for a Chapel with an Altarpiece of the Crucifixion*, ca. 1582–84. Pen and brown ink and brown wash over black chalk, heightened with white, 28.2 x 21.3 cm (11⅛ x 8⅜ in.). Albertina, Vienna, inv. no. 820

sacristy of the Oratory of San Giovanni Decollato, and there is no reason to doubt his connection of it to a *Crucifixion* for the nearby Carcere Nuove for which Zucchi received payments in 1584: the confraternity of San Giovanni Decollato tended to prisoners in the Carcere, and it is hardly surprising that a painting from the disused prison would have wound up at the Oratory.[7] The drawing is apparently a study for a chapel in which a preexisting Crucifix was to be attached to a wall where Zucchi was to paint the flanking figures. This is not the case with Zucchi's *Crucifixion* in San Giovanni Decollato, nor with Cesare Nebbia's altarpiece of the same subject in the church, although Zucchi's painted *Ascension* in the church surrounds a much older painted icon. Accordingly, as Pillsbury has noted, the compositional similarity of the *Crucifixion* drawing to the San Giovanni Decollato chapels suggests that it might have been an unused early scheme for the altarpiece ultimately painted by Nebbia in 1582–83.[8] From 1582 on, Zucchi was primarily occupied with the tribune of Santo Spirito in Sassia, which may explain why the commission passed to Nebbia.[9] In any case, the small copper *Crucifixion* here is likely to date from the moment when Zucchi was working on these other versions of the subject, with which it agrees in style as well as composition; a date of ca. 1583 accords, too, with the comparisons made previously between the *Crucifixion* and other paintings by Zucchi from the early 1580s.

JJM

1. Edmund Pillsbury, "The Cabinet Paintings of Jacopo Zucchi: Their Meaning and Function," *Monuments et mémoires* 63 (1980): pp. 189–96. For the *Assembly of the Gods*, see *Art for Yale: Collecting for a New Century*, exh. cat. (New Haven, Conn., 2007), pp. 225, 395.
2. E. P. Bowron, in *Copper as Canvas: Two Centuries of Masterpiece Paintings on Copper, 1575–1775*, exh. cat. (New York, 1999), pp. 9–30. For the Parmigianino, see David Ekserdijan's catalogue entry, in Christie's, London, sale cat. (July 6, 2006), lot 44.
3. John Marciari, "Girolamo Muziano and Art in Rome, ca. 1550–1600," (PH.D. diss., Yale University, 2000), pp. 222–24.
4. Pillsbury, "Cabinet Paintings of Jacopo Zucchi," pp. 207–9.
5. Michel Hochmann, ed., *Villa Medici: Il sogno di un cardinale*, exh. cat. (Rome, 1999), no. 80.
6. Antonio Vannugli, "Per Jacopo Zucchi: Un 'Annunciazione' a Bagnoregio ed altre opere," *Prospettiva* 75/76 (1994): pp. 161–73. For new information on the Patrizi altarpiece, see Suzanne Boorsch and John Marciari, *Master Drawings from the Yale University Art Gallery*, exh. cat. (New Haven, Conn., 2006), pp. 16 and 32–33n.46.
7. Edmund Pillsbury, "Jacopo Zucchi in S. Spirito in Sassia," *Burlington Magazine* 116 (1974): p. 438.
8. Edmund Pillsbury, "Drawings by Jacopo Zucchi," *Master Drawings* 12 (1974): pp. 15–16.
9. Patrizia Tosini, in *Roma di Sisto V: Le arti e la cultura*, ed. Maria Louisa Madonna, exh. cat. (Rome, 1993), p. 207.

Alessandro Allori

Florence, 1535–1607

38. *Christ Carrying the Cross*, ca. 1591–95

Oil on copper, 21 x 14.5 cm (8¼ x 5¾ in.)

PROVENANCE: Sotheby's, London, April 19, 1989, lot 7

BIBLIOGRAPHY: Simona Lecchini Giovannoni, *Alessandro Allori* (Turin, 1991), no. 167

CONDITION: The paint surface is in excellent condition, with only a small retouch on the palm of Christ's left hand. There is an old inventory number, "57," on the verso.

Along with Jacopo Zucchi (see no. 37), Alessandro Allori was one of the first artists to make regular use of copper panels as supports for oil paintings. Allori's first certain example, the *Hercules Crowned by the Muses* in the Galleria degli Uffizi, Florence, seems to date to 1567–68 and was part of a set that included Giorgio Vasari's *Forge of Vulcan* and Agnolo Bronzino's *Allegory of Felicity*, also now in the Uffizi.[1] The medium's smooth surface befitted the jewel-like colors and marmoreal figures found in much Florentine painting of the midcinquecento, and especially in the cabinet paintings for the *studiolo* of Francesco I and other private rooms in the Medici palaces; the slate supports also used for the *studiolo* (begun 1569) are an analogous technique. Like Zucchi, Allori generally used copper for two types of subjects: small-scale mythologies and devotional works. The mythological compositions were usually created for the coppers, but the sacred scenes were most often based on compositions designed for works on a much larger scale. Allori seems to have begun the practice of creating reduced replications as early as the 1570s, for his *Adoration of the Magi* copper in the Musée du Louvre, Paris, seems to relate to a lost painting sent to Palermo around 1570, the composition of which is known through drawings; the style of the Louvre painting, however, seems to be that which Allori used in the later 1570s (as has also been suggested by Elizabeth Pilliod), and Allori might have produced it when he began thinking about his second altarpiece for Palermo, the 1578 *Adoration*.[2] Another of Allori's early devotional coppers, the *Saint Jerome* in a New York private collection, similarly relates to a fresco done at the same moment in the later 1570s, and there are numerous later examples.[3] Despite reproducing compositions, however, the coppers should be considered as more than merely small-scale copies; certain compositions required adaptation to fit the different format of the small panels, and some of the reductions include significant changes that shift the narrative emphasis of the scenes. Just as the technique of these paintings served as the model for many examples in the next generation, so too the practice of small-scale replication would become commonplace in the seicento (see, for example, nos. 43–44). The coppers were surely intended for connoisseurs, and, at least some of the time, the patrons of public altarpieces must have desired reductions of those pictures for their private collections.

The *Christ Carrying the Cross* relates to another version of the composition, a painting signed and dated 1604 in the Galleria Doria-Pamphilj, Rome (fig. 1); the Feigen version is not dated but is signed at lower right, "AAFF," an abbreviation for "Alexander Allorius Florentinus faciebat," which the artist inscribed on other paintings.[4] The Doria-Pamphilj painting is not much larger than the Feigen version, but the differences between the two make the latter a much tighter composition, one in which all the emphasis is at the center, where Christ meets His mother's gaze. In contrast, the Virgin is hidden in shadow in the Doria-Pamphilj painting, and the arrangement of the ancillary figures draws the eye to the margins of the picture. Although more elaborate, the greater number of figures in the Doria-Pamphilj painting lends the work a miniaturist aspect, and the panel loses the dramatic impact of the pared-down Feigen version. Even the Doria-Pamphilj version, however, might be considered a reduction, for Allori had originally invented the composition for a tapestry cartoon, one of a set of four scenes from the Passion of Christ that he designed between 1591 and 1602.[5] Neither the cartoon of the corresponding scene, for which Allori was paid on August 5, 1602, nor any of Allori's preparatory drawings for it seem to have survived, but the tapestry is in the deposits of Palazzo Pitti, Florence (fig. 2). The Rome painting, with its great number of figures, is closely based on the tapestry or its cartoon. It has generally been thought that the Feigen painting derives from the Doria-Pamphilj panel, but some parts of the present work are closer to the tapestry itself and suggest that it could derive directly from Allori's drawings rather than from the Doria-Pamphilj version. The figure of Simon of Cyrene at left, for example, with his right leg bent at the knee (and not extended as in the Doria-Pamphilj painting), is more like the tapestry, and there are four figures seen below the Cross in the Feigen painting, as also in the tapestry, while the Doria-Pamphilj painting has only one. In sum, the Feigen copper does not derive from the Rome painting but, rather, directly from Allori's tapestry drawings.

Allori's frequent repetition of successful compositions—in large-scale works as well as in small-scale coppers—makes for difficulty in establishing the date of some works, including the painting at hand. It is nonetheless here proposed that the Feigen copper was created significantly earlier than the Rome version, in the early or mid-1590s when Allori began designing the Passion tapestries, rather than around 1602 when he finally executed the cartoon for those tapestries, or 1604 when he made the Rome painting. Allori tended to adapt individual figures from one painting to the next, and a comparison of figures might lend support to an earlier date for the *Christ Carrying the Cross*. The figure of Simon of Cyrene, for example, is very close to that of Lazarus in Allori's *Resurrection of Lazarus* in Sant'Agostino, Montepulciano, which is signed and dated 1593.[6] Beyond the comparison of this figure, however, close compositional and stylistic similarities exist between the Feigen copper and other paintings of the 1590s, including the *Christ and the Canaanite Woman* in San Giovannino degli Scolopi, the *Saint James Healing a Cripple* in Santa Maria Novella of 1592, and the copper *Calling of Saint Peter* of 1596 in the Uffizi, all in Florence.[7] Allori's works of the 1590s still tend to have the abstracted faces seen in the Feigen painting, while works of the artist's final decade more often include naturalistic, portraitlike heads, which are absent from the present painting. Many of the works of the 1590s likewise include impressionistic blue-green landscapes like that seen here. Finally, the palette and even the mode of painting in the Feigen copper are entirely different from those in the Doria-Pamphilj version: the latter painting is built with lights laid over darks, whereas the Feigen version is built up with layers of transparent oil glazes. In sum, the style of the Feigen *Christ Carrying the Cross* has far more to do with Allori's works of the early and mid-1590s than with those of ca. 1605, and it appears to have been produced close to the time when Allori received the commission for the Passion tapestries, and not when he delivered the cartoon for the corresponding scene a decade later. Accordingly, rather than merely a replication of the larger tapestry design, the Feigen copper might be considered the artist's first version of the subject, one necessarily elaborated and embellished for the large scale (365 x 353 cm) tapestries.   JJM

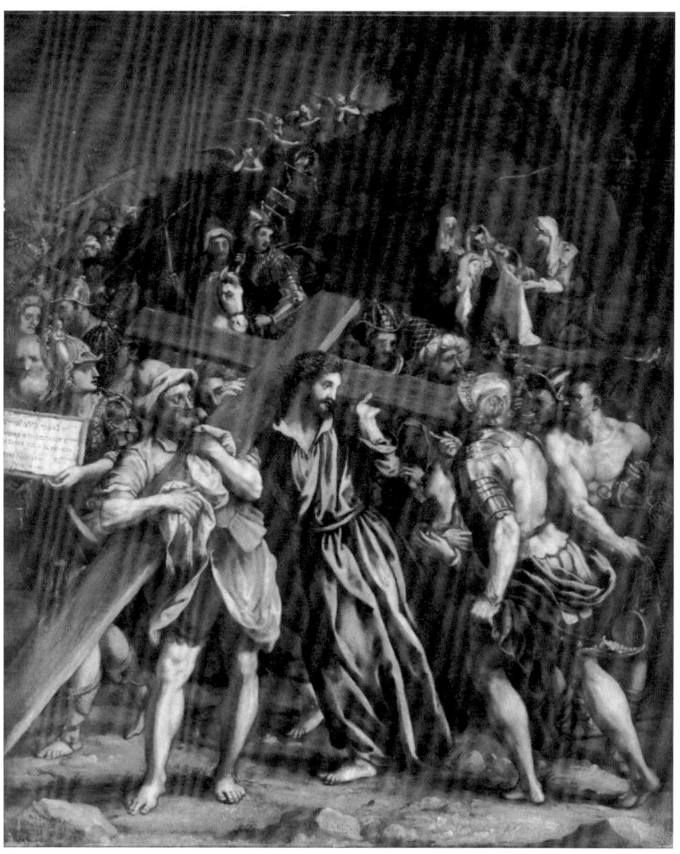

Fig. 1. Alessandro Allori, *Christ Carrying the Cross*, 1604. Oil on panel, 57 x 47 cm (22½ x 18½ in.). Galleria Doria-Pamphilj, Rome

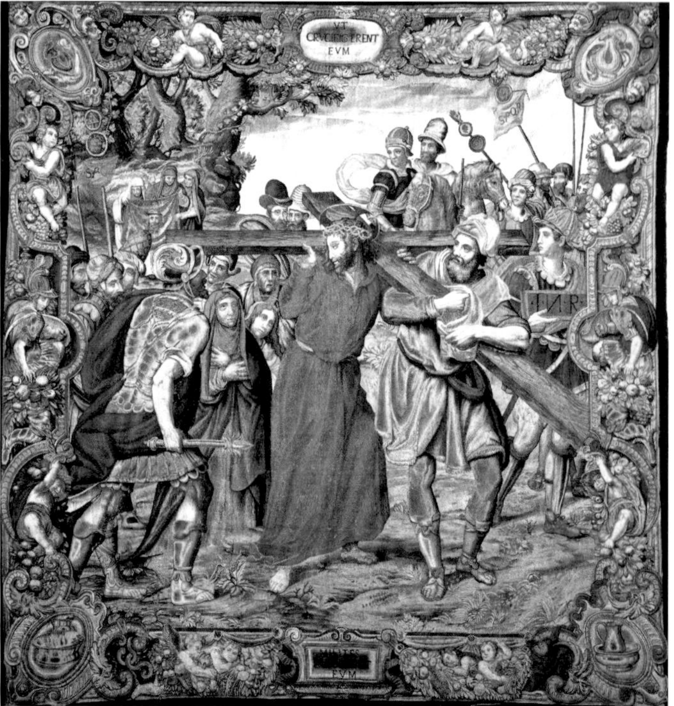

Fig. 2. After Alessandro Allori, *Christ Carrying the Cross*, ca. 1602. Tapestry in silk and gold, 365 x 353 cm (143¾ x 139 in.). Palazzo Pitti, Florence

1. For the *Hercules*, see Simona Lecchini Giovannoni, *Alessandro Allori* (Turin, 1991), no. 23; the dating and attribution of no. 7 in that catalogue, also a painting on copper, are questionable. On these early coppers, see Alesssandro Cecchi, "Invenzioni per quadri di Don Vincenzo Borghini," *Paragone* 383–85 (1982): pp. 89–96; see also *Copper as Canvas: Two Centuries of Masterpiece Paintings on Copper, 1575–1775*, exh. cat. (New York, 1999) for the history of painting on copper.

2. On the *Adoration of the Magi* drawings, see Lecchini Giovannoni, *Alessandro Allori*, nos. 34–35. For Pilliod's comments, see Elizabeth Pilliod, review of *Alessandro Allori*, by Simona Lecchini Giovannoni, *Burlington Magazine* 134 (1992): p. 729. On the 1578 *Adoration*, see Lecchini Giovannoni, *Alessandro Allori*, no. 64.

3. For the *Saint Jerome*, see *The Medici, Michelangelo, and the Art of Late Renaissance Florence*, exh. cat. (New Haven, Conn., 2002), no. 2.

4. For the Doria-Pamphilj painting, see Lecchini Giovannoni, *Alessandro Allori*, no. 166.

5. Ibid., no. 129.

6. Ibid., no. 132. Both figures ultimately derive, of course, from one at lower left in Michelangelo's *Last Judgment*, of which Allori's drawn copy is in the Musée du Louvre, Paris, inv. no. 830.

7. Ibid., nos. 113, 124, and 142.

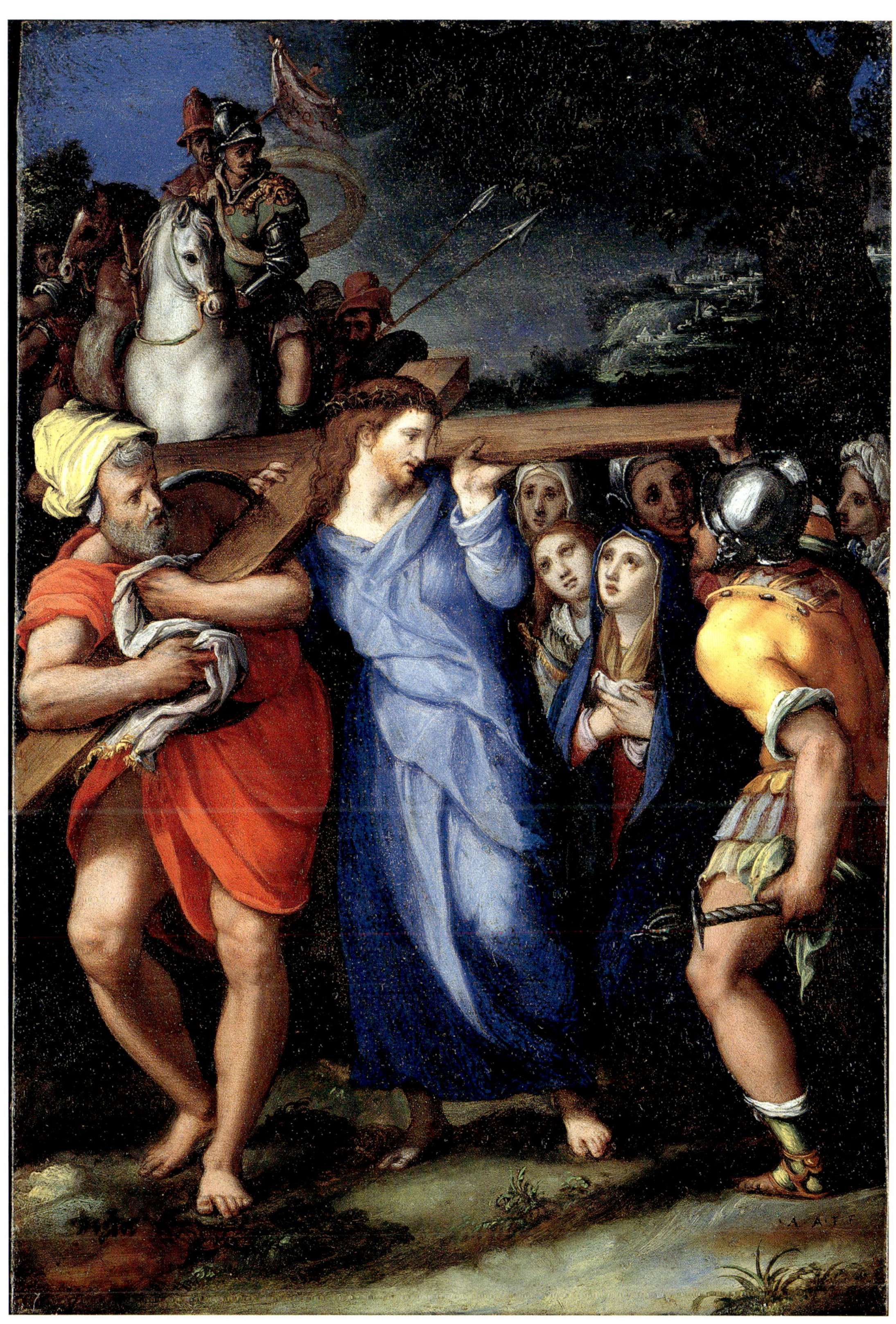

Annibale Carracci

Bologna, 1560–1609

39. *Virgin and Child with Saint Lucy and the Young Saint John the Baptist,* ca. 1587–88

Oil on panel, 78.5 x 63 cm (30⅞ x 23¾ in.)

PROVENANCE: Sampieri collection, Bologna; Gavin Hamilton; Francis Basset, 1st Baron Basset, England; by descent to Arthur Francis Basset, Tehidy, near Camborne, Cornwall, England (his sale, Christie's, London, January 9, 1920, lot 88 [sold to Everitt]); Phillips, London, December 8, 1987, lot 69 (as "Sisto Badalocchio").

The provenance of this panel has hitherto been traced only to A. F. Basset's sale of 1920, but the work was previously offered for sale at Christie's, London, May 8, 1824, lot 41 (as "Ludovico Carracci") but was bought in. The catalogue of the 1824 auction indicates the picture had been purchased from Gavin Hamilton (1723–1798), which in turn demonstrates that the panel was acquired for the Basset family by Francis Basset, Baron de Dunstanville of Tehidy and Baron Basset of Stratton (1757–1835), who began acquiring art during his Grand Tour in 1777–78. Many (perhaps all) of his purchases from that trip were sent home on the ship *Westmorland,* which was captured by privateers and sold to Spain.[1] Basset returned to Italy in 1788 and possibly acquired more pictures on this second trip, but he is also known to have made many purchases in London during the first decades of the nineteenth century. The Carracci is not among the pictures noted at Tehidy by Brayley and Britton in 1809 and might have been acquired later.[2]

BIBLIOGRAPHY: Richard L. Feigen & Co., *Seven Highly Important Pictures* (New York, 1988), no. 3; Daniele Benati, "I dipinti sugli altari," in Amedeo Benati and Daniele Benati, *La Parrocchia di Sassomolare,* Quaderni del Circolo Culturale Castel d'Aiano 13 (Castel d'Aiano [Bologna], 1998), pp. 76–77; Daniele Benati, "L'oratorio di San Rocco: Il ruolo di Reggio nella prima attività di Annibale Carracci," in *Il seicento a Reggio: La storia, la città, gli artisti,* ed. Paola Ceschi Lavagetto (Reggio, Italy, 1999), p. 54; Daniele Benati, Diane De Grazia, and Gail Feigenbaum, eds., *The Drawings of Annibale Carracci,* exh. cat. (Washington, D.C., 1999), p. 46; Daniele Benati and Carla Bernardini, *I dipinti della Pinacoteca Civica di Budrio* (Bologna, 2005), p. 192; Daniele Benati and Eugenio Riccòmini, eds., *Annibale Carracci,* exh. cat. (Milan, 2006), p. 186, no. 4.1; Aidan Weston-Lewis, "The Annibale Carracci Exhibition in Bologna and Rome," *Burlington Magazine* 149 (2007): p. 259

CONDITION: The panel has a few minor cracks and numerous wormholes but is secure and stable. There are a few small areas of retouching.

With his *Crucifixion* of 1583 (Santa Maria della Carità, Bologna), Annibale Carracci brought to religious painting the radically naturalistic style that he had developed in earlier works such as his *Butcher Shop* of ca. 1582–83 (Christ Church Picture Gallery, Oxford). Although the *Crucifixion* was harshly criticized by the leading Bolognese artists of the older generation, the unveiling two years later of Annibale's *Baptism* (San Gregorio, Bologna) revealed that the *Crucifixion* had been merely the first glimpse of the revolution that the artist would bring about in painting in Bologna and beyond. Infused with the study of Correggio, of Venetian art from earlier in the cinquecento, and of contemporary paintings by Federico Barocci, Annibale constructed the *Baptism* from a series of monumental life drawings, creating a work that—in its combination of a powerful, high-minded style with solid, muscular figures and intimate, naturalistic touches—prefigured religious art for the following generation.

Up to 1585, the Carracci workshop had operated on a basically unified front, but in the following years, Annibale's ascendancy over his elder brother, Agostino, and cousin Ludovico was ever more evident. Given his growing fame, and perhaps also to have some freedom from Ludovico's control over the family workshop, Annibale began to accept commissions for projects outside Bologna. Executing his remarkable *Pietà* of 1585 for the Capuchin church in Parma, he would have had ample opportunity to study the works of Correggio, and the various strains of influence from the Parmese artist are evident in Annibale's works of the following years: the *Mystic Marriage of Saint Catherine* (Museo di Capodimonte, Naples), which was probably executed for Ranuccio Farnese around 1586, the destroyed Bridgewater House *Pietà,* and the *Assumption* and *Madonna of Saint Matthew* painted for Reggio Emilia in 1587–88 (both now Gemäldegalerie, Dresden).

The present work was surely also painted during this period. Its tender intimacy compares closely to the aforementioned pictures in betraying the influence of Correggio. The figure of Saint John at lower left has an obvious relationship to the angel at lower center in the *Madonna of Saint Matthew,* for example, while the heads of Christ and of the angel in the background might be compared to those of the Parma *Pietà.* While allowing for the differences of support, the handling of paint resembles that in the *Venus with a Satyr and Cupid* (Galleria degli Uffizi, Florence) and *San Ludovico Altarpiece* (Pinacoteca Nazionale, Bologna), both

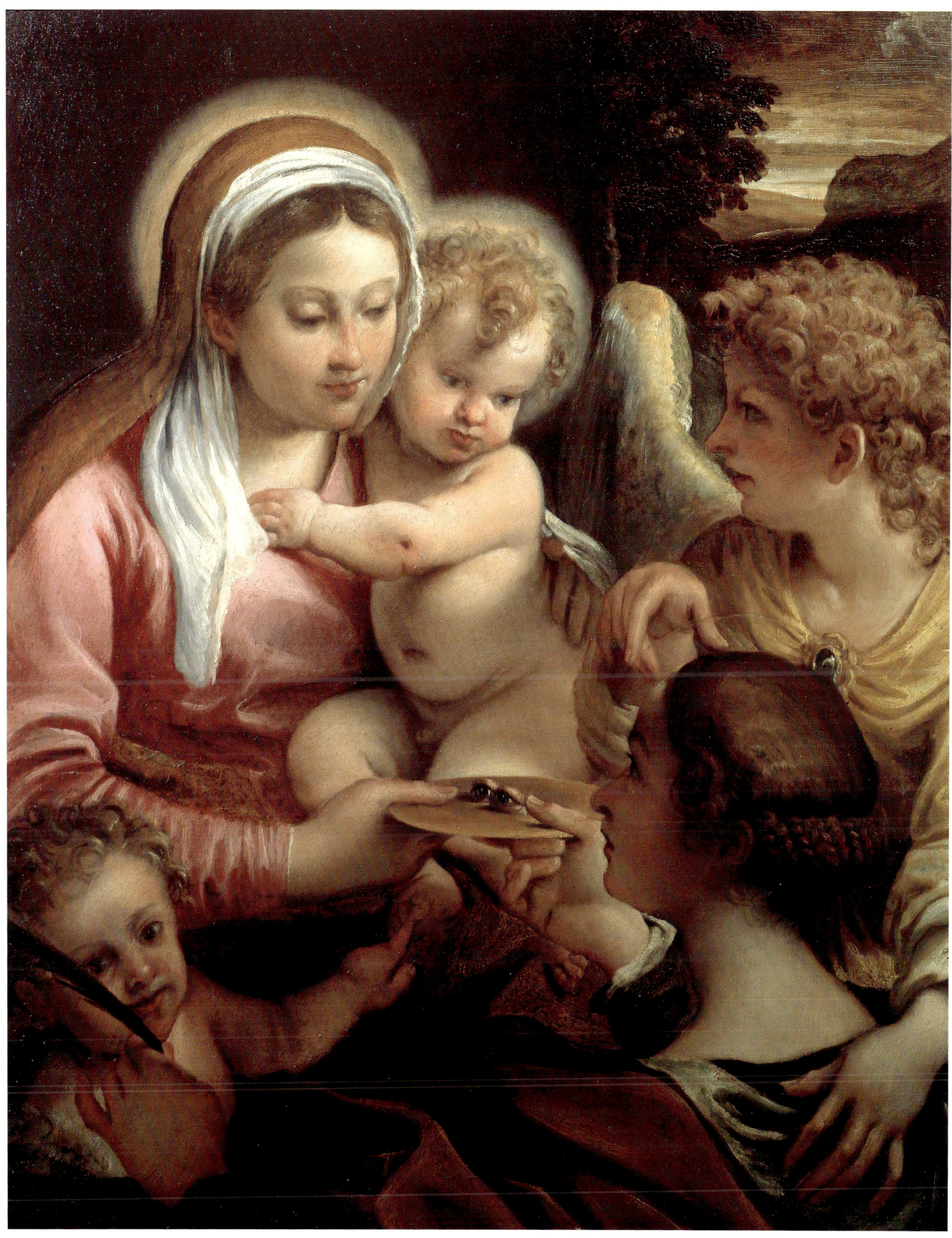

ca. 1589. Although an earlier date of ca. 1584–85 was initially proposed for the Feigen panel upon its rediscovery in the late 1980s, the work's facture, a suave combination of Parmese and Venetian styles, has led to a now-general consensus that it dates to the latter half of the decade.

Painted at a time when Annibale was traveling to Parma, Reggio, and elsewhere, the Feigen panel was nonetheless probably made for a Bolognese patron. It is unrecorded by Malvasia and other early writers, but it exists in at least four early copies, suggesting that it hung in a reasonably prominent location in the city.[3] When the picture was placed at auction in 1824, the catalogue noted that the Scottish painter-cum-dealer Gavin Hamilton had bought the work from the Zampieri collection. "Zampieri" is surely a reference to the Sampieri collection, for the spellings are used interchangeably in British guidebooks and travel diaries of the period. In 1811 Eugène de Beauharnais, the French Viceroy of Italy, acquired the highlights of that collection in his efforts to establish a national gallery of art; these include some of the greatest Bolognese paintings now in the Brera. There are, however, a number of works in the earlier inventories of the palace that were not part of the collection acquired by Beauharnais, and it is possible that Gavin Hamilton, who remained in Italy until his death in 1798, had previously been able to purchase them. It is impossible to discern when the work had entered the Sampieri collection, but it is hardly implausible to suggest that it could have been commissioned by the Abbate Astorre di Vincenzo Sampieri, an important patron of the Carracci. In either case, the presence of the work in the Palazzo Sampieri, one of the primary private collections in Bologna until its dispersal, can explain why there are multiple copies; another of Annibale's Sampieri paintings, the *Burial of Christ* on copper of 1594–95 (Metropolitan Museum of Art, New York) likewise exists in numerous copies.[4] This is also the case with Ludovico Carracci's *Saint Jerome*, another picture from the Palazzo Sampieri.[5]

When offered for sale in 1824, the present panel was attributed to Ludovico Carracci, presumably maintaining the attribution it had when purchased by Hamilton and sold to Francis Basset. Given the misattribution and the Sampieri provenance, the panel is possibly the often-noted but otherwise lost half-length *Madonna and Child with Figures* "come il naturale" by Ludovico recorded in the Palazzo Sampieri by Oretti in the 1760s or 1770s and in the published inventory of 1795.[6] Giacomo Gatti's guide of 1803, however, repeats the reference: if Gatti actually saw the picture at that date, after Hamilton's death, it obviously could not be the work that Hamilton purchased, but Gatti might simply have relied on the earlier published references when compiling his guide.[7] It is also possible that Gatti saw a copy, for Hamilton is known to have commissioned copies to replace pictures that he was interested in buying.[8] Alternately, Hamilton could have purchased the work before the aforementioned inventories were made.

The *Virgin and Child with Saint Lucy and the Young Saint John the Baptist* is the earliest known painting by Annibale on a panel rather than canvas support. It was perhaps an experiment inspired by the work of Correggio and Parmigianino that Annibale would have seen in Parma or elsewhere in Emilia-Romagna: Correggio's similarly scaled *Mystic Marriage of Saint Catherine* (Musée du Louvre, Paris), which was in Modena until the end of the sixteenth century, might serve as one point of comparison. Alternately, panel might have been used at the request of the patron, as was surely the case for Annibale's late panel paintings including the Cerasi chapel *Assumption* (Santa Maria del Popolo, Rome) and the *Domine quo Vadis* (National Gallery, London). The technique was not one to which Annibale would often return, although one wonders whether the manipulation of paint on the smooth panel did not lead him to the frequent use of copper supports in the following years.   JJM

1. José M. Luzón Nogué, ed., *El Westmorland: Recuerdos del Gran Tour*, exh. cat. (Madrid, 2002).

2. Edward Wedlake Brayley and John Britton, *The Beauties of England and Wales* (London, 1809), 2: pp. 506–7.

3. Celide Masini, ed., *Gli splendori della Vergogna: La collezione dei dipinti dell'Opera Pia dei Poveri Vergognosi*, exh. cat. (Bologna, 1995), no. 16; Daniele Benati, "I dipinti sugli altari," in Amedeo Benati and Daniele Benati, *La Parrocchia di Sassomolare*, Quaderni del Circolo Culturale Castel d'Aiano 13 (Castel d'Aiano [Bologna], 1998), pp. 75–77; and Daniele Benati and Carla Bernardini, *I dipinti della Pinacoteca Civica di Budrio* (Bologna, 2005), p. 192.

4. Keith Christiansen, "Annibale Carracci's 'Burial of Christ' Rediscovered," *Burlington Magazine* 141 (1999): pp. 414–18.

5. Formerly in the Feigen collection, the *Saint Jerome* was returned to the heirs of Max Stern when it was discovered that the painting had been part of the forced sale of Stern's property in 1937.

6. Marcello Oretti, *Marcello Oretti e il patrimonio artistico privato bolognese: Bologna Biblioteca Comunale, MS. B.104*, ed. Emilia Calbi and Daniela Scaglietti Kelescian (Bologna, 1984), p. 66; and *Descrizione italiana e francese di tutto ciò che si contiene nella Galleria del Sig. Marchese Senatore Luigi Sampieri* (Bologna, 1795). See also Alessandro Brogi, *Ludovico Carracci (1555–1619)* (Bologna, 2001), 1: p. 288, no. P56, with earlier bibliography.

7. Giacomo Gatti, *Descrizione delle più rare cose di Bologna, e suoi subborghi* (Bologna, 1803), p. 169.

8. David Irwin, "Gavin Hamilton: Archaeologist, Painter, and Dealer," *Art Bulletin* 44 (1962): p. 98n.83; and John Ingamells, *A Dictionary of British and Irish Travellers in Italy, 1701–1800* (New Haven, Conn., 1997), pp. 447–50.

Ludovico Carracci

Bologna, 1555–1619

40. *Alexander the Great and Thaïs,*
ca. 1609–12

Oil on canvas, 130 x 169 cm (51¼ x 66½ in.)

PROVENANCE: probably commissioned by Marchese Alessandro Tanari (1548–1639), Palazzo Tanari, Bologna, and first recorded in his posthumous inventory, 1640; by descent in the Tanari family; from whom purchased in 1827/28 by James Irving for Sir William Forbes, 7th Bt. of Pitsligo (1759–1828); by whom bequeathed to Sir John Forbes, 8th Bt. (1804–1866); offered in the sale of Sir William Forbes's pictures at Rainey's, London, June 2, 1842, lot 7, bought in; by inheritance to John Forbes's daughter Harriet Williamina Forbes Trefusis, Baroness Clinton (d. 1869); by inheritance (either directly from his mother or through his father, 20th Baron Clinton [d. 1904]) to Charles John Robert Hepburn-Stuart-Forbes-Trefusis, 21st Baron Clinton; by inheritance to his daughter Fenella Hepburn-Stuart-Forbes-Trefusis (Mrs. John Herbert Bowes-Lyon); by gift to her daughter Diana Cinderella Bowes-Lyon (Mrs. Peter Somervell); Sotheby's, London, March 19, 1975, lot 61; Colnaghi, London

BIBLIOGRAPHY: Vincenzo Pisani, Inventory of the Paintings of Alessandro Tanari, May 9, 1640, published in Luisa Ciammitti, *Tre artisti nella Bologna dei Bentivoglio: Ercole Robert, La cappella Garganelli in San Pietro* (Bologna, 1985), 208; Carlo Cesare Malvasia, *Felsina pittrice: Vite de' pittori Bolognesi* (Bologna, 1678), 1: p. 495; Marcello Oretti, *Le pitture che si ammirano nelli palaggi e case de' nobili della città di Bologna*, Biblioteca Comunale, Bologna, MS B.104, ca. 1760–80, p. 140, reprinted in Marcello Oretti, *Marcello Oretti e il patrimonio artistico privato bolognese: Bologna, Biblioteca Comunale, MS. B.104*, ed. Emilia Calbi and Daniela Scaglietti Kelescian (Bologna, 1984), p. 68; Ferdinando Belvisi, *Elogio storico del pittore Lodovico Carracci* (Bologna, 1825), p. 53; Colnaghi, London, *Italian Paintings, 1550–1780*, sale cat. (1976), no. 7; Babette Bohn, "The Drawings of Ludovico Carracci" (PH.D. diss., Columbia University, 1982), p. 108; Hugh Brigstocke, *William Buchanan and the Nineteenth-Century Art Trade* (London, 1982), pp. 27, 481; Clovis Whitfield, in Colnaghi, London, *Discoveries from the Cinquecento*, sale cat. (1982), pp. 30–31, no. 14; Gail Feigenbaum, "Lodovico Carracci: A Study of His Later Career and a Catalogue of His Paintings" (PH.D. diss., Princeton University, 1984), pp. 96–100, 428–29, no. 128; Babette Bohn, "Ludovico's Last Decade," *Master Drawings* 25 (1987): p. 228; Gail Feigenbaum, "The 'Kiss of Judas' by Lodovico Carracci," *Record of the Art Museum, Princeton University* 48 (1989): p. 17nn.28–29; Andrea Emiliani, ed., *Ludovico Carracci*, exh. cat. (Bologna, 1993), pp. 139–40, no. 64; Erich Schleier, review of *Ludovico Carracci*, by Andrea Emiliani, *Burlington Magazine* 136 (1994): p. 263; Diane De Grazia and Eric Garberson, *Italian Paintings of the Seventeenth and Eighteenth Centuries: The*

Collections of the National Gallery of Art, Systematic Catalogue (New York, 1996), pp. 52, 54n.34; Keith Christiansen, "Ludovico Carracci's Newly Recovered 'Lamentation,'" *Burlington Magazine* 142 (2000): pp. 416–18; Anne Summerscale, *Malvasia's Life of the Carracci: Commentary and Translation* (University Park, Pa., 2000), pp. 313–24; Alessandro Brogi, *Ludovico Carracci (1555–1619)* (Bologna, 2001), 1: pp. 212–13, no. 98; Keith Christiansen, "A Late Masterpiece by Ludovico Carracci: The Tanari 'Denial of Peter,'" *Burlington Magazine* 145 (2003): p. 23

CONDITION: The painting is on a heavy-gauge linen canvas woven in a checkered pattern, with original seams at approximately 12 cm from the top and bottom edges. Although relined, there is no visible flattening of the painted surface. There are marginal losses at the edges and one horizontal loss approximately 15 to 20 cm from the top, but the painting can be described as in a superior state of preservation.

A prime example of Ludovico Carracci's late style, *Alexander the Great and Thaïs* is like many of the artist's works from around 1610 characterized by a closely cropped and dramatically lit composition, with an emphasis on muscular forms—Ludovico's paintings from his last decade are often described as peopled by gigantic or colossal figures—and on boldly modeled draperies, in contrast to the gentler forms of his earlier work. As has often been noted, Ludovico has pared down the scene, thus emphasizing the psychology of the characters rather than narrative detail, and this also seems to follow a broader trend in his later work. The *Alexander and Thaïs* has much in common, in particular, with the paintings that Ludovico executed for the cathedral in Piacenza in 1605–9, and the general tendency has been to place this canvas around 1609, just following that project.

The picture was first recorded in the Palazzo Tanari in Bologna in 1640, where it hung as an overdoor and was paired with Ludovico's since-lost *Alexander the Great and the Wife of Darius*.[1] A third painting by Ludovico, depicting the birth of Alexander the Great, was also in the palace. The three Alexander the Great paintings were surely commissioned by Alessandro Tanari, who must have chosen subjects connected to his namesake. Although the pendant picture of *Alexander and the Wife of Darius* would have provided a well-known image of Alexander's virtue, the *Alexander and Thaïs* would seem an unusual exemplum. As related by Plutarch and other ancient sources, at the banquet celebrating Alexander's victory over the Persians, the Attic courtesan Thaïs proposed that it was not victory enough merely to celebrate in the palace of Xerxes, the Persian king; instead, as punishment for the Persians' burning of Athens, Alexander and his army should burn the palace. In his drunkenness, Alexander agreed and led the arsonist crowd (the torches held by the protagonists and the troops in the background of the Feigen painting allude to the continuation of the story), but the fire was uncontrolled and the entire city of Persepolis burned to the ground. Thaïs, upright and alert in contrast to the reeling form of Alexander, is shown as the villain here, and the serpent-entwined handle of the wine jug that Alexander overturns suggests a connection between her conduct and Eve's role in the temptation of Adam. Nonetheless, the drunken impetuosity of Alexander in the Feigen canvas argues against a moralizing scheme for the ensemble, and indeed, Alessandro Tanari seems to have planned a personal but not particularly serious program in his choice of subjects. Upon his marriage to Diana Barbieri in January 1589, he commissioned a painting on copper depicting the Marriage of the Virgin, probably that formerly in the Pouncey collection (now National Gallery, London). He later commissioned a *Diana and Actaeon* from Annibale Carracci (now lost), as well as Annibale's painting of ca. 1595 in the National Gallery of Art, Washington, D.C. (fig. 1), commonly called *Venus Adorned by the Graces,* but in the 1640 Tanari inventory, and in the seventeenth- and eighteenth-century accounts of Carlo Cesare Malvasia and Marcello Oretti, identified as *Diana Adorned by Her Attendant Virgins.* This identification of the subject has been discounted by modern scholars but should probably be reconsidered, as Keith Christiansen has also argued.[2] Indeed, the traditional identification

fits perfectly with the series of subjects commissioned by Alexander Tanari and his wife, Diana.

Annibale's panel (later transferred to canvas) also hung as an overdoor in the Palazzo Tanari, accompanied by Ludovico's canvases and by a since-lost *Venus and Vulcan* by Agostino Carracci. What has not hitherto been noted, however, is that Ludovico's *Alexander* canvas of ca. 1609 matches the dimensions of Annibale's *Venus* (or more properly, *Diana*), which had been painted over a decade earlier, before Annibale's departure for Rome. This strongly suggests that Ludovico's painting was specifically commissioned to hang in an arrangement with Annibale's earlier work; it also reinforces the argument that the Washington painting depicts Diana, the obvious pendant to the *Alexander* canvas. The 1640 Tanari inventory was made at the Palazzo Tanari in via Galliera, but this building was begun only in 1612, later than the *Alexander and Thaïs* is generally dated, and it is unclear whether the ensemble was first assembled in the older Palazzo Tanari on the Strada Maggiore, or whether Ludovico's pictures were commissioned for the new palace.[3] There is enough similarity between the *Alexander and Thaïs* and the *Saint Sebastian Thrown in the Cloaca Maxima* of 1612 (J. Paul Getty Museum, Los Angeles), to admit the possibility that the former could have been made as late as 1611–12, with the new palace in mind; Babette Bohn, moreover, has argued that the *Alexander and Thaïs* could be as late as 1616.[4] Christiansen has similarly argued that Ludovico's *Birth of Alexander,* in which Diana figures and which would thus seem to be part of the Alexander–Diana ensemble, probably dates to ca. 1611–12, although the work is only known from the compositional drawing now at the Royal Collection at Windsor.[5] As a counterargument, it should

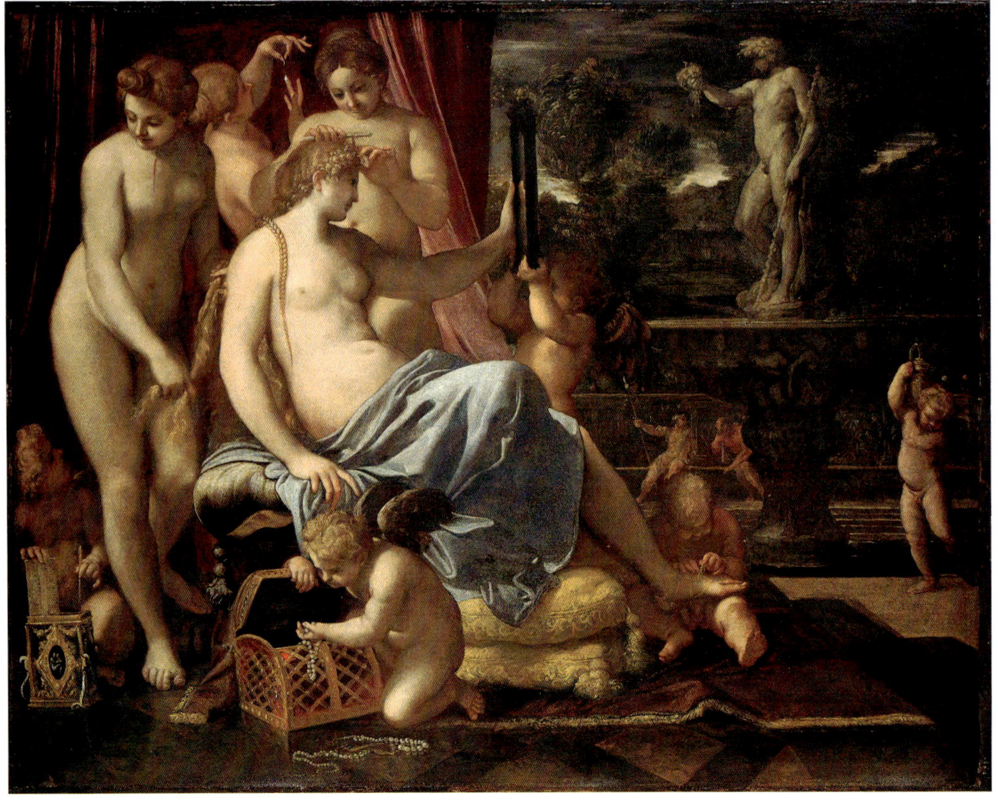

Fig. 1. Annibale Carracci, *Venus Adorned by the Graces (or, Diana Adorned by Her Attendant Virgins),* ca. 1595. Oil on panel transferred to canvas, 132.8 x 170.4 cm (52¼ x 67⅛ in.). Samuel H. Kress Collection, Courtesy of the Board of Trustees, National Gallery of Art, Washington, D.C.

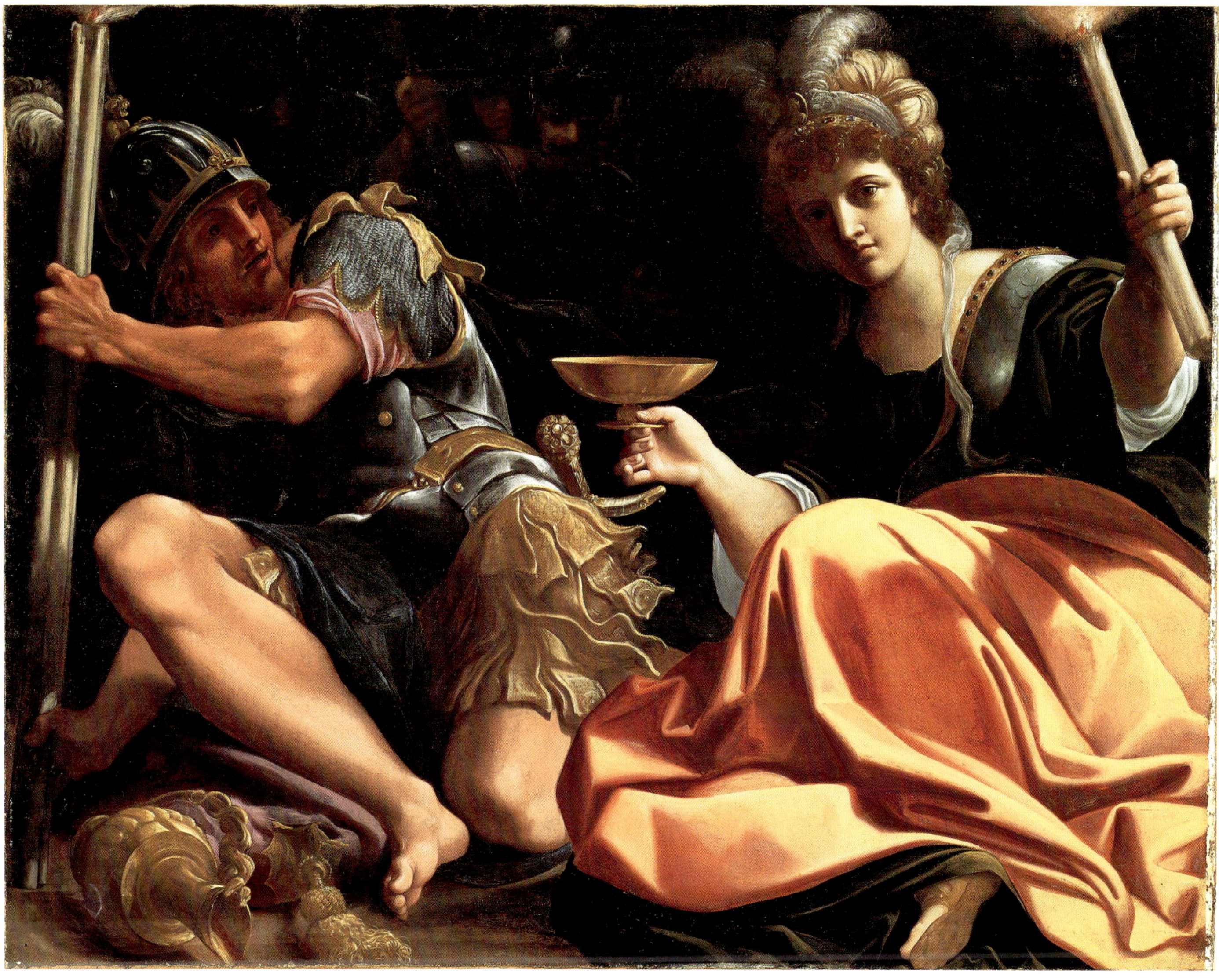

be recalled that Ludovico had previously painted a chimney
with an *Alexander and Thaïs* in 1592 at the Palazzo Luchini
in Bologna (now Palazzo Zambeccari-Francia), a version that
emphasizes the burning of Persepolis, so that the decision in
1611–12 to choose the much less obviously incendiary *Birth
of Alexander* for a chimney at the new Palazzo Tanari could
have been due to Ludovico's having previously painted the
Feigen canvas for an ensemble first assembled in the Strada
Maggiore palace.

Whatever the date of his commission for Ludovico's *Alexander and Thaïs*, Alessandro Tanari now appears to have
been one of the most important and sustained patrons of the
Carracci, at least as important as the more often recognized
Abbate Sampieri. There were thirteen works by Ludovico in
Tanari's posthumous inventory, as well as three by Annibale
and three by Agostino, to say nothing of the many works by
other artists, all of which led Malvasia to describe the Palazzo
Tanari as a "museo insigne" (renowned museum).[6] The works
by Ludovico ranged in date from the very early *Lamentation* of ca. 1582 (Metropolitan Museum of Art, New York)

to late works like the *Alexander and Thaïs* and the *Denial of
Peter* (private collection), and Tanari was also responsible for
Ludovico's final commission, the enormous *Annunciation* in
San Pietro, Bologna.[7]
      JJM

1. Carlo Cesare Malvasia, *Felsina pittrice: Vite de' pittori Bolognesi*
   (Bologna, 1678), 1: p. 495.
2. Keith Christiansen, "Ludovico Carracci's Newly Recovered 'Lamentation,'"
   Burlington Magazine 142 (2000): p. 417.
3. Ibid., p. 417n.7, clarifies the previously confused history of the new palace's
   construction.
4. Babette Bohn, "Ludovico's Last Decade," *Master Drawings* 25 (1987):
   pp. 228, 235n.30. Babette Bohn, "The Drawings of Ludovico Carracci"
   (PH.D. diss., Columbia University, 1982), p. 108, gives, however, the date
   as ca. 1610.
5. Christiansen, "Ludovico Carracci's Newly Recovered 'Lamentation,'"
   pp. 417–18; and Keith Christiansen, "A Late Masterpiece by Ludovico
   Carracci: The Tanari 'Denial of Peter,'" *Burlington Magazine* 145 (2003):
   pp. 23–28.
6. Malvasia, *Felsina pittrice*, 1: pp. 353–59.
7. See Christiansen, "Ludovico Carracci's Newly Recovered 'Lamentation,'"
   pp. 416–22; and Christiansen, "A Late Masterpiece by Ludovico Carracci,"
   pp. 22–29, for further comments on Tanari.

Bartolomeo Schedoni

Modena and Parma, 1578–1615

41. *The Holy Family with Saint John the Baptist*, ca. 1605–10

Oil on panel, 29 x 24 cm (11½ x 9⅞ in.)

PROVENANCE: Phillip's, London, July 6, 1993, lot 262 (as "Studio of Schedoni").

Schedoni's frequent repetition of this composition makes it impossible to reconstruct further provenance.

BIBLIOGRAPHY: unpublished

CONDITION: The primary support of the painting is a fruit-wood panel with a horizontally oriented grain; the panel has been thinned to a thickness of approximately 0.3 cm and was at some point backed with a vertically grained hardwood panel. The tension created by the conflicting warp and shrinking of the differently grained panels caused the original panel to split and the paint surface to blister. In 1993–94 the hardwood backing was removed and replaced with a new basswood support, and the blistering paint was reattached. The panel is most damaged at the upper and lower third (the inscription on the *cartellino* at lower right has been worn away), but the center of the image is well preserved.

Born in Modena in 1578, Bartolomeo Schedoni was the son of a mask maker employed by the Este and Farnese courts in Modena and Parma. He displayed impressive talents even at a young age and was sent by Ranuccio Farnese in 1595 to study with Federico Zuccaro in Rome.[1] He was back in Parma by 1597, and this Roman sojourn seems to have had little impact, for Schedoni's paintings show no influence of Zuccaro and remain instead grounded in the Emilian tradition, with Correggio and Ludovico Carracci as the most obvious sources of his style. Schedoni's was a dissolute lifestyle, and gambling and fighting led several times to his imprisonment.[2] In 1600, after one such incarceration, he left Parma and went to Modena, where until 1607 he was in the employ of Cesare d'Este. He later returned to Parma, where he spent the remaining years of his life once again in the service of the Farnese, until the time of his premature death—possibly by suicide—in 1615. It has often been suggested that Schedoni's violent life is difficult to reconcile with the sweet sensibility and delicate style of his art, but the intimacy and warmth of the *Holy Family with Saint John the Baptist* is typical of the artist's work.

Although Schedoni was for most of his career associated with the ducal courts, he also created a very large number of small devotional pictures like the present work, a production that was probably outside his regular court patronage but that would have supplied him with a steady additional income for a rather small investment of time.[3] Schedoni's large output of these small, easily saleable pictures was likely to have been an expedient way of raising money to pay off his well-documented gambling debts, a parallel to the better-known case of Guido Reni.[4] In the final decade of his life, from 1607–15, Schedoni's contract with Ranuccio Farnese stipulated that he could work for other patrons only if the Duke allowed it.[5] On the one hand, Farnese may have been trying to limit Schedoni's notably broad production, but on the other hand, it is clear that the contract did not prohibit Schedoni from continuing to produce many small-scale pictures.

Images of the Holy Family can well be described as Schedoni's bread and butter. He created many different variants on the subject, but at some point in his career he settled into a practice of repetition.[6] The artist's technical proficiency allowed him to maintain a high level of quality through many such examples, but he seems not to have invested much inventive energy in the pictures, instead repeating a few basic compositions over and over again. One iteration of the composition showed the Holy Family with the Virgin teaching the Christ Child (and sometimes also Saint John the Baptist) how to read; the best-known examples of this type are those from the Mahon Collection in the National Gallery, London, and at the Ashmolean Museum, Oxford.[7] Another version, best known from an example in the Musée du Louvre, Paris, shows Joseph and the Virgin in half-length, with the latter embracing a standing Christ Child.[8] Still closer to the Feigen example is a composition that shows the young John the Baptist at left, and a Virgin and Child similar to the Feigen picture, but with Joseph in the background at right, behind the Virgin's shoulder.[9] The Feigen composition is, however, the most popular variant. The following list, which includes autograph versions, studio copies, and perhaps also later copies, provides a sample that might give some idea of how many replicas must have been produced: Hermitage, St. Petersburg (oil on panel, transferred to canvas, 66 x 50 cm); Szépművészeti Múzeum, Budapest (oil on canvas, 37 x 31 cm); Museo Civico, Modena (oil on canvas, 91 x 75 cm); Museo Diocesano, Reggio Emilia (oil on canvas, 93 x 87 cm); formerly in the Hartveld collection, Antwerp (oil on canvas, 106 x 91 cm); formerly in the Earl of Yarborough collection, sold Christie's, London, July 12, 1929, lot 94 (oil on canvas[?], 102 x 84 cm); Sotheby's, Monaco, June 15, 1990, lot 219 (oil on canvas, 23 x 19 cm); Christie's, Rome, April 8, 1991, lot 198 (oil on canvas, 24 x 20 cm); Sotheby's, London, May 11, 1995, lot 85 (oil on canvas, 100 x 84 cm); Finarte Semenzato, Venice, June 17, 2003, lot 605 (oil on canvas, 30 x 25 cm).[10]

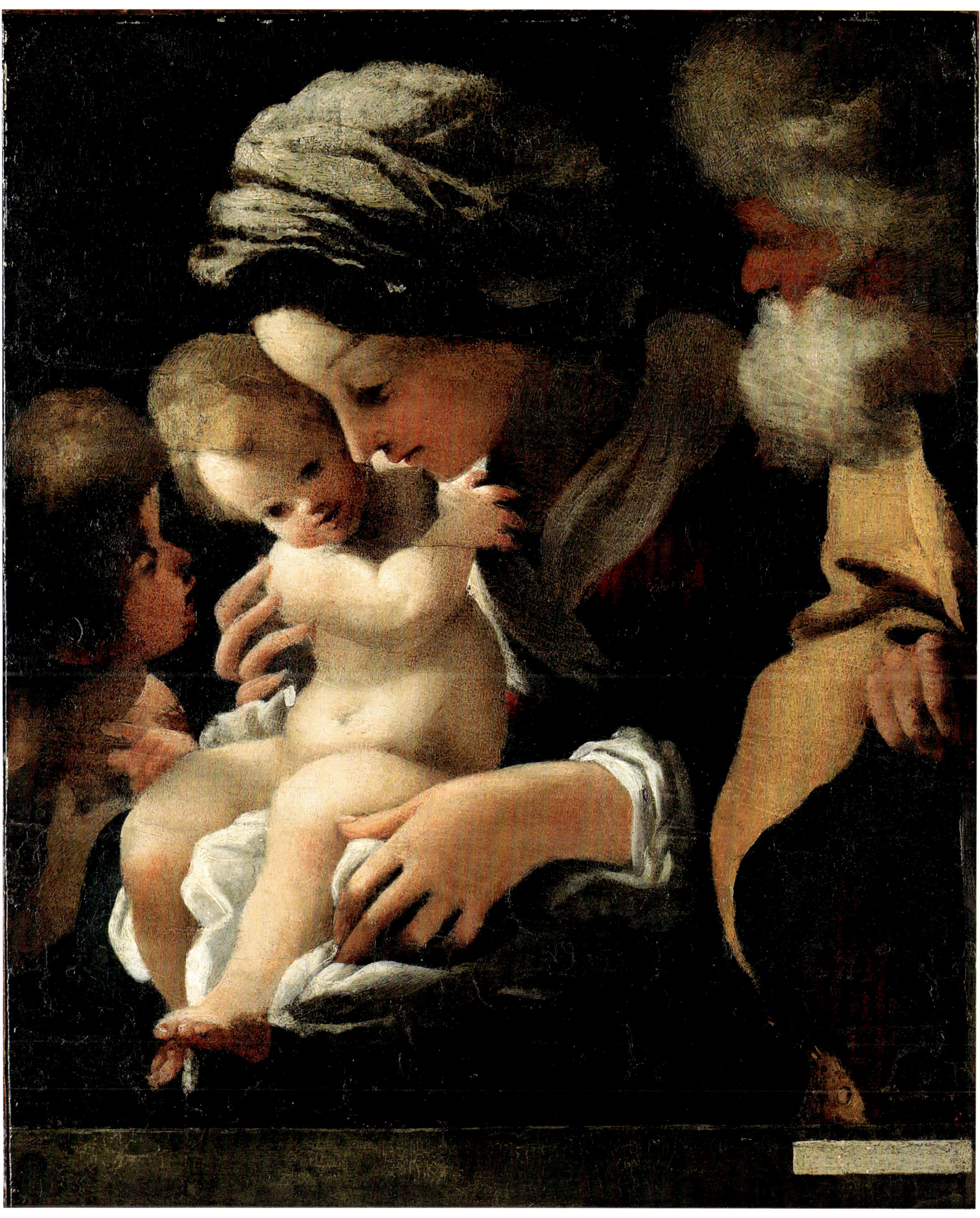

Schedoni's characteristic painterly style is evident in many autograph paintings, but he must also have had a workshop responsible for the equally large number of mediocre examples. The Feigen composition, it might be observed in the preceding list, was made at two scales, one roughly 30 cm tall, and another more like 100 cm high. The majority of known examples are on canvas, but Dwight Miller has noted that many of the best versions—those most likely to have been produced by Schedoni himself—are on panel. The fruitwood support of the Feigen picture is relatively unusual for an Italian artist, but the Mahon painting, one of the examples universally accepted as by the master himself, is likewise on fruitwood. The Feigen picture, too, seems unquestionably to be by Schedoni, as has also been confirmed by Miller.[11]

Schedoni's practice of replicating his composition makes difficult any attempt to date his paintings. The presence in the Galleria Estense, Modena, of one replica of the Feigen painting cannot be used to suggest that the composition was one painted during the Modena period 1600–1607, for a second example, in the Museo Civico, Modena, from the Campori Collection, has a provenance trail leading back to Parma. The Farnese account books, however, allow precise dating of several key pictures from the period 1607–15, including the *Charity* at the Museo di Capodimonte, Naples, and the *Entombment* in the Galleria Nazionale, Parma. These late works are notable for their crystalline forms and stark lighting, qualities also evident in the Louvre *Holy Family*. Schedoni's earlier style has much more in common with Correggio and with Ludovico Carracci and is characterized by a more painterly application of paint, by a lighting scheme that is dramatic but without the preternatural brightness of the late works, and by a tendency for a softer focus than is seen in the crisp forms of the late pictures. The Feigen panel would thus to the present author seem most likely to fall into this earlier period, perhaps around 1605, although the composition has been dated to ca. 1610 by others.[12]   JJM

1. Dwight Miller, "A Roman Sojourn of Bartolomeo Schedone and Other Documents Relative to the Early Phase of His Career," *Burlington Magazine* 115 (1973): pp. 650–52.
2. See Dwight Miller, "Bartolomeo Schedoni in Modena: The Earlier Phase of His Work," *Burlington Magazine* 121 (1979): pp. 76–94.
3. Dwight Miller, in *The Age of Correggio and the Carracci: Emilian Painting of the Sixteenth and Seventeenth Centuries*, exh. cat. (Washington, D.C., 1986), pp. 526–27.
4. For Reni's gambling and its relationship to his painting practice, see Richard E. Spear, *The "Divine" Guido: Religion, Sex, Money, and Art in the World of Guido Reni* (New Haven, Conn., 1997).
5. Antonio Gualtiero Lodi, *Bartolomeo Schedoni, 1578–1615: Notizie e documenti* (Modena, 1978), pp. 51–52; and Gabriele Finaldi and Michael Kitson, *Discovering the Italian Baroque: The Denis Mahon Collection*, exh. cat. (London, 1997), p. 156.
6. Rolf Kultzen, "Variationen über das Thema der Heiligen Familie bei Bartolomeo Schedoni," *Münchner Jahrbuch der bildenden Kunst* 21 (1970): pp. 167–79; Miller, "Bartolomeo Schedoni in Modena," pp. 76–94; Federica Dallasta and Cristina Cecchinelli, *Bartolomeo Schedoni: Pittore emiliano* (Colorno [Parma], 1999); and Emilio Negro and Nicosetta Roio, *Bartolomeo Schedoni, 1578–1615* (Modena, 2000).
7. See Finaldi and Kitson, *Discovering the Italian Baroque*, p. 156, no. 74; and Negro and Roio, *Bartolomeo Schedoni*, no. 42.
8. Negro and Roio, *Bartolomeo Schedoni*, p. 85, no. 30.
9. One frequently cited example is in the Galleria Estense, Modena; see Dallasta and Cecchinelli, *Bartolomeo Schedoni: Pittore emiliano*, no. 17. See also Federica Dallasta and Cristina Cecchinelli, *Bartolomeo Schedoni a Parma (1607–1615): Pittura e controriforma alla corte di Ranuccio I Farnese* (Colorno [Parma], 2002).
10. In addition to the list here, see Dallasta and Cecchinelli, *Bartolomeo Schedoni: Pittore emiliano*, no. 62; Negro and Roio, *Bartolomeo Schedoni*, p. 83, no. 27; and Daniele Benati and Lucia Peruzzi, *Musei Civici di Modena: I dipinti antichi* (Modena, 2005), no. 32.
11. Dwight Miller, letter to Richard L. Feigen, September 15, 1993, Richard L. Feigen Co. files.
12. Negro and Roio, *Bartolomeo Schedoni*, p. 83, no. 27.

Alessandro Turchi, called l'Orbetto
Verona and Rome, 1578–1649

42. *The Adoration of the Shepherds,*
ca. 1610–15

Oil on copper, 28 x 23 cm (11 x 9 in.)

PROVENANCE: Bonham's, London, December 15, 1977, lot 31

BIBLIOGRAPHY: Daniela Scaglietti Kelescian, ed., *Alessandro Turchi, detto l'Orbetto, 1578–1649*, exh. cat. (Milan, 1999), no. 9

CONDITION: The paint surface is well preserved, exhibiting only minor flaking losses in the upper left quadrant and in the sleeve of the kneeling shepherd.

Alessandro Turchi is typical of the generation of painters who came of age in Verona in the years just after 1600. He studied in the workshop of Felice Brusasorci, as did his contemporaries Marcantonio Bassetti and Pasquale Ottino, but all three painters were equally under the influence of Paolo Farinati, Jacopo Bassano, Palma Giovane, and especially Paolo Veronese. Turchi, Bassetti, and Ottino all traveled to Rome, where they were further influenced by the works of Caravaggio, Annibale Carracci, and, most of all, Carlo Saraceni, with

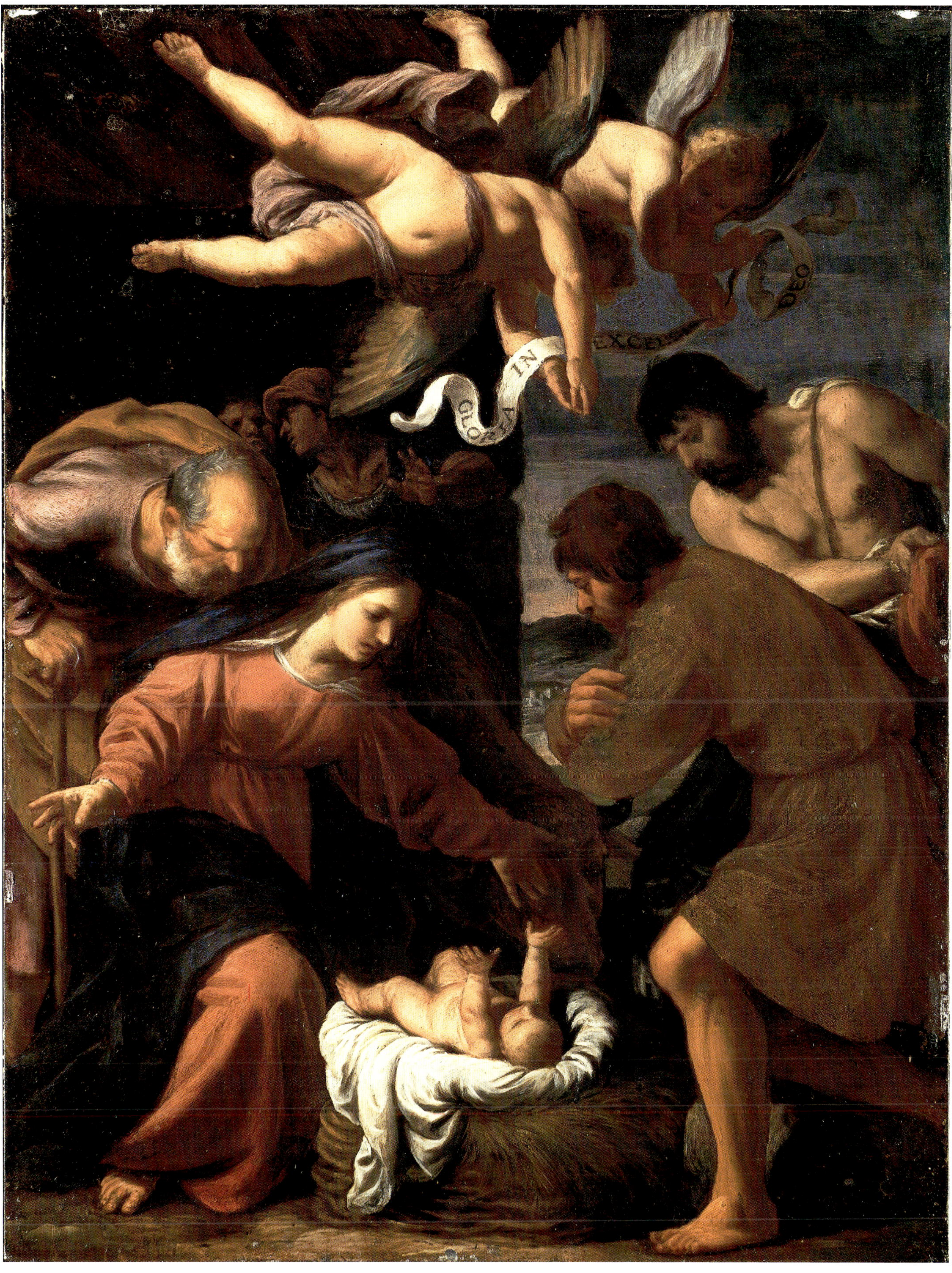

GLORIA IN
EXCELSIS DEO

whom Turchi and Bassetti worked in the Sala Regia in the Palazzo del Quirinale.[1] Unlike his Veronese colleagues, Turchi remained in Rome, where he received a steady run of commissions for altarpieces and cabinet paintings, and where he was eventually, in 1637, elected *principe* of the Accademia di San Luca.

Turchi spent the majority of his career in Rome, and he has—at least since so-labeled by Roberto Longhi—often been discussed as a primarily Caravaggesque painter, but many of the elements of his style were already in place before he arrived in the papal city.[2] The *Adoration of the Shepherds*, for example, with its figures set against a dark background and painted in the luminous and precise style offered by the copper support, has everything to do with the traditions of Verona, where copper and slate had been in common use for at least a generation.[3] One particular characteristic of the paintings on slate by the artists of Verona is that the surface of the stone was often allowed to show, with the polished black

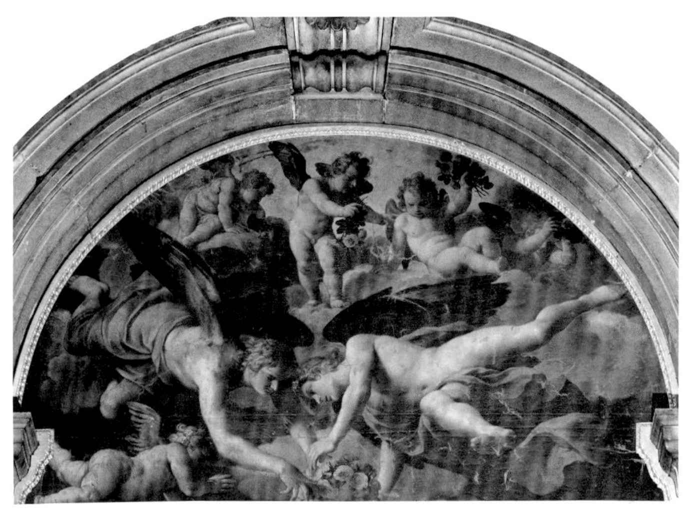

Fig. 2. Alessandro Turchi, *Angels with Rose Garlands*, ca. 1607. Oil on canvas, 160 x 239 cm (63 x 94⅛ in.), lunette. Santa Anastasia, Verona

background thus standing as a foil to brightly painted figures.[4] This approach probably underlies the deep chiaroscuro of the Feigen *Adoration*, although it is on copper rather than slate.

In a style that might be labeled as "classicizing *caravaggismo*," the painting can be compared with Saraceni's Roman works, but it is difficult to establish whether the copper was painted in Rome or, more likely, in Verona shortly before Turchi's departure. The relative simplification of the composition would point to a date right around 1614, the year of Turchi's departure for Rome, and might be contrasted, despite the difference of scale, with the far busier composition of Turchi's *Adoration of the Shepherds* painted for the church of San Fermo in Verona, in 1608 (fig. 1).[5] The energy of the composition and the figure types of the Feigen painting can be compared, though, to the *Saint Augustine Meditating on the Trinity* at Santi Apostoli in Verona, probably painted around 1613.[6] As noted by Daniela Scaglietti Kelescian, the angel at top left in the Feigen painting is directly related to that at right in Turchi's *Angels with Rose Garlands*, painted for Santa Anastasia in Verona, around 1607 (fig. 2).[7] Yet, Scaglietti Kelescian dates the similar *Adoration of the Shepherds* slate in Dresden (fig. 3) to Turchi's first years in Rome.[8] The distinction between Turchi's latest paintings in Verona and his first works in Rome would seem a matter of splitting hairs, but one of the few questions that remains about Turchi's development concerns the impact on the artist of Roman painting, so some further clarification of this period would still be desirable.[9] The work in Rome of Northern Italian and Northern European artists like Turchi, Saraceni, and Adam Elsheimer—to say nothing of Peter Paul Rubens or Caravaggio—points toward the relative breakdown of regional styles in the early years of the seicento.

In the end, the Feigen *Adoration of the Shepherds* seems best to fit somewhere ca. 1610–15, spanning the end of Turchi's Verona period and his first years in Rome, although this is later than Scaglietti Kelescian's preferred dating of

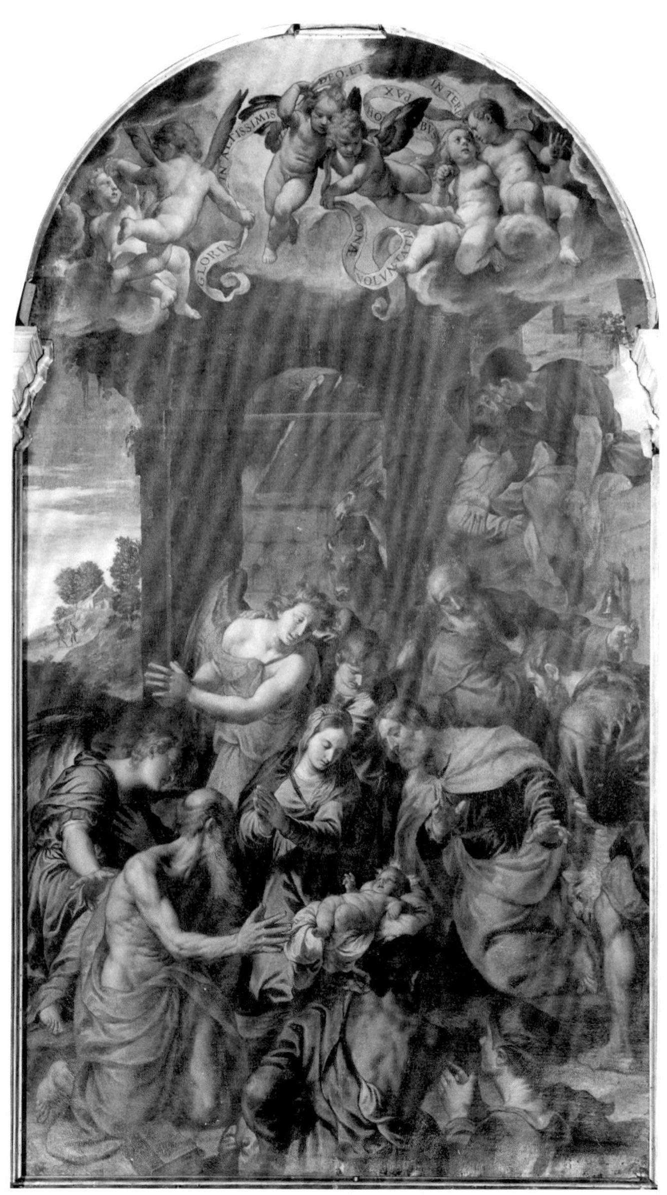

Fig. 1. Alessandro Turchi, *The Adoration of the Shepherds*, 1608. Oil on canvas, 413 x 235 cm (162⅞ x 92½ in.). San Fermo, Verona

"before 1610."[10] The present author would likewise place another *Adoration of the Shepherds*, in the Castelvecchio, Verona, in the second decade.[11] This painting on slate is related to the Feigen copper, for the putto at left in the former mimics the pose of the more mature angel in the latter, and the Christ Child in both paintings reaches similarly upward from almost identical basket-mangers. Despite Scaglietti Kelescian's description of the Dresden picture (and, by implication, the Feigen version) as "ancora cinquecentesca, brusasorciana," both compositions seem somewhat advanced beyond the more mannered ("cinquecentesque") figures in works like the San Fermo painting of 1608 and the *Madonna and Child in Glory* of ca. 1607 (Castelvecchio, Verona).[12] Whatever the date, the similarity of the Feigen *Adoration* to the Santa Anastasia *Angels* and other paintings makes the attribution certain, and it has not been questioned by modern scholars (an old inscription on the verso, however, attributes the picture to Scarsellino).

Turchi took up the subject of the *Adoration of the Shepherds* several times. In addition to the previously mentioned pictures, other important examples include a late altarpiece and several related studies and/or reduced *ricordi*.[13] Finally, another *Adoration of the Shepherds* in the Fitzwilliam Museum at Cambridge, also on copper, has generally been attributed to Turchi and deserves some mention here, in part because it has not been included in most of the literature on the artist (it is absent from the catalogues of the Turchi exhibitions of 1974 and 1999). It is, nonetheless, somewhat difficult to reconcile the attribution of the Fitzwilliam and the Feigen paintings. The Fitzwilliam painting must be either a very early work by Turchi, or else instead by one of his Veronese contemporaries, perhaps Marcantonio Bassetti, whose works are closer to Northern Italian predecessors and thus compare well to the more painterly approach seen in this version of the subject; any discussion of the attribution is complicated, however, by the fact that the Fitzwilliam painting appears to be a copy after a lost altarpiece by Bassano.[14]   JJM

1. Older sources, particularly Dal Pozzo, *Vite de' pittori . . . Veronesi* (Verona, 1718), held that Turchi had been associated with Saraceni in Verona, but this is now seen as unlikely, as noted by Daniela Scaglietti Kelescian, in *Cinquant'anni di pittura veronese, 1580–1630*, ed. Licisco Magagnato, exh. cat. ([Vicenza], Italy, 1974), pp. 107–8.

2. Roberto Longhi, *Precisioni nelle gallerie italiane: 1, R. Galleria Borghese* (Rome, 1928), pp. 60–74.

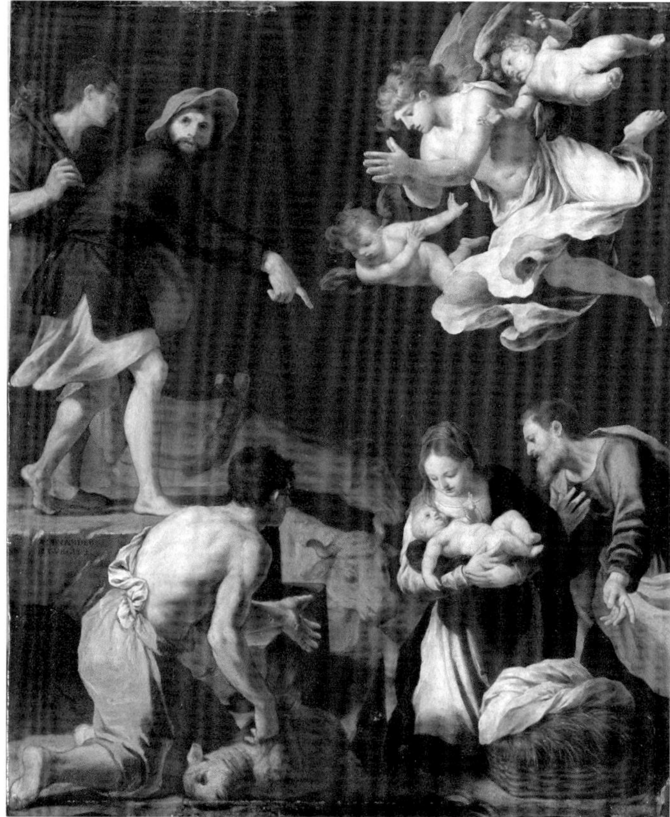

Fig. 3. Alessandro Turchi, *The Adoration of the Shepherds*, ca. 1614. Oil on slate, 45 x 37.5 cm (17¾ x 14¾ in.). Gemäldegalerie, Dresden, inv. no. 515

3. See, for example, *Pittura su pietra*, exh. cat. (Florence, 1970).

4. Beverly Louise Brown, ed., *The Genius of Rome, 1592–1623*, exh. cat. (London, 2001), nos. 73 and 115, are typical examples.

5. Daniela Scaglietti Kelescian, ed., *Alessandro Turchi, detto l'Orbetto, 1578–1649*, exh. cat. (Milan, 1999), no. 80.

6. Ibid., no. 85, correcting an earlier dating of 1619–20 put forth in Magagnato, *Cinquant'anni di pittura veronese*, no. 96.

7. Scaglietti Kelescian, *Alessandro Turchi*, no. 79. Both pictures, incidentally, demonstrate the young Turchi's study of Peter Paul Rubens's *Gonzaga Family in Adoration of the Trinity* in nearby Mantua.

8. Ibid., no. 14.

9. *Pace* Bernard Aikema, review of *Alessandro Turchi, detto l'Orbetto, 1578–1649*, by Daniela Scaglietti Kelescian, *Burlington Magazine* 142 (2000): p. 638, who argues that "Turchi's oeuvre is well documented and presents few problems of dating."

10. Scaglietti Kelescian, *Alessandro Turchi*, no. 9.

11. Ibid., no. 70.

12. Ibid., no. 4.

13. Ibid., no. 89.

14. See Hugh Macandrew, "A Silver Basin Designed by Strozzi," *Burlington Magazine* 113 (1971): pp. 7–8.

Carlo Saraceni

Venice and Rome, ca. 1579–1620

43. *The Dormition of the Virgin*, 1612 (not in exhibition)

Oil on canvas, 305 x 231 cm (120 x 91 in.)

PROVENANCE: commissioned for the Cherubini chapel, Santa Maria della Scala, Rome, but removed ca. 1612; sold by the artist to Sebastian Füll, Munich(?); Electoral Collection, Heidelberg, by 1679; Orléans Collection, Versailles, France, by December 7, 1692, and by descent; with the rest of the Orléans Collection it passed in 1792 to the banker Walkuers, then to Laborde de Méréville, then to a consortium in England led by the Duke of Bridgewater, Lord Carlisle, and Lord Gower; Frederick, 5th Earl of Carlisle, Castle Howard, England, purchased 1798; by descent to the 9th Earl of Carlisle, by whom given to Ampleforth Abbey, York, England, in 1890; Heim Gallery, London

BIBLIOGRAPHY: see no. 44

CONDITION: An inscription on the reverse of the canvas records that it was relined in 1792. The underlying original version (with the Virgin's eyes closed and her head slumped) is evident on the painting's surface.

44. *The Dormition of the Virgin*, ca. 1612–15

Oil on copper, 45.6 x 28.1 cm (18 x 11⅛ in.)

PROVENANCE: Sir Peter Lely, London (his posthumous sale, London, April 18, 1682); Christopher Batt, London (his sale, Langford, London, April 14–15, 1756, lot 2); Alfred Scharf, London; private collection, Chicago; private collection, New York

BIBLIOGRAPHY: Giovanni Baglione, *Le vite de' pittori, scultori, et architetti . . .* (Rome, 1642), p. 146; Joachim von Sandrart, *Teutsche Akademie* (Nuremberg, Germany, 1679), modern edition, ed. A. R. Peltzer (Munich, 1925), 2: p. 312; Gustav Friedrich Waagen, *Treasures of Art in Great Britain* (London, 1854), 2: p. 495; 3: pp. 324–25; Leopold von Ranke, *Französische Geschichte*, vol. 5 (Stuttgart, Germany, 1861), pp. 339–40; Amadore Porcella, *Carlo Saraceni* (Venice, 1929), pp. 26–28; B. Heinrich, "Carlo Saraceni," in Ulrich Thieme and Felix Becker, *Allgemeines Lexikon der bildenden Künstler von der Antike bis zur Gegenwart*, vol. 29 (Leipzig, Germany, 1935), pp. 459–60; Tancred Borenius, "Editorial: Sir Peter Lely's Collection," *Burlington Magazine* 83 (1943): p. 186n.17; Eve Borsook, "Documents Concerning the Artistic Associates of Santa Maria della Scala in Rome," *Burlington Magazine* 96 (1954): pp. 270–75; Benedict Nicolson, "Current and Forthcoming Exhibitions," *Burlington Magazine* 106 (1964): p. 349; Alfred Moir, *The Italian Followers of Caravaggio* (Cambridge, Mass., 1967), 2: p. 100; Anna Ottani Cavina, *Carlo Saraceni* (Milan, 1968), no. 92, see also nos. 9, 37, 69, 82; Fioravante Martinelli, *Roma ornata dall'architettura, pittura, e scoltura*, undated manuscript published in *Roma nel seicento*, ed. Cesare D'Onofrio (Rome, 1969), p. 134; Benedict Nicolson, review of *Carlo Saraceni*, by Anna Ottani Cavina, *Burlington Magazine* 112 (1970): pp. 312–15; Benedict Nicolson, *The International Caravaggesque Movement* (Oxford, 1979), p. 87; Maurizio Marini, "Caravaggio e il naturalismo naturale," in *Storia dell'arte italiana* (Turin, 1981), 6, pt. 1: p. 389; Benedict Nicolson, *Caravaggism in Europe*, 2nd ed., rev. and enlarged by Luisa Vertova (Turin, 1989), 1: p. 170, no. 175; Pamela Askew, *Caravaggio's "Death of the Virgin"* (Princeton, N.J., 1990), pp. 65–66, 168–69; John Gash, review of *Identificazione di un Caravaggio: Nuove tecnologie per una rilettura del "San Giovanni Battista,"* by Giampaolo Correale, *Caravaggio's "Death of the Virgin,"* by Pamela Askew, and *Caravage, "La mort de la Vierge": Une Madone sans dignité,* by Stéphane Loire and Arnauld Brejon de Lavergnée, *Burlington Magazine* 134 (1992): p. 187; Maria Giulia Aurigemma, "Carlo Saraceni, un Veneziano a Roma," in *Caravaggio e il Caravaggismo*, ed. Giovanni Capitelli and Caterina Volpe (Rome, 1995), p. 120; Catherine Puglisi, *Caravaggio* (London, 1998); Edgar Peters Bowron, in *Copper as Canvas: Two Centuries of Masterpiece Paintings on Copper, 1370–1400*, exh. cat. (New York, 1999), p. 277; Larry Silver, "Caravaggism's Missing Link, or What ter Brugghen Brought Home from Rome," *Pantheon* 58 (2000): pp. 188–90; *Caravaggio e l'Europa: Il movimento caravaggesco internazionale da Caravaggio a Mattia Preti,* exh. cat. (Milan, 2005), p. 240; Keith Christiansen, "Going for Baroque: Bringing 17th Century Masters to the Met," *Metropolitan Museum of Art Bulletin* (winter 2005): pp. 21–22

CONDITION: Despite a few small flaking losses of the sort common in paintings on copper, the work is in good condition. It was last treated in 1998. There is a visible pentiment: the pair of hands that appears behind the apostle furthest at the right (over Saint John the Evangelist's shoulder) in the altarpiece was initially present in the copper as well but has been painted out.

In June of 1601, Caravaggio signed a contract with Laerzio Cherubini to paint, within one year's time, a large canvas with "the death, or the transit, of the Virgin" for the church of Santa Maria della Scala in Rome.[1] A successful lawyer and businessman, Cherubini was a devout Catholic and one of the three custodians of the church of Santa Maria della Scala, which had been recently given to the Discalced Carmelites. The church and convent had as its mission the protection both of young women in danger of falling into prostitution

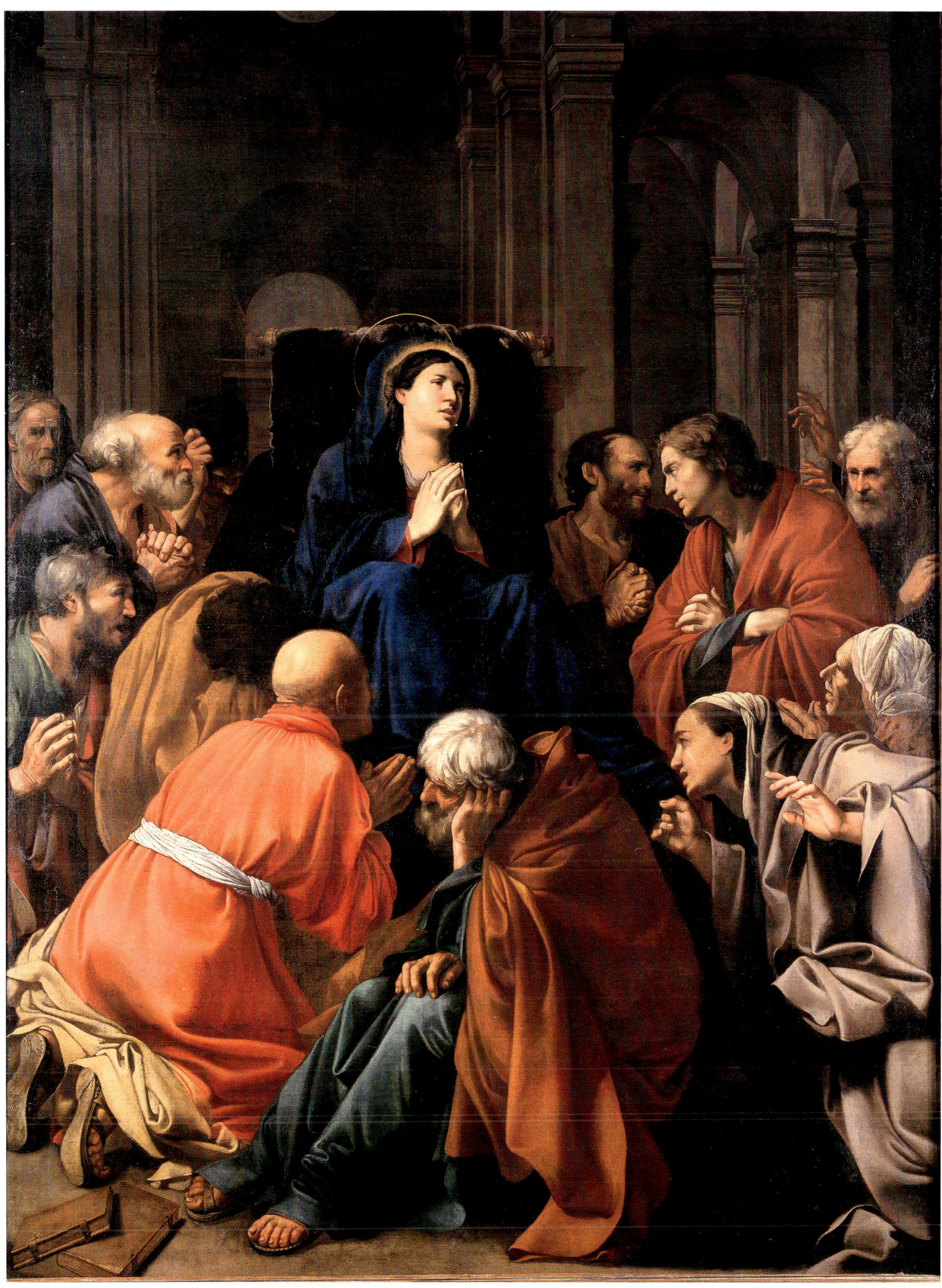

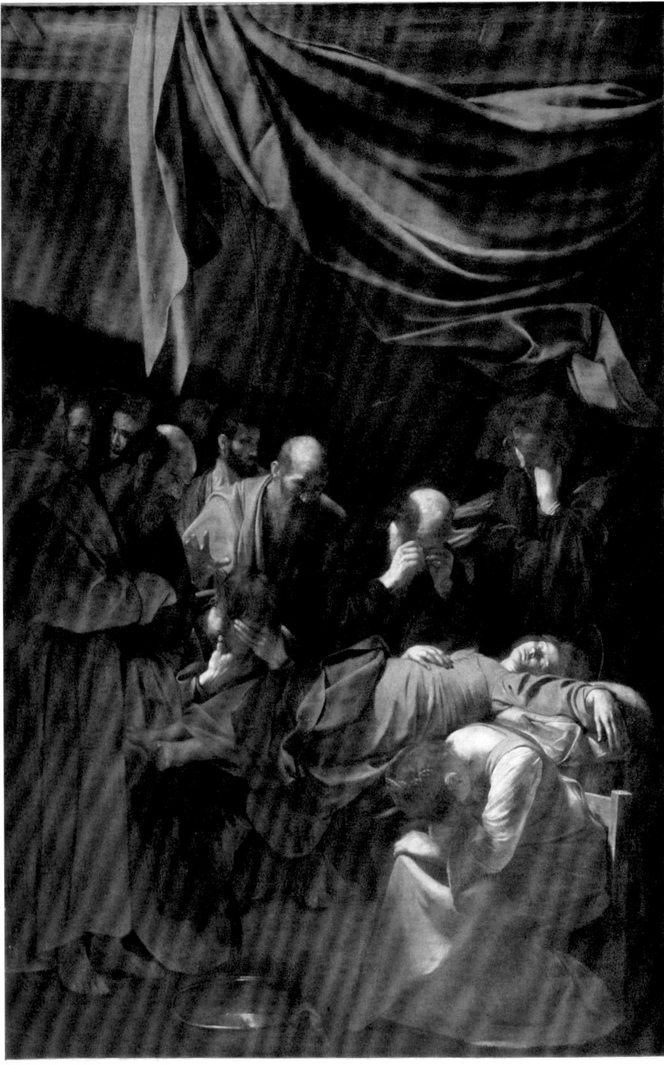

Fig. 1. Michelangelo Merisi, called Caravaggio, *The Dormition of the Virgin*, 1601–1605/6. Oil on canvas, 369 x 245 cm (145¼ x 96 in.). Musée du Louvre, Paris, Louis XIV Collections, inv. no. 54

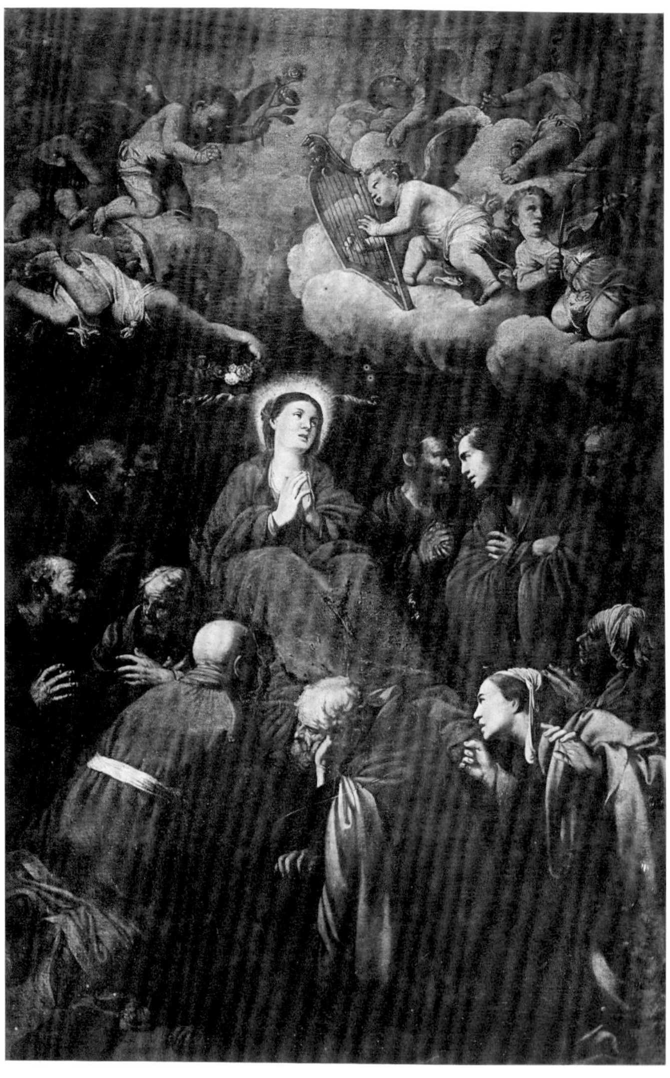

Fig. 2. Carlo Saraceni, *The Dormition of the Virgin*, 1612. Oil on canvas, 459 x 273 cm (180¾ x 107½ in.). Santa Maria della Scala, Rome

and of the *malmariate*, wives who had been abused or abandoned. We do not know exactly when Caravaggio delivered the painting, but it seems likely that more than the allotted year passed before the project was completed.[2] Caravaggio's career was then in rapid ascent: his works for the Contarelli chapel in San Luigi dei Francesci had been unveiled shortly before he signed the contract with Cherubini, and his laterals for the Cerasi chapel in Santa Maria del Popolo were nearing completion and would be installed in the following month.

Caravaggio's *Dormition of the Virgin* (fig. 1) is an extraordinary painting, a quiet study of grief and contemplation completely devoid of the obvious rhetoric in so many early Baroque paintings. By 1606, however, the year in which Caravaggio fled Rome, the picture had been removed from the church and was up for sale on the Roman art market. According to Giulio Mancini, the Carmelites thought that the Virgin was modeled on a prostitute.[3] They also—at least according to Giovanni Baglione and Giovan Pietro Bellori (both writing long after the fact)—complained about the bare feet, the

swollen stomach and bloated body of a dead woman, and the apparent poverty of the Virgin, all of which were summed up in the pronouncement that the painting lacked the proper decorum.[4] Yet, the canvas may have remained in the church for several years before criticism led to its removal, and the complaints about it may have had as much to do with Caravaggio's scandal-plagued lifestyle as with the actual iconography. Vincenzo Giustiniani had been chosen to assess the completed *Dormition of the Virgin* to determine the final price owed to Caravaggio; he assigned it a fairly high price of 280 *scudi*, which Cherubini apparently paid, for he was later eager to recoup the cost when the painting was placed on sale. Finally, the work was highly esteemed by many in Rome, and Peter Paul Rubens eventually recommended it to the duke of Mantua, who had his agent acquire the painting.

The Carmelites and/or Cherubini next handed the altarpiece commission to Carlo Saraceni.[5] Born in Venice, Saraceni had arrived in Rome around 1598, but he was not an obvious choice for the commission. Most of his work during his first

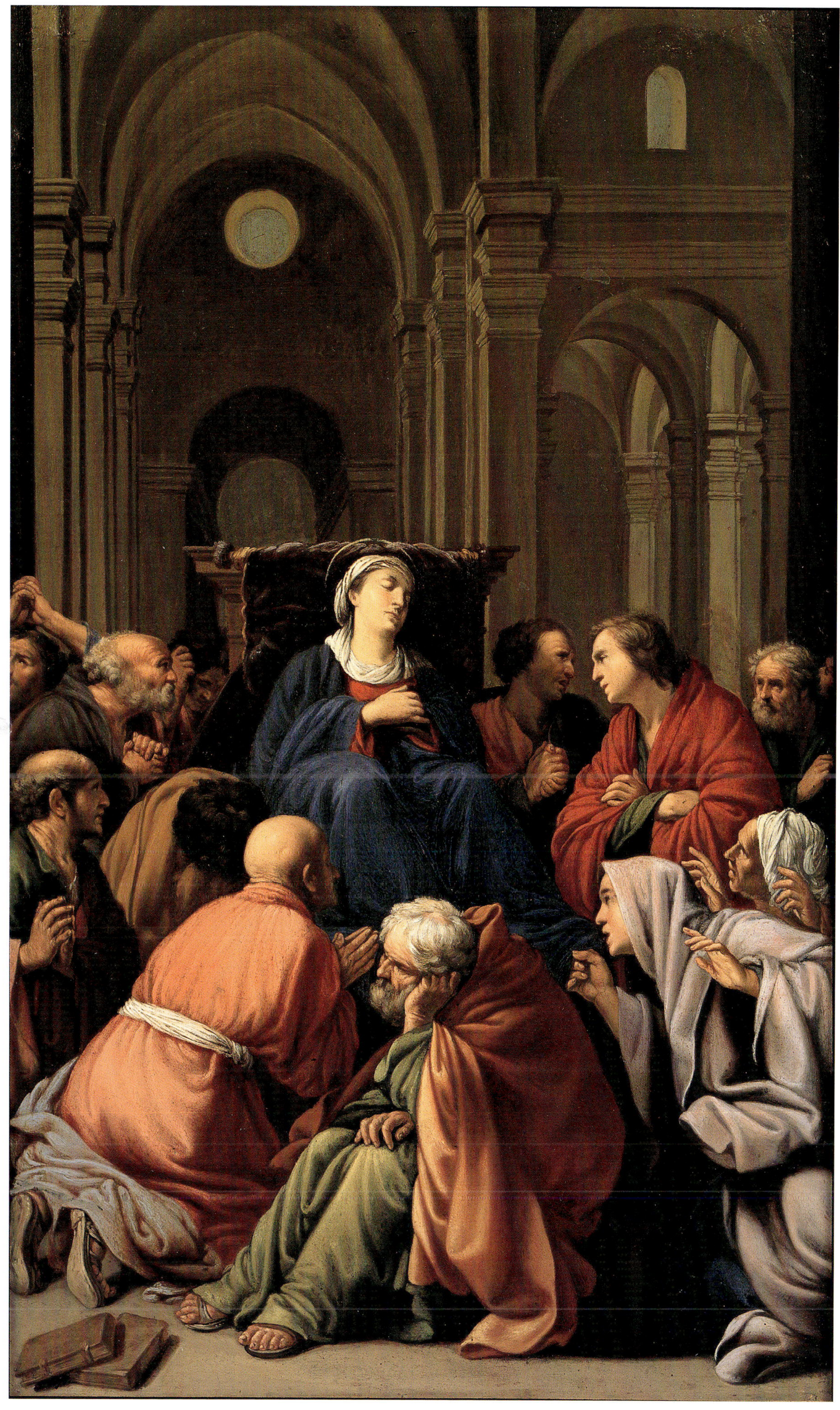

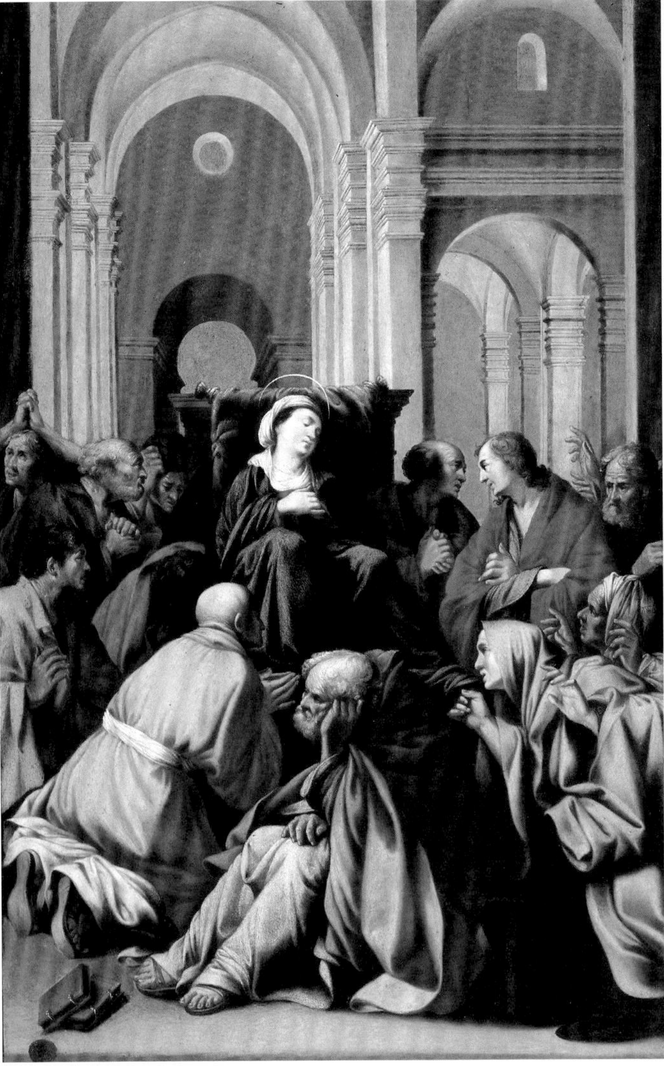

Fig. 3. Carlo Saraceni, *The Dormition of the Virgin*, ca. 1612. Oil on copper, 45.6 x 28 cm (18 x 11 in.). Alte Pinakothek, Bayerische Staatsgemäldesammlungen, Munich

decade in Rome consisted of small-scale cabinet paintings, and the *Dormition of the Virgin* may have been his first Roman commission for an altarpiece on this scale, although his *Rest on the Flight into Egypt* in the monastery of San Romualdo in Frascati is signed and dated 1606. It is not entirely clear when Saraceni received the commission, but at least a few years seem to have passed between the rejection and sale of Caravaggio's painting and the hiring of Saraceni; he delivered the altarpiece in 1612.[6]

Saraceni's altarpiece—the painting now in the Feigen collection (no. 43)—was also rejected by the Carmelites. If the accounts of Mancini, Baglione, and Bellori are to be trusted, Caravaggio's painting had failed mainly for reasons of decorum: the model for the Virgin was recognizable, and the depiction of the Virgin did not preserve sufficient dignity. Saraceni's first painting for Santa Maria della Scala, however, seems to have been rejected on the basis of more subtle theological points. Although he depicted the Virgin in a seated position and not as a prone corpse, her eyes were closed and her head was slumped; she would have seemed to be sleep-

ing, as if Saraceni was determined to depict not the Death but the Dormition of the Virgin. The traces of this original version are clearly evident on the surface of the painting even today, but Saraceni then changed the painting to show the Virgin with her eyes open and her head upright. This, too, failed to please the Carmelites. He eventually painted a completely new canvas, which remains in the church today (fig. 2). This final version replaced the architectural background of the original composition with a glory of angels. Showing neither the Death nor the Dormition of the Virgin, the final painting instead depicts the transit of the Virgin into Heaven.

Despite what is often written about the first two paintings by Caravaggio and Saraceni, there was a long tradition of showing the Virgin as a dead body. Examples range from the triptych that Petrus Christus sent to Sicily in the late fifteenth century (Timken Museum of Art, San Diego) to Federico Zuccaro's fresco in the Trinità dei Monti in Rome, painted in 1589, not long before Caravaggio's altarpiece. Moreover, the stipulation in the contract that Caravaggio could paint either the death or transit (*mortem sive transitem*) indicates that either could be acceptable, and in his great contemporary history of the early church, the *Annales ecclesiastici* (published between 1589 and 1607), Cardinal Baronius specifically explained that Mary had been human and so had died a mortal death. Too little is known about the Carmelites of Santa Maria della Scala to understand why they were so particular about the iconography of their painting; nor is there any explanation of why they were not more specific earlier in the process, if the precise iconographic details were so vitally important.

The rejection of the first two paintings (the second of which was revised before it was rejected) nonetheless fits into a broader pattern of conflicts between church officials and painters in early seicento Rome. Caravaggio's difficulties are the best known. In addition to the *Dormition of the Virgin*, the first version of his Contarelli chapel *Saint Matthew Writing the Gospel* and his *Virgin and Child with Saint Anne* for the Vatican had also been removed from the chapels for which they were made. Another, less well-known example is that of Scipione Pulzone's altarpiece for the Chapel of the Angels in the Gesù, which was originally accepted and installed in the church, but which nine years later was deemed indecorous and removed. Much of the problem was naturalism. Pulzone's altarpieces depicted the archangels, but to judge from his contemporary works and from written sources, the angels were so naturalistic that they seemed like portraits, in which case their nudity was shocking.[7] Similarly, Caravaggio's tendency to adopt aspects of the less-than-pristine life of contemporary Rome in his biblical narratives may have made the paintings more immediate to some viewers, but they seemed instead to others, especially clerics, to belittle the sacred events being shown. Yet, while Saraceni's first altarpiece was much influenced by the naturalism of Caravaggio's work, that naturalism was tempered—as it often is in Saraceni's art— by the bright colors, high finish, and greater tendency to use rhetorical gestures that came from the study also of his Venetian forebears, of Adam Elsheimer, and of the Carracci. These may not have adequately diffused for the Carmelites the inherently naturalistic conceit of Saraceni's first *Dormition*: the event is depicted as if happening more or less in contemporary Rome and in a setting not unlike the church of Santa Maria della Scala, and the apostles and Mary Magdalen are shown as rather ordinary people. The addition of the Glory of Angels in the final painting may have been a solution to mitigate the immediacy of the first two versions. It should be noted though, as Eve Borsook first argued in 1954, that the simple fact of the painting's Caravaggesque style was not inherently an issue, for the church was filled with works by artists working in one or another variety of *caravaggismo*.[8]

Fioravante Martinelli records that Saraceni's original painting was greatly praised during the "poco tempo" that it was placed on the altar, but that following the complaints of the Carmelite fathers, Saraceni sent his first painting home to Venice, painted the second version "in a few days," and received a payment of 300 *scudi*.[9] In any case, the painting was next definitively recorded in Germany in 1679 in the Palatine collections at Heidelberg; from there, the chain of provenance is complete down to the present day. It is possible that the original, rejected altarpiece might have been the *Death of the Virgin* recorded in the posthumous inventory of Saraceni's studio, a painting that was to be sent to Sebastian Füll in Munich, although Anna Ottani Cavina argues instead that this was more likely to be the small version on copper now in the Alte Pinakothek, Munich (fig. 3).[10]

Numerous additional versions of the subject by Saraceni are known, including the version on copper also in the Feigen collection (no. 44), the aforementioned version in Munich, and one in the Gallerie dell'Accademia, Venice. These small-scale replicas are figments of an increasingly common phenomenon in seicento Rome. One imagines that some of them were made for patrons who commissioned altarpieces: the large altarpiece would go to the church, and the smaller replica would be taken home by the patron. Saraceni may also have been inspired to paint the delicate, jewel-like coppers in emulation of the work of his sometime-associate Adam Elsheimer. In the case of Saraceni's *Dormition of the Virgin*, moreover, the existence of several autograph replicas suggests that they served another function, something akin to reproductive engravings, although they were far more precious objects than any print would have been. Given that Saraceni first repainted the original altarpiece and then sent it to Venice, it seems that one of the copper versions was, in turn, the model for the reproductive engraving made by Jean Le Clerc in 1619. Finally, in addition to the coppers in Venice, Munich, and the Feigen collection, there are additional versions—on copper, canvas, and panel—that seem not to be by Saraceni himself, but by his workshop or followers, further testament to the appreciation for, and fame of, his altarpiece, despite its rejection by the priests of Santa Maria della Scala.[11]   JJM

1. There is much discussion of Caravaggio's altarpiece and its rejection by the Carmelites. The longest treatment is Pamela Askew, *Caravaggio's "Death of the Virgin"* (Princeton, N.J., 1990). For recent summaries, with references to earlier literature, see Catherine Puglisi, *Caravaggio* (London, 1988), pp. 185–88; and Helen Langdon, *Caravaggio: A Life* (London, 1998), pp. 226–29, 246–51.

2. The discovery of the 1601 contract has not mitigated the general tendency of scholars to place the work in 1605–6, just prior to its known sale in 1606. In recent years, however, a date of ca. 1601–3 has been proposed, which also seems to the present author better to fit the style of the painting. If this date is accepted, the painting would have remained on the altar for three years before its removal. See also Langdon, *Caravaggio*, p. 410n.44.

3. Giulio Mancini, *Considerazioni sulla pittura*, ed. Adriana Marucchi (Rome, 1956), 1: p. 224.

4. Giovanni Baglione, *Le vite de' pittori, scultori, et architetti . . .* (Rome, 1642), p. 138; and Giovan Pietro Bellori, *Le vite de' pittori, scultori, et architetti moderni* (Rome, 1672), p. 213.

5. Cherubini did not die until 1626, and Fioravante Martinelli, in his *Roma ornata dall'architettura, pittura, e scoltura*, undated manuscript published in *Roma nel seicento*, ed. Cesare D'Onofrio (Rome, 1969), p. 134, suggests that Cherubini commissioned Saraceni.

6. A date of ca. 1610–12 is most often assigned to the painting.

7. Baglione, in *Vite de' pittori* (p. 54), for example, writes that the angels were "beautifully painted, but because they were taken from life, representing various people known to all, the picture was removed to avoid scandal."

8. Eve Borsook, "Documents Concerning the Artistic Associates of Santa Maria della Scala in Rome," *Burlington Magazine* 96 (1954): pp. 270–75.

9. Martinelli, *Roma ornata*, p. 134. The 300 *scudi* sum compares to the 280 *scudi* paid to Caravaggio and seems to have been a standard figure for the church; Cristoforo Roncalli was also paid 300 *scudi* for his altarpiece in the first chapel on the left, as noted in Borsook, "Documents Concerning the Artistic Associates," pp. 270–71.

10. Anna Ottani Cavina, *Carlo Saraceni* (Milan, 1968), no. 37.

11. Ibid. See nos. 9, 37, and 82, as well as a list of nonautograph replicas under no. 69.

Domenico Zampieri, called Domenichino

Bologna, 1581–1641

45. *Landscape with a Hermit*, ca. 1615–20

Oil on canvas, 40.5 x 53 cm (16 x 20⅞ in.)

PROVENANCE: Everard Jabach, Paris, no. 582 (inventory 1696; see de Grouchy, "Everhard Jabach," in bibliography); acquired in Stowe-on-the-Wold, Gloucestershire, England, March 1973

BIBLIOGRAPHY: Vicomte de Grouchy, "Everhard Jabach, collectionneur parisien (1695)," *Mémoires de la Société de l'Histoire de Paris et de l'Île de France* 21 (1894): p. 278, no. 582; George Gent, "Lost Domenichino Is Found and Bought for $392," *New York Times* (June 19, 1973): p. 32; Mead Art Museum, *Major Themes in Roman Baroque Art from Regional Collections*, exh. cat. (Amherst, Mass., 1974), no. 83; Luigi Salerno, *Pittori di paesaggio del seicento a Roma/Landscape Painters of the Seventeenth Century in Rome*, trans. Clovis Whitfield and Catherine Enggass, vol. 1 (Rome, 1976), 1: pp. 81, 102, no. 19.3; Richard E. Spear, *Domenichino* (New Haven, Conn., 1982), 1: p. 317 (as "misattributed to Domenichino"); Luigi Salerno, review of *Domenichino*, by Richard E. Spear, *Storia dell'arte* 50 (1984): p. 88; Arnauld Brejon de Lavergnée, *L'inventaire Le Brun de 1683: La collection des tableaux de Louis XIV* (Paris, 1987), p. 297 (as "copy after Domenichino"); Clovis Whitfield, "Les paysages du Dominiquin et de Viola," *Monuments et mémoires* 69 (1988): p. 106n.92 (as "Grimaldi?"); Richard E. Spear,

"Domenichino addenda," *Burlington Magazine* 131 (1989): p. 11n.44 (as "copy after Domenichino"); Stéphane Loire, *École italienne, XVIIe siècle: 1. Bologne*, Musée du Louvre, Département des Peintures (Paris, 1996), pp. 214, 216 (as "copy after Domenichino")

CONDITION: When acquired in 1973, the canvas was paste lined and the paint layer had cupping, cracking, and scattered cleavage. The canvas was wax resin lined to new linen, and discolored varnish and retouchings were removed and replaced. It was cleaned again in 1986 to remove varnish bloom.

The austere, classically structured *Landscape with a Hermit* is among the most powerful of Domenichino's landscape compositions. Always more a painter of frescoes and altarpieces, Domenichino was nonetheless one of the great landscape painters of his time and worked in the genre throughout his career, although most of his landscapes are undocumented and their dating—as indeed, their attribution—remains problematic. His earliest essays in the genre, including the *Landscape with a Ford* (Galleria Doria-Pamphilj, Rome), are obviously inspired by Annibale Carracci and must have been

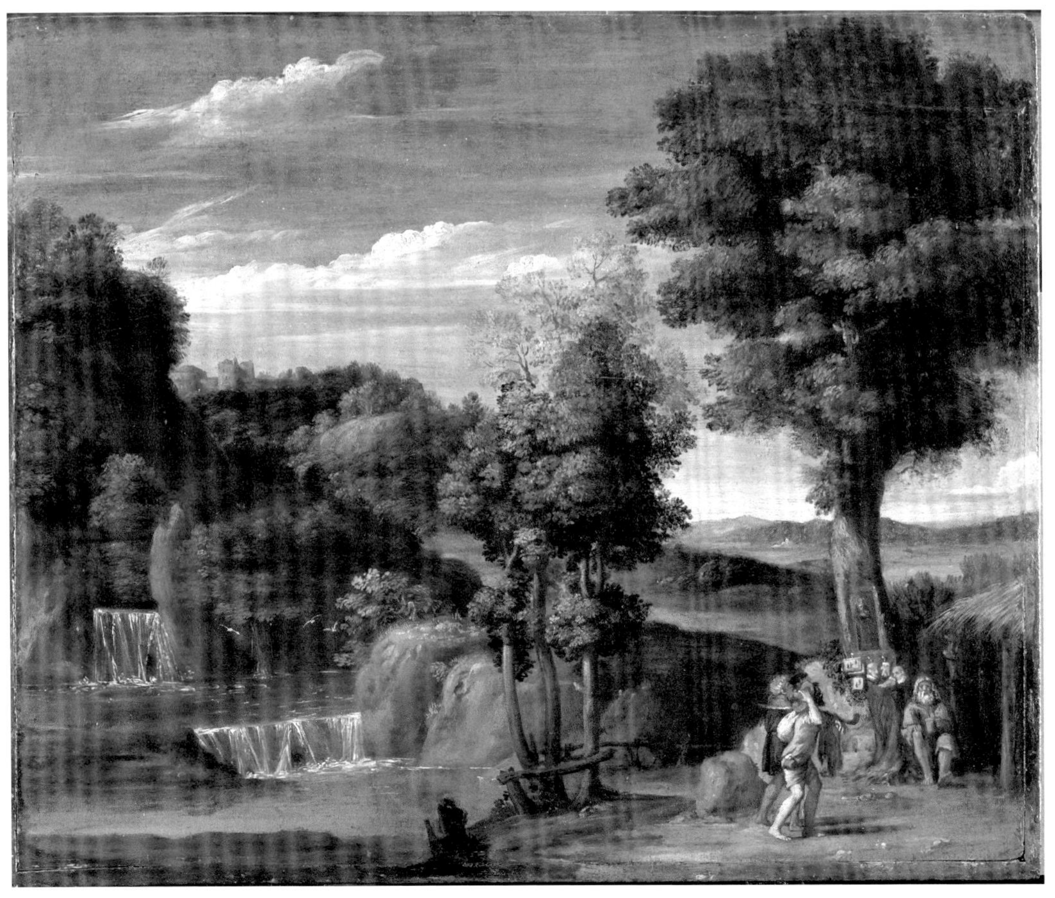

Fig. 1. After(?) Domenico Zampieri, called Domenichino, *Landscape with a Hermit*. Oil on panel, 30 x 37 cm (11⅞ x 14⅝ in.). Musée du Louvre, Paris, Louis XIV Collections, inv. no. 211

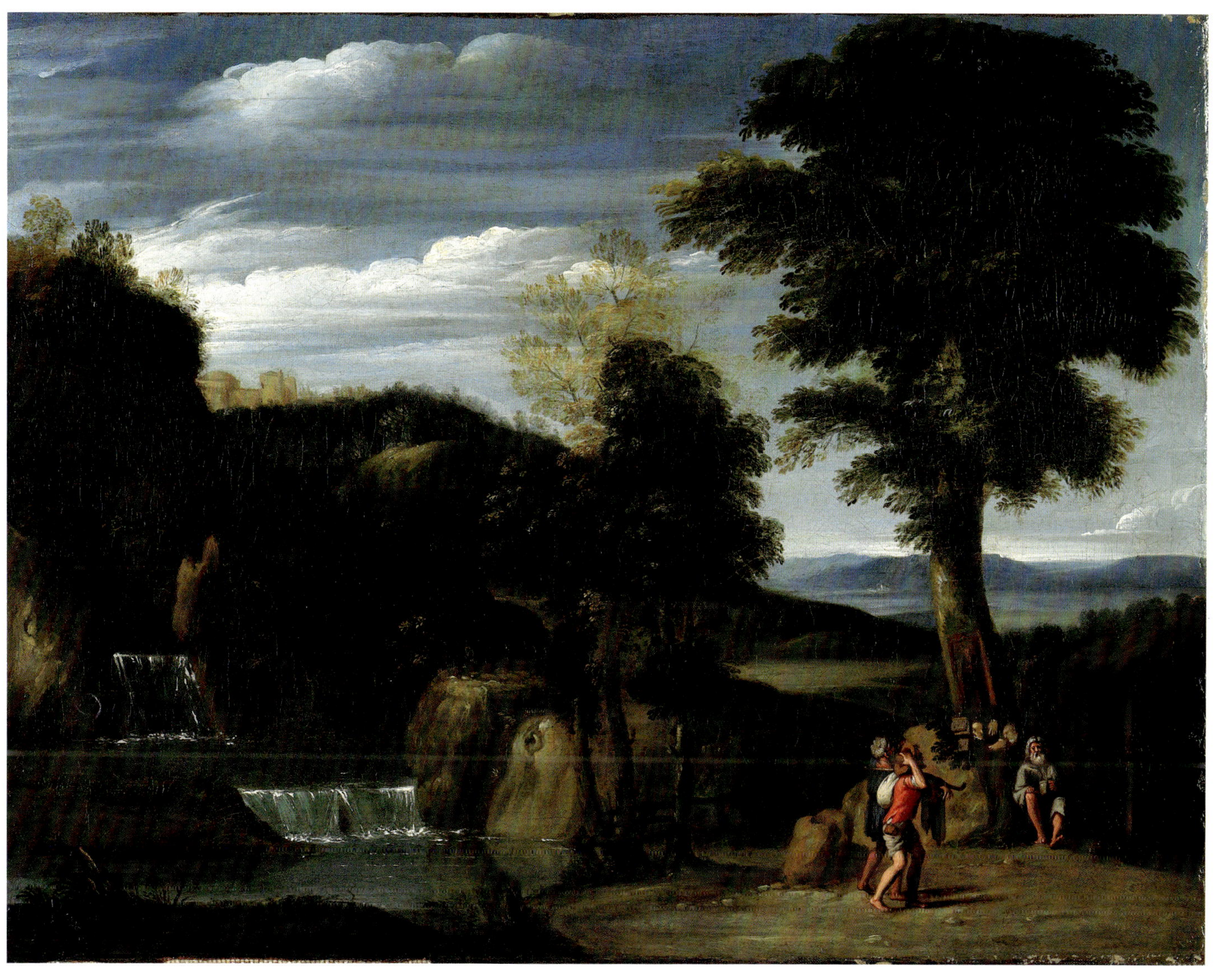

made soon after Domenichino joined Annibale in Rome in 1602. A handful of these early landscapes are anecdotal celebrations of nature—river and hunting scenes that recall works like Annibale's *River Landscape* (National Gallery of Art, Washington, D.C.)—but Domenichino was generally interested in a grander, more heroic view of landscape. He quickly moved from the virtually subjectless landscape to those with biblical and mythological subject matter and, especially in the following decades, stripped away much of the naturalistic detail seen in the early works in favor of clearer, architectonic spatial structures. Where figures serve mainly to enliven the early natural views, the later landscapes seem inextricably linked to their figural subjects. In the present example, for instance, the landscape is a fundamental element of the quasi-

narrative subject; rather than merely a setting, the landscape is an essential element of the story. No literary source for the scene has been identified, but the man seated beside the rustic hut at right must be a hermit, having removed himself from the distant town at upper left; he has become a natural monument of a sort, like the tree under which he sits and like Saint Anthony Abbot, who is depicted on the rustic tabernacle. (Adam Elsheimer's *Saint Christopher* in the Hermitage, which has a tabernacle similarly attached to a tree in the background, might have served as inspiration.[1]) The two men arriving at the scene seem awed, and one reaches to remove his hat, as if in reverence to the sacred ground he has entered. The fence and stream, as much as the votive offerings on the tree, emphasize the sense that the hermit occupies some

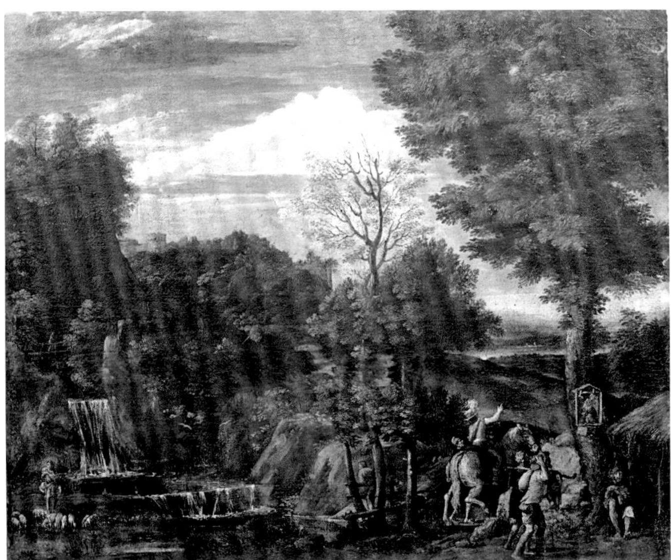

Fig. 2. Pietro Paolo Bonzi, *Landscape with a Hermit*, ca. 1620–25. Oil on canvas, 47 x 59 cm (18½ x 23¼ in.). Galleria Doria-Pamphilj, Rome

reserved precinct. The structured space and high tone compare to those in Domenichino's landscapes of the later 1610s and early 1620s, including the large Hercules landscapes in the Musée du Louvre, Paris, and a date of ca. 1615–20 seems most probable for the present work. Whatever their date, landscapes such as this, in which the landscape and figures together create tone and subject, must be considered important models for Claude Lorrain and Nicolas Poussin later in the century and bear witness to John Pope-Hennessy's claim that "Domenichino was probably the most important landscape painter of his time."[2]

This composition exists in three versions: the present work, a reduced (30 x 37 cm) example in the Louvre (fig. 1), and an enlarged (47 x 59 cm) version in the Galleria Doria-Pamphilj, Rome (fig. 2). Formerly attributed to Domenichino and to Agostino Tassi, the Doria-Pamphilj version is now generally considered the work of Pietro Paolo Bonzi, also known as the Gobbo dei Carracci, although it has also been called the work of Giovanni Battista Viola, Bonzi's master and another follower of Domenichino.[3] The addition to the scene of an elegantly dressed horsewoman at right, a man leaning on the fence, and a shepherd and flocks at left are discordant notes, not only because of their problematic scale, but more importantly, because they clearly misinterpret the tone of the hermit landscape, the very meaning of the picture. Such misunderstandings are typical of Viola and Bonzi, who often constructed pastiches of this type, drawing landscapes and/or figures from the paintings of Annibale and Domenichino with little regard to the original intent or combined reading of those elements. According to Richard Spear, both the Feigen and Louvre pictures are simplified versions of the Doria-Pamphilj painting, a view to which no subsequent author has subscribed.[4] Indeed, any argument that the Feigen and Louvre paintings are a simplified version of the Rome painting is

untenable, as is any discussion about the attribution of the former paintings that is based on that argument. Clovis Whitfield's suggestion that the composition is based on a print by Antonio Tempesta is, likewise, not to be sustained.[5]

Where the Doria-Pamphilj painting is surely a later painting based on the present composition, the attributions of the Louvre and Feigen versions, which are virtually identical although of different sizes, are a much more contentious matter. The Feigen version has been accepted as Domenichino's original by Luigi Salerno and others, but Arnauld Brejon de Lavergnée catalogued the Louvre version as "Domenichino(?)," citing the Doria-Pamphilj variant but not the Feigen version.[6] More recently, Stéphane Loire has argued that the Louvre version is original, a view now accepted by Denis Mahon, who formerly accepted the Feigen painting as Domenichino's own.[7]

When the Feigen painting was acquired it had been relined, but during conservation the inscription "jabach no. 582" was discovered on the back of the original canvas. The number corresponds to the entry in the 1696 posthumous inventory of Everard Jabach's collection, "un aveugle assis au pied d'un arbre où il y a une chapelle avec des signes de miracles et deux paisans passans devant" (a blind man seated at the foot of a tree, where there is a chapel with votives, and two peasants passing nearby). Much of Jabach's collection was sold to Louis XIV, and Loire and others imply that the Feigen painting is a copy that Jabach had made when he sold the original to the king in 1671. Spear argues, similarly, that the work is inventoried in the Jabach collection "among a long list of pictures that basically were copies."[8] Yet, Jabach seems sometimes to have sold a copy and to have reserved the original for himself, and one wonders whether that might not have been the case here.[9] While many of the pictures in the Jabach inventory are specifically described as copies (e.g., nos. 578–79, which are described as "de Francisque [Millet] après Carache"), that is not the case for this work, which is not even attributed in the inventory (it should be noted that the work at the Louvre was long attributed to Annibale). Likewise, the low appraisal of its value cannot rule out the possibility of its being the original, for if Jabach had retained the original for himself, that fact would not necessarily have been known by his son, who had to travel from Cologne to Paris in order to draw up the posthumous inventory of the collection in 1696. As a parallel case, a number of drawings in the Louvre that were also sold by Jabach to Louis XIV are clearly copies but were not described as such when sold; the originals that have been traced are in various collections, which suggests that they remained in Jabach's possession until his third collection was dispersed after his death.[10] In sum, even at the risk of accepting what are admittedly slim possibilities, there are enough questions about the inscription, and about Jabach's dealings, to prohibit any identification of the Feigen or Louvre version as the original on the basis of documentary evidence alone.

The Louvre version is painted on panel, an extremely unusual support for Domenichino, all of whose unreservedly accepted landscapes are on canvas or copper. Panel is the support, however, of the *Saint Jerome* landscape in Glasgow, a picture accepted as Domenichino's own by all save Pope-Hennessy.[11] In support of the Louvre version, it might be argued that the delineation of waves and reflections in the water at left and the foliage on the hills of the middle distance are perhaps more sharply rendered. Moreover, a number of details in the Louvre version—the birds over the pool, and the gray-lined clouds high in the sky at left—are in the Doria-Pamphilj picture (which would have been produced in Rome from the original) but not in the Feigen version. Yet, the issue here is one of conservation: the Louvre painting's surface is frankly in better condition than that of the Feigen painting, and it is entirely plausible that some of these details have been lost from the latter.

The support, moreover, demands fuller consideration than it has hitherto been given. Not only is the Louvre version on panel, but also the panel consists of a central plank with enlargements added around the edge. These additions are in oak, which would be highly unusual for an Italian painting. What is more, the central part of the panel is of a different wood, as yet unidentified, but seemingly not poplar.[12] The very materials used would argue for this being the copy produced in France in the later seventeenth century. In contrast, the Feigen painting is on a twill canvas that seems to be of Italian manufacture; this would not absolutely prohibit it from being a copy made in France, but it does support the case for its being the original.[13] In sum, the evidence of documents, style, and materials does not all point to a single conclusion. While it seems probable that the Feigen canvas is the original version, the matter might be settled only after both are carefully studied side by side.   JJM

1. For the Hermitage work, see Rüdiger Klessmann et al., *Adam Elsheimer, 1578–1610*, exh. cat. (London, 2006), no. 13.
2. John Pope-Hennessy, "The Sensuous and the Cerebral," *Times Literary Supplement* (March 25, 1983): p. 305.
3. For the Pietro Paolo Bonzi attribution, see Teresa Pugliatti, "Pietro Paolo Bonzi Paesista," *Quaderni dell'Istituto di Storia dell'Arte Medievale e Moderna . . . Università di Messina* 1 (1975): pp. 18–19; and Luigi Salerno, *Pittori di paesaggio del seicento a Roma/Landscape Painters of the Seventeenth Century in Rome*, trans. Clovis Whitfield and Catherine Enggass (Rome, 1976), 1: pp. 102, 111, no. 23.11. For the Giovanni Battista Viola attribution, see Clovis Whitfield, "Les paysages du Dominiquin et de Viola," *Monuments et mémoires* 69 (1988): p. 106; and Beverly Louise Brown, ed., *The Genius of Rome, 1592–1623*, exh. cat. (London, 2001), p. 197.
4. Richard E. Spear, *Domenichino* (New Haven, Conn., 1982), 1: pp. 317–18.
5. The print by Tempesta is Bartsch 1176.
6. Arnauld Brejon de Lavergnée, *L'inventaire Le Brun de 1683: La collection des tableaux de Louis XIV* (Paris, 1987), p. 296, no. 260.
7. Stéphane Loire, *École italienne, XVIIe siècle: 1. Bologne*, Musée du Louvre, Département des Peintures (Paris, 1996), pp. 214–16; and Loire, review of *Domenichino 1581–1641*, by Richard E. Spear et al., *Burlington Magazine* 139 (1997): p. 222.
8. Spear, *Domenichino*, 1: p. 317.
9. Brejon de Lavergnée, *Inventaire Le Brun*, pp. 54–61; and Catherine Monbeig Goguel, "Taste and Trade: The Retouched Drawings in the Everard Jabach Collection," *Burlington Magazine* 130 (1988): pp. 829–30.
10. Roseline Bacou, "Everard Jabach: Dessins de la seconde collection," *Revue de l'art* 40–41 (1978): pp. 141–50.
11. Richard E. Spear et al., *Domenichino, 1581–1641*, exh. cat. (Milan, 1996), no. 18. See also Pope-Hennessy, "The Sensuous and the Cerebral," p. 305; and Richard E. Spear, "Domenichino Addenda," *Burlington Magazine* 131 (1989): p. 15, under no. 44.
12. I am grateful to Stéphane Loire, Chief Conservator, Department of Paintings, Musée du Louvre, Paris, for supplying this information (e-mail to the author), which was omitted in his 1997 catalogue.
13. An examination of the canvas undertaken by the Institut Textile de France in November 1996 identified hemp fibers that likewise suggest an Italian rather than French origin for the canvas.

Giovanni Francesco Barbieri, called Guercino

Cento and Bologna, 1591–1666

46. *Vanitas Still Life*, ca. 1620

Oil on canvas, 30.5 x 39 cm (12 x 15⅜ in.)

PROVENANCE: Church of the Santissima Trinità dei Cappuccini, Cento, Italy; Bolognini-Amorini collection, Bologna, 19th century(?); private collection, Zurich

BIBLIOGRAPHY: Francesco Algarotti, *Opere del conte Algarotti*, vol. 8 (Livorno, 1764–65), p. 132; Orazio Carlo Righetti, manuscript continuation of his *Pitture di Cento e le vite in compendio di vari incisori e pittori della stessa città* (Ferrara, Italy, 1768), Archivio Comunale, Cento, MS 164, fol. 148; Adamo Chiusole, *Itinerario delle pitture, sculture, ed architetture più rare di molte città d'Italia* (Vicenza, Italy, 1782), pp. 146–47; Carlo Cesare Malvasia, *Felsina pittrice: Vite de' pittori Bolognesi*, ed. Giampietro Zanotti et al. (Bologna, 1841), p. 279; Gaetano Atti, *Intorno alla vita e alle opere di Gianfrancesco Barbieri* (Rome, 1861), p. 142; Luigi Salerno, *I dipinti del Guercino* (Rome, 1988), p. 127, no. 49; Stéphane Loire, "Études récentes sur le Guerchin," *Storia dell'arte* 67 (1989): p. 269; Luigi Salerno, *Nuovi studi su la natura morta italiana/New Studies on Italian Still Life Painting* (Rome, 1989), p. 138; David M. Stone, *Guercino: Catalogo completo* (Florence, 1991), p. 80, no. 58

CONDITION: The canvas was relined in the eighteenth or nineteenth century. The paint surface is well preserved beneath a discolored varnish, with a small retouched loss at the left edge above the vase of roses and some abrasion and retouchings in the bottom left and right corners.

A long inscription in a nineteenth-century hand is attached to the back of this painting and tells much of its known history:

> As one reads in a note in the new edition of the Felsina pittrice on page 279, we must not omit mention of a small painting in the sacristy of the Capuchin church (at Cento) representing a skull with an hourglass, much praised by Algarotti (Opere, ed. Palese, T. VIII, p. 132) but in the time of the French invasion lost without anyone having known who took it—thus being remarked that in the present little painting there is the particular practical imprimature of Guercino's early works, and that the roses are very much the same as those scattered beside the sepulcher of the Blessed Virgin Assumed into Heaven, a famous work of Guercino in the Casa Tanara. It is thus judged by the most intelligent critics that this little picture is that of which the note in Malvasia speaks, as does Algarotti in his letter of 27 September 1760 to Giampietro Zanotti, in addition to the remark under other circumstances and judgment already pronounced by Giuseppe Sedazzi.

The new edition of Carlo Cesare Malvasia's *Felsina pittrice* mentioned in the inscription is that published in 1841, and, in fact, much of the inscription paraphrases a footnote from that edition. As noted there, the painting is described by a number of eighteenth-century sources. Lost from view around 1796, the canvas went untraced until published by Luigi Salerno in 1988, and it has since been universally accepted as the painting from the Capuchin church in Cento. As recognized by the author of the inscription, the work bears comparison with the paintings of Guercino's early career. The roses of the Casa Tanari *Assunta* of 1623 (now State Hermitage Museum, St. Petersburg) are indeed similar, as the inscription notes, and further connections may be made to a number of paintings done around 1620. The skull recalls that in the foreground of Guercino's *Et in Arcadia Ego* of ca. 1618 (fig. 1) and that in the *Magdalen* of ca. 1624 (Blanton Museum of Art, Austin, Texas, from the Suida-Manning collection), and the juxtaposition of the skull and book is found in a number of paintings including the *Vision of Saint Jerome* in the versions of ca. 1619–20 (Musée du Louvre, Paris) and ca. 1621 (Pushkin Museum of Fine Arts, Moscow).

Although highly naturalistic still-life elements are continually found in the foregrounds of Guercino's paintings, especially early in his career, the *Vanitas* is the only independent still life that is generally accepted as his work. It has been suggested that the canvas began as a study of the

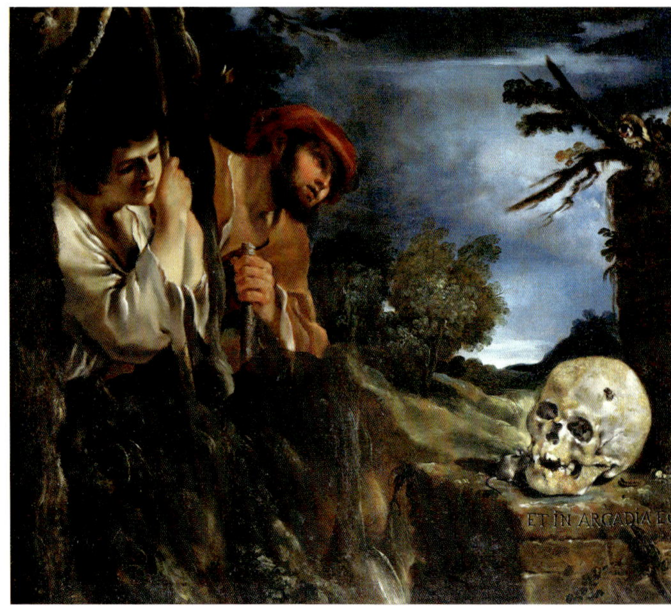

Fig. 1. Giovanni Francesco Barbieri, called Guercino, *Et in Arcadia Ego*, ca. 1618. Oil on canvas, 78 x 89.1 cm (30¾ x 35⅛ in.). Galleria Nazionale d'Arte Antica, Rome

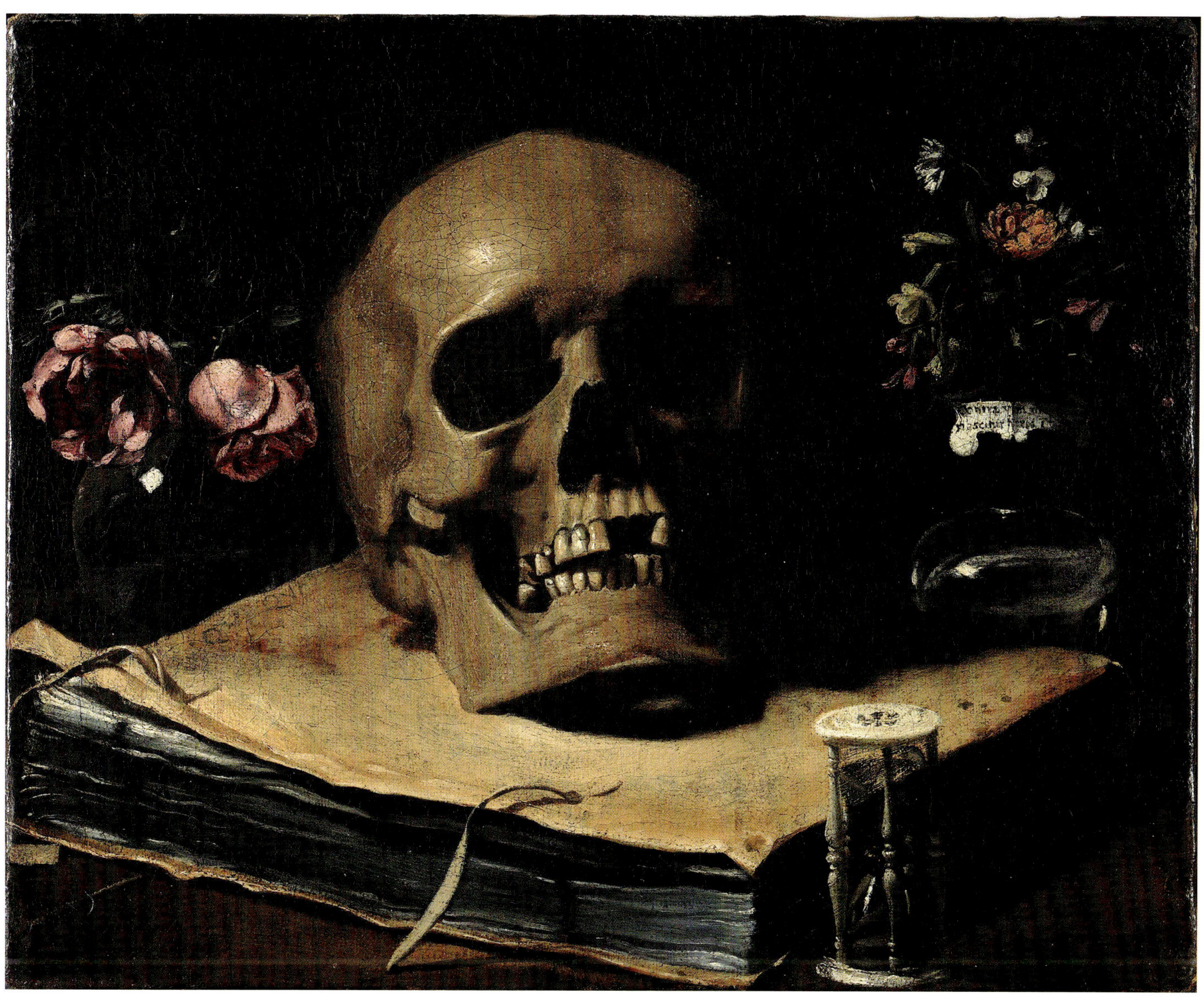

skull and books, and that the flowers were added later, but the flowers seem an integral part of the composition here (as also noted by Salerno), and there are no comparable oil studies by Guercino to support the hypothesis that this began as a kind of oil sketch.[1] Guercino not infrequently reused motifs from one painting to the next at this point in his career: the shepherds of the *Et in Arcadia Ego* come from his *Apollo Flaying Marsyas* (Palazzo Pitti, Florence) also of 1618, and the aforementioned *Magdalen* is derived from a figure in the *Resurrection of Lazarus* (Musée du Louvre, Paris) of 1619. Whatever its relationship to the other paintings, that is, the *Vanitas* should be considered a finished work in its own right, rather than a kind of preparatory study.

Guercino was probably aware of the developing genre of still life through the work of painters of the previous generation, including that of Vincenzo Campi, Bartolomeo Passarotti, and perhaps also Carlo Antonio Procaccini (the brother of Camillo and Giulio Cesare Procaccini), whom Malvasia identifies as a still-life specialist, although none of his works

has been identified; Caravaggio and his followers, especially Tommaso Salini and Pietro Paolo Bonzi (il Gobbo dei Carracci) also experimented with still-life painting in the decades after 1600.[2] It is difficult, though, to identify a direct source for the *Vanitas*. The skull, hourglass, book, and drooping flowers now seem standard motifs in paintings of the subject (the inscription on the vase at right, now illegible, was surely an epigraph on the theme), but independent *Vanitas* still lifes are far more common in Northern European than in Italian painting before and during Guercino's time. The constituent motifs appear in Italian depictions of Saint Jerome and Saint Francis, and also in portraits—and on portrait covers—given over to a *memento mori* theme.[3] Jacopo Ligozzi depicted a skull and book on the cover or verso of several of his portraits, but there are also a number of similar *Vanitas* images by him that are of a horizontal format, and on copper, and thus seem to have been made as independent paintings rather than as portrait covers.[4] These are probably the closest precedents to Guercino's canvas, but given the skull in Guercino's ca. 1618 *Et in Arcadia*

Ego, itself a meditation on death, it is perhaps unnecessary to seek any further visual source for a motif that was equally a common literary trope. Roberto Longhi long ago suggested that Caravaggio's still-life paintings had relatively little to do with precedents in Northern art or with *ekphrastic* passages from ancient literature, and that the paintings instead derived from the artist's experimental approach to image making.[5] Even if Guercino had seen some still-life paintings by the previous generation of Emilian artists, something similar might be argued for the *Vanitas*, which has little to do with the paintings by the Campi or Passarotti and is instead likely to have been devised by Guercino in relation to the *Et in Arcadia Ego* and similar compositions.

The canvas was first recorded in the sacristy of the Capuchin church at Cento, but that was already over a century after Guercino's death, and nothing is known of the circumstances under which Guercino painted it. It comes from the early part of his career, before the period covered by his surviving account book. The artist's earliest documented commission for the Capuchins at Cento, the *Virgin and Child* now in the

Cento Pinacoteca, dates to 1629, but this picture can have little to do with that commission.[6] Finally, it bears noting that Guercino's younger brother, Paolo Antonio Barbieri, was a still-life specialist, but he need not be considered in relation to the Feigen painting, for Paolo Antonio's paintings are in a broader, flatter style than that seen here.[7]   J J M

1. Luigi Salerno, *Nuovi studi su la natura morta italiana/New Studies on Italian Still Life Painting* (Rome, 1989), p. 138.
2. See John T. Spike, *Italian Still Life Paintings from Three Centuries,* exh. cat. (Florence, 1983).
3. Alberto Veca, *Vanitas: Il simbolismo del tempo,* exh. cat. (Bergamo, 1981).
4. See, for example, Pierluigi Carofano, ed., *Luca e Ombra: Caravaggismo e naturalismo nella pittura toscana del seicento,* exh. cat. (Pisa, 2005), p. 18, no. 6.
5. Roberto Longhi, "Un momento importante nella storia della 'natura morta,'" *Paragone* 1 (1950): pp. 34–39.
6. For the Cento *Virgin and Child,* see Luigi Salerno, *I dipinti del Guercino* (Rome, 1988), no. 126.
7. Emilio Negro, Massimo Pirondini, and Nicosetta Roio, *La scuola del Guercino* (Modena, 2004), pp. 83–99.

Orazio Gentileschi

Pisa, active in Rome, Genoa, Paris, and London, 1563–1639

47. *Danaë and the Shower of Gold*, 1621–22

Oil on canvas, 161.3 x 226.7 cm (63½ x 89¼ in.)

PROVENANCE: commissioned by Giovanni Antonio Sauli, Genoa; by descent, in Palazzo Sauli, Genoa, to at least 1818; by descent (see below) to Marchesa Carlotta Giustiniani Cattaneo-Adorno, the Villa di Arenzano, near Genoa, in whose possession the painting was noted in 1975; Thomas P. Grange, London, 1975–78

BIBLIOGRAPHY: Raffaello Soprani, *Vite de' pittori, scultori, ed architetti genovesi* (Genoa, 1674), p. 317; 2nd ed., rev. by Carlo Giuseppe Ratti (Genoa, 1768), 1: p. 452; Carlo Giuseppe Ratti, *Instruzione di quanto può vedersi di più bello in Genova . . .* (Genoa, 1780), p. 112; Alessandro da Morrona, *Pisa illustrata nelle arti del disegno* (Livorno, 1812), 2: p. 258; Wilhelm Suida, *Genua* (Leipzig, Germany, 1906), p. 156; Hermann Voss, *Die Malerei des Barock in Rom* (Berlin, 1925), p. 460; Alfred Moir, *The Italian Followers of Caravaggio* (Cambridge, Mass., 1967), 1: p. 197; 2: p. 78; R. Ward Bissell, "Orazio Gentileschi and the Theme of 'Lot and His Daughters,'" *Bulletin of the National Gallery of Canada* 14 (1969): pp. 20, 30–31; Ennio Poleggi and Fiorelli Caraceni Poleggi, eds., *Descrizione della città di Genova da un anonimo del 1818,* 2nd ed. (Genoa, 1974), p. 79; Benedict Nicolson, *The International Caravaggesque Movement* (Oxford, 1979), pp. 51–52; R. Ward Bissell, *Orazio Gentileschi and the Poetic Tradition in Caravaggesque Painting* (University Park, Pa., 1981), pp. 176–77; Cleveland Museum of Art, *Catalogue of Paintings,* pt. 3, *European Paintings of the 16th, 17th, and 18th Centuries* (Cleveland, 1982), pp. 46–47; Benedict Nicolson, "Orazio Gentileschi and Giovanni Antonio Sauli," *Artibus et historiae* 6, no. 12 (1985): pp. 9–25; Mary D. Garrard, *Artemisia Gentileschi: The Image of the Female Hero in Italian Baroque Art* (Princeton, N.J., 1989), p. 242; Benedict Nicolson, *Caravaggism in Europe,* 2nd ed., rev. and enlarged by Luisa Vertova (Turin, 1989), 1: p. 112; Judith W. Mann, "The Gentileschi 'Danaë' in the Saint Louis Art Museum: Orazio or Artemisia," *Apollo* 143, no. 412 (1996): p. 41; Susan J. Barnes et al., eds., *Van Dyck a Genova: Grande pittura e collezionismo,* exh. cat. (Milan, 1997), p. 160; R. Ward Bissell, *Artemisia Gentileschi and the Authority of Art* (University Park, Pa., 1999), pp. 6–7, 49–50, 302; Keith Christiansen and Judith W. Mann, *Orazio and Artemisia Gentileschi,* exh. cat. (New York, 2001), pp. 21–23, 30–33, 166, 172–73, 178–80, 193–94; Mark Leonard, Narayan Khandekar, and Dawson W. Carr, " 'Amber Varnish' and Orazio Gentileschi's 'Lot and His Daughters,'" *Burlington Magazine* 143 (2001): pp. 4–10;

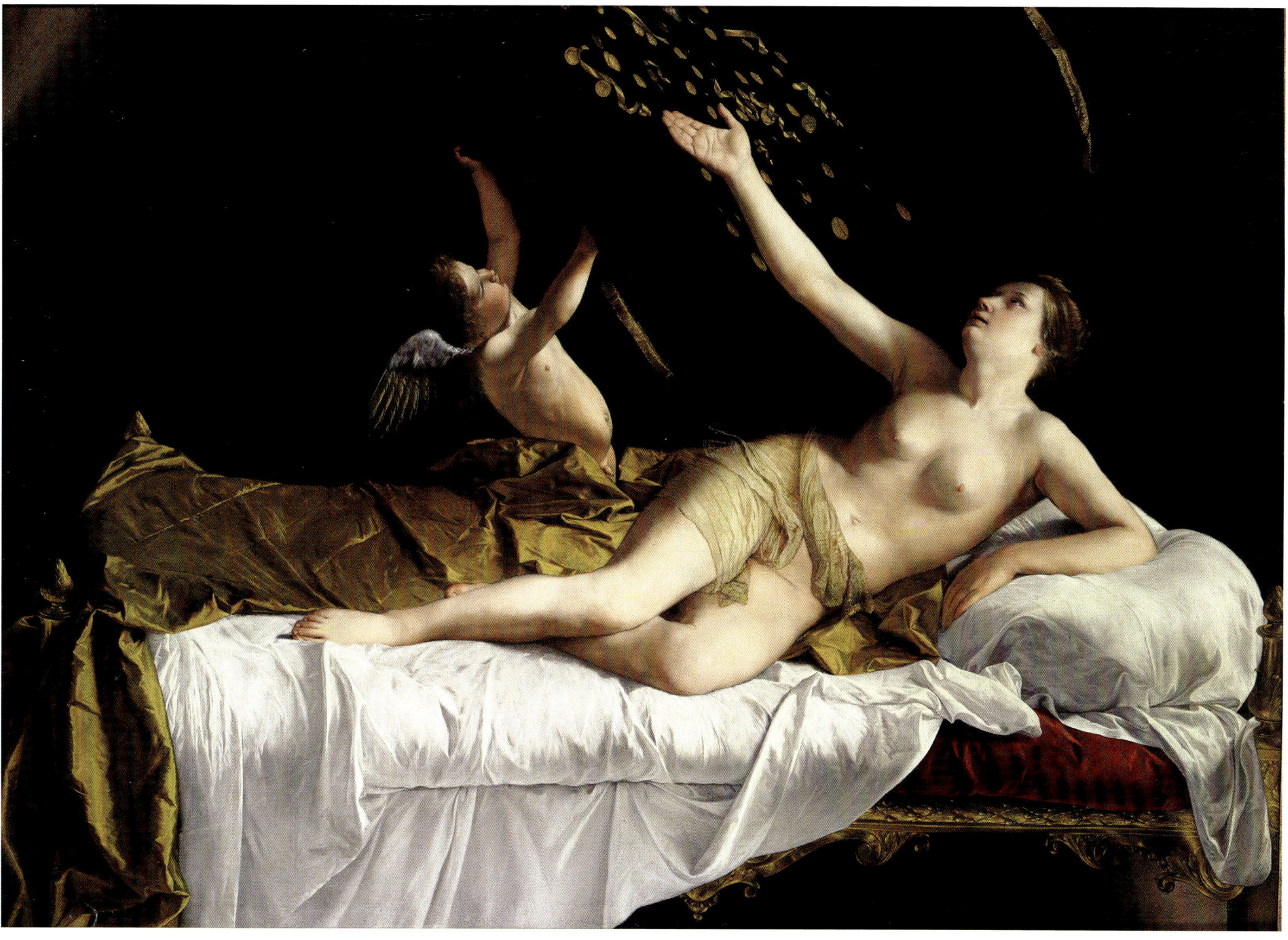

Patrick Matthiesen, letter to the editor, *Burlington Magazine* 143 (2001): p. 162; Marzia Cataldi Gallo, "The Sauli Collection: Two Unpublished Letters and a Portrait by Orazio Gentileschi," *Burlington Magazine* 145 (2003): pp. 349–51

CONDITION: The painting is relatively free of large, major areas of loss, although there are many minor areas of loss and abrasion that were repaired in 1999–2001, when a discolored layer of varnish was removed, revealing extensive discolored retouching.[1] The drapery of the background has oxidized to a dark brown color, but cross-section samples and pigment analysis reveal that it would originally have been a much brighter green. The canvas appears to retain its original dimensions, although it has been cut diagonally at all four corners; similar diagonal cuts are found in the lower corners of Gentileschi's ex-Sauli *Lot and His Daughters* (J. Paul Getty Museum, Los Angeles) and *Penitent Magdalen* (private collection, New York), which constituted a set with the Feigen *Danaë*.[2]

As has often been noted, X-radiographs of the painting reveal several changes, including the shifting of Danaë's left hand and forearm, as well as revisions to the figure of Cupid and to the white drapery.

Orazio Gentileschi's *Danaë* is in many senses the very epitome of secular painting in seventeenth-century Italy. Cupid draws back a curtain, allowing Jupiter, in the form of a shower of gold, to enter the room where Danaë has been confined by her father, King Acrisius (fearing a prophecy that he would be killed by Danaë's child, Acrisius attempted to shut his daughter away from the world). A study in the theatrical poetics of Baroque painting, Gentileschi's composition is at once both dramatic and serene. For all the evident animation of the scene, with the tumbling gold depicted just as it reaches Danaë, her reaction is less natural than rhetorical. As he so often does in his paintings, Gentileschi combines the seductive, naturalistic touches of Caravaggesque painting with a more high-minded approach to narrative. Regarding the former, the painting is a study in texture, as if to convey not only the different light-reflecting properties but also the very different feel of flesh, satin, linen, and metal. Even the gold appears in varied forms: the gilding of the furniture, the threads woven into the transparent veil across Danaë's waist, the falling coins, and—perhaps most exceptionally—the twirling ribbons and shavings that fall amid the coins, which seem to be an unprecedented motif

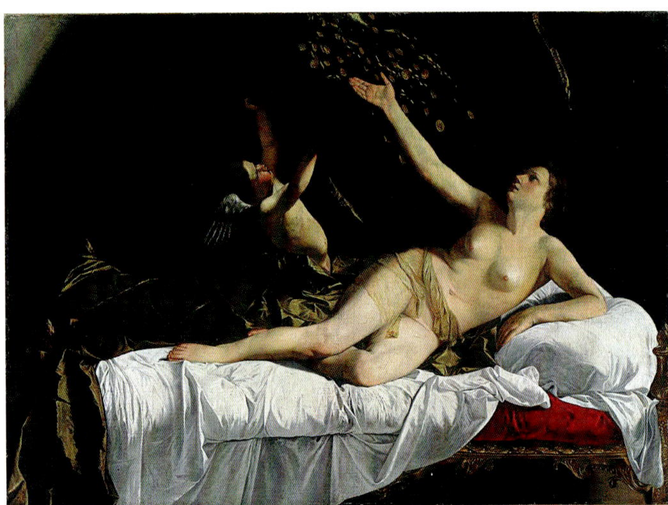

Fig. 1. Orazio Gentileschi, *Danaë*, ca. 1623. Oil on canvas, 162 x 228.5 cm (63¾ x 90 in.). Cleveland Museum of Art, inv. no. 1971.101

despite the popularity of the subject for at least a century prior to the creation of this painting.

Like so many cabinet paintings of the age, particularly those on this grand scale, Gentileschi's *Danaë* should be considered not as a work in isolation, but rather, as a work made in competition with similar works by contemporaries and rivals. Indeed, in this painting, probably the first that Gentileschi made in Genoa, he seems to have set out to rival the most sensational paintings made for Genoa in the years just prior to his arrival there in 1621. These included two massive altarpieces in the Church of the Gesù—Guido Reni's *Assumption of the Virgin*, installed in 1617–18, and Peter Paul Rubens's *Miracle of Saint Ignatius of Loyola*, which arrived in 1620—as well as the portraits that Rubens had painted during his earlier trips to Genoa, and probably also those that Anthony Van Dyck began in 1621.[3] All of the above are, like the *Danaë*, notable for their sublime studies in light, texture, and the bravura depiction of draperies. Gentileschi also clearly had in mind some major precedents for the subject that he had seen in Rome, including Titian's famous depiction, then in the Palazzo Farnese (now Museo di Capodimonte, Naples).[4] Titian's painting underscores the erotic potential for this subject, but Gentileschi offers instead a relatively chaste Danaë, with a restraint that presents a very different story than does the sensual abandon of Titian's woman. The point of reference for the "chaste Danaë" is, nonetheless, perfectly clear: a painting designed by Annibale Carracci, and perhaps executed jointly by Carracci and Francesco Albani, which was formerly in Bridgewater House, London.[5]

The *Danaë* was part of a series of paintings made in Genoa for Gio Antonio Sauli, and the "chaste interpretation" of the subject is particularly interesting when one considers it alongside the two other paintings by Gentileschi with which it hung in the Palazzo Sauli: the *Penitent Magdalen* (no. 48, fig. 1) and the *Lot and His Daughters* (J. Paul Getty Museum, Los Angeles). Although the paintings have been trimmed to

various degrees, it is unlikely that they were ever exactly the same size. Yet, they seem to have been conceived as a set. All three focus on women of ambiguous virtue, and, as has been noted before, one subject is from the Old Testament, one from the New Testament, and one from classical mythology; it has also been said that one subject is erotic (Danaë), one moral (Lot), and one devotional (Magdalen).[6] It is difficult to know how seriously the project was guided by iconographic, programmatic concerns, and the set might have been considered as much a variation on a visual theme as on subject matter. The *Magdalen*, for example, was clearly made from the same cartoon—albeit with minor adjustments—that Gentileschi used for the *Danaë*. Yet, the tone of the *Danaë* should probably be considered at least in part due to its planned juxtaposition, for it makes a notable contrast with another of Orazio's reclining nude women, the overtly erotic *Cleopatra* that Gentileschi may have brought to Genoa with him.[7]

Sauli had gone to Rome in 1621 as part of a delegation sent from Genoa to the newly elected Pope Gregory XV and, while there, had become a passionate admirer of Gentileschi's work. He took steps to bring the artist to Genoa, and Orazio arrived by the end of 1621.[8] As recently as 2001, Mary Newcome echoed Benedict Nicolson's summary of Sauli as a "shadowy personality," but recent investigations into the Sauli archive have helped shed some light on the patron and his relationship with the painter.[9] Marzia Cataldi Gallo has explained that "it seems likely that Gentileschi acted as advisor to Sauli while he was setting up his picture gallery, and that their relationship, based on a mixture of respect, friendship, and financial considerations, continued after Gentileschi's departure for London and almost until his death."[10]

As is well known, Gentileschi repeated the composition of the *Danaë* and the other Sauli paintings. This was hardly an uncommon practice in the seventeenth century. Apart from the different notions of originality then held, the movement of artists and paintings around Europe presented the artist with the opportunity to recycle successful compositions, for as a general rule, few patrons in London or Paris would have had the opportunity to see a painting in Genoa. Whether the various repetitions of Gentileschi's compositions are simple copies, second versions by the artist, or versions created under his supervision remains the subject of debate. Certainly, there are examples of all three categories, and Gentileschi's practice of reusing his cartoons, so well documented by Keith Christiansen, does not resolve the matter but merely shows that many of the versions must have been created in Gentileschi's studio.[11]

There is another version of the *Danaë* at the Cleveland Museum of Art (fig. 1), which, upon its rediscovery in 1971 (five years before the Feigen painting came to light), was generally thought to be the lost original.[12] Even before the Gentileschi exhibition of 2001, however, close examination of the paintings over the previous decades had made clear that the Feigen version was the original painting. Not only does the Cleveland painting lack some of the obvious pentimenti of the Feigen version, but also it is executed in a harder manner that appears to result from its having been made to follow an already-resolved composition. The 2001 exhibition, furthermore, provided a memorable opportunity to see the two paintings in the same room, and the difference between the good Cleveland replica and inspired Feigen original was all too clear. The Cleveland painting is nonetheless universally believed to be by Gentileschi himself.

Recent research into the Sauli family and its descendants would seem to present an unbroken chain of provenance for the Feigen picture, from Palazzo Sauli to the present, offering further, if unnecessary, proof of its status. Despite much discussion of the provenance of the painting as it came to be identified as the Sauli original, its location and ownership between 1818 and 1975, the year when it was recorded in the collection of Carlotta Giustiniani Cattaneo-Adorno, have not hitherto been entirely clarified. The painting was probably removed from the Palazzo Sauli in 1852, when the palace was sold by Costantino Sauli. Costantino's goods were divided among his three daughters: Maria, who was unmarried; Bianca, who married Domenico de Mari; and Luisa, who married Francesco Camillo Pallavicino. Luisa's daughter Maria Teresa married Lazzaro Negrotto Cambiaso; their son was Pierfrancesco (also known as Pierino) Negrotto Cambiaso (1867–1925), who was also ultimately named heir to his aunt Maria, thus reuniting many of the Sauli possessions. In 1924 Pierfrancesco Negrotto Cambiaso married Matilda Giustiniani Durazzo Pallavicini, who inherited his goods after his death;[13] she, however, died childless and bequeathed her possessions to her niece, Carlotta Giustiniani Cattaneo-Adorno, in whose villa at Arenzano the work was rediscovered.[14] While there is no specific documentary reference to the *Danaë* between 1818 and 1975, this trail of family and property would explain how the ex-Sauli painting came into the possession of Carlotta Giustiniani Cattaneo-Adorno. The *Magdalen*, moreover, was recorded in the palace of Pierfrancesco Negrotto Cambiaso by Wilhelm Suida in 1906, which would likewise support this reconstruction.[15] This would thus present a virtually unbroken chain of provenance for the painting from its commission by Sauli to the present.[16]

Questions nonetheless remain concerning the other paintings that Sauli commissioned from Gentileschi. The completed chain of provenance does not, for example, account for the substitution of the original Sauli *Lot and His Daughters* now at the Getty with the version that was discovered in Arenzano in 1975 (now Thyssen-Bornemisza Museum of Art, Madrid).[17] By the eighteenth century, however, the Sauli inventories already included references to "copies" of the Gentileschi histories.[18] At least some of these copies were part of a group of pictures that Francesco Maria Sauli (the son of Gio Antonio) inherited from his cousin, Antonio II Grimaldi Cebà, and it is reasonable to suspect that Gio Antonio Sauli had copies of his masterpieces made for his sister Maria (the

mother of Cebà). In support of this argument, it can be noted that an inventory of 1735 measured the copies as 5 x 7 *palmi*, roughly 124 x 175 cm, which corresponds closely with the 120 x 169 cm dimensions of the Thyssen *Lot*. While it does not explain when the switch was made, it does seem likely that at some point, the original *Lot* was sold by the Sauli descendants, and that the copy was subsequently kept with the *Danaë* and *Magdalen* until all three were rediscovered.[19] Alessandro da Morrona in 1792 could find only the *Danaë* in the Palazzo Sauli, although in 1818, an anonymous author recorded all three paintings.[20] This last author, furthermore, noted the "excellent condition" of the *Lot*, echoing an observation that Carlo Giuseppe Ratti had made in 1780, when he described the picture as "più conservati" than the other two paintings. It is tempting to propose that the Thyssen painting had already been substituted for the original by the time it was seen by Ratti and that its different provenance as well as its notably higher-pitched color tone underlie the comments about its condition, although it is perhaps difficult to reconcile this with Ratti's praise of the painting as one of Gentileschi's finest works.

JJM

1. At the time, it was noted that R. Ward Bissell's commentary about the condition, including his idea that a section of cloth had been overpainted where Gentileschi had intended a shadow, is not entirely accurate.

2. See Mark Leonard, Narayan Khandekar, and Dawson W. Carr, " 'Amber Varnish' and Orazio Gentileschi's 'Lot and His Daughters,' " *Burlington Magazine* 143 (2001): pp. 4–10.

3. See, for similar comments, Keith Christiansen and Judith W. Mann, *Orazio and Artemisia Gentileschi*, exh. cat. (New York, 2001), pp. 178–80. Van Dyck's *Portrait of Agostino Pallavicini* (J. Paul Getty Museum, Los Angeles) is often cited as one of Gentileschi's models, but while the portrait may have been started as early as 1621, it was probably not finished until 1623, when the *Danaë* was already complete.

4. See Mary Newcome, "Orazio Gentileschi in Genoa," in Christiansen and Mann, *Orazio and Artemisia Gentileschi*, pp. 165–71.

5. For Carracci's *Danaë*, and for further comments on the iconography, see Madlyn Millner Kahn, "Danaë: Virtuous, Voluptuous, Venal Woman," *Art Bulletin* 60 (1978): pp. 43–55, esp. pp. 50–51, figs. 9–10. The Bridgewater *Danaë* was destroyed in the Second World War; the preparatory drawing survives in the Royal Collection at Windsor and has recently been discussed in Daniele Benati et al., *The Drawings of Annibale Carracci*, exh. cat. (Washington, D.C., 1999), pp. 278–79, no. 90. For iconographic discussions of Gentileschi's *Danaë*, see also Judith W. Mann, "The Gentileschi *Danaë* in the Saint Louis Art Museum: Orazio or Artemisia," *Apollo* 143, no. 412 (1996): pp. 40–41.

6. Christiansen and Mann, *Orazio and Artemisia Gentileschi*, pp. 172–73.

7. The *Cleopatra* (formerly collection of Amadeo Morandotti, now collection of Gerolamo Etro) entered the Genoese collection of Pietro Gentile at an unknown date. The present author agrees entirely with Keith Christiansen on the attribution of the painting to Orazio rather than Artemisia, for which see Christiansen and Mann, *Orazio and Artemisia Gentileschi*, pp. 97–100, no. 17, and Keith Christiansen, "Becoming Artemisia. Afterthoughts on the Gentileschi Exhibition," *Metropolitan Museum of Art Journal* 39 (2004): pp. 101–26, esp. pp. 109–11. For a contrary view, see Christiansen and Mann, *Orazio and Artemisia Gentileschi*, pp. 302–5, no. 53. Regarding the related painting in Saint Louis, for which see Mann, "Gentileschi *Danaë*," and Christiansen and Mann, *Orazio and Artemisia Gentileschi*, pp. 305–8, no. 54, the experience of seeing the painting in the exhibition in 2001 raised for the present author the question of whether this painting is neither by Orazio nor Artemisia, but might instead be a copy after a lost work by one of them.

8. Raffaello Soprani, *Vite de' pittori, scultori, ed architetti genovesi* (Genoa, 1674), p. 317; 2nd ed., rev. by Carlo Giuseppe Ratti (Genoa, 1768), 1: pp. 223–31. Most of our information on Sauli, and on Gentileschi's time in Genoa, comes from Sorprani and Ratti. See also Benedict Nicolson, "Orazio Gentileschi and Giovanni Antonio Sauli," *Artibus et historiae* 6, no. 12 (1985): pp. 9–25.

9. Christiansen and Mann, *Orazio and Artemisia Gentileschi*, p. 166, echoing Nicolson, "Orazio Gentileschi and Giovanni Antonio Sauli," p. 12.

10. Marzia Cataldi Gallo, "The Sauli Collection: Two Unpublished Letters and a Portrait by Orazio Gentileschi," *Burlington Magazine* 145 (2003): p. 345.

11. For a good summary of the problem in general, see Keith Christiansen, "The Art of Orazio Gentileschi," in Christiansen and Mann, *Orazio and Artemisia Gentileschi*, pp. 3–37, esp. pp. 21–31. See also Aidan Weston-Lewis, "Orazio Gentileschi's Two Versions of 'The Finding of Moses' Reassessed," *Apollo* 145, no. 424 (1997): pp. 27–35; and Gabriele Finaldi, ed., *Orazio Gentileschi at the Court of Charles I*, exh. cat. (London, 1999).

12. This was not a universal conclusion. Carlo Volpe (in his "Annotazioni sulla mostra caravaggesca di Cleveland," *Paragone* 263 [1972]: pp. 50–69), for example, questioned the identification.

13. Marco Bologna, ed., *L'archivio della famiglia Sauli di Genova*, Atti della Società Ligure di Storia Patria n.s. 40 (114), fasc. 2 (Genoa, 2000), pp. 32–35; and Gallo, "The Sauli Collection," p. 350.

14. For clarification on this point, see Patrick Matthiesen, letter to the editor, *Burlington Magazine* 143 (2001): p. 162.

15. Wilhelm Suida, *Genua* (Leipzig, Germany, 1906), pp. 156, 203; and Hermann Voss, *Die Malerei des Barock in Rom* (Berlin, 1925), p. 460.

16. As a point of clarification, it should be stressed that the provenance of these paintings is entirely different from that of the four other paintings by Orazio and Artemisia Gentileschi that were in the Palazzo Cattaneo-Adorno by 1846; see Christiansen and Mann, *Orazio and Artemisia Gentileschi*, p. 166. Those paintings came from the collection of Pietro Maria Gentile, not that of the Sauli family.

17. Leonard, Khandekar, and Carr, " 'Amber Varnish,' " pp. 4–10, demonstrates that the Getty painting is the Sauli original version of the *Lot and His Daughters*.

18. Gallo, "The Sauli Collection," pp. 349–50.

19. As noted by Leonard, Khandekar, and Carr, in " 'Amber Varnish,' " pp. 4–5, the first modern reference to the Getty painting was in 1910, when it was owned by a Genoese collector named Teophilatos. In the 1920s, it hung in a villa at Diano Marina, near Imperiale on the Ligurian Riviera. The villa's British owner, Margaret Pole, took the painting to England between 1925 and 1928; the Getty subsequently acquired the painting from her heirs.

20. See Alessandro da Morrona, *Pisa illustrata nelle arti del disegno* (Livorno, 1812), 2: p. 258; and Ennio Poleggi and Fiorelli Caraceni Poleggi, eds., *Descrizione della città di Genova da un anonimo del 1818*, 2nd ed. (Genoa, 1974), p. 79.

Orazio Gentileschi
Pisa, active in Rome, Genoa, Paris, and London, 1563–1639

48. *The Penitent Magdalen*, ca. 1628

Oil on canvas, 130.5 x 206 cm (51$\frac{1}{2}$ x 81 in.)

PROVENANCE: possibly the painting of this subject made for King Charles I of England; M. Le Monnier, Paris; from whom acquired, probably under the advice of Quentin Crawford, by Thomas Bruce, 7th Earl of Elgin and 11th Earl of Kincardine, Broomhall, near Dunfermline, Fife, Scotland, 1805; by descent to Andrew Bruce, 11th Earl of Elgin and 15th Earl of Kincardine, Broomhall, Dunfermline, Fife; Christie's, London, June 28, 1974, lot 115

BIBLIOGRAPHY: Joachim von Sandrart, *Academie der Bau-, Bild-, und Mahlerey-Kunste von 1675*, ed. A. R. Peltzer (Munich, 1925), p. 166; Charles Sterling, "Gentileschi in France," *Burlington Magazine* 101 (1958): p. 117; Benedict Nicholson, "Some Little Known Pictures at the Royal Academy," *Burlington Magazine* 102 (1960): p. 79; Alfred Moir, *The Italian Followers of Caravaggio* (Cambridge, Mass., 1967), 2: p. 77 (erroneously listed twice, as 10.b.ii and 10.b.iii); Benedict Nicolson, *The International Caravaggesque Movement* (Oxford, 1979), p. 53; R. Ward Bissell, *Orazio Gentileschi and the Poetic Tradition in Caravaggesque Painting* (University Park, Pa., 1981), pp. 181–82, no. 55; Benedict Nicolson, "Orazio Gentileschi and Giovanni Antonio Sauli," *Artibus et historiae* 6, no. 12 (1985): pp. 9–25; Mary D. Garrard, *Artemisia Gentileschi: The Image of the Female Hero in Italian Baroque Art* (Princeton, N.J., 1989), p. 106; Benedict Nicolson, *Caravaggism in Europe*, 2nd ed., rev. and enlarged by Luisa Vertova (Turin, 1989), p. 115; Keith Christiansen and Judith W. Mann, *Orazio and Artemisia Gentileschi*, exh. cat. (New York, 2001), pp. 174–78; Mark Leonard, Narayan Khandekar, and Dawson W. Carr, " 'Amber Varnish' and Orazio Gentileschi's 'Lot and His Daughters,' " *Burlington Magazine* 143 (2001): p. 4

CONDITION: When owned by the Lords Elgin, the breasts of the Magdalen were covered by a garment that had been painted onto the figure at some unknown date; this was removed before the painting was sold at Christie's in 1974. There are still areas of damage to the painting that retain old retouching; these include the hands and feet of the figure. Other areas of the painting—the book, foliage, and drapery, for example—suffer from the loss of surface layers that would have refined the forms.

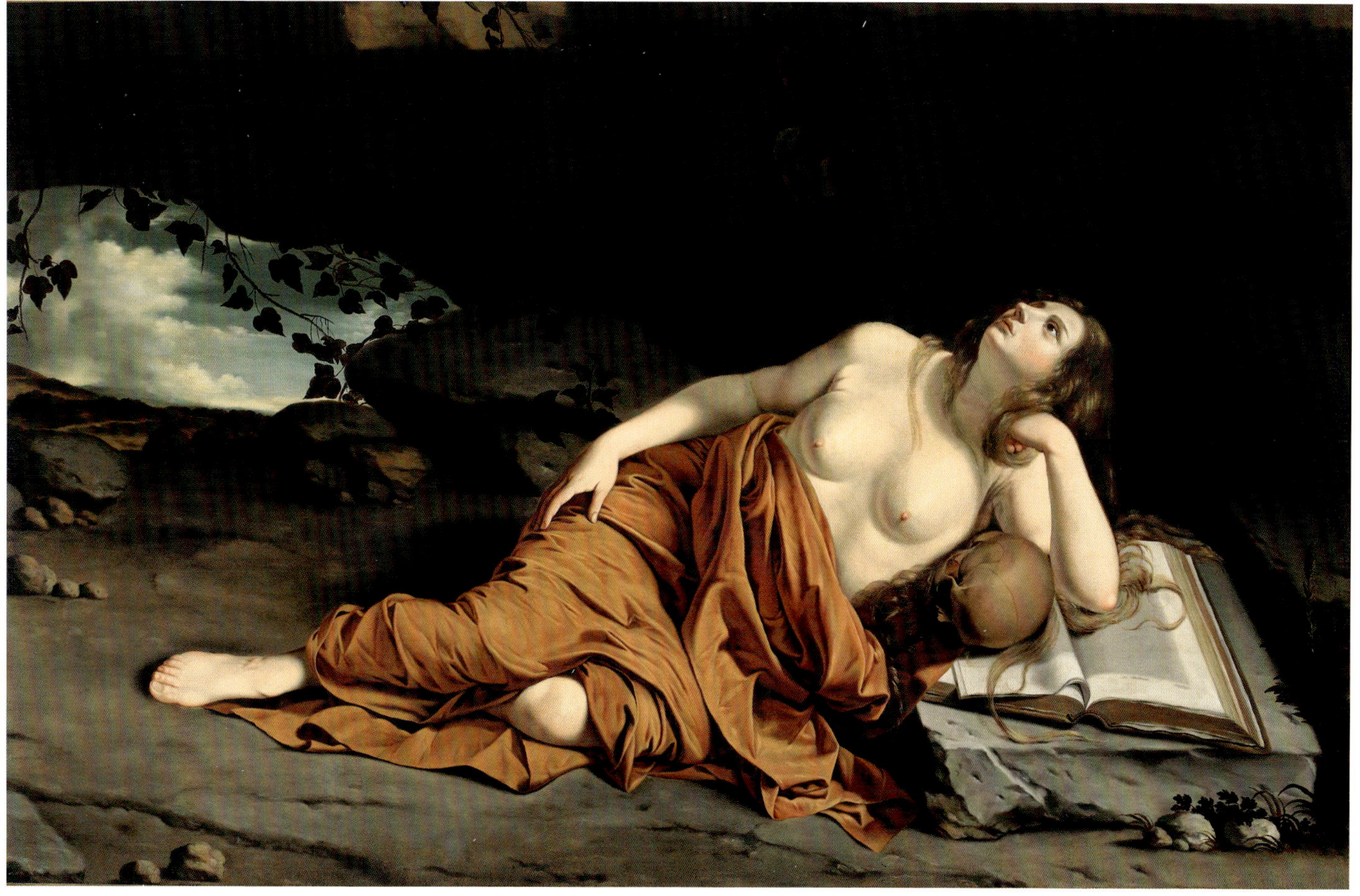

The Feigen *Penitent Magdalen* is the latest of the three known autograph versions of the composition painted by Orazio Gentileschi. Despite a few scattered references to a Roman version of the subject, the artist's original painting of the full-length Magdalen in a landscape is probably the example made to hang alongside the Feigen *Danae* (no. 47) and the *Lot and His Daughters* (J. Paul Getty Museum, Los Angeles) in the palace of Gio Antonio Sauli (fig. 1).[1] The *Danaë* and *Magdalen* make a particularly notable juxtaposition. Not only are the reclining subjects in both canvases based on the same cartoon, but the two works operate with a similar ambiguity of interpretation. Gentileschi's *Danaë*,

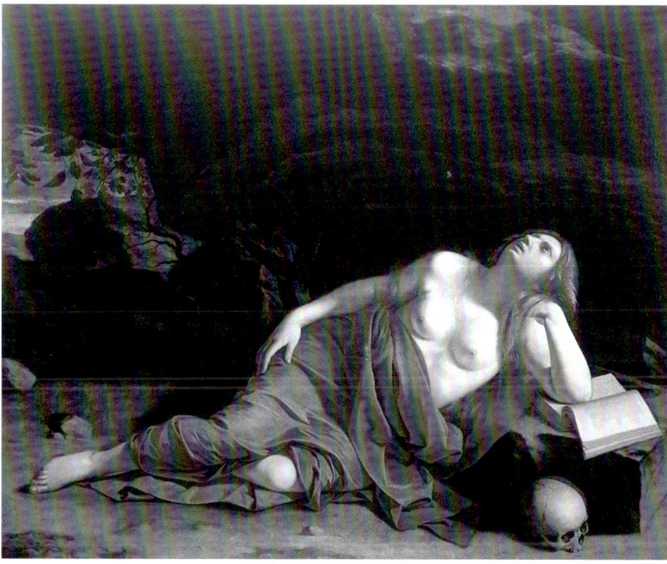

Fig. 1. Orazio Gentileschi, *The Penitent Magdalen*, 1622–23. Oil on canvas, 149.5 x 183 cm (58⅞ x 72 in.). Private collection

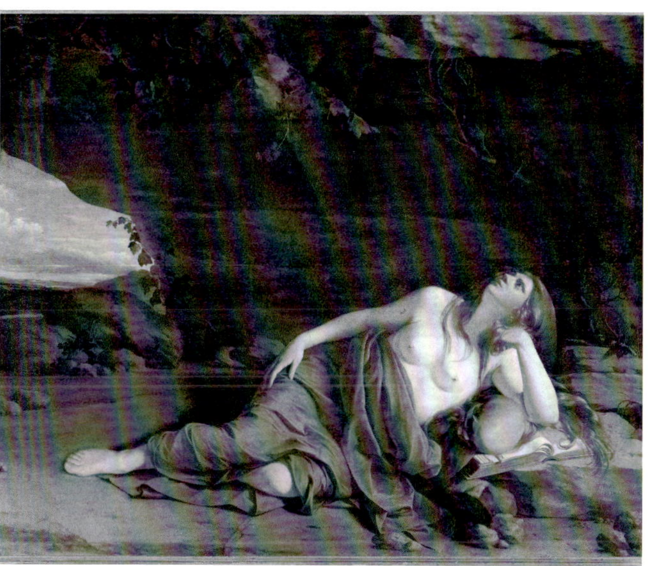

Fig. 2. Orazio Gentileschi, *The Penitent Magdalen*, ca. 1622–23. Oil on canvas, 163 x 208 cm (64¼ x 81⅞ in.). Kunsthistorisches Museum, Vienna, Picture Gallery

that is, offers a relatively chaste interpretation of an overtly erotic subject; in contrast, the nominally devotional *Magdalen* is presented in a more or less overtly erotic manner.[2] The Sauli paintings were among Gentileschi's most esteemed works, and there are both autograph replicas and later copies of all three canvases. Gentileschi's practice of reusing his cartoons has been well documented in recent years by Keith Christiansen, and the replication of the Sauli *Danaë* has already been discussed herein (see no. 47). Whereas both the Feigen and Cleveland *Danaë* seem to have been executed in Genoa for Genoese clients, however, the case of the *Magdalen* is more complicated.

The *Penitent Magdalen* now in Vienna (fig. 2) was by the late 1620s in the London collection of George Villiers, 1st Duke of Buckingham, and it is generally presumed to have been one of the two canvases sent by Gentileschi prior to his arrival in London.[3] (The other is almost certainly the *Rest on the Flight into Egypt* that still hangs as the pendant to the *Magdalen* in Vienna.[4]) The painter and the duke met in Paris in 1625, and Buckingham was responsible for bringing Gentileschi to London the following year. It has thus often been suggested that Gentileschi executed Buckingham's paintings during his stay in Paris, but the most recent examinations of the Vienna *Magdalen* seem to favor Genoa as its likely place of origin, and some scholars have even suggested that the Vienna painting might antedate the Sauli version. There is also a possibility that Gentileschi sent the two paintings from Genoa to Marie de' Medici in Paris in an attempt to win patronage at the French court, and that Marie de' Medici and/or Cardinal Richelieu in turn presented the paintings to Buckingham, but the evidence is too fragmentary to reconstruct the situation with any certainty.[5]

Gentileschi made further versions of these compositions after his arrival in England. During his visit to London in 1628, Joachim von Sandrart recorded that he saw in Gentileschi's studio two paintings being made for King Charles I, a "penitent Magdalen in contemplation, lying on the ground" and a "Mary sitting on the ground, the Child drinking from her breast, the old Joseph however lying to the rear and resting his head on a Sack."[6] It is clear from Sandrart's descriptions that the two paintings for Charles I must have been replicas of the two canvases owned by Buckingham. Sandrart also recorded a painting of *Lot and His Daughters* that was likewise destined for the king. The *Lot and His Daughters* remained in the Royal Collection at Windsor Castle through the 1640s, was acquired by William Latham in the Commonwealth sale of the king's goods, and in 1654 was sold by Latham to the Spanish Ambassador in London; taken back to Spain, the painting is now at the Museo de Bellas Artes de Bilbao.[7] Charles I's *Rest on the Flight* is recorded in the inventory of the Royal Collection drawn up in 1637–39 by Abraham van der Doort but is absent from later royal inventories; it is generally believed, though, to be the version of the subject now in the Musée

du Louvre, Paris, which King Louis XIV acquired from Everard Jabach in 1671.[8] Of King Charles I's *Magdalen*, however, there is no further trace in any royal inventory or other English document.

The Feigen *Magdalen* is, nonetheless, almost certainly the painting that Sandrart saw being painted for King Charles I. One would expect it to have remained together with the king's *Rest on the Flight*, just as Buckingham's versions remained together, and although the painting is not mentioned in the van der Doort inventory, that inventory is notably incomplete. While the chain of provenance for the Feigen painting begins in Paris only in 1805, it might be suggested that the canvas went to Paris along with the now-Louvre *Rest on the Flight* and that they were separated once there. Documentary evidence aside, certain details of the Feigen *Magdalen* would seem to connect it with the other paintings for Charles I. The trailing strands of ivy that frame the view of the sky offer one such example, for the foliage is different in earlier versions of the *Magdalen*, and it is absent from most versions of the *Rest on the Flight*, but it compares closely in the two canvases. Moreover, the view of the distant sky, present in the earliest Italian versions of the *Rest on the Flight* (for example, the one now in the City Museum and Art Gallery, Birmingham, England) is absent from the ex-Buckingham painting now in Vienna.[9] Given that the *Magdalen* and *Rest on the Flight* were not originally conceived as a pair, but only became one through their juxtaposition in Buckingham's collection, Gentileschi may have thus reinserted the view of the sky, and framed it with ivy, as a means of making Charles I's paintings into pendants. These changes were perhaps also meant to have the two paintings seem to constitute a set with the contemporary *Lot and His Daughters* for Charles I, which also includes a similar view of the sky at upper left. The three canvases are not the same size, but Gentileschi generally was not particularly concerned that pendant pictures had identical dimensions, a fact to which the different-sized Sauli paintings can attest.

Gentileschi's English paintings tend to share certain stylistic traits: a blonder tonality than his Italian canvases, an often uneasy spatial relationship between the figures and their settings, and a tendency toward a rather loose psychological focus. Michael Levey belittled the paintings as "costume drama almost absurdly lacking in real significance."[10] This dismissal is unfair, but there is a clear shift in Gentileschi's working practice in this last phase of his career, one that might be demonstrated by the comparison of his earlier *Lot and His Daughters* (particularly the version at the Getty Museum) and the late version of the composition that he made in England now in Bilbao. In the case of the Feigen *Magdalen* and Louvre *Rest on the Flight*, moreover, where Gentileschi did not devise new compositions but instead made his third or fourth nearly identical iterations of the subjects, it is hard not to sense a relative lack of inspiration on the part of the artist.[11] The poor state of the Feigen *Magdalen*, from which surface glazes are clearly missing, only emphasizes the artist's growing detachment.

Condition aside, it is difficult to explain why Gentileschi would not have devoted greater energy to these early royal projects. He had been brought to London by Buckingham and was housed under Buckingham's roof at York House on the Strand, but he must have moved to England with the intention of winning royal commissions. Moreover, London in the late 1620s and early 1630s was an incredible crucible of artistic activity. Peter Paul Rubens and Anthony van Dyck, with whose work Gentileschi's would have been compared in Rome, Genoa, and Paris, were present in the city for part of that time, and supplied pictures even when absent. Gerrit von Honthorst was also in London in 1628, and Charles I continued to commission work from artists like Daniel Mytens, who had been in England since 1618, but whose work continued to develop according to the latest fashions. Guercino declined Charles I's invitation to come to London, but pictures by him, and by others of Gentileschi's contemporaries including Caravaggio, Giovanni Baglione, and Guido Reni arrived in London in the 1620s and 1630s. The milieu deserves further consideration, for the works of the Flemish painters, for example, have tended to be treated in isolation from those of the Italians.[12] What is nonetheless clear is that Gentileschi's English period must be seen against this background. The abstracted forms of these late works are probably at least in part a reaction against the florid style of Rubens and van Dyck. They fit, too, into a broader pan-European stylistic shift away from Caravaggesque naturalism and early Baroque drama, and toward the classicizing mode also evident in the later works of Reni, Guercino, Simon Vouet, and others. It would be impossible to argue that the Feigen *Magdalen* should be counted among Gentileschi's masterpieces, but the work—and the Louvre *Rest on the Flight*, which was probably its original pendant—can well be conceived as pictures from the transitional moment when Gentileschi began to develop the style that would characterize his final decade.   JJM

1. R. Ward Bissell, *Orazio Gentileschi and the Poetic Tradition in Caravaggesque Painting* (University Park, Pa., 1981), p. 174, suggests the possibility that the Sauli picture was painted in Rome or was based on an earlier Roman painting, views which have not met with acceptance in the scholarship in recent years, in part because Bissell submits as evidence for a Roman *Magdalen* the painting now in the Pinacoteca, Lucca, which seems to be little more than a copy of the ex-Sauli version; see Keith Christiansen and Judith W. Mann, *Orazio and Artemisia Gentileschi,* exh. cat. (New York, 2001), pp. 174–80.

2. See Christiansen and Mann, *Orazio and Artemisia Gentileschi,* pp. 174–77; see also, for other treatments of the Magdalen, Bernard Aikema, "Titian's Mary Magdalen in the Palazzo Pitti: An Ambiguous Painting and Its Critics," *Journal of the Warburg and Courtauld Institutes* 57 (1994): pp. 48–59.

3. The paintings are first recorded in the Buckingham collection after the first duke was assassinated in 1628, but they are universally thought to have been commissioned, or at least collected, by him and not by his young son or his widow.

4. Christiansen and Mann, *Orazio and Artemisia Gentileschi,* pp. 217–20, no. 45.

5. Ibid., pp. 177n.15, 217–20; *Caravaggio e l'Europa: Il movimento caravaggesco internazionale da Caravaggio a Mattia Preti,* exh. cat. (Milan, 2005), p. 192; and Gabriele Finaldi, ed., *Orazio Gentileschi at the Court of Charles I,* exh. cat. (London, 1999), p. 17.

6. Joachim von Sandrart, *Academie der Bau-, Bild-, und Mahlerey-Kunste von 1675,* ed. A. R. Peltzer (Munich, 1925), p. 166; reprinted in Finaldi, *Orazio Gentileschi,* pp. 101–2. Although Sandrart's text was not printed until much later, he was in London only in 1628, which gives a date for the reference.

7. Christiansen and Mann, *Orazio and Artemisia Gentileschi,* pp. 232–34, no. 46; and Finaldi, *Orazio Gentileschi,* pp. 22–23, 66–67.

8. Christiansen and Mann, *Orazio and Artemisia Gentileschi,* pp. 218, 220n.17.

9. For the Birmingham painting, see Christiansen and Mann, *Orazio and Artemisia Gentileschi,* pp. 160–63, no. 34.

10. Michael Levey, *The Later Italian Paintings in the Collection of Her Majesty the Queen* (London, 1964), p. 13; see also Christiansen and Mann, *Orazio and Artemisia Gentileschi,* p. 242.

11. Similarly, Keith Christiansen, in Christiansen and Mann, *Orazio and Artemisia Gentileschi,* p. 220n.17, writes of the Louvre painting, "I find this a rather disappointing picture—the modeling is dull and the treatment of light uninspired."

12. Two recent exhibitions on Gentileschi, however, have begun the process. See Finaldi, *Orazio Gentileschi,* as well as Gabriele Finaldi and Jeremy Wood, "Orazio Gentileschi at the Court of Charles I," in Christiansen and Mann, *Orazio and Artemisia Gentileschi,* pp. 223–31.

Giovanni Lanfranco

Parma and Rome, 1582–1647

49. *Christ Appearing to the Magdalen (Noli me tangere)*, ca. 1646

Oil on copper, 23 x 20 cm (9 x 7⅞ in.)

PROVENANCE: Maria Maddalena Farnese, Palazzo Ducale, Parma (inventory 1693); to her brother Antonio Farnese, Palazzo Ducale, Parma (inventories 1708, 1731); Carlo di Borbone, later King Charles III of Spain, who inherited the Farnese title in 1731 (inventory 1736), Parma and Naples (the painting was brought to Naples by 1745, probably in 1736, but is unrecorded in subsequent inventories and was perhaps taken from Naples by French troops ca. 1797); private collection, England; Sotheby's, London, December 6, 1972, lot 59; Herner Wengraf, London

BIBLIOGRAPHY: A. J. Dézallier d'Argenville, *Abrégé de la vie des plus fameux peintres . . .* (Paris, 1745–52), 1: p. 305; (Paris, 1762), 2: p. 146; Erich Schleier, "Two Lanfranco Paintings from the Farnese Collections," *J. B. Speed Art Museum Bulletin* 32, no. 1 (1979): pp. 2–15; John T. Spike, *Italian Baroque Paintings from New York Private Collections*, exh. cat. (Princeton, N.J., 1980), no. 27; Giuseppe Bertini, *La galleria del Duca di Parma: Storia di una collezione* (Bologna, 1987), p. 117; Emilio Negro and Massimo Pirondini, *La scuola dei Carracci: I seguaci di Annibale e Agostino* (Modena, 1995), p. 192; Lucia Fornari Scianchi and Nicola Spinosa, eds., *I Farnese: Art e collezionismo*, exh. cat. (Milan, 1995), no. 113; Erich Schleier, ed., *Giovanni Lanfranco: Un pittore barocco tra Parma, Roma, e Napoli*, exh. cat. (Milan, 2001), no. 107

CONDITION: The four corners of the copper support have been bent from some early framing system, and minor losses in these areas have been retouched. Scattered pinpoint flaking losses in the shadow of Christ's leg and garment have been retouched. The paint surface otherwise is in excellent condition.

Giovanni Lanfranco was born in Parma but as a youth served as a page to Count Orazio Scotti in Piacenza. Recognizing the young Lanfranco's artistic talents, Scotti arranged for an apprenticeship with Agostino Carracci in Parma. After Agostino's death in 1602, Duke Ranuccio Farnese sent Lanfranco to Rome, where he painted alongside Annibale Carracci in the Palazzo Farnese. He was closely associated

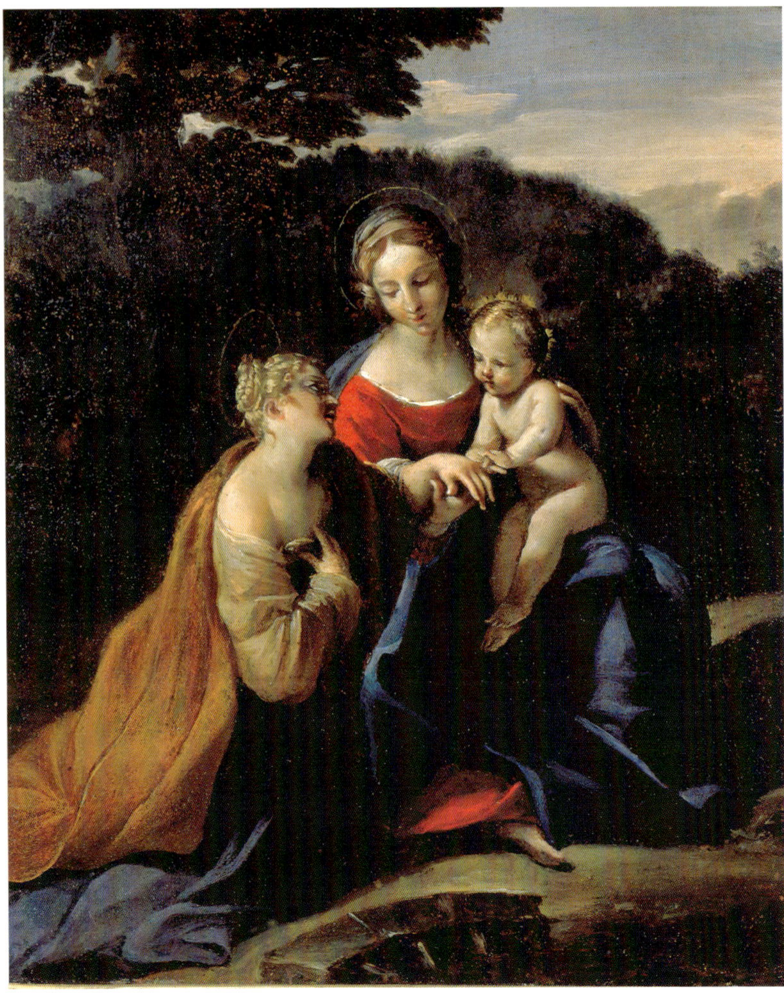

Fig. 1. Giovanni Lanfranco, *The Mystic Marriage of Saint Catherine*, ca. 1646. Oil on copper, 22.9 x 19.2 cm (9 x 7⅞ in.). Speed Art Museum, Louisville, Ky.

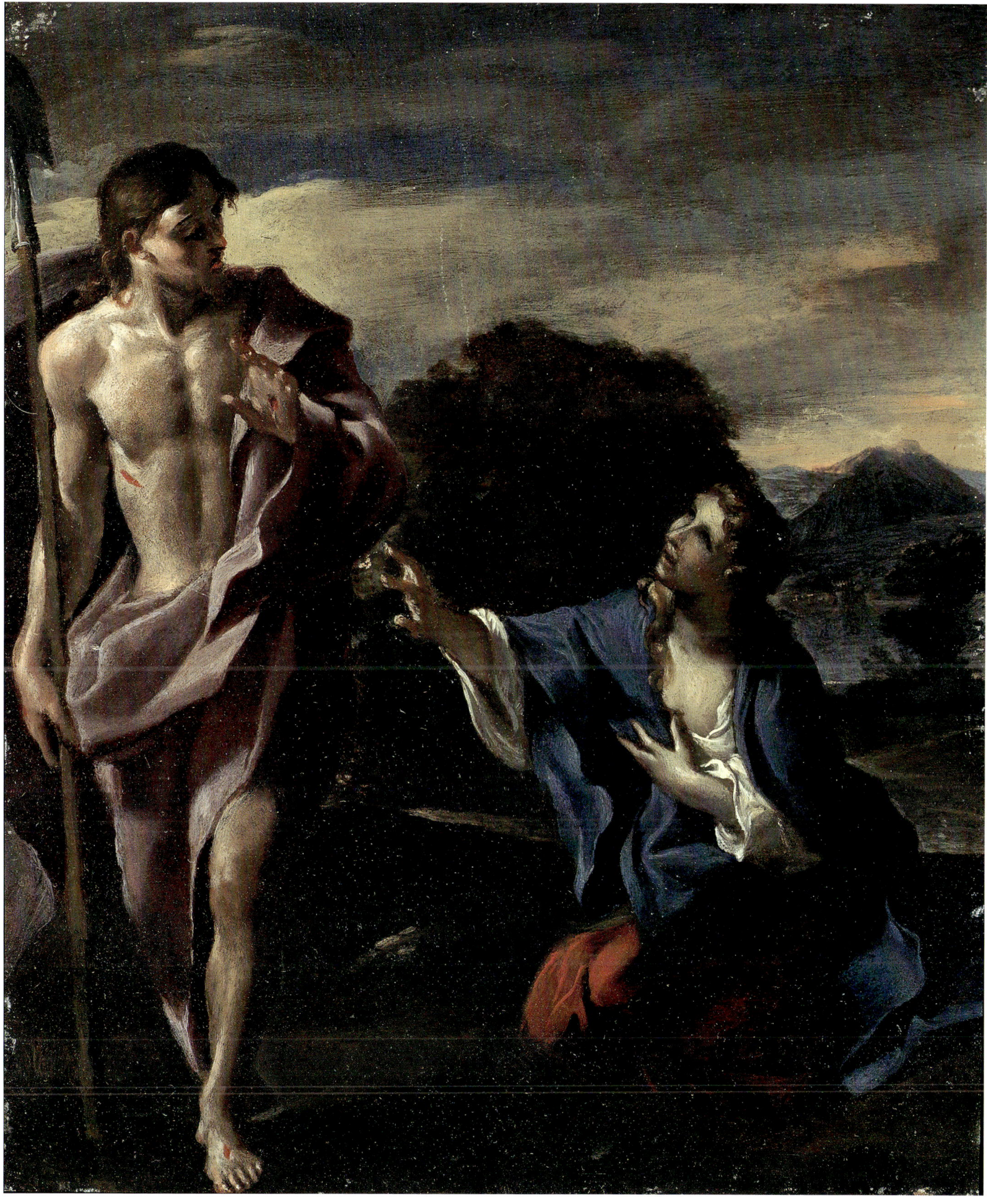

with Sisto Badalocchio and also worked with Guido Reni in Rome, but even at this early stage of his career, Lanfranco demonstrated a stylistic independence from the Carracci, however much he may have adopted their general classicizing trend. After Annibale's death, moreover, Lanfranco returned to Emilia, where his study of Correggio led him to a mode of painting emotional figures and fluttering draperies closer to those of Ludovico Carracci. Back in Rome by 1612, Lanfranco painted the illusionistic, Correggesque frescoes at the Bongiovanni chapel in Sant'Agostino and, following the praise for that small project, the enormous dome of Sant'Andrea della Valle. He thereafter enjoyed continual success in both Rome and Naples. He is best known even today for his large-scale fresco projects, but throughout his career he was also active in the production of large altarpieces and cabinet pictures as well as diminutive paintings on copper, like the *Noli me tangere*.

Thirty years ago, not long after this painting came to light, Erich Schleier identified it as the pendant to a *Mystic Marriage of Saint Catherine* that the Speed Art Museum, Louisville, Kentucky, had acquired several years earlier (fig. 1). Not only are the two paintings on copper panels of exactly the same dimensions, but their subjects likewise point to their having been made as a pair. Schleier further traced the paintings to the Farnese collection inventories of the seventeenth and eighteenth centuries, confirming that the small copper panels were indeed pendants.[1] They are first recorded in the Farnese inventory of 1693, when they were in the apartment of Maria Maddalena Farnese, and are listed together in subsequent inventories; they are also identified as having the same ebony and gold frame. With the extinction of the male Farnese line in 1731 with the death of Duke Antonio, the collections passed to Carlo, the son of King Philip V of Spain and Elisabetta Farnese. The panels were presumably transferred to Naples with the rest of the Farnese collections by 1736, when Carlo di Borbone, the future King Charles III of Spain, ceded Parma to the Holy Roman Emperor in exchange for his recognition as king of Naples. As late as the 1762 French edition of A. J. Dézallier d'Argenville's *Abrégé de la vie des plus fameux peintres . . .*, the paintings were described as being in "la galerie du Duc de Parme," but the 1767 German edition of the book makes clear that the panels had arrived in Naples.[2]

No documentary evidence exists for the paintings prior to the 1693 inventory, although scholarly consensus has been to date the paintings to the very last years of Lanfranco's career. John Spike noted, for example, that "the expressive liberties that Lanfranco allows himself in his anatomical draftsmanship does evoke the late style of the series of canvases that he and assistants painted for the Duomo at Pozzuoli in the 1640s."[3] Moreover, a drawing in the Royal Collection at Windsor Castle is preparatory for the figures of the Magdalen and Christ, and Schleier noted that the drawing is likewise in a style associated with Lanfranco's later work.[4]

Lanfranco was mainly in Naples between 1634 and 1646, although he returned to Rome in 1646 and spent the last year of his life there. While in Naples, he sent altarpieces to several north Italian cities, and he could have sent the *Noli me tangere* and *Mystic Marriage* from Naples to the Duke of Parma, but it is perhaps more likely that Lanfranco painted the small coppers while in Rome. In support of this argument, Schleier cites a "free, almost contemporary copy of the Louisville picture" in the Gemäldegalerie, Berlin, of which both materials and style seem to link to a Roman artist of the mid-seventeenth century. Neither the copy nor the originals seem likely, judging by their style, to have been painted prior to Lanfranco's 1634 departure from Rome; Schleier's conclusion is thus that the originals were probably made in 1646–47, when Lanfranco returned to the papal city.[5]

What has not before been noted, furthermore, is that the two female saints who are the subjects of the panels—Saints Catherine and Mary Magdalen—are the name saints of Caterina and Maria Maddalena Farnese, the two daughters of Duke Odoardo Farnese and his wife, Margherita de' Medici. It would thus seem likely that the panels were a commission from the duke or duchess. Caterina, the younger daughter, was born in 1637, when Lanfranco was already in Naples; conversely, Odoardo died suddenly in September 1646, which was probably before (or just as) Lanfranco returned to Rome. The panels may have been commissioned by the duke during Lanfranco's time in Naples, but no other Farnese commissions have been linked to that period, during much of which the duke was primarily occupied with the War of Castro. The most likely scenario is thus that the panels were made upon Lanfranco's return to Rome and that they were a commission from or for the newly widowed duchess in 1646–47.   JJM

1. Erich Schleier, "Two Lanfranco Paintings from the Farnese Collections," *J. B. Speed Art Museum Bulletin* 32, no. 1 (1979): pp. 2–15.

2. A. J. Dézallier d'Argenville, *Abrégé de la vie des plus fameux peintres . . .* (Paris, 1762), 2: p. 146; and A. J. Dézallier d'Argenville, *Leben der berühmtesten Maler*, ed. and trans. J. J. Volkmann (Leipzig, Germany, 1767–68), 2: p. 200.

3. John T. Spike, *Italian Baroque Paintings from New York Private Collections*, exh. cat. (Princeton, N.J., 1980), p. 72.

4. Schleier, "Two Lanfranco Paintings," pp. 3–7, figs. 4–5. The drawing was first published by Anthony Blunt and H. L. Cooke (in *The Roman Drawings of the XVII and XVIII Centuries in the Collection of Her Majesty the Queen at Windsor Castle* [London, 1960], p. 46, no. 147) as preparatory for the 1607–8 *Annunciation* in the State Hermitage Museum, St. Petersburg; Erich Schleier (in "Lanfranco's 'Notte' for the Marchese Sannesi and Some Early Drawings," *Burlington Magazine* 104 [1962]: p. 252n.50) soon rejected that connection. In 1972, when the *Noli me tangere* copper appeared at auction, Philip Pouncey's note in the auction catalogue correctly linked the painting with the Windsor sheet; see Sotheby's, London, sale cat. (December 6, 1972), lot 59. Schleier, in "Two Lanfranco Paintings," also noted that a *Head of Christ* drawing in Stockholm (Nationalmuseum, inv. no. c6990) might be preparatory for the *Noli me tangere*.

5. Schleier, "Two Lanfranco Paintings," p. 5.

Carlo Dolci

Florence, 1616–1686

50. *Saint Jerome in Penitence*, 1647

Oil on panel, 29 x 21.5 cm (11½ x 8½ in.), oval

PROVENANCE: Mrs. E. Hooper, Vancouver; Sotheby's, London, April 6, 1977, lot 2

BIBLIOGRAPHY: Charles McCorquodale, ed., *Painting in Florence, 1600–1700*, exh. cat. (London, 1979), p. 48; Charles McCorquodale, "Some Unpublished Works by Carlo Dolci," *Burlington Magazine* 121 (1979): pp. 145–46; John T. Spike, *Italian Baroque Paintings from New York Private Collections*, exh. cat. (Princeton, N.J., 1980), no. 18; Giuseppe Cantelli, *Repertorio della pittura fiorentina del seicento* (Fiesole, Italy, 1983), p. 72; Alessandro Parronchi and Anthea Brook, eds., *Il seicento fiorentino: Arte a Firenze da Ferdinando I a Cosimo III*, exh. cat. (Florence, 1986), 3: p. 82; Mina Gregori and Erich Schleier, eds., *La pittura in Italia: Il seicento* (Milan, 1988), 2: p. 726; Maria B. Guerrieri Borsoi, "Dolci, Carlo," in *Dizionario biografico degli italiani*, vol. 40 (Rome, 1991), p. 422; Francesca Baldassari, *Carlo Dolci* (Turin, 1995), pp. 101–3, no. 72; Charles McCorquodale, "Carlo Dolci," in *Grove Dictionary of Art* (New York, 1996), 9: pp. 76–79; Francesca Baldassari, *Un inedito San Girolamo e altre aggiunte al catalogo di Carlo Dolci*, exh. cat. (Siena, 2002), pp. 14–16

CONDITION: Described by Giuseppe Cantelli as "guasto" (broken, or ruined), an opinion based on the panel's appearance at auction in 1977, the work underwent conservation treatment soon after it was acquired but required only cleaning and minor inpainting.[1] The thinly applied paint surface is in excellent condition. A vertical check in the panel passing through the knee, chest, and right eye of the saint has not resulted in any visible paint loss. Small retouches are restricted to the bottom edge of the panel and minor flaking losses in the purple drapery.

Carlo Dolci, one of the premier painters of seventeenth-century Florence, was an artist of profound piety and extraordinary technique. He was during his lifetime, and for a century afterward, one of the most highly esteemed Italian artists—much appreciated in particular by British collectors in the eighteenth century—but the intense and personal religiosity of so many of Dolci's paintings, as well as the vast number of copies and paintings by followers that were sold as Dolci's own work, led to his much-diminished reputation by the mid-twentieth century. As the catalogue of his work continues to be clarified, the amazing virtuosity of Dolci, a child prodigy who enjoyed a long career in his native Florence, is once again apparent. As has always been noted in the literature on the artist, beginning with the biography written by his friend and pupil Filippo Baldinucci, the devout Dolci strove to paint images that would evoke religious sentiment in their viewers. That ambition is evident here, in the pathos of the penitent ascetic Jerome, who turns away from the brilliantly lit landscape at left and instead faces the shadowy right side of the composition, where the most prominent object is the precisely rendered skull serving as a *memento mori*.

Dolci studied with Jacopo Vignali and was also obviously influenced by Matteo Rosselli and Francesco Curradi, but he also looked back to previous generations, and his work might be considered the culmination of the Florentine traditions of the later cinquecento and early seicento. As for all Florentine painters of the later Renaissance, elegant design and brilliant color are one constant of Dolci's art. His "ability to render mystical events arrestingly tangible," in Charles McCorquodale's felicitous description, depended partly on the adoption of a pictorial strategy found in the work of many Florentines working at the end of the cinquecento: the depiction of marginal figures in sacred narratives in what might best be described as "contemporary fancy dress."[2] Indeed, Dolci was a diligent student of Florentine art, an active and noted copyist of fifteenth- and sixteenth-century paintings, and he would sometimes begin his own works by adapting a figure, or an entire composition, from a painting of an earlier generation. This is the case with the Feigen *Saint Jerome*, which as McCorquodale noted long ago, is based on a much larger painting of 1603 by Cigoli (fig. 1).[3] Cigoli was an artist of certain interest to Dolci, and his *Christ in the House of the Pharisee* (Corsham Court, Wiltshire, England), painted also in the 1640s, is likewise based on a composition by Cigoli.[4]

Like a number of paintings by Dolci, the *Saint Jerome* bears on the reverse an inscription in the artist's hand. Some of these inscriptions note the date on which the painting was begun, with a reference to the saint whose feast was celebrated on that day. In this case, however, the inscription is more suggestive, indicating that Dolci painted the work in payment for a debt:

> 1647 a di 14 di Febbraio restano
> che questo farsi per ultimo giorno e di quanto
> gli fussi stato debitore sin a questo giorno

On the basis of the inscription, McCorquodale linked the panel with "a Saint Jerome in the act of beating his breast with a stone" that Dolci, according to Baldinucci, painted for his physician, Antonio Lorenzi.[5] Dolci sold other paintings to Lorenzi in the later 1640s, including the aforementioned *Christ in the House of the Pharisee*, but as Francesca Baldassari has noted, Baldinucci identified the Lorenzi painting as a "mezza figura quanto il naturale"—a half-length—which

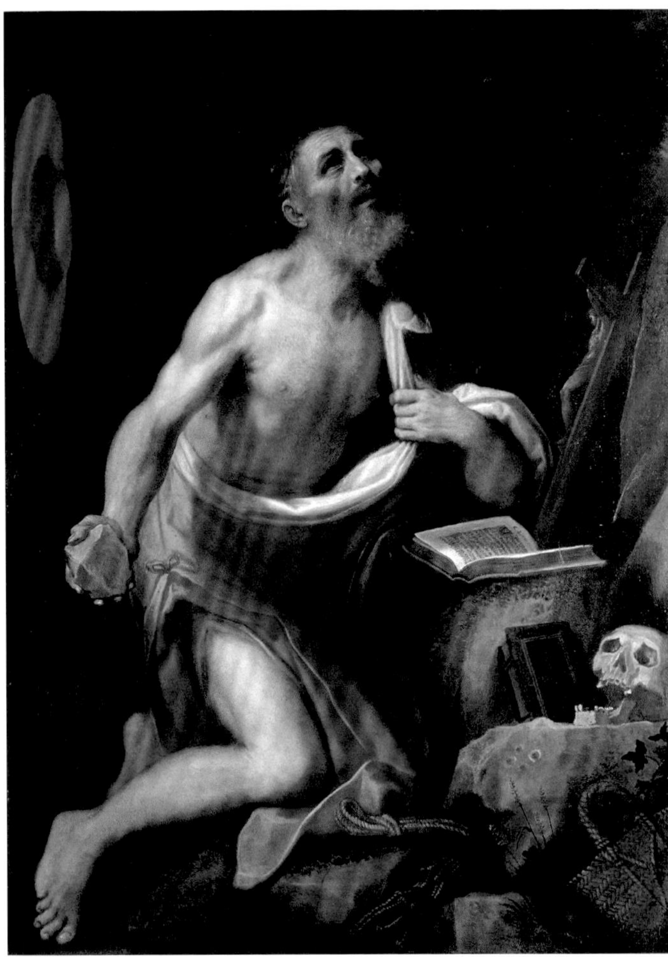

Fig. 1. Ludovico Cardi, called il Cigoli, *Saint Jerome in Penitence*, 1603. Oil on canvas, 162 x 120 cm (63¾ x 47¼ in.). Fondazione Cassa di Risparmio, Pisa

cannot be linked to the Feigen *Saint Jerome*.[6] The circumstances of the painting's creation remain a mystery. There is no reason to doubt, however, the date of the inscription, and this serves as a benchmark for dating a group of similar small paintings that Dolci made with a feathery, free brushwork that is far less familiar than the marmoreal surfaces, devoid of any visible brushstrokes, that most often characterize Dolci's work.[7]

J J M

1. Giuseppe Cantelli, *Repertorio della pittura fiorentina del seicento* (Fiesole, Italy, 1983), p. 72.

2. Charles McCorquodale, ed., *Painting in Florence, 1600–1700*, exh. cat. (London, 1979), p. 44. See, for example, the man raising the Cross in Dolci's *Martyrdom of Saint Andrew* (versions in the Palazzo Pitti, Florence, and the Birmingham Museum of Art, Alabama), or the elaborately patterned dress of figures in Dolci's *Adoration of the Magi* (National Gallery, London).

3. The signed and dated painting by Cigoli was traced by McCorquodale to the sale at Sotheby's, Florence, June 6, 1980, lot 534.

4. McCorquodale, *Painting in Florence*, p. 44.

5. Charles McCorquodale, "Some Unpublished Works by Carlo Dolci," *Burlington Magazine* 121 (1979): p. 145; and Filippo Baldinucci, *Notizie (1681–1728)*, ed. F. Ranalli (Florence, 1847), 5: p. 351.

6. There are at least three versions of the *Christ in the House of the Pharisee*; that in the Methuen collection at Corsham Court has traditionally been identified as the Lorenzi version, but Francesca Baldassari (in *Carlo Dolci* [Turin, 1995], pp. 94–98, nos. 62–64) instead identifies the version in Clergy House, London, as the Lorenzi original. The Lorenzi *Saint Jerome* has not been identified. Neither of the known half-length depictions of Saint Jerome by Dolci (one in a private collection, see Baldassari, *Carlo Dolci*, no. 21; the other identified by Baldassari in *Carlo Dolci*, no. 101, as with Colnaghi, but later in the Koelliker collection and recently sold at Sotheby's, New York, January 29, 2009, lot 27) shows the saint beating his breast.

7. McCorquodale, "Some Unpublished Works," pp. 145–46.

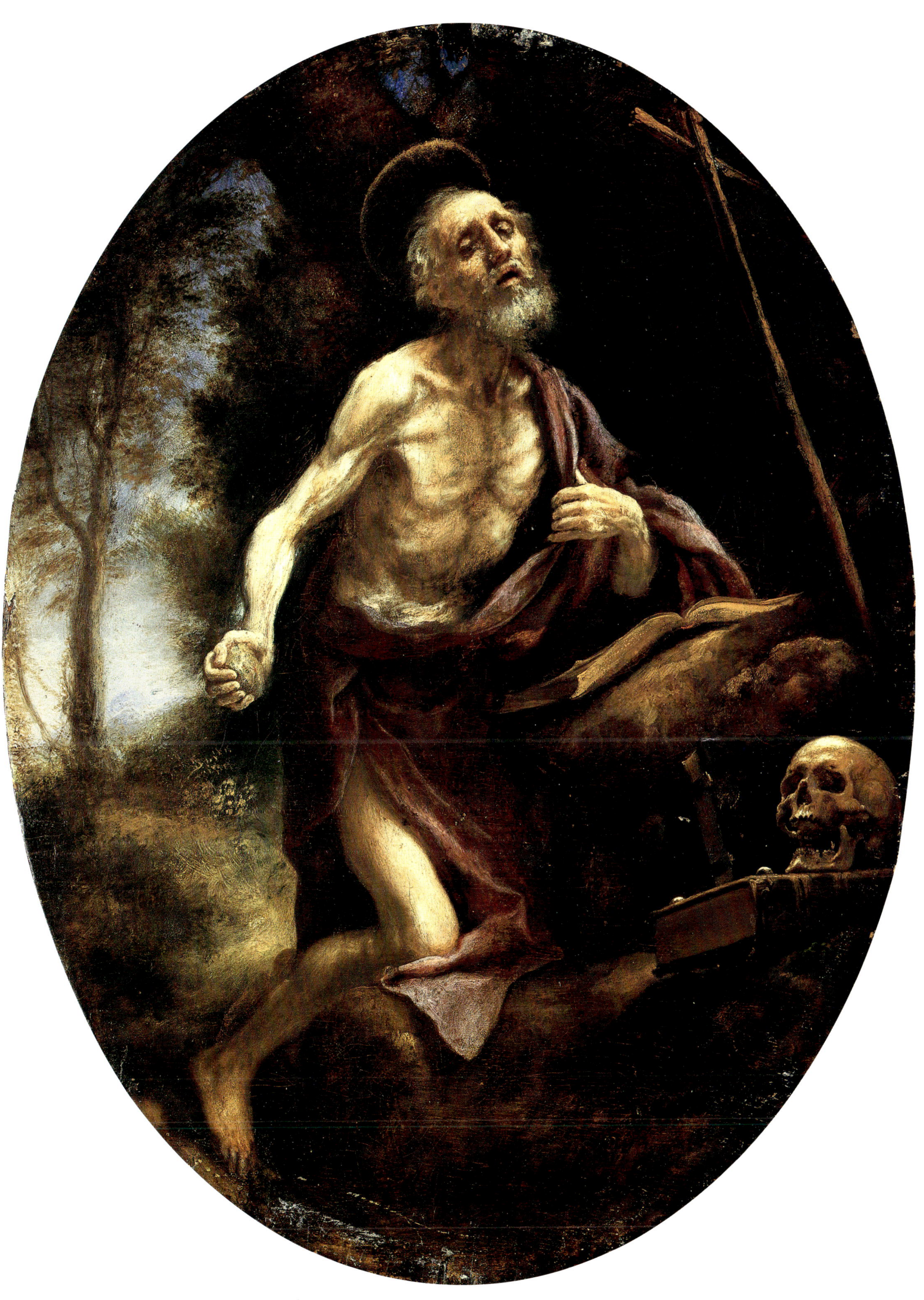

APPENDIX: RECENT ACQUISITIONS

Appendix 1

Master of Paciano
Perugia, active ca. 1320–50

Matricola of the Confraternity of Saint Benedict, ca. 1330–40

Tempera on parchment, 33 x 22.4 cm (13 x 8¼ in.)

PROVENANCE: Don Gioacchino Cotogni, Perugia, 18th century; private collection, Lugano, Switzerland; Sam Fogg, London

BIBLIOGRAPHY: Filippo Todini, "Miniature del Maestro di Paciano," *Esercizi* 3 (1980): p. 39; Filippo Todini, *La pittura umbra dal duecento al primo cinquecento* (Milan, 1989), 1: p. 163; 2: p. 120, fig. 252; Marina Subbuoni, *La miniatura perugina del trecento* (Perugia, 2003), pp. 109, 122–23, 328; Elvio Lunghi, in *Dizionario biografico dei miniatori italiani: Secoli IX–XVI*, ed. Milvia Bollati (Milan, 2004), p. 696

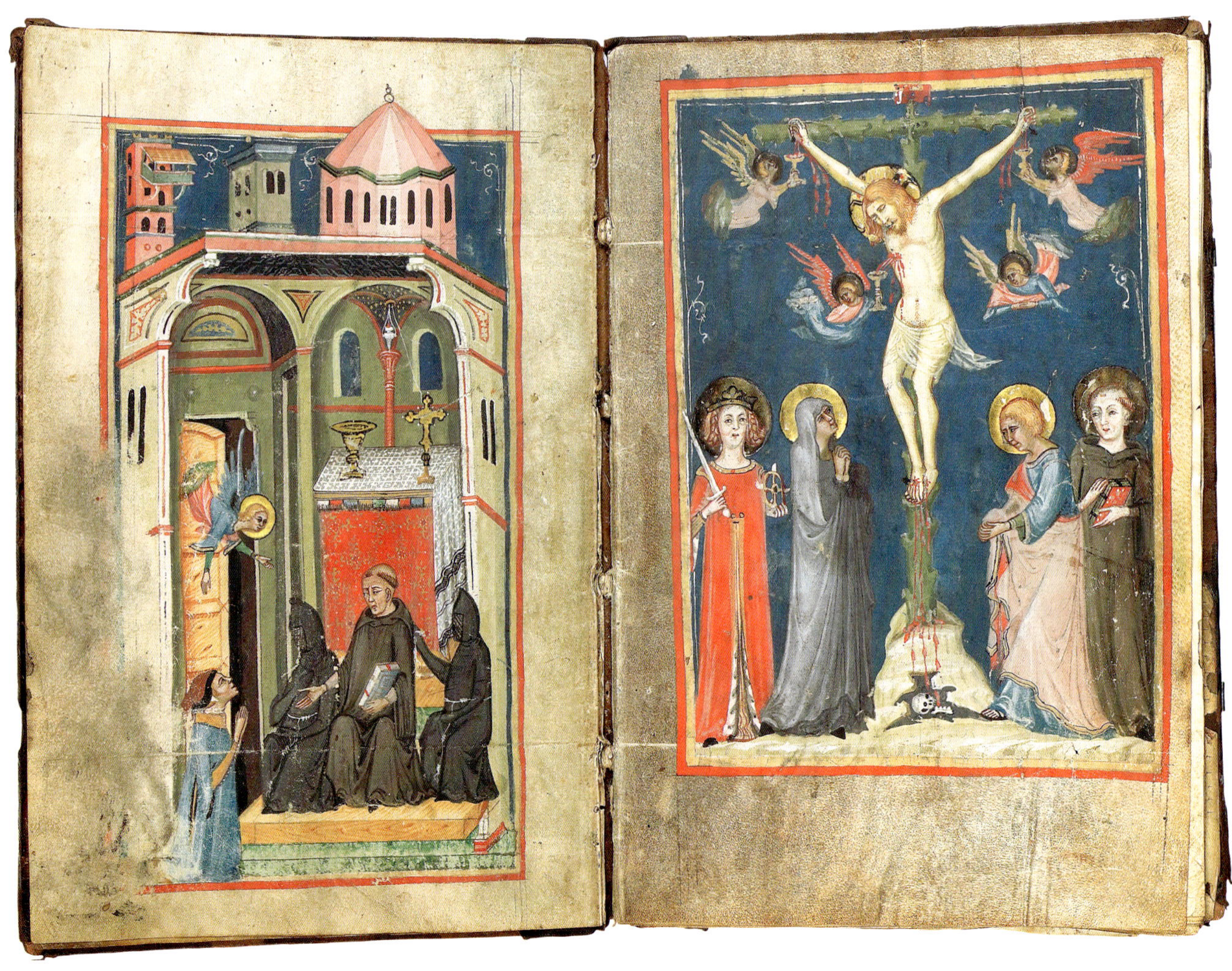

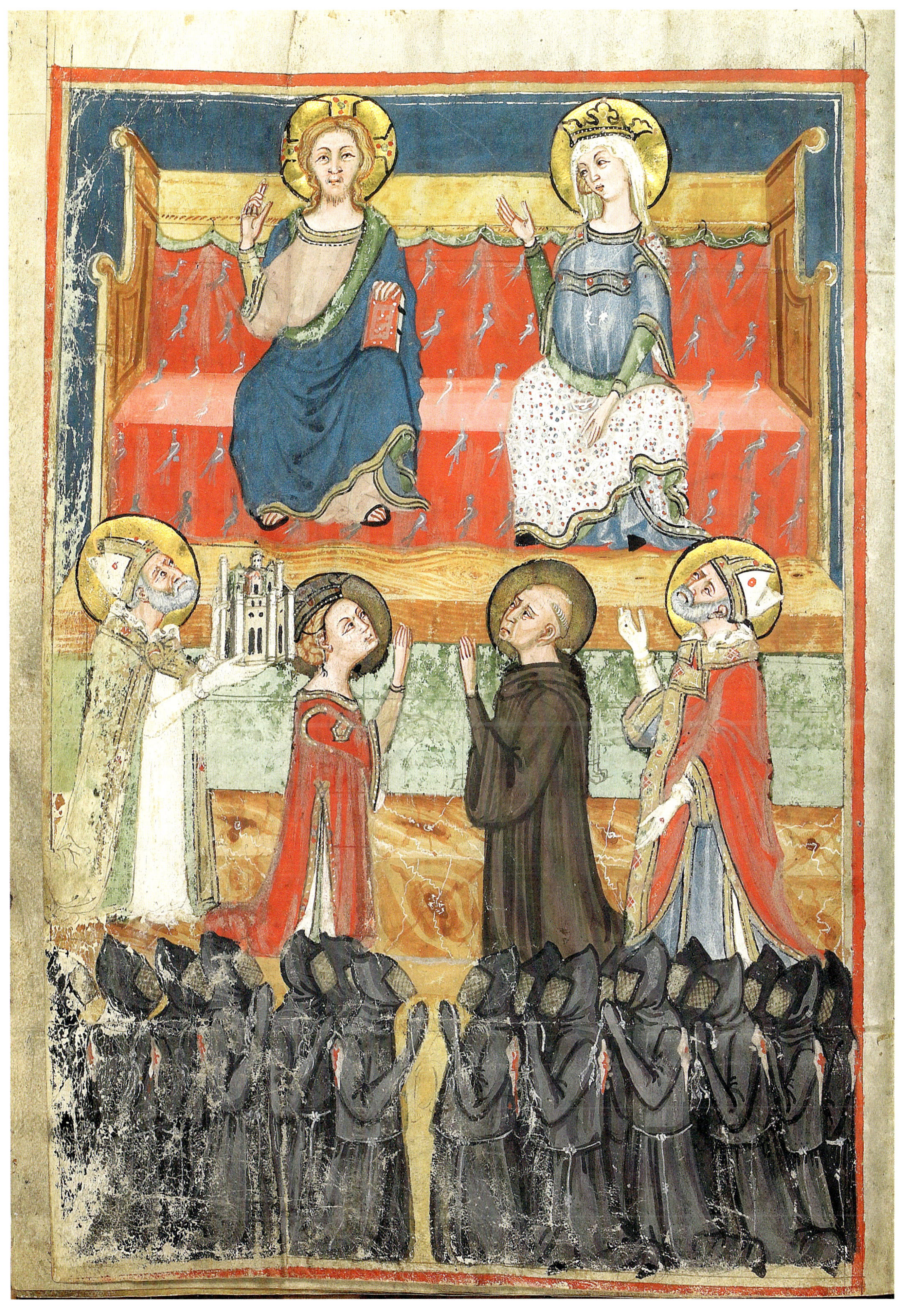

<h1 style="text-align:center">Appendix 2</h1>

Circle of Ambrogio Lorenzetti

Siena, active by 1319–died 1348

The Annunciatory Angel, ca. 1340–45

Tempera on panel, 46.1 x 18.1 cm (18⅛ x 7⅛ in.)

Provenance: Asta Antiquariato Boetto, Genoa, September 29, 2008, lot 98

Bibliography: unpublished

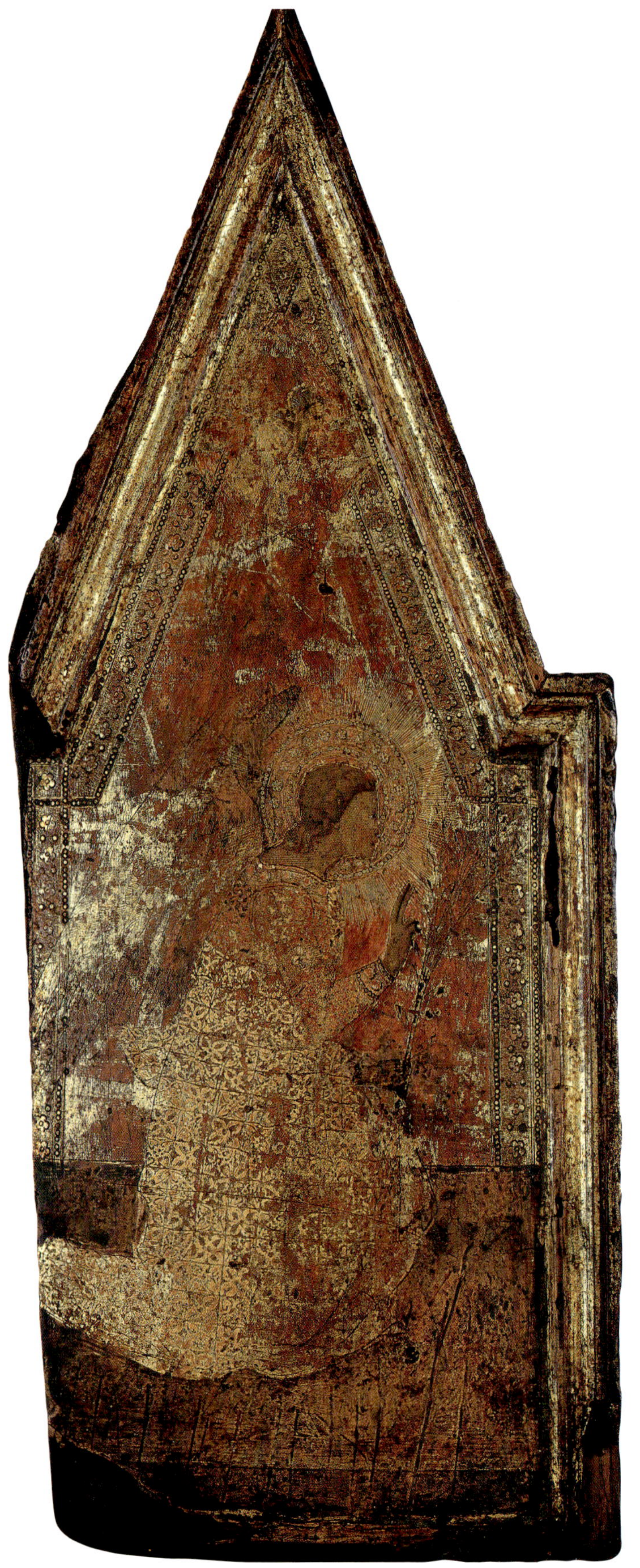

Appendix 3

Andrea di Bartolo
Siena, active by 1389–died 1428

Saint Stephen and *Saint Lawrence*, ca. 1390–1400

Tempera on panel, 33 x 12 cm (13 x 4¾ in.), each

Provenance: Sotheby's, London, October 29, 2009, lot 73

Bibliography: unpublished

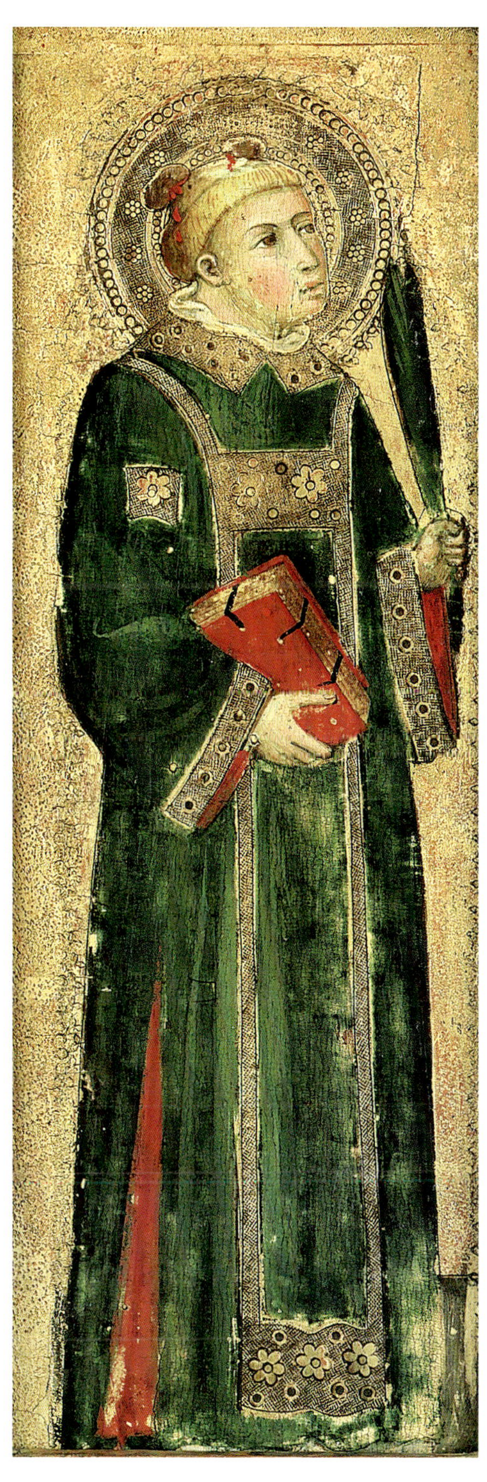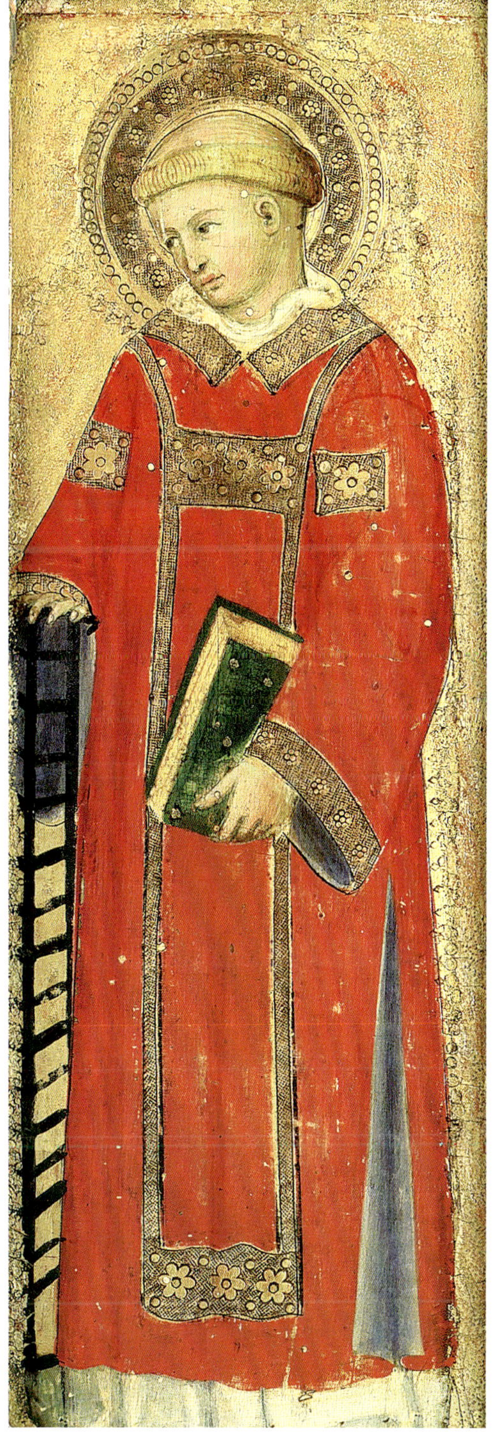

Appendix 4

Neri di Bicci(?)
Florence, 1419–1492/93

The Crucifixion, ca. 1440–50

Tempera on panel, 45.8 x 35.8 cm (18 x 14⅛ in.), overall;
33.5 x 23.3 cm (13¼ x 9⅛ in.), picture surface

Provenance: Guidalotti family, Florence or Perugia;
Sebastiano Genovini; Ubaldo Manucchi; Christie's, London,
July 9, 2008, lot 250

Bibliography: unpublished

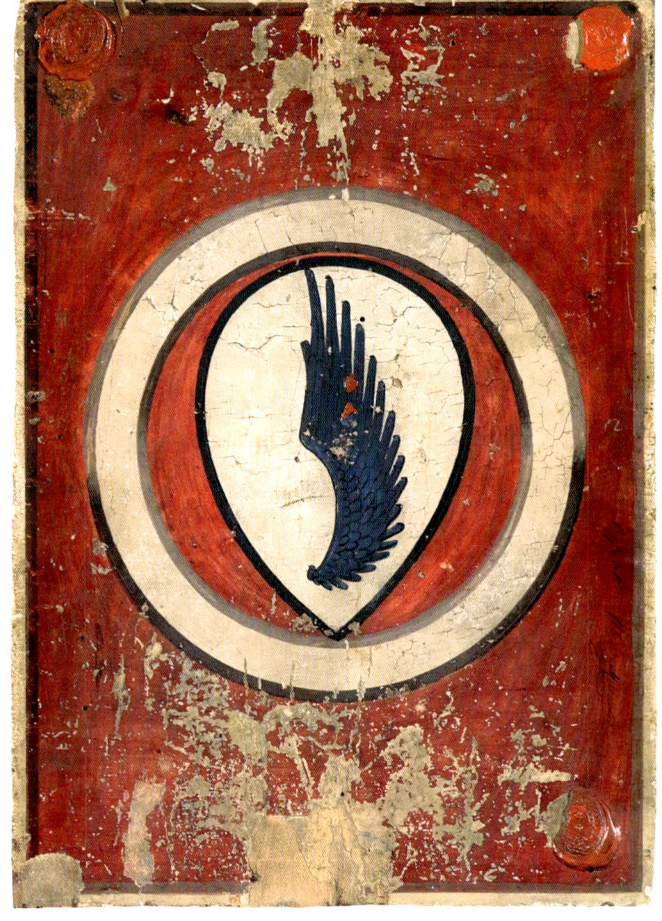

Appendix 4 Verso

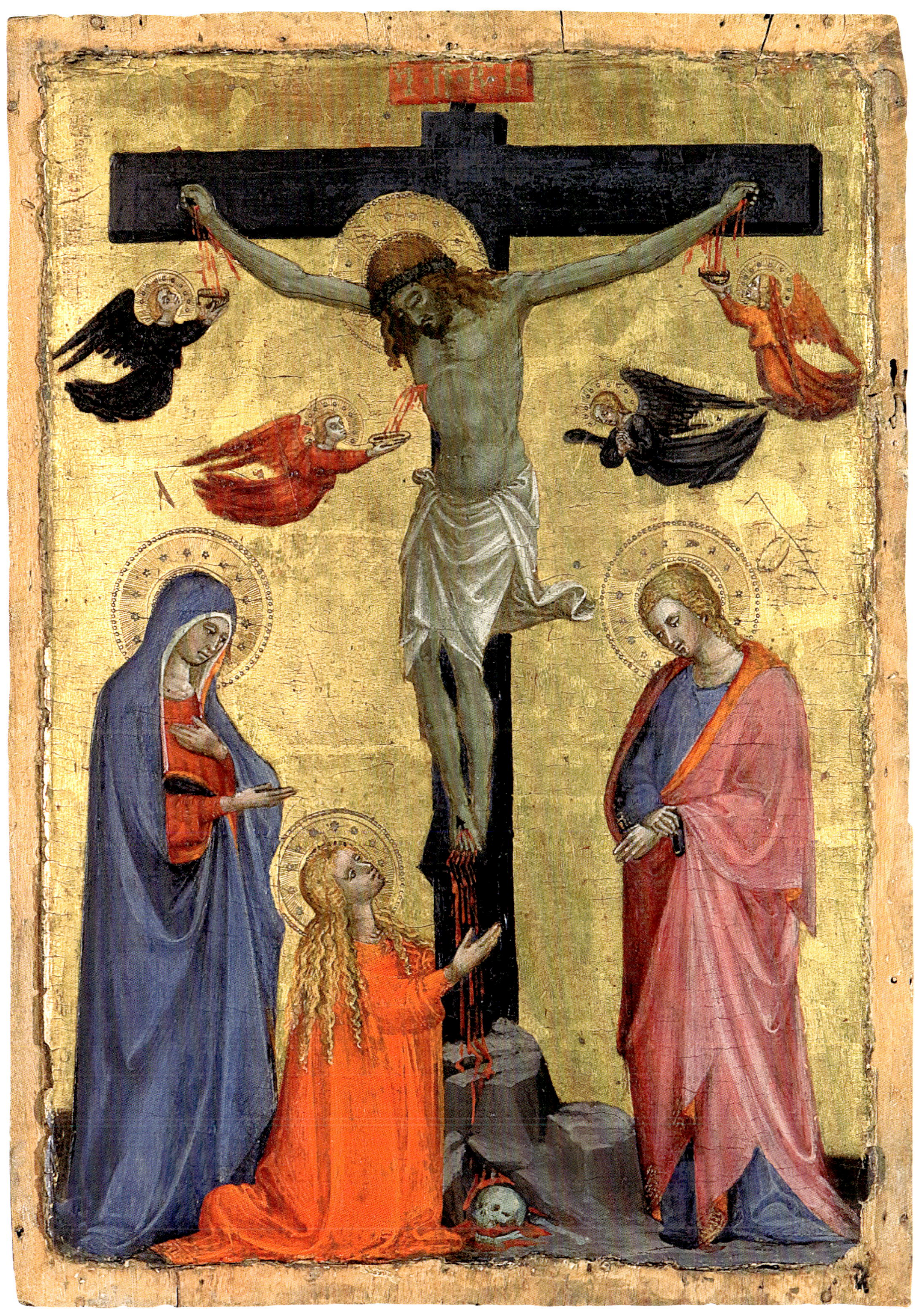

Appendix 5

Bernardino Fungai

Siena, 1460–1516

Ecce Homo, ca. 1495–1500

Tempera and oil on panel, 67.4 x 50.8 cm (26½ x 20 in.),
overall; 56 x 39.5 cm (22 x 15½ in.), picture surface

PROVENANCE: Piccolomini family, Siena; Sotheby's, Milan,
June 9, 2009, lot 11

BIBLIOGRAPHY: unpublished

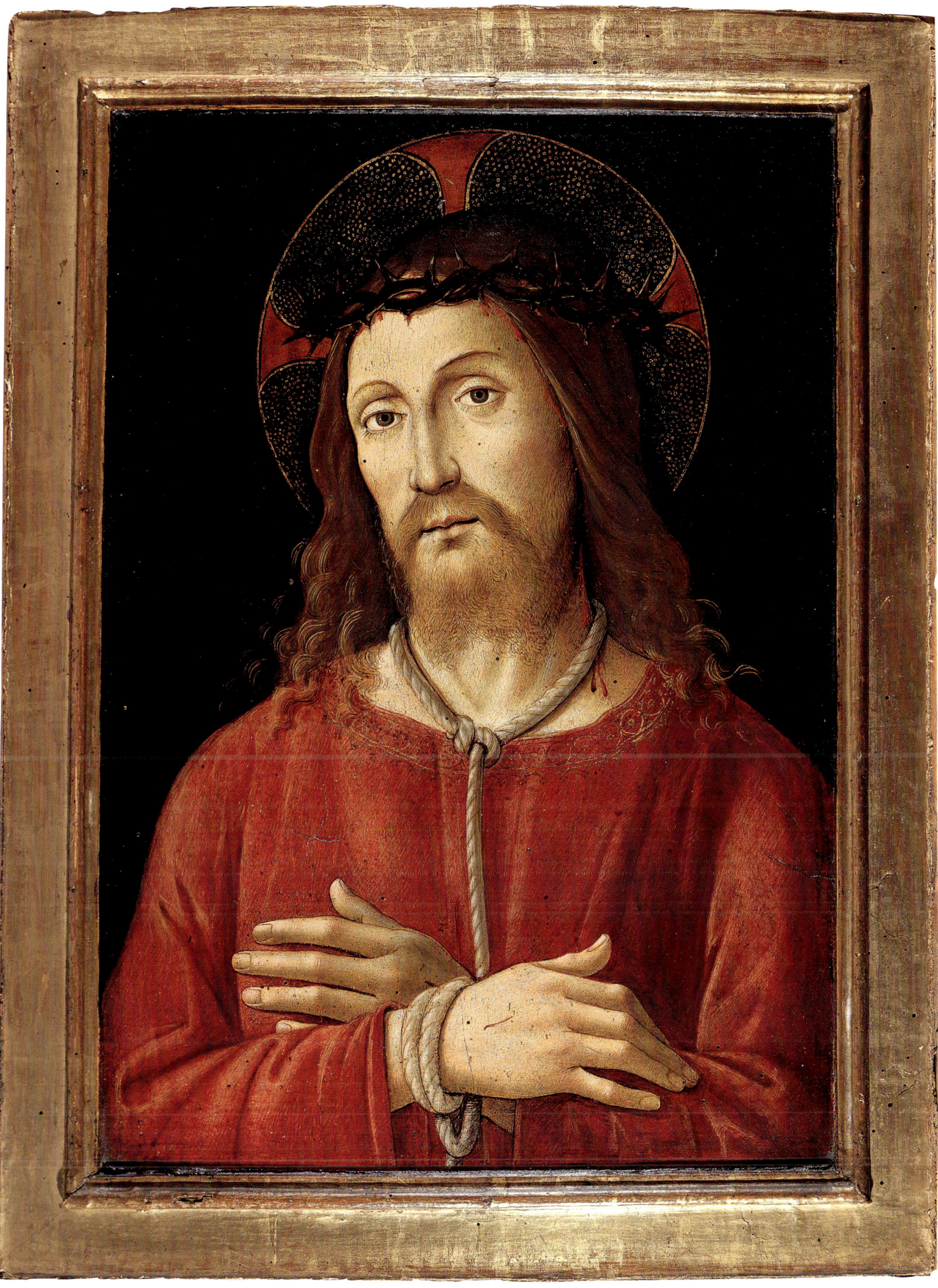

Index

Photo Credits

Albertina Museum, Vienna: no. 37, fig. 2

Alinari/Art Resource, New York: no. 2, fig. 1; no. 11, fig. 4

The Baltimore Museum of Art, Maryland: no. 32, fig. 5

Bildarchiv Preussischer Kulturbesitz/Art Resource, New York: no. 10b, fig. 1; no. 42, fig. 3; nos. 43–44, fig. 3

The Bridgeman Art Library International Ltd.: no. 14b, fig. 2

Cameraphoto Arte, Venice/Art Resource, New York: no. 42, fig. 2

Courtesy of Christie's, Fine Art Auctions, Ltd.: no. 29, fig. 1; no. 32, fig. 2

The Cleveland Museum of Art: no. 47, fig. 1

© 1998 The Detroit Institute of Arts: no. 29, fig. 3

El Paso Museum of Art, Gift of the Samuel H. Kress Foundation: no. 32, fig. 3; no. 32, fig. 4

© Richard L. Feigen & Co., New York: app. 2–5; no. 1; no. 2; no. 3a; no. 3b; no. 6; no. 7; no. 11; no. 12 (verso); no. 21; no. 22; no. 25; no. 32; no. 33; no. 34; no. 36; no. 37; no. 38; no. 39; no. 40; no. 42; nos. 43–44; no. 49; no. 50

Fine Arts Museums of San Francisco: no. 22, fig. 4

Courtesy of Mark Fisch, Continental Properties, New York: no. 48, fig. 1

Courtesy of Sam Fogg, London: app. 1

Galleria Doria-Pamphilj, Rome: no. 38, fig. 1

© Christopher Gardner, Deep River, Conn.: no. a; no. 4b; no. 5; no. 8; no. 9; no. 10a; no. 10b; no. 13; no. 17; no. 18; no. 19; no. 20; no. 23 (verso); no. 25; no. 26; no. 28; no. 29; no. 31; no. 35; no. 41; no. 45; no. 46; no. 48

The J. Paul Getty Museum, Los Angeles: no. 15, fig. 1

Gronchi Fotoarte, Pisa: no. 50, fig. 1

Imaging Department © President and Fellows of Harvard College: no. 18, fig. 3; no. 23, fig. 1

Istituto Centrale per il Catalogo e la Documentazione, Rome: no. 37, fig. 1; nos. 43–44, fig. 2; no. 45, fig. 2

Kimbell Art Museum, Fort Worth, Texas/Art Resource, New York: no. 22, fig. 1

Kunsthistorisches Museum, Vienna: no. 36, fig. 1

The Metropolitan Museum of Art, New York, The Image Library: no. 24, fig. 1; no. 47

Courtesy of Moretti Fine Art Ltd.: no. 32, fig. 1

Museo Poldi Pezzoli, Milan: no. 33, fig. 1

Imaging Department, Museum of Fine Arts, Boston: no. 12, fig. 1

© National Gallery, London/Art Resource, New York: no. 10b, fig. 2; no. 19, fig. 1

Courtesy of the Board of Trustees, the National Gallery of Art, Washington: no. 40, fig. 1

National Gallery of Ireland, Dublin: no. 14b, fig. 1

The Nelson-Atkins Museum of Art, Kansas City, Missouri, Photograph by Mel McLean: no. 18, fig. 2

Courtesy of the Board of Trustees, Norton-Simon Museum: no. 19, fig. 2

The Philadelphia Museum of Art: no. 8, fig. 1; no. 18, fig. 4; no. 22, fig. 3; no. 29, fig. 2

Réunion des Musées Nationaux/Art Resource, New York: no. 30, fig. 1; nos. 43–44, fig. 1; no. 45, fig. 1

Scala/Art Resource, New York: no. 20, fig. 1

Scala/Ministero per i Beni e le Attività culturali/Art Resource, New York: no. 22, fig. 2; no. 46, fig. 1

La Soprintendenza per il Patrimonio storico, artistico e demoetnoantropologico del Veneto, Ministero per I Beni e le Attività Culturali: no. 34, fig. 1; no. 42, fig. 1

Soprintendenza Speciale per il Polo Museale Fiorentino: no. 38, fig. 2

Collection of The Speed Art Museum, Louisville, Kentucky: no. 49, fig. 1

Courtesy of Staatliche Museen zu Berlin, Gemäldegalerie: no. 11, fig. 1

Courtesy of the Strossmayer Gallery, Zagreb: no. 11, fig. 3

© Ville de Nice, Musée des Beaux-Arts Jules Chéret, Nice: no. 20, fig. 2

Yale University Art Gallery, New Haven, Conn.: no. 3a, fig. 1